Narrating Mothers

Narrating Mothers

Theorizing Maternal Subjectivities

Edited by
Brenda O. Daly
Maureen T. Reddy

The University of Tennessee Press / Knoxville

Library of Congress Cataloging in Publication Data

Narrating mothers : theorizing maternal subjectivities / edited by
  Brenda O. Daly and Maureen T. Reddy.
     p.   cm.
  Includes bibliographical references and index.
  ISBN 0-87049-705-7 (cloth : alk. pa.)
  ISBN 0-87049-706-5 (pbk. : alk. pa.)
    1. Mothers in literature. 2. Women in literature. 3. Fiction—
Women authors—History and criticism. 4. Motherhood in literature.
I. Daly, Brenda O., 1955–   . II. Reddy, Maureen T.
PN56.5.M67N37   1991
823.009'9287—dc20   90–27053   CIP

Contents

Part III. Mothers Transforming Practices

Figures

___

Preface

Narrating Mothers began in a confluence of tensions and outright contradictions: between our shared view that the novel is a form open to women's revisions and the view of some feminist critics that the novel is "male-devised" and therefore uncongenial to women's stories; between our "private" lives and our academic work; between the deep pleasures of the actual experience of mothering and the pain of the oppressive institution, which often seemed to demand impossible choices (mother or write, mother or work, your child or yourself). Individually, we turned to the emerging work on the novel and on motherhood by feminist writers and scholars in order to understand these issues better, and to attempt some resolution of them. Our academic work began to move toward the problems of motherhood. Inspired by Dale Spender's *Mothers of the Novel* and by our own reading and experience, together we planned a session on "Mothers and the Novel" for the 1987 convention of the Modern Language Association, where we met and talked with many women who were thinking about similar issues. Tillie Olsen was especially encouraging at that convention. Ultimately we decided to do a book on the subject. As our work progressed, we began to consider not only the novel, but also other kinds of narratives. *Narrating Mothers* is the result of this process.

We have greatly enjoyed the dialogue—with each other, our contributors, colleagues, and friends—that working on *Narrating Mothering* has inspired, and we want to thank the many people who have helped and encouraged us during the gestation of this collection. We are grateful to Shirley Nelson Garner for encouraging us to go forward with a collection of essays and to Carol Wallace Orr for her faith in the project. The readers of our initial proposal, Elizabeth Abel, Cathy Davidson, Jane Tompkins, and an anonymous reviewer, offered sympathetic criticism and helpful suggestions that we believe made the collection much better than the one we originally had envisioned. Elizabeth Flynn, Betsy Postow, and Ellen Cronan Rose read both that proposal and a first draft of the manuscript, providing enormously useful critiques and great encouragement. We thank them all. We also wish to thank Paula Bennett and Ruth Perry for careful readings and extensive comments on the introduction. We are grateful as well to Katherine Sotol for suggesting artists for our cover illustration, Karen Murphy for research assistance, Billie Green for typing, and Norma Michalski for proofing.

Brenda Daly would like to thank Katherine Hayles of the University of Iowa for help with the proposal for *Narrating Mothers*; Jane Smiley of Iowa State University (ISU) for suggestions on the introduction; and Kathy Hickok, former chair of women's studies at ISU, for information regarding a key essay in this collection. She also thanks ISU's Feminist Reading Group for its lively discussion of many issues related to mothering, and the ISU English Department for research release time to complete the book. Beyond the university, women in the Ames community have supported this project through their invitations to speak to the American Association of University Women and the Ames-ISU YWCA. The National Women's Studies Association provided the opportunity to present essays from *Narrating Mothers* at its 1989 conference, where a number of women in the audience made valuable comments. Through the years, Brenda has benefited from the maternal thinking of numerous friends whom she would like to name here: Ann Hebert, Laurin Porter, Carol Lerfald, Margaret Soli, and, most of all, Maureen Reddy.

Maureen Reddy would like to thank Judith Arcana for lively correspondence on many aspects of feminist mothering; Jane Lazarre, whose work and life are an ongoing inspiration; and Sara Ruddick, who has been a constant source of encouragement, support, clear thinking, and energizing conversations. She also thanks her colleagues in the English Department at Rhode Island College, especially Joan Dagle, Carolyn Swift, and Barbara Schapiro, who asked thoughtful questions and gave good advice on an early draft of her essay. Marlene Lopes, research librarian at Rhode Island College, gave important help, as did the Rhode Island College Faculty Research Fund. Maureen is also grateful to her research assistants, Kim Baker, Cynthia Boland, and Barbara Silliman. And deepest thanks go to Brenda Daly for her friendship, which made working on this project a real pleasure.

We dedicate *Narrating Mothers* to our mothers, Arline Oland and Joann Reddy, and to our children, Stephan Daly and Brendan Reddy-Best.

Narrating Mothers

Introduction
___
Narrating Mothers:
Theorizing Maternal Subjectivities

Brenda O. Daly and Maureen T. Reddy

In *Inventing Motherhood*, Ann Dally argues that, even in the late twentieth century, "many women find it impossible to be committed to both feminism and motherhood because the two have not been reconciled" (168–69). Dally attributes this failure to reconcile feminism and motherhood to the relative paucity of feminist texts written by mothers (168), but we find that numerous feminist books either by or about mothers (sometimes both) have appeared, especially in the past decade. Yet Dally is certainly right in saying that motherhood remains an "area in which there is the greatest inequality" (168): the "feminization of poverty" might better be called "the maternalization of poverty," for instance; and racism, sex discrimination, and homophobia often disproportionately affect mothers. Nevertheless, in the larger culture's debates on these topics, mothers' voices continue to be ignored. Even in women's accounts of motherhood, maternal perspectives are strangely absent. We most often hear daughters' voices in both literary and theoretical texts about mothers, mothering, and motherhood, even in those written by feminists who are mothers.

In her foreword to *Of Woman Born*, Adrienne Rich says that the question *"But what was it like for women?"* was always in her mind as she researched and wrote (xviii; emphasis in original). Yet the very phrasing of the question that animated her landmark work illustrates a representative slippage from "mothers" to "women": the subjectivity of mothers often disappears from even the most sensitive feminist discussions of mothering. Rich's definition of motherhood as "the *potential relationship* of any woman to her powers of reproduction and to children" (xv; emphasis in original) seems to explain this elision as a deliberate choice, since Rich focuses throughout her book on the ways in which all women can be seen as mothers, whether they give birth, care for children, or do neither. Unfortunately, however, this deliberately broad, inclusive definition leads unintentionally but seemingly inexorably to a displacement that foregrounds the subjectivity of daughters.

Feminist theorists for some time have been analyzing the effects on women (and men) of the traditional construction of motherhood; the work of Nancy Chodorow, Dorothy Dinnerstein, and Carol Gilligan is now widely known. All three have been taken to task by other feminists—most recently by Elizabeth Spelman in her critique of theorizing—for the ethnocentricity of their studies; all three books are based on examinations of white, middle-class, Euroamerican experience. Black feminists have pointed to the differences in African-American constructions of motherhood and experiences of mothering from the models used by Chodorow, Dinnerstein, and Gilligan. So far as we are aware, though, no critic has explored fully the varying degrees of "daughter-centricity" of these studies; that is, all three write from a *daughter's* perspective, paying attention mostly to the effects of current conditions of mothering on children's progression into adulthood. In feminist psychoanalytic studies, we frequently learn less about what it is like to mother than about what it is like to be mothered, even when the author has both experiences.

This daughter-centricity in some cases may be deliberate, a necessary step in a political analysis of motherhood. As Judith Arcana points out in *Our Mothers' Daughters*:

> Of all the roles women are required to fill in this society, daughterhood is universal. Being born, every woman is another woman's daughter. Should her mother die, or leave her when she is a child, she is yet raised up by the society as a "daughter." Even if she becomes a mother, she remains a daughter. (4)

Feminists sometimes have used the universal experience of daughterhood as the basis of a critique of patriarchally defined motherhood, with the feminist daughter analyzing the social conditions which must change if motherhood is to be redefined. However, not all daughter-centric accounts of mothering move through the daughter's experience to the mother's, as does Arcana's; many remain uninterested in the mother's subjectivity. Why?

Jessica Benjamin offers an answer in *The Bonds of Love*, when she acknowledges that the perception of the mother in psychology as principally "an object for her child's demands" is "deeply embedded in the culture as a whole" (23–24). Benjamin shows how the oedipal theory, from which the rest of psychoanalytic theory developed, depends upon denying mothers' subjectivity. In a related project, *The Mother/Daughter Plot: Narrative, Psychoanalysis, Feminism*, Marianne Hirsch goes back to Sophocles's *Oedipus Rex* to demonstrate how the very structures of myths preclude our even imagining mothers' stories. Jocasta's story, Hirsch says, "cannot be filled in because we have no framework with which to do it *from her perspective*"; to know this story, "we would have to *begin* with the mother, not the son or the father" (4–5; emphasis in original)—or the daughter, for that matter. Few fictional or theoretical works *begin* with the mother in her own right, from her own perspective, and those that do seldom hold fast to a maternal perspective; further, when texts do maintain this perspective, readers and critics tend to suppress the centrality of mothering.

Feminist avoidance of the maternal, Hirsch argues, is rooted in four areas: (1) since motherhood "remains a patriarchal construction," women identify their mothers with victimization and martyrdom; (2) feminist writings demonstrate "a discomfort with the vulnerability and lack of control" that are aspects of maternity; (3) women, both feminist and nonfeminist, display a "fear of and discomfort with the body" that Elizabeth Spelman has named "somatophobia";[1] and (4) feminist ambivalence about power, authority, and anger causes a separation between feminist discourse and maternal discourse (165–66). Hirsch asserts that, "before feminists generally can claim power— without intense ambivalence," we must confront our fantasies of the maternal, rather than denying our fears and anger (167). We agree with Hirsch, and we believe that this collection of essays, in which maternal subjectivity is central, will contribute to this project. Our contributors focus primarily upon redefinitions of motherhood dating from feminism's "second wave," from the mid-1960s to the present, in North America and the United Kingdom.

The child-centricity of most feminist and nonfeminist accounts of mothering deflects feminist attention from central questions: What are the effects of current conditions of mothering *on mothers*? And how might *mothers* benefit from a revisioning of motherhood? A number of women writers have consciously taken maternal perspectives in their fiction and autobiographies, and in their classrooms as well. It is these writers whose work most of the essays in *Narrating Mothers* explore. What visions of mothering do they offer? What revisions of motherhood do their works suggest? The fifteen essays in this book address these questions, finding widely varied answers from the perspectives of diverse theories and genres.

Like Sara Ruddick's *Maternal Thinking: Toward a Politics of Peace* and the essays in Joyce Trebilcot's edited volume, *Mothering*, the essays in this volume attempt to articulate maternal perspectives in the hope that the actual practice of mothering might give rise to other possible ways of constructing motherhood and to other-than-patriarchal ways of thinking that could have a transformative effect on literary, political, and social conditions.

Rather than seeing motherhood as biologically predetermined and central to all women's lives, we, like Rich, see motherhood as a potential relationship rooted in female physicality; but we also see it as a choice essentially *separate* from biology, drawing a distinction here between the ability to give birth and the decision to care for children. Although giving birth is indeed a part of mothering, it is caregiving that *defines* the act of mothering, and caregiving is a choice open both to those who give birth and those who do not. In this sense, Ruddick says, all mothers are adoptive mothers, meaning that one "adopts" the child—whether one has given birth to that child or not—when one chooses to care for that child. We think this notion of "adoption" may serve as the foundation of a transformation of motherhood, as it is predicated upon the necessity of choice and thereby rejects essentialist views of women.

Crucial issues here are who makes that choice and under what conditions. The question of choice becomes increasingly urgent with the advent of new reproductive technologies that threaten to make the ancient fantasy of "single male parenthood, in which reproduction has nothing to do with women" (O'Brien, *Politics of Reproduction*, 127), a reality. The language of the reproductive technocrats—in which eggs are "harvested" and so on—presumes the absence of the mother as a speaking, involved subject; instead, as Gena Corea has shown, she is a "machine" whose role is that of passive object of scientific experimentation. Similarly, the language of so-called surrogacy contracts separates the mother not only from her child, but from her own uterus, her own body.[2] Women need to challenge this vocabulary, and they are doing so, in this volume and elsewhere. One important recent challenge to such language is *Recreating Motherhood: Ideology and Technology in a Patriarchal Society*, wherein Barbara Katz Rothman offers the concept of relatedness as the basis of a woman-centered understanding of motherhood, including abortion, adoption, and "surrogacy":

> There is much in the experience of motherhood that fights against alienation, that fights against seeing things and people as separate, but rather fosters a vision of connection. . . . Motherhood is an experience of interpersonal connection. (88–89)

Any effort at redefining motherhood must include some consideration of childbirth's meaning. While giving birth is not everything, it is far indeed from being nothing either. If we turn to imaginative literature, we often find childbirth as metaphor, not as narrated experience: the cliche of the creative process is one in which the (usually male) artist gives birth to a work of art. Mary O'Brien, in *The Politics of Reproduction*, traces this familiar metaphor back as far as Plato. In the *Timaeus*, Plato inverts "the reality of maternity as opposed to the ideality of paternity," thereby making "motherhood . . . passively abstract while male creative imagination becomes a potent and regenerative force" (O'Brien, 125). For centuries, male metaphors have dominated our language and our consciousnesses, but O'Brien believes that a revolution in the politics of reproduction will also revolutionize consciousness, perhaps as radically as it was once transformed by male knowledge of and control over men's participation in reproduction. Thus, as women challenge male metaphors of birth, they also transform human consciousness.

In *Bearing the Word*, Margaret Homans argues that women writers tend to privilege the literal, a strategy that often leaves them with no figurative ground on which to stand. However, given the Lacanian model that Homans employs — a model that views women as the unconscious of language — we find her conclusions inevitable. In fact, many discourses, rather than a single "Symbolic," have defined motherhood, and in the gaps between the various official discourses — religious, legal, medical, psychoanalytic, etc. — women have managed to tell stories of mothering. However, the discourse of actual mothers must be disentangled from psychoanalytic terminology, such as the pre-Symbolic, before feminists can begin to hear the double-voiced discourse of mothers. As Hirsch says, "Feminists are in the process of inventing new theories and new fictions that might be maternal without falling into essentialism, that might act out the mother's contradictory double position" (*Mother/Daughter Plot*, 198). We shall return to this notion of the double position and the double-voiced discourse of maternal subjectivity, but one brief example may be useful here. In "From the Poets in the Kitchen," Paule Marshall speaks of the advantages for girls, who later become mothers and/or writers, of having listened to kitchen talk among women. Besides "instilling in [Marshall] an appreciation for ordinary speech" (205), this talk also introduced her to a subjectivity that "had never heard of the mind/body split" (213). Furthermore, in adjectives such as "'beautiful-ugly': the beautiful-ugly dress, the beautiful-ugly car," she heard a dualistic discourse that we think may be one characteristic of maternal speech and writing.

Significantly, the women whose writing is analyzed in *Narrating Mothers* resist binary logic, particularly the injunction to either mother or write, in order to assert the value of *both* procreation *and* creation. To insist upon a dialogic (both/and) rather than a monologic (either/or) subject, these mother/writers must simultaneously disrupt narratives that silence mothers and invent a different notion of character, or subjectivity. Jessica Benjamin argues that we must invent an "*inter*subjective" psychology to replace the Freudian "*intra*subjective" psychology that has silenced mothers, denying them subjectivity. Unfortunately, though, as women writers strive to transform the Freudian subject — with his well-bounded ego — into a subject whose consciousness is relational, or intersubjective, critics often confuse this more fluid consciousness with the pre-Symbolic. But as Nel Noddings has pointed out in *Caring*, motherhood is not a role, it is a relationship. Parents and teachers, according to Noddings, must see "with two pairs of eyes" (70). We see feminists, in a variety of disciplines, redefining motherhood and teaching in terms of this duality. Noddings points out that "the work of the teacher is facilitated by her dual vision" (70). Using similar terminology, Kathryn Rabuzzi emphasizes in *Motherself* that maternal consciousness is "dual" and therefore different from "the single-minded purposiveness of the unitary self" (57). Likewise, what Julia Kristeva (following Mikhail Bakhtin) calls the "dialogic" text and what Hirsch calls "double-voiced" selfhood are not the same as the fluid, preverbal state of childhood consciousness.

In *Boundaries of the Self*, Roberta Rubenstein recommends that what we stereotypically identify as "masculine" and "feminine" modes might be better termed "agency" and "communion" to differentiate opposing ways of relating to experience (191). We believe that the communal self is identified in our culture with the flesh, and thus with "Woman" (in the mythical sense). Consequently, the communal self is assumed to be an inferior, pre-Symbolic consciousness associated with the "lack of separation" in the undifferentiated child. Somatophobia is one consequence of the silencing of maternal voices in our culture as the bounded self—the self of "agency"—struggles to deny its participation in matter and mortality. As Rubenstein says, "In a given culture, the proportion of activity accorded members of each gender in each mode may be strictly set; furthermore, the culture itself may be characterized by emphasis on one more than the other" (191). The Western literary canon has privileged one mode—the male mode of agency—just as classroom discourse frequently has privileged one voice, rather than voices in dialogue. Noddings identifies the practice of dialogue as a maternal mode often absent in the classroom, just as the communal mode often is undervalued in society. Thus, as Noddings says, "We may have to struggle through a tremendous upheaval before mother and father are heard equally in the schools" (183).

A number of writers in this collection use various strategies to signify the communal mode—which in our culture tends to be associated with the maternal—as necessary for preserving a healthy planet on which to raise healthy children. Some of our essayists identify this collective or communal self to praise it; others find the fluid, unbounded self dangerous to children, linking it, for example, to boundary violations such as incest. Although this topic needs further investigation, we think that perverted agency—and not communal selfhood—is the cause of such boundary transgressions. Yet, as Roberta Rubenstein demonstrates, "The very concept of the boundary itself is fluid"(8), and women writers seem to be preoccupied with boundaries of various kinds: physical boundaries (as in pregnancy); psychological boundaries; relational boundaries (as in the experiences of attachment, union, separation, and loss); and the boundaries of families and cultures.

Minimally, truly feminist theories of motherhood would assess the boundaries, values, and meanings of motherhood in accordance with mothers' own testimony about the meanings of pregnancy, childbirth, and childcare. A feminist theory would value mothers' labor and language and insist upon their access to language. This concern is central in the essays in *The (M)Other Tongue*, a groundbreaking collection of feminist psychoanalytic criticism edited by Shirley Nelson Garner, Clare Kahane, and Madelon Sprengnether, yet psychoanalytic theories of language remain highly problematic for mothers, as we have suggested. At present, the branch of feminist literary theory most directly concerned with the question of maternal language posits the mother's language as a nonverbal one limited to the preoedipal period, with some theorists going so far as to assert that the mother's bodily fluids are her language. If the only maternal language imaginable, or at least admissible, is a preoedipal, nonverbal one, then mothers are effectively silenced and barred from public discourse,[3] a move that serves patriarchal control of mothers and of motherhood.

In order really to hear mothers' voices, feminists have to recognize the actual limitations both of mothers' power and of their powerlessness. Gloria Joseph persuasively argues that black daughters, as witnesses of racism directed at their mothers, earlier come to know the real boundaries of their mothers' power in the world and therefore tend to produce fewer victim/powerless daughter narratives—ones that posit the mother as all-powerful and therefore as all-responsible—than do white women (95–105). Numerous women writers explore the powerful/powerless paradox and its implications both for the practice of mothering and for the writing mother. How are mothers affected by theories of motherhood? This question arises in some form in most of the essays collected here. Several women writers discussed in this volume create mothers who actively resist the powerful/powerless split, who reach out to other mothers in attempts to subvert patriarchal power through female alliances, who perceive mothering not strictly in biological or in property terms but also in social terms, as a collective (social, public) responsibility. These mothers find in the practice of mothering a model for social and political action. These fictional mothers extend their love of their own children outward, finding in that very intense personal love a less personal but nonetheless powerful love of *all* children and concern for the future of the human race.

The idea of mothering as a collective responsibility is a revolutionary one in Western society, as it runs precisely counter to capitalist, patriarchal prescriptions for motherhood; it is not, however, a new idea, as it has historically been familiar in African and African-American cultures.[4] Patricia Hill Collins, in "The Meaning of Motherhood in Black Culture and Black Mother/Daughter Relationships," describes the importance to African-American communities of "othermothers" and "community othermothers." According to

Collins, "'othermothers,' women who assist bloodmothers by sharing mothering responsibilities, traditionally have been central to the institution of Black
motherhood" (5). Black women's experiences as, or knowledge of, othermothers
provide models for social activism, wherein community othermothers take
public responsibility for *all* black children. Under patriarchal capitalism,
motherhood is largely about private property: the children are the property
of the father who "loans" them temporarily to the mother, whose duty is to
raise those children according to the father's law. In turn, private property
and the whole notion of ownership are about competition; the idea is to
amass more, or at least better, property than that held by others, because property is power. Motherhood under the law of the white father requires that
the mother love her own children to the exclusion of others, that she place
her own children above other children, and that she see her own children's
claims as *a priori* more valid than the claims of other children.[5] Seeing motherhood as a collective responsibility leads mothers to see other mothers' children as being equally entitled to claims on mothers' care as their own children are.

While resisting the powerful/powerless split and challenging traditional
constructions of motherhood, women writers simultaneously attack the
other familiar binary oppositions of mother/father, private/public, and, most
important for our own work, the injunction from fathers to mothers: either
mother or write. Most of these writers mother *and* write, as did many of their
predecessors and as do many of their characters. For centuries, women have
been told that they may have books or babies, but not both, a doctrine that
Ursula Le Guin—along with many of the writers in this collection—recognizes as false: "just the flip side of the theory that books come from the
scrotum" (36). As Le Guin points out, "The books-or-babies myth is not only
a misogynistic hang-up, it can be a feminist one" (37). Like Le Guin, many
of the writers/mothers whose work gives rise to *Narrating Mothers* surely
would agree with Alicia Ostriker's assertion that mothering, far from disabling the woman writer, *enables* her:

> The advantage of motherhood for a woman artist is that it puts her in im-
> mediate and inescapable contact with the sources of life, death, beauty,
> growth, corruption. . . . If the woman artist has been trained to believe that
> the activities of motherhood are trivial, tangential to the main issues of
> life, irrelevant to the great themes of literature, she should untrain herself.
> The training is misogynist, it protects and perpetuates systems of thought
> and feeling which prefer violence and death to love and birth, and it is a
> lie. (Quoted in LeGuin, 36)

At the same time, practical limits do exist: a woman who must stand ironing all day cannot also both write *and* care for her children.

The tension between figurative and literal creation is evident in the words of two Boston-area women writers interviewed by Ruth Perry for *The Women's Review of Books* in 1988. Echoing Ostriker's comments, but also drawing attention to their daily "Balancing Acts" (the title of the piece), both Kathi Aguero and Marea Gordett say that mothering has changed their writing. Gordett finds herself turning toward fiction, because she believes that in fiction she can "respond to some of the issues of motherhood . . . that maybe I can't in poetry" (29).

But the connection between fiction and motherhood is more vexed than Gordett's remark implies. Even though (public) autobiography is a genre no freer from history—and from male-devised conventions—than fiction, it enjoys a privileged status among some feminist scholars. By contrast, the novel is often suspect. Judith Fetterley concludes in *Provisions* that nineteenth-century stories by women "could perhaps be better told" in those genres "less clearly marked" and "less formalized, less pretentious, and less predetermined, and therefore more open, fluid and malleable to their uses" than the novel (15). Yet, as Marianne Hirsch claims, women novelists are employing post-modern strategies to break down conventional boundaries that have defined women in binary terms. In a section of *The Mother/Daughter Plot* called "Postmodern Plots," Hirsch describes how the ideology of realistic novels has come under close scrutiny in contemporary novels, as women writers reformulate the boundaries between public and private, mothers and daughters, past and present, myth and history. Despite the fluid boundaries in works by Margaret Atwood, Marguerite Duras, and Christa Wolf, for instance, Hirsch does not describe their investigations of subject formation in Lacanian terms:

> Although I identify in these texts some of the literary strategies we have come to identify as postmodernist—polyvalence, multiplicity, fluidity, indeterminacy, open-endedness, fragmentation—I do not connect them with what Lacan identifies as the slippage of the signified, the play of the signifier, or the irreducible, unbridgeable bar between signifier and signified. (139)

Instead, Hirsch argues that this deconstruction of the subject leads to a reformulation of the subject who "returns to raise the political, historical, and social question of subjectivity" (139). Certainly such a postmodern project is useful for creating spaces in which to allow mothers to speak for themselves.

It is important to know, however, that efforts to claim subjectivity for mothers do not originate in the twentieth century. Many nineteenth-century women writers imagined themselves as mother-authors. Despite the subversiveness of this authorial act, Margaret Homans demonstrates in *Bearing the Word* that these women often were deeply conservative in their portrayals of motherhood, locating maternal power within the images of patriarchal religion but at the same time insisting that such spiritual power had the capacity to transform life on earth. As twentieth-century readers and writers, feminists may not share these views of maternal power; however, the representation of that power in ninetenth-century fiction enables us to deconstruct motherhood as a patriarchal institution and to understand the ideology of realistic novels. Postmodern strategies enable twentieth-century novelists to question, resist, and transform what Mikhail Bakhtin describes as "that sturdy skeleton of plot and composition, that we have grown to expect from the novel as a genre" (22).

Of course, the ideology of narrative forms is not confined to the novel; other genres, such as autobiographies and biographies, also pose problems for women writers, with conventions dictating the kind of self the writer must present. As Doris Sommers says in "Not Just a Personal Story," autobiography "became really popular during the Renaissance and Reformation when self-made men became the rage" (111). She therefore asks of the genre: "Is it the model for imperializing the consciousness of colonized peoples, replacing their collective potential with a cult of individuality and even loneliness?" (111). Yet most of the essays in *Life/Lines*, a volume edited by Bella Brodzki and Celeste Schenck, in which the Sommers essay appears, assert that women autobiographers construct a different subject, a subject whose identity is grounded in relationships. This relationship may be with a transcendent being, a spouse, children, or community; but, as Bella Brodzki states in her introduction to *Life/Lines*, "This self-definition of identity in relation to significant others is the most pervasive feature of female autobiography" (8). As Roberta Rubenstein says of writers like Maxine Hong Kingston and Leslie Marmon Silko, in order to reweave boundaries of selfhood that move beyond the binary opposites of culture and gender, it is necessary to extend "the boundaries of narrative form" (205).

Clearly, women writers, including those in this collection, *are* revising the conventions of prose narratives, such as the autobiography and the novel, in order to tell stories of mothering. Often, however, they do so only to find resistance from readers who have been taught to read as men and who expect to be told the "classic" tales of adventure and romance, in which the hero (or heroine) is seeking to establish a sense of self—or agency or individuality— through "murdering" the mother (not just the father, as Freud would have us believe). Such *bildungsromans* have been mistaken as the core plot of the novel, and often of autobiographies and biographies as well, but of course this story is only one of many these genres are capable of telling. Indeed,

Rachel Blau DuPlessis sees "the project of twentieth-century writers [as being] to solve the contradiction between love and quest and to replace the alternate endings in marriage and death that are their cultural legacy from nineteenth-century life and letters by offering a different set of choices" (4). One such choice, of course, is to begin with a mother's voice, thereby demonstrating that women do not become mute after marriage and childbirth.

We agree with Marianne Hirsch that "feminism might begin by listening to the stories that mothers have to tell, and by creating spaces in which mothers might articulate those stories" (*The Mother/Daughter Plot*, 167). Sometimes these spaces occur in the gaps, or discontinuities, between different discourses—religion, law, medicine, folktales, kitchen talk—but readers who look only for unity may not hear what Roberta Rubenstein calls "the maternal subtext" (235). In the classical story of Demeter and Persephone, or its "inversion," states Rubenstein, women writers frequently explore issues of selfhood, "including attitudes toward sexuality, procreation, relationship, and autonomy" (235). If we read only as daughters, we may fail to hear what mothers are trying to say. Because we believe, as Rubenstein suggests, that the mother-daughter relationship is often "a paradigm of conflicting cultural messages" (237), we think that, as readers and as teachers, we need to become alert to this site of contradiction.

We find that narratives in which mothers are split into "good" and "bad" often articulate these conflicts. When the woman writer assumes the maternal point of view, her quest may involve a confrontation with the "bad" mother, who is at once her own childhood memories of an archaic mother *and* an aspect of her present—perhaps her own maturation and aging—which requires psychic integration. Such an integration may free the mother-author from society's misogyny and somatophobia; thus, it is important for us as readers to understand that, as Rubenstein says, "Allusions to or incorporations of myths, fairy tales, legends and classical motifs frequently suggest attempts to mediate contradiction: to get not only 'beyond language' but beyond culture to resolve the dilemmas faced by the central characters" (238). As the mother-author mediates conflicting messages, or contradictions, from the culture, she often puts boundaries into play in what Bakhtin calls a "carnivalization" of discourses. But if readers interpret such moments of boundary transgression exclusively in psychoanalytic terms—as a regression to the pre-Symbolic—the subversive impulse behind such linguistic play may be silenced by readers. Readers may, for instance, wish to silence the contradictions in postmodern texts, rather than confronting the problems they pose, such as the problem of redefining maternal subjectivity. As Rubenstein suggests, "The willingness to accommodate rather than resolve contradiction . . . indicates the characters' refusal of dualistic modes of thought themselves" (238). Instead, the character, quite possibly the mother-narrator, may embrace the "both/and," the "beautiful-ugly," of dialogic consciousness.

The hybrid forms of writing that women authors often produce are textual symptoms of the effort to reformulate the subject (maternal or otherwise). The boundaries between genres are fluid: maternal fiction is often highly autobiographical, autobiographies frequently employ fictional strategies, collections of short stories often read more as novels, and the text of the feminist classroom sometimes reads as a confrontation between mother/teachers and daughter (or son)/students. Therefore we have concluded that in the process of redefining mothering it is also necessary to redefine genres and their conventions. Since Oedipal narratives silence the voices of mothers, we must listen for maternal stories in postmodern plots where selfhood is constructed, or reconstructed, in more complex patterns.

As Hirsch emphasizes, this project requires that we "develop a more complicated model of identity and self-consciousness" (The Mother/Daughter Plot, 194). This selfhood, she says, "would have to balance the personal with the political, the subjective experience with the cognitive process of identification with various group identities. It would have to include a consciousness of oppression and political struggle. It would have to be both familial and extra-familial" (194). This notion of the postmodern is, as Hirsch states, not simply aesthetic but also political.

In short, we have only begun to map the psychic geography of maternal consciousness, but it appears to us to be more complex than we might at first have imagined. If we follow the way of mothers, dislodging mothers from their place in our psychic and cultural past in order to relocate the voices of mothers in our collective future, we may begin to understand this more complex consciousness. Since, as Ruddick notes, it frequently surprises people that mothers do, in fact, think, merely to claim that maternal thinking is complex is to court disbelief. Nevertheless, relational consciousness, which insists upon acknowledging the subjectivity of the (m)other, moves beyond dualism, embracing the both/and: the "beautiful-ugly," for instance, or the "good/bad" mother. Frequently, as Jessica Benjamin tells us in The Bonds of Love, this consciousness is represented in spatial terms (127), and we must look for these open spaces to find what Benjamin calls "the dance of mutual recognition" (130). In this dance, Benjamin says, "when the totality of space between, outside, and within our bodies becomes the site of pleasure, then desire escapes the borders of the imperial phallus and resides on the shores of endless worlds" (130). We turn now to the writers in this volume who are exploring together these shores of "endless worlds."

Essays in part 1 of *Narrating Mothers*, "Mothers Redefining Authority," posit considerable differences between how mothers are defined according to official discourses and how mother-novelists and autobiographers view mothers. Mother-writers' questions, such as under what social conditions women mother, lead to new definitions of maternal authority. As Elaine Hansen says, in her analysis of Marge Piercy's *Woman on the Edge of Time* and Margaret Atwood's *The Handmaid's Tale*, "Both novels clearly resist and deconstruct the mythic duality, paradox, or splitting of the mother, her omnipotence and powerlessness, her overshadowing presence and her fundamental absence." Hansen also finds that both Piercy and Atwood challenge the notion that motherhood and writing are incompatible; however, under conditions of patriarchy, it appears to be the absence of their children that enables mothers to write.

In her essay, "Mother Right/Write Revisited: *Beloved* and *Dessa Rose* and the Construction of Motherhood in Black Women's Fiction," Carole Boyce Davies asserts that accounts of mothering must include race and history in their analyses. In both novels, Davies finds the question of "mother rights" closely linked to the power of mothers to write. According to Davies, Morrison's text speaks "double-voicedly" in order to critique "exclusive mother-love as it asserts the necessity for Black women to claim something as theirs," and Williams examines motherhood as a contradictory site of power and powerlessness for black women.

Through an analysis of a mother-authored autobiography, in her essay Jane McDonnell is "reclaiming the voice of the mother against the discourse of the experts." In this case, the expert is Bruno Bettelheim, who claims that "refrigerator mothers" cause autism in children, a mother-blaming view challenged by Clara Claiborne Park's *The Seige*, which describes how a mother sees her autistic daughter. Like Hansen, McDonnell finds considerable difference between the way the mother-writer defines her maternal authority and the way the male expert defines his. The mother-author is humbler, less arrogant, but, at the same time, she is less frequently read and is assumed to be a less reliable narrator. McDonnell's essay responds to Sara Ruddick's call for work that "tests and extends the insights of some feminist literature," literature that often assumes a child's "predictable growth" in white, middle-class conditions.

In her analysis of another maternal autobiography, Shirley Nelson Garner argues that mothering and writing are compatible activities for Maya Angelou, but under conditions very different from those assumed by psychoanalytic discourse. Even in the writing of D. W. Winnicott, which shows considerable interest in supporting mothers' authority, the assumption is that mothering is "natural" and, where a father provides economic and emotional protection, the "good enough" mother is possible. Garner demonstrates how Angelou's autobiography puts such assumptions into question.

In "Her Mother's Language," Cecelia Konchar Farr takes up the question of the power of mothers to write and thereby to rewrite the mythology of motherhood. Farr sees in E.M. Broner's *Her Mothers* an example of Helene Cixous's call for a liberating "mother-language," a subversive language that escapes the oppressive phallocentric determinism of the Symbolic, as defined by Jacques Lacan. Farr identifies these subversive strategies as linked to the pre-Symbolic, thus displaying a lack of differentiation among characters, shifting points of view, disruptions of the narrative, and a multiplicity of forms.

The essays in part 2, "Mothers Mapping Boundaries," explore a variety of types of boundaries: those between mothers and daughters, for example, and those between the autonomous and the social, or relational, self. The essayists also explore boundaries within the self, between the "good" and "bad" fantasy mother, between the self-as-artist and the self-as-mother, between the mother-author and the mother-nurturer. Physical and psychic boundaries also are scrutinized, as are the boundaries between cultures, between biological and adoptive mothers, between Native-American and Euroamerican conceptions of maternity, and between mothers of different social classes.

Quite possibly, what patriarchal myths consider a "good" mother is, from the perspectives of mothers and their children as well, "bad." This possibility is one that Mary Jane Elkins considers in her analysis of Margaret Drabble's fiction. According to Elkins, Drabble's later novels explore the social and psychological boundaries between "good" and "bad" mothers. Elkins demonstrates the frequency with which Drabble creates confrontational scenes between "good" mothers who, in contrast to the patriarchal ideal, have interests other than mothering and therefore a healthy sense of detachment from their children, and "bad" mothers who sacrifice themselves to motherhood and as a consequence have no boundaries themselves and do not respect their children's boundaries. Often in Drabble's fiction, mothers who show signs of madness are in fact not mad but in quest of the mother-monster, the witch of fairy tales who is inside all mothers. Successful mothers in Drabble's fiction, according to Elkins, confront this monster, successfully integrating the "good" and the "bad" mothers. But this psychic journey, which remaps the boundaries of maternal consciousness, has its objective correlative in actual mothers who are separated from each other by conventional definitions of good and evil and so fail to give attention to the social conditions of their mothering.

Paula Bennett notes an important danger in romanticizing fluid ego boundaries: the danger of boundary violation, particularly within families. Bennett examines the work of Virginia Woolf and Toni Morrison, arguing that, in *To the Lighthouse* and *The Bluest Eye*, mothers who ally themselves with patriarchal power and who therefore lack authentic authority may deprive their daughters of the ability to set appropriate boundaries. The lack of boundaries characterizes incestuous families, as Bennett emphasizes, and fluid boundaries between characters may be a symptom of this problem. Under conditions of patriarchy, the permeable boundaries that make mothers receptive to the needs of children may at the same time render them vulnerable to the predations of those with more bounded selves.

Gayle Greene finds in Doris Lessing's novels, particularly the pseudonymous work, *The Diaries of Jane Somers*, considerable ambivalence toward boundaries, toward separation and merging, that may help to account for Lessing's aversion toward feminism. Greene also finds in Lessing's fiction the notion that encounters with the fantasy mother may lead us to special powers, powers long repressed in Western culture, which may lead the way into a different future.

Judith Roof's essay, "'This Is Not for You': The Sexuality of Mothering," explores the boundaries of feminist psychoanalytic theory, which ignores the reality that some mothers are lesbian. Roof also examines the boundaries of two prototypical lesbian novels, in which mothers are defined by absence: lesbians disappear from the mothering theory created by heterosexual writers, while mothers disappear from lesbian narratives. Between the boundaries of these two discourses, Roof investigates the meaning of desire.

Hertha Wong's analysis of Louise Erdrich's fiction shows how differences in culture create differences in formulating boundaries of identity. In Native-American cultures, which value "interconnections rather than ruptures, cooperation rather than individualism," Wong finds that what is often perceived as boundary confusion in white society can be understood instead as a sense of relatedness. Wong finds Native Americans in Erdrich's fiction defining simply as "Indian" what white culture defines as "feminine." Yet even among the Chippewa, the communal self has become a burden, a source of vulnerability. As Wong says, "Having had their totem/family identities destroyed by Euroamerican domination, these characters must reformulate notions of self, family, and community," a task that frequently falls to mothers. Mothers are central in Erdrich's fiction, and the novelist's use of multiple points of view in a series of interconnected narratives reflects the Chippewa sense of identity in family and tribe.

When mothers write, they not only reformulate the boundaries of self and world, they also transform linguistic and social practices. In part 3, "Mothers Transforming Practices," we examine a variety of different practices: of writing, reading, teaching, and, of course, mothering itself. These five essays concern themselves with the barriers—sometimes within mothers, sometimes outside—to acting collectively as mothers to effect change in the world.

Judith Arcana finds that, in the fiction of Grace Paley, the boundaries among mothering, writing, and social activism undergo creative change. Arcana tells us, for example, that Paley's writing about mothers, who have figured centrally in her fiction, was encouraged by the feminist movement. Although Paley initially experienced a sharp division between her writing and her activism, largely due to the constraints of formalistic, apolitical conventions, she has so broadened the terms of mothering that she now sees maternal nurturance as "necessary on a global scale," according to Arcana. Like Margaret Drabble, Alice Walker, Marge Piercy, and other writers discussed in this volume, Paley refuses the public-private boundary, bringing mothers into a community, portraying mothers as talking with each other and as sharing the responsibility of making the world a safe and healthy place for the raising of children.

Yet feminists' fantasies of maternal perfectability inhibit this movement toward shared responsibility for mothering. For example, as Ruth Perry reads Mary Gordon's *Men and Angels*, this novel explores myths of maternal omnipotence. A "meditation about the relation between motherhood and work," *Men and Angels* also illustrates how the act of writing continues the act of mothering. As Perry says, "Gordon talks about writing as if it were a kind of mothering," and her relationship to her characters is like that of a mother who cares for her children but who also gives them independence.

In her essay, Maureen Reddy argues that we must learn new reading strategies in order to understand maternal narratives. She suggests that feminists use Sara Ruddick's theory of maternal thinking as a strategy for reading texts that centralize maternal subjectivity, in this instance novels by Jane Lazarre and Alice Walker. She further argues that maternal thinking, particularly the concept of "attentive love," may teach white women how to read texts by black women. Attentive love, as defined by Ruddick, is a kind of loving detachment, which "seeks to understand difference but not to change it." This stance, which mothers practice in raising children, Reddy seeks to broaden by applying it to reading. As Reddy argues, critics of works written from the perspectives of mothers frequently find it dificult to categorize that work, and faulty categorization often leads to reader confusion and even hostility.

Brenda Daly's essay describes Alice Walker's *Meridian* as a novel that tells the story of the Civil Rights Movement "according to mothers." At the same time, Daly reports that her efforts to teach this novel have demonstrated the difficulty of teaching students to read maternally. Like Reddy, Daly believes that maternal reading can be taught, but it is far more complex than she originally had anticipated. In her three efforts at teaching *Meridian*, Daly has found that gender is the most significant variable in how students read, but race, age, and the experience of mothering also make a difference.

In the essay that concludes this volume, Sheryl O'Donnell demonstrates how a transformation in student readers may be nurtured in a feminist classroom. O'Donnell's analysis of the feminist-classroom-as-text shows how students of both genders resist the political dimensions of the act of reading. O'Donnell suggests that feminist teachers must analyze their own fantasies of the teacher as a "good mother" with "grateful daughters and sons" in order to come to terms with resistance and hostility from students. In addition, O'Donnell shows how student journals, which so often become stories of victimization, may be nurtured by feminist teachers who encourage students to transform victimization into protest and self-assertion. Competition in the classroom may inhibit such collective self-revision, but O'Donnell demonstrates that student journals, by providing students with opportunities to tell their own stories, including mother-blaming stories, may become occasions for freeing students from their childish fantasies of omnipotent mothers.

Perhaps these opportunities for self-revision will lead students to move beyond romantic tales depicting flights from the mother or more violent stories of slaying the mother—for example, the tale of Perseus's slaying of Medusa. As we confront our fantasy mothers—at once monstrous and omnipotent—we may slay our own fears of freedom, so that people of both genders may engage in the task of imagining what it means to mother children. One of the most challenging tasks will be the education of male imaginations. For centuries women have been required to read from the point of view of men (and fathers); now it is time for men to learn to read as women (and mothers) if we are to survive. Sons and daughters must learn to imagine the complexities of what Sara Ruddick calls "preservative love," if we are to bring the capacity for nurturing life into the public sphere from which it has been excluded for centuries. Now that feminists have learned the significance of gender in the reading process—an awareness signaled by such texts as *Gender and Reading*—surely we will find strategies for addressing the complexities of motherhood. Such complexities sometimes are suppressed in more traditional classrooms, where the search for textual unity may lead to a blurring of those discourses which currently control definitions of motherhood.

We must begin to investigate where students take the classroom discourse of motherhood, as Sheryl O'Donnell suggests, to understand where students take this knowledge and how they negotiate the contradictions they experience in different discourse communities. The feminist classroom should not become a "bounded text," as O'Donnell emphasizes, since the work of redefining motherhood has implications far beyond the doors of classrooms and outside the covers of academic books and journals. We have placed O'Donnell's essay last in this volume in order to underscore the fact that learning to hear the voices of mothers and learning to speak as mothers are absolutely necessary projects if feminists are successfully to combat the threats posed to our very lives by the resurgence of the political Right. We need more narratives of mothers' experiences of mothering and working and writing— activities not sharply divided, as we learn from many of the essays in this volume—and we need to pay attention to those narratives. We need to recognize the silencing of mothers that is implicit in calls for a return to traditionalism and to "classical" canons. We also need to see the ideological intersection of this silencing with the denial of mothers' needs in the federal government's refusal to enact decent childcare legislation and in the Supreme Court's erosion of *Roe v. Wade*. The antichoice movement is only the most recent and the most currently visible incarnation of familiar social forces that attempt to define and control motherhood. We should take care to remember that what happens to mothers happens to us all.

Notes

1. In *Of Woman Born*, Adrienne Rich says of this somatophobia:

> The fear and hatred of our bodies has often crippled our brains. Some of the most brilliant women of our time are still trying to think from somewhere outside their female bodies—hence they are merely producing old forms of intellection. . . . The physical organization which has meant, for generations of women, unchosen, indentured motherhood is still a female resource barely touched upon or understood. We have tended either to *become* our bodies—blindly, slavishly, in obedience to male theories about us—or to try to exist in spite of them. (291)

2. Gena Corea extensively analyzes the implications of this language in *The Mother Machine*; see also Phyllis Chesler's analysis of the Whitehead-Stern contract in *The Sacred Bond* and Barbara Katz Rothman's chapter on surrogacy in *Recreating Motherhood*.

3. Nina Baym makes a similar point in "The Madwoman and Her Languages," 55–56.

4. See Gloria Joseph on collective mothering in African-American communities, 75–76.

5. Ruddick, *Maternal Thinking: Toward a Politics of Peace*, links this construction of motherhood to racism and to war (56–57). See also Claudia Koonz, *Mothers in the Fatherland: Women, the Family, and Nazi Politics*. This law does not usually apply to mothers of color, a lack of application that has its own pain.

Part I

Mothers
Redefining Authority

Chapter 1

Mothers Tomorrow and Mothers Yesterday, But Never Mothers Today:
Woman on the Edge of Time and The Handmaid's Tale

Elaine Tuttle Hansen

As observers of history from various perspectives have noted, few writers have been mothers; many theorists also argue that culture and language have been founded on the absence of the mother. In response to this disabling conjunction of real and symbolic circumstances in which discourse of and about mothering has been enmeshed, feminists now are concerned to rewrite the old story, to imagine maternity differently. One difficulty we face in this project is theorizing the relations between the two positions or ideas, each already destabilized and problematized by feminist thought, signified by the terms "maternal" and "feminine," "mother(ing)" and "woman." To put it one way, only biological women give birth, but not all biological women are, can be, or choose to be mothers, and not all who mother give birth, or are women. Another difficulty entails the frequently noted gap between theoretical and ideological constructions — feminist or not feminist — and experience, between the institution of motherhood and the fraught myths of the mother, on the one hand, and the "practice" of mothering as lived in disparate cultural, socioeconomic, and psychic circumstances, on the other.[1] Such issues underlie and give rise to the spectrum of opinion seen over the course of the past two decades of feminist debate (and often within positions held by individual debaters), ranging from earlier repudiations of the burdens of motherhood through later celebrations of maternity as the empowering female difference, even the privileged aesthetic position within language or a visionary political standpoint, to recent critiques of such privileging. At the same time, across such divisions in modern feminist opinion about the maternal, some have seen a pervasive failure to revise patriarchal notions of the mother and her role. Contemporary Western feminist thought has been charged with being not only a white middle-class movement, but a white middle-class daughter's movement.[2]

Where is the missing mother, in writing, in theory? When will her story be told? When it is, will it give us answers to questions with long histories, yet still vital to feminist inquiry? When the mother's voice is heard, will it speak of a special access through the maternal to the world of imaginative vision, a place somewhere else, outside phallogocentrism? Or will it speak of (and/or somehow from) the fissure between mothering and writing? If most participants in the debate over issues such as these could agree on one thing, it might be that a lot simply remains to be seen, and with this in mind, some feminist critics have turned to the most recent writing by women who are mothers or who write about mothering from their evolving understanding of the maternal.[3] The two novels I read here, Marge Piercy's *Woman on the Edge of Time* (1976), with its utopian vision, and Margaret Atwood's *The Handmaid's Tale* (1985), a dystopian nightmare, explicitly speculate about what mothering might look like in the future, and how we might get there. In the first part of the following discussion, I explore the ways in which each novel gives a particular, compelling voice to the so-called missing mother in its critique of present social arrangements. The protagonists in both are mothers, and their behavior and experience as such in past, present, and future time are a crucial focus of representation. Women's relation to biological reproduction is also the central political issue, the perceived locus of power, in both utopian and dystopian fantasies; moreover, the relation of actual mothering and imaginative creativity is examined in both narratives. At the same time, as I suggest in the second and concluding part of this essay, what seems most intriguing and open to me is that both these mothers' stories center on their inability to mother, and specifically on the tragic loss of a female child. In these texts the missing mother speaks above all to lament the missing daughter, and thus both novels problematize any simple substitution of the mother-daughter bond for the old stories of mother-son, father-daughter, and father-son relations.

In *Woman on the Edge of Time*, the story's problems and solutions and the protagonist's weaknesses and strengths are imbricated, in both the realistic and the fantastic plots, with her maternal experiences—her local and specific behavior *as* a mother and the ideological and theoretical notions of what it means to (be a) mother that she represents. In the present time of the story, sometime in the second half of the twentieth century—I'll call this "real time," for short—Connie Ramos is an unfit Chicana mother, previously committed to a mental hospital for abusing her four-year old daughter, Angelina, who was subsequently taken from her for adoption by a middle-class white couple. Connie is read by the so-called caring professions into whose hands she falls as "socially disorganized" (377), a rubric that at least accounts for the contradictory observations the professionals themselves make—she is "cooperative," they note at one point, but then later she is described as "hostile and suspicious toward authority" (379). The final diagnosis at Bellevue is "Schizophrenia, undiff. type 295.90" (378); at Rockover State Psychiatric Hospital, "Paranoid schizophrenia, type 295.3" (379). Such dehumanizing labels are offered only at the very end of the novel, however, in a brief epilogue of sorts, closing the fictional story with a few putatively official files on the case after Connie has willfully committed subversive acts that, the narrative implies, put her beyond the imaginative reach of novel writing, fictional authority, or readerly apprehension. The main story that precedes, the bulk of the novel, indicts not Connie but, among other things, the crude and cruel ignorance of institutional psychiatry and social work. Novel writing and fantasy-making are thus set in relief by the epilogue as discursive modes that see the mother unofficially, differently, more compassionately, and more honestly.

As the official, reductive diagnosis in fact suggests, Connie in the realistic story embodies all that is normally perceived as paradoxical in our culture's paranoid and schizophrenic myths about mothers and mothering: she is passive, submissive to the will of others, empathic, self-sacrificing; she is tough, violent, resistant to the will of others, self-absorbed. Her behavior is not represented by the novel, however, as an index of some internal, individual bind or an inevitable split, for good or bad, constitutive or otherwise, in the maternal as type of the subject.[4] The point instead is that the negative consequences of the apparent dichotomy in Connie's personality and behavior are a function of the social and political context in which this woman is positioned as a mother. Her anger and violence are viewed both as self-implosive reflexes of her oppression and as tools of empowerment. Taught by her ethnic and class background to be a good woman — a passive, submissive, complicitous victim — Connie is brutalized and abandoned by a series of men and institutions who are allegedly her protectors: her father, brother, lovers, husbands, professors, doctors; her family, the welfare state, the hospitals she is imprisoned in. She is in turn unable to nurture and hold onto her child. She sees herself in this daughter, and comes to believe, after she loses the girl, that some of her neglect and even rage against the child was self-abusive: "She should have loved her better; but to love you must love yourself, she knew that now, especially to love a daughter you see as yourself reborn" (62).

Seen from the more enlightened perspective afforded by the novel's interwoven construction of a utopian community, moreover, Connie the schizophrenic Chicana is not merely situated in a truer history, but redefined as "an unusual and powerful mix" of these qualities we usually consider to be in binary, gender-specific, and irreconcilable opposition. And both sets of qualities are necessary in present and future time, the novel further suggests, to the successful rearrangement and revaluing of mothering practices, on which a better society for all depends.

The opening episode of the real-time plot anticipates the possibility toward which the story relentlessly moves: Connie's utter oppression and, above all, the fact that she is deprived of her daughter or any other person to love and protect are precisely what fuel crimes of justified violence against her immediate oppressors. The loss of the daughter, then, incites the mother's narrative here, though not in a straightforward way. In the first chapter, we witness the act that causes Connie to be reinstitutionalized, as she smashes an empty wine jug into the handsome, evil face of her niece's pimp, Geraldo.[5] The instrument of violence she chooses—presumably because it is nearest to hand—carries marked symbolic weight. As we learn a little later, the bottle, one of the few decorations in Connie's bleak two-room flat, contained dried flowers and grasses gathered on a rare family outing, a picnic with her estranged brother, Luis (or Lewis, as he wishes to be called), her niece Dolly, and Dolly's baby daughter Nita. What Connie remembers most about this picnic is that Nita, just learning to walk, fell asleep in her arms, and that she was allowed to hold her: "She had sat on the blanket burning, transfigured with holding that small sweet-breathing flush-faced morsel" (34). It is the erotic, sensual, "transfiguring" possibility of holding an infant that Connie unwittingly throws away, in effect, when she scatters the "nostalgic grasses" (16) and breaks the wine jug over Geraldo's nose. At the same time, in committing this act she takes the offensive as a mother and on behalf of mothers and mothering. She is rightfully protecting not herself, but her niece Dolly, the unloved and illegitimate daughter of the same brother who later betrays Connie, a woman whom she views as "her almost child" (20). Dolly, moreover, has come to her aunt pregnant and bleeding from Geraldo's beating, because he wants to abort the baby he has fathered on her, and so Connie defends her niece both as almost daughter and as almost mother. The wine bottle itself also foreshadows the smaller bottle, disguised as a container of herbal shampoo, in which Connie will conceal the poison she uses in the matching act of violence that closes her story. Both wine jug and shampoo bottle—emptied, curvilinear spaces no longer holding what they were designed to contain; fragile, easily shattered, yet dangerous vessels—clearly image the female womb itself as a weapon.

Connie is beaten and once again incarcerated for her opening act of maternal violence. As she lies strapped to a hospital bed, drugged and untreated for burns and broken ribs, she articulates her own understanding of both the difference and the connection between the anger that previously caused her to lose her daughter and the rage that she has now turned on the pimp:

> She hated Geraldo and it was right for her to hate him. Attacking him was different from turning her anger, her sorrow, her loss of Claud into self-hatred, into speed and downers, into booze, into wine, into seeing herself in Angelina and abusing that self born again into the dirty world. Yes, this time was different. She had struck out not at herself, not at herself in another, but at Geraldo, the enemy. (19–20)

It is perhaps the greater distance between niece and aunt that enables her to fight for Dolly, whereas she could only see her hated, defeated self in Angelina, her birth daughter.[6] Later in this passage, Connie goes on to think, mistakenly, that this time will be different, too, in that she will know how to convince the authorities that she is sane, so that she can "get out fast." The story demonstrates instead that she will never get out. In the present time of social injustice and inhumanity, a mother's righteous, deadly anger cannot disguise itself as sanity and will not serve to reunite her with her lost daughter, save her niece, or allow her niece to mother again.[7] In Connie's last reported act, she attacks the enemy again, this time more seriously and successfully and self-destructively, as she poisons several of the doctors who are carrying out mind-control experiments on mental patients like herself. Connie's premeditated murder is depicted as both heroic and self-sacrificial; as a piece of political commentary, the novel thereby registers the powers, limits, and costs of maternal violence in the realistic context.

In the utopian plot that intersects and shapes Connie's real-time experience, her qualities and capacities are again inextricably connected to her maternal experience and to our paradoxical stereotypes of the mother, but her talents are used and valued differently, just as mothering is practiced differently, in the future world. Connie turns out to be one of a handful of people in our time who can travel to the future, *because* they are passive, submissive, penetrable. In the terminology of time-travel here, Connie is a natural receiver, and her friend who fetches her from the future, Luciente, notes: "It's odd. . . . Most we've reached are females, and many of those in mental hospitals and prisons" (196). The novel thus debunks the mythic opposition between mental creativity and the self-denying, other-oriented side of mothering, just as it perhaps invokes another myth about creativity and madness, and certainly anticipates in its own way recent theories, like those of Julia Kristeva and Helene Cixous, attributing special imaginative and discursive powers to the feminine/maternal. In Connie's case, a narrative pattern further emphasizes the link between the maternal self and the experience of time travel. This pattern is established at the moment of "first contact" with the future: Luciente initially appears immediately *after* Connie has passed a playground full of brown-skinned girls that she imagines to be just about her daughter's age by now. She weeps with pain at the loss of Angelina, and with characteristic self-reproach thinks herself "sentimental": "Anybody would think that she had loved her daughter." In the next sentence, Luciente comes through: "A shadow across her" (40). Again, the second time they make contact, Connie is in the hospital, locked in seclusion, still physically suffering from the burns and beatings and mentally reliving the horrible moment when she hit Angie too hard and the child fell and broke her wrist. To forget the pain of losing the girl, this time she consciously lets herself feel Luciente's approach (and on this visit she travels to Matapoisett herself for the first time; 60–63). Later, when she learns to travel in time easily, she summons Luciente, for example, when she wants to stop herself from dwelling on memories of Angelina (113).

Through this strategy of initiating time travel (like the story itself), with memories of the lost daughter (a strategy that also serves to fill readers in on the history of Connie's case, well after we are already on her side), the novel equates the "unfit" mother's mental receptivity with her maternal experience, and revalues both—from a utopian point of view—as keys to the future. The narrative insists at the same time, however, both that Connie's maternal experience was not a positive force in her own life, and that she is not merely a receiver. In this way the novel does not simply propose that we can rewrite the victimization of women into a potential source of strength and power; maternal powerlessness, as it is experienced in the here and now, blocks the road to the future even as it opens the way by goading Connie into revolutionary violence. While Connie's constant recall of Angie may trigger her imaginative insights into the future, but just as often the pain of those memories stays with her in future time and, when it becomes too strong, breaks the psychic connection. When, for example, Connie visits the utopian "brooder," a building full of tanks where fetuses gestate, and learns with initial disgust that in the future world each test-tube baby will have three co-mothers of either gender, she weeps again for Angie and recalls bearing and nursing the child so intensely that she suddenly finds herself back in the mental hospital. Again and again, if Connie remembers the reality of her disabled mothering or the injustices of motherhood as an institution in real time, the link is broken (see 114, 125–27, 160, 183). Furthermore, gradually it becomes clearer that Connie is not just a receiver; often, as I noted before, to forget present pain she learns to thrust herself into the future (and on one occasion she even manages to get into the wrong future, without Luciente, possibly in the alternative universe that the utopians are fighting against). Luciente than realizes that Connie is a potent force in her own right: "Grasp, you could be a sender too. What a powerful and unusual mix" (113).

But again: only in utopia is this mixture of passivity and activity, of maternal empathy and maternal violence, viewed as a positive, powerful conjunction rather than a pathology or psychosis; and Connie and the novel, both committed to political action, cannot remain in the future. Just as her feelings of anger and pain can break the connection, so, too, as her real-time purposiveness and outwardly-directed rage take shape, she travels less and less frequently, and Luciente comments on the unreachable "hardness" in her mind (370). After Connie has irrevocably committed herself to murder—the insecticide is already in the doctors' coffee maker—her time-travel ends, and the novel has only a few pages to go: "She thought of Luciente, but she could no longer reach over. She could no longer catch. She had annealed her mind and she was not a receptive woman. She had hardened" (375).

What, here, is Piercy's prescription for feminist action? In the quest for an end to domination, is she actually urging the separation of mothering and being a biological mother, suggesting that women have to give up their special, sometimes celebrated powers of receptivity/creativity, putative reflexes of their physiological capacity to give birth, as Connie does, and as the women of the future have done?[8] Is she in fact inscribing the incompatibility between mothering/imagining and social reform or political change? This particular possibility is contradicted within the novel itself by Luciente's valorization of the imagination as a way to the better future—"The vestiges of old ways will fade. . . . We can only know what we can truly imagine. Finally what we see comes from ourselves" (328). And the novel, I think, does not mean to urge women to stop either mothering or imagining to take up revolutionary, guerrilla warfare. Instead, it realistically apprehends the complexities and compromises of trying to take care of children, do creative work, and/or be politically active; and it resists the notion that the power of (maternal/feminine) imagination it both idealizes and embodies is sufficient unto itself, independent of political purpose and action. Above all, *Woman on the Edge of Time* insists on the necessity of redefining motherhood, so that it is a collective as well as a personal project, and so that good mothering, like good art-making and good political action, recognizes, legitimates, and fosters the "powerful mix" that Connie, a sender and a receiver, would be in a better world.

It is important to emphasize that this is more like a prescription for parthenogenesis than one for androgyny, for Piercy does not attribute one set of binary traits to women and another to men, and urge that they be combined into a fuller human essense.[9] Instead, the novel locates the "powerful mix" most specifically *within* what is falsely conceived, and punished, as the mythic maternal split or paradox. Child abuser and sterile woman, Connie is still the constantly evolving figure of the caring mother, and remains committed to mothering even as her notion of what that means, like her own behavior, changes. Notably, it is only after Connie has convinced herself that her daughter Angie has been reborn in Luciente's daughter, Dawn (140), that she is able to free herself sufficiently from her own complicity and self-loathing to think of fighting back. Giving Angie to the future and assenting to its utopian repudiation of the biological role of women as mothers are turning points for Connie; thereafter, she dreams of becoming a comother herself (249), and the last thing she sees in Matapoisett, before she poisons the doctor's coffee, is Dawn/Angie. It is made pointedly clear that Connie knows the difference between her real loss and this imaginative substitution—again, the visionary imagination is not romanticized as an escape or retreat to an alternative reality in this novel—but the utopian dream nevertheless fires the real act of subversion. She tells a fellow inmate, "I dreamed of my daughter, safe, happy, in another place"; then she acknowledges that it is her absolute loss of anyone to love that empowers her vengeance: "If only they had left me something. . . . Only one person to love. . . . For that love I'd have borne it all and I'd never have fought back. . . . But I have nothing. Why shouldn't I strike back?"(372).

In real time, then, Connie has suffered for trying to embody, all too well but not exclusively, one side of the falsely dichotomous maternal personality, the one most overtly enjoined upon women in patriarchal prescriptions for motherhood, marked by passivity, vulnerability, empathy, lack of self-control, irrationality. These are also the qualities that empower her fantastic journey in time, but the novel does not sentimentalize or idealize even as it identifies with and revalues these capacities. Instead, it sugests that Connie has other valuable strengths, complementary in theory and in Matapoisett, that would make her a good mother if she were allowed to develop them, just as they make her a good sender: her aggression, her emotional and physical endurance, her drive to protect those she loves and to fight for her beliefs. But in real time, she can only be punished for those qualities, and the novel finally refuses to let us forget that Connie, mired in the historical specificity of her oppression as a female member of an ethnic minority, never will mother her own birth-daughter. And, indeed, once her final heroic act is committed, she is forever lost to us as well, cast beyond even the imaginative grasp of novelist and readers; we too are painfully lopped off from relationship with Connie and exiled into the position of reading the official files.

In *The Handmaid's Tale*, published almost a decade after *Woman on the Edge of Time*, the problem of women's biological link to mothering, solved in Piercy's utopian world by politically motivated renunciation and socially controlled technology, is even more obviously and singlemindedly at the center of the story. The dystopia Atwood constructs might have been designed to illustrate by counter-example Piercy's suggestion that we will get to a better world, one without injustice and inequality, when women give up their own apparent power, the capacity to give birth. For in the future-world of the early Gilead era, mothering (and the institutions that control it, including marriage and domestic life) is women's *only* (illusory) power. In a fantastic caricature of actual surrogacy practices brought to national attention shortly after the publication of the novel in the Baby M case, the gestational and caregiving aspects of maternal experience are strictly divided among women, through a system sanctioned by association with the Old Testament version of surrogacy practiced by Rachel, Jacob, and Bilhah. Quite literally, Gilead's women of childbearing years recite the ancient words of Rachel quoted in one of the novel's epigraphs: "Give me children, or else I die" (Genesis 30:1). Atwood's protagonist, known only as Offred (not her own name, but the name derived from the Commander she currently serves,[10] for survival depends completely on her biological capacity to give birth. The state protects her only because she once bore a child, a daughter earlier confiscated and given to a childless couple of the elite, and because she still has viable ovaries. If she or any Handmaid fails to conceive and bear a healthy child after three postings with aging, probably sterile leaders of the regime, she will at best be deported to "the Colonies," where many varieties of the powerless clean up toxic wastes until they die hideous deaths.

Concomitantly, all the old lines of gender difference are redrawn and reinforced by the totalitarian, patriarchal regime of Gilead, one of whose first important steps, we learn, was to fire all women from their jobs and freeze their financial assets. Ludicrously and cruelly, women who have argued against feminist reform and for conservative values that privatize and domesticate the female have been taken all too literally. Serena Joy, the wife in the Handmaid's household, is a former television personality who once made speeches, the Handmaid recalls, "about the sanctity of the home, about how women should stay home" (60). "How furious she must be," the Handmaid thinks, "now that she's been taken at her word"(61).

Atwood's novel thus seems to conflate both traditional misogynist and recent feminist notions of the special difference and power of the female body and the sacred, redeeming experience of maternity, and pushes them to one horrifying, logical extreme. Her pessimistic insistence on the ease with which feminist gains of the very recent past could be swept away seems only more and more percipient and urgent as political events develop at the end of the 1980s. As a dystopia, the *Handmaid's Tale* offers nothing like the programmatic recipe for change that is available in the utopian fantasy of Piercy's work; however, Atwood's indictment of this baldly patriarchal state's control over the female body and its reproductive powers is at least as biting as Piercy's earlier, perhaps more optimistic vision.

Like the earlier novel, Atwood's has a crucial epilogue, "Historical Notes on *The Handmaid's Tale.*" Later I shall return to a comparison of the two epilogues; at this point I merely note that in tone and interpretive function the "Historical Notes" are complex and unsettling. Here we are offered a brief glimpse of a better future (the year is 2195), wherein both male and female academics with Third-World and First-World surnames analyze the tale itself, at a conference of the Gileadean Research Association. But in this short episode, it is not clear how much things have changed: the male keynote speaker's references to putatively obsolete sexist language, for instance, evoke laughter and applause (381). And what are we to make of the speaker's apolitical stance, when he eschews "passing moral judgment upon the Gileadeans" and says, "'Our job is not to censure but to understand.' (*Applause.*)" (383)? Up to this point, the nightmare of the Handmaid's story had left me feeling that the job of getting out of Gilead and into any remotely tolerable future would have required not just censure, but subversion and revolutionary violence; is Atwood just satirizing academic complacence?[11] Like *Woman on the Edge of Time*, the Handmaid's story itself implies that there are limits to "understanding," that empathy has to be prepared to harden itself when revolution is called for.

While, as a satire, this novel does not spell out a program for avoiding the grim possibility it imagines, it is not therefore less interesting or available to feminist interpretation. Two timely questions about mothering in particular seem to me addressed here, questions that Piercy's more confidently (but not simplistically) prescriptive utopian work cannot raise in the same way. First, how are we to read Atwood's play with the metafictional capacities of narrative (and of first-person narrative in particular)? The speaker is an archly self-conscious one who often pauses to discuss her distaste for the story she must tell, or to assess the difficulty of telling the truth, or to offer alternative versions of certain episodes. And twice at least these passages toy with that old idea, implicated in the link between Connie Ramos's receptivity and her time-traveling capacity, that the (female) artist's storytelling is a type of reproduction, a metaphorical surrogate mothering, so to speak, in its own right. At these moments, the narrator speculates whether the imaginative artist can, in telling her story, create her audience, bring it into being; and on each occasion, the answer seems to be different.

In the first of these passages, the narrator remembers how her captors convinced her to become a Handmaid: they showed her a picture of her daughter with another woman, presumably her adoptive mother, and they told her, "You are unfit, but you want the best for her. Don't you?" She reports that her reply was "You've killed her," and adds, "She was wearing a dress I'd never seen, white and down to the ground." Then immediately follows this typical digression:

> I would like to believe this is a story I'm telling. I need to believe it. I must believe it. Those who can believe that such stories are only stories have a better chance. . . .
> It isn't a story I'm telling. . . .
> . . . But if it's a story, even in my head, I must be telling it to someone. You don't tell a story only to yourself. There's always someone else.

Even when there is no one.

A story is like a letter. *Dear You,* I'll say. Just *you,* without a name. Attaching a name attaches *you* to the world of fact, which is riskier, more hazardous: who knows what the chances are out there, of survival, yours? I will say *you, you,* like an old love song. *You* can mean more than one.

You can mean thousands.

I'm not in any immediate danger, I'll say to you.

I'll pretend you can hear me.

But it's no good, because I know you can't. (52–53)

This characteristic passage is interesting for several reasons, as the speaker moves back and forth in her efforts to find in discourse the control she has lost over her life, but all that I want to call attention to now is her struggle, at this point an avowedly futile one, to create an audience, a listener, "someone else," *you,* perhaps, in psychoanalytic terms, the "other." Here this effort can be read as a (failed) metaphor or displacement of maternal reproduction, coming as it does immediately after the memory of her daughter's picture and her own disbelief in the daughter's existence. The narrator can no longer care for or even, it seems, imagine the possibility of her lost child; in present time, she is also waiting and desperately hoping to give birth to another child, one who in turn will be taken from her as soon as it is born. Storytelling is thus implicitly seen here as a bereaved mother's necessary self-deception, a compensatory, imaginative giving birth to "someone" even as the "unfit" mother/narrator despairs that she will ever mother again, or that someone, anyone, can hear her words.

In a subsequent passage, by contrast, the teller's power to give birth to an audience, to imagine the other, is more firmly maintained. Almost three hundred pages later, near the end of the novel, chapter 41 begins, again, *"I wish this story were different"* (343). The Handmaid apologizes:

I'm sorry there is so much pain in this story. I'm sorry it's in fragments, like a body caught in crossfire or pulled apart by force. But there is nothing I can do to change it.

I've tried to put some of the good things in as well. Flowers, for instance, because where would we be without them?

Nevertheless it hurts me to tell it over, over again. Once was enough; wasn't once enough for me at the time? But I keep on going with this sad and hungry and sordid, this limping and mutilated story, because after all I want you to hear it, as I will hear yours too if I ever get the chance, if I meet you or if you escape, in the future or in heaven or in prison or underground, some other place. . . . By telling you anything at all I'm at least believing in you, I believe you're there, I believe you into being. Because I'm telling you this story I will your existence. I tell, therefore you are. (343–44)

The Handmaid still associates telling her story with her pain and lack of control; the most painful parts of the story (to me, at least, and this is another point I return to later) involve the loss of her child. Now, however, the fragmented story is literally compared to the female body in Gilead, divided "like a body caught in crossfire or pulled apart by force," and the product of her virtually forced narrative labor is a more solid "you" and "your existence," critically situated in "some other place." In this passage, the narrator suggests that artistic creativity, doomed here to repeat a painful experience, does not constitute merely an imaginative escape from the present (as it did not, finally, in *Woman on the Edge of Time*, either), nor does it offer the female artist a positive, liberating alternative to mothering (which throughout the novel, in the present time of utter oppression or in past reveries of relative freedom, is never seen as a burden, but as a privilege). It is instead, in its own right, a giving birth to you, to someone else, to alternatives and to new conjunctions and relationships in the future. Whether this represents anything more than the narrator's passing mood we cannot know; but to the extent that the tale itself survives to be read—as the epilogue insists that it does—the Handmaid as storyteller has mothered, in this sense; tale and epilogue together could embody her final optimistic notion here, "I tell, therefore you are," and "you" may include her lost daughter, her future offspring, her fictional readers who are brought to life in the epilogue, and her real readers. To the question of how maternity and creativity are related, then, it could be argued that the *Handmaid's Tale* offers at least once a tentative version of an answer as complicated and affirmative in its own way as Piercy's. Without freezing "the mother" into a particular position, the novel may manage to suggest that mothering and storytelling are analogous, not mutually exclusive, activities, that mothers can and do create, and that creativity itself— here embodied in a woman who has mothered and may mother, but does not mother now—entails much the same relation to the future and the possibility of a "someone else, *You*" as giving birth and/or giving care to a child.

Shortly I want to explore more implications of the two novels' common situation, the foregrounded inability of the mother to mother. First, however, let me briefly consider a related issue that *The Handmaid's Tale* raises: the question of what it means to mother (and, again, by one reading that the novel sometimes endorses, to tell stories), what qualities and characteristics are essential to or desirable in a good, or even just good enough, mother. In Connie Ramos, we see a woman who embodies and reconciles both sides of the mythic mother, her power and her powerlessness, her "clean anger" and her remarkable empathy. In the Handmaid as she displays herself to us, we have no such "unusual and powerful mix," but rather a woman who is much more ordinary, the typical protagonist that we have come to know since the stolid Marian of Atwood's first novel, *The Edible Woman*, whom one recent reviewer has called "the Atwood woman" (Yglesias, 3). She is both less power-less and less powerful than Connie. On the one hand, she is not drugged, nor considered insane; she has an education and is white and therefore genet-ically acceptable for the elite position of Handmaid; in the "normal" world of pre-Gileadan society, she had a job and money of her own. Her memories of motherhood imply that she had no serious problems, as Connie did, in loving her daughter adequately.

On the other hand, it sometimes seems that her strongest emotion in cap-tivity is boredom. She never tries to escape; she contemplates a variety of subversive, criminal acts but never commits them, is always cautious, or almost always. The most dangerous thing she does is to risk her life for sex-ual satisfaction by carrying on an affair with Nick, the man who may betray her or may save her, but whom she cannot resist; in the end, she simply waits, to be destroyed or rescued, by the man. She speaks of herself as a coward, terrified of pain, who wants to survive; to that end she often tries hard not to feel, and certainly seems to succeed in suppressing any signs of the rage that empowers Connie. In the very beginning, she announces: "I try not to think too much. Like other things, thought must be rationed. There's a lot that doesn't bear thinking about. Thinking can hurt your chances, and I intend to last" (10). Like most of Atwood's earlier heroines, here and else-where she is aware of, even at times seems eager to foreground, with deadpan humor, her own ordinariness, her limits and weaknesses, her failures of cour-age and wit. When the Commander takes her to an illegal nightclub, she calms her nervousness: "All you have to do, I tell myself, is keep your mouth shut and look stupid. It shouldn't be that hard" (306). And she admits to admiring what she cannot be, the heroine that she sees in her friend Moira, and worries about the double standard she holds for herself, on the one hand, and for Moira, on the other:

> How can I expect her to go on, with my idea of her courage, live it through, act it out, when I myself do not?
> I don't want her to be like me. Give in, go along, save her skin. That is what it comes down to. I want gallantry from her, swashbuckling, heroism, single-handed combat. Something I lack. (324)

What this narrator *is* capable of, or guilty of, by her own account, is not the kind of overtly criminal, antisocial, self-destructive behavior of a woman like Connie, but normal, "usual" behavior. Commenting on her past life, she says: "We lived, as usual, by ignoring. Ignoring isn't the same as ignorance, you have to work at it" (74). Now, however, although she tries not to think or feel too much, because she understands how dangerous that would be, she does want to know, or at least this is what she finds herself telling the Commander that she wants—after she has asked for and been given hand lotion (243). But still, any use of the knowledge she knows might be important seems just beyond her capacity. When, for instance, she finally admits to understanding what has been obvious to the reader for some time, that there is an underground resistance and that her walking partner is a member, she is given a chance to join their efforts. Her partner urges her to use her nightly secret meetings to find out something about the Commander; "'Find out what?' I say" (289). At best, she is not "an unusual and powerful mix" of what we perceive as dualities, like Connie, but someone caught in the middle between knowledge and ignorance, action and inaction, anger and numbness, resistance and submission, all too aware of what she lacks but incapable of changing. As she says, "I would like to be ignorant. Then I would not know how ignorant I was" (340).

What do we make of such a heroine, whose stupidity and complicity (or at least failure to fight back) seems to be, as she says in one of the last of her self-criticisms, "the point"?[12] Is she another one of Atwood's depressing postfeminist types, from whom women readers can take no pleasure, no positive inspiration?[13] How do we read her ambivalence about heterosexual relations, and about feminism itself, seen particularly in her portrayal of her own lost mother, who chose to be a single parent, as a somewhat pathetic and stereotyped seventies radical? And, more pertinently, how does her story recast the myth of the mother; what does the novel say to late-twentieth-century mother theory, particularly when read in the context of the earlier utopian vision of *Woman on the Edge of Time?* In opposite ways, I suggest, both novels clearly resist and deconstruct the mythic duality, paradox, or splitting of the mother, her omnipotence and her powerlessness, her overshadowing presence and her fundamental absence. While Connie as mother is both powerful—as a time-traveler, as a grandstanding liberation hero who embodies our ideas of courage—and powerless, imprisoned for life, the Handmaid is, more realistically, more pessimistically, neither. Concomitantly, in her postmodern blandness, paralyzing rather than dynamic ambivalence, ordinariness and willful lack of power, the Handmaid counters and interrogates the myth of the mother's ultimate responsibility, just as comothering in Matapoisett, again in a more positive and idealized fashion, models collective responsibility for its children. Susan Rubin Suleiman has asked why women are reluctant to give up this myth of ultimate or absolute responsibility ("On Maternal Splitting," 30 ff.) Perhaps it is because giving up the myth leaves us with unsettling fictional characters like the Handmaid. As Atwood's protagonist says, "Those who can believe that such stories are only stories have a better chance"; while Connie's heroism offers hope to everyone but herself, it is perhaps harder to believe that the Handmaid's story is only a story.[14] The possibility that both novels speak to the difficulty and useful-ness of giving up the mother's ultimate responsibility emerges with greater complexity if we unpack more fully now some ways of responding to the story of the missing daughter, as each novel carefully inscribes it.

As I have suggested in the preceding discussion, the mother's being de-prived of her child by a repressive patriarchal state and by the institutions it designates to "protect" women is crucial to each novel's critique of patri-archy. In the dominant ideology of Piercy's real-time America and Atwood's not-so-far-off Gilead, Adrienne Rich's assertion is borne out: "The loss of the daughter to the mother, the mother to the daughter, is the essential female tragedy," (Of Woman Born, 240). Writing in the 1970s, Rich argues that "there is not presently enduring recognition of mother-daughter passion and rapture," a recognition she believes anciently was expressed in the myth of Demeter and Kore (240ff.). In the separation of Connie from Angelina and of the Hand-maid from her daughter, we now have two potent evocations of the mother-daughter story, indeed a tale of "essential female tragedy"—"essential," that is, given the ideology and practice of motherhood that both novels stren-uously indict. Now, in conclusion, I return to this issue, and, with some of the open-endedness that both narratives structurally enjoin upon us, I sug-gest some (not all) of the ways I can imagine reading the story of the missing daughter as it is told here.

It could be argued, for instance, that by telling the mother's story as a tale of the inability to mother, these novels express and sustain the ambivalence about mothering that historically has been expressed in many myths and nar-ratives, and that late-twentieth-century feminists have reiterated in their movement from rejecting to celebrating (and then rejecting again) the mater-nal. As Woman on the Edge of Time in particular insists, this ambivalence itself may be attributable to the material conditions under which we mother, but this makes it all the more real and problematical to feminism in theory and in practice. Along these lines, one of the first readings of these stories that occurred to me was that in both cases, the loss of the protagonist's child solved the mother's practical problem of what to do with the kids while hav-ing either a utopian or dystopian vision. Flippantly (and admittedly from the position of a mother of two young daughters), I noted that the absence of her child effectively emancipated each protagonist from the cares and constraints of mothering a preschooler on her journey into the future. Were Connie still single-handedly in charge of Angelina, her expeditions to Matapoissett would be impossible; she would hardly have the free time necessary for a quick nap, let alone an extended daydream or out-of-body experience (who would babysit during her sudden transports?). Suppose the Handmaid, in turn, had found herself in the position of an Econowife in Gilead—one of those women she sees at a distance on the street, lower class, unattractively dressed, who have to be wives, bear children, and care for them all at the same time. In such circumstances, the escape that makes it possible for her to transmit her story—and hence the very premise on which the tale is founded—would be far less likely to be undertaken. She would hardly have opportunity or time, again, for an affair with a man like Nick, the Eye who rescues this odd princess, once from sexual deprivation and then from Gilead; and any life underground would be difficult to imagine with a young daughter in tow. The impossibility of escaping patriarchal captors *with* a child is literalized in the most prominent and painful episode the Handmaid relives, when she and her husband tried to escape across the border. If the child could have run faster— or if the Handmaid hadn't been responsible for the child at all—couldn't she have made it to safety? Did her husband, who apparently left her to carry the little girl, possibly sprint across the border?

The loss and absence of the child might then be critiqued as a less-than-fully-satisfactory solution to the problems, both literal and symbolic, of combining motherhood and creativity; on the question of whether female artists can mother (or whether mothers can be artists), that is, both novels may hedge by developing figures of the visionary or storyteller who *have* mothered, who love their daughters and long to mother, but who do not *now*, in the time of visioning or speaking, mother. If this is the case, then do these stories really give us the mother's story that feminists have called for, or do they only seem to? Is there still no literary representation of the actual, daily, ordinary aspects of the mother's story? Do these novels testify to the joys of motherhood as a theory and the impossibility of mothering as a practice? Or, and at the same time, by avoiding writing about mothering directly, do they avoid the risks of sentimentalizing the experience, too?[15]

Another (in no way incompatible) reading of the loss of the daughter as a sign of the complexity of our culture's ambivalence about mothers and mothering is this: it is a manifestation, and perhaps then an exorcism, of potent fears—first, fears that if the child doesn't kill or silence the mother/ writer, the mother/writer will neglect, abuse, and/or kill her child; and, second, any mother's seemingly inevitable fears of losing her child.[16] No matter how perfect the world became, children would be vulnerable to our self-centered desires, and there is still war, even in Matapoisett. But if we imagine the worst, perhaps it will not happen; things never happen as we worry and dream that they will. Atwood's novel gives a special place to the anxieties of maternal experience in the very first memory of her daughter that the narrator shares, a typically mundane one that contains, like most ordinary life, a record of real and imaginary terror. As she purchases a chicken wrapped in paper for her Gileadean household, she recalls the plastic shopping bags of former times, which she used to save, for no reason, until the pile under the sink spilled out onto the floor. Then her husband would throw them all out: "She [the first cryptic reference to the never named daughter] could get one of those over her head, he'd say. You know how kids like to play. She never would, I'd say. She's too old. (Or too smart, or too lucky.) But I would feel a chill of fear, and then guilt for having been so careless. It was true, I took too much for granted; I trusted fate back then" (37).

In both novels, there is this reminder that mothers, while or because they live with the all-too-easily-evoked guilt and fear of loss, also take too much for granted. This is especially true of Connie, who never fully comprehends what her child means to her, how much she loves her, until she cannot have her. In this way an aspect of precisely the everyday, confounding experience of mothering, as I and several people I know feel it, seems to be captured: when we are with our children, they are often irritating, demanding, boring, unreasonable, unlovable. How much more we feel our love when they are asleep, at daycare, at a distance; when we look at a picture of them; when we feel that intense chill of fear as we read a newspaper story about a missing child or hear a television report about an abused one.

The reasons why both women can't mother, in the narrative time of each novel, may also in some sense indict the complicity of mothers in the institutions that make mothering so difficult and conflictual. Neither novel should be accused of encouraging us to blame the victim, I hasten to point out. Connie's oppressors are so vividly realized and horrible, Gilead so terrifyingly powerful and plausible, that I find it hard to imagine readers (although they may well exist) who would feel, on the whole, anything but sympathy for the protagonists and anger at the injustices done to them. At the same time, it is clear to Connie herself that she lost Angie, in part at least, because she chose to mourn her dead lover, Claud, at the expense of nurturing the child. The Handmaid is guilty, as I have suggested, of taking too much for granted and, more seriously, perhaps, of "ignoring"—if she had paid attention, could she have seen what was coming sooner, taken her child across the border before it was so risky to do so? Did she, like Connie, put her relationship with her husband first? Did she fail her daughter in trusting a man to protect her, to make arrangements for their escape that obviously were not adequate?

And/or we can read these mothers' fears, failures, and losses of their daughters in yet another way. This way brings me back to the two problems of imagining and imaging maternity and its relation to discourse differently that I noted at the beginning of this essay: (1) the difficulty of theorizing the relations between "the maternal" and "the feminine," given that *only* women give birth but *not all* women are (birth) mothers; and (2) the gap between theorizing the maternal and practicing mothering. Read with an eye to these issues, the characterization of Connie and the Handmaid, as women who have mothered in the past and who show us what mothering might look like in the future but who do not mother in the present, may at once figure and circumvent (rather than just hedge, as I suggested earlier) the first difficulty. Connie and the Handmaid—situated as they are in each narrative as mothers of missing daughters—speak for and about both women (and men) who mother and women who don't mother. They thereby comprehend a versatile, fluid, unsettled relation of maternity and femaleness or femininity and resist any fixing of the mother or motherhood as a complete human identity, a transcendent or full or atemporal, ahistorical essence. Evaluating and critiquing "the maternal metaphor" in French feminism, along with metonymic American feminist alternatives that she also sees as "utopian," Domna C. Stanton has argued that "an initial counter-valorization of the maternal-feminine as a negation/subversion of paternal hierarchies" is an important first step, "an enabling mythology"; "but the moment the maternal emerges as a new dominance, it must be put into question before it congeals as feminine essence, as unchanging in-difference" (174). *Woman on the Edge of Time* and *The Handmaid's Tale* individually and collectively give flesh to this argument, demonstrating both the positive (Connie's enabling time-travel) and negative (Gilead's surrogacy practices) effects of "counter-valorization of the maternal-feminine" and, through the situation of Connie and the Handmaid in narrative time, putting any congealed notion of the maternal (be it patriarchal or feminist) into question.

In this putting maternal dominance into question, as I argued earlier, *Woman on the Edge of Time* and *The Handmaid's Tale* also subvert the mythic notion that the single figure or person of the mother—as biological birth-giver and/or caretaker and/or position in language—has or should have complete and only individual responsibility for the care of the child. By virtue of this interrogation of old myths about mothers, the novels question whether any single theory (or any one reading) can be ultimately responsible for meaning, can completely contain or even accurately describe motherhood. They suggest in particular that the relations between mothering and novel-writing, between maternity and creativity, are consequential and also always mobile, precarious, uneven relations, rooted in personal and social histories of great complexity, as resistant to theoretical resolution as they often are to practical combination. Thus our maternal figures, Connie and the Handmaid, also are figures for the creative, imaginative faculty, as I have read them to be, but the analogy between protagonist and visionary artist can be taken only so far in each case. Neither protagonist has complete responsibility for the story, and neither's voice or narrative corresponds exactly to the novel as a whole. Connie's story is told in a third-person voice that sees almost exclusively from her point of view and records her innermost thoughts, but sees other things too—possibly more than Connie does. The Handmaid is a first-person narrator, but her tale is followed by a story of how its transmission was effected by other hands. And on this point, the epilogues in both novels take on common significance: in both cases, the main story, a fantasy, is thus closed by the fictive voices of official, nonfictional discourse, the putative institutional files on Connie, the imaginary proceedings of the conference of the Gileadean Research Association. As I noted with reference to Piercy's novel, this valorizes the fantasy by demonstrating how much more believably it speaks, how thoroughly the novel escapes and subverts other discourses that try to read and theorize about the protagonists' experiences.

At the same time, the presence of the epilogue in each novel also serves to establish a difference and a distance between novelist and character; and this gap itself suggests, among other things, that full understanding of the fictional character exceeds authorial or readerly control, and that the novelists thus see not exactly *with* their characters, but *as* their characters see: partially, in detail, never in full control or totalizing comprehension. So, for example, the central, supposedly visionary heroine of *Woman on the Edge of Time* is often and increasingly, both by psychiatric diagnosis and by her own account, "confused." One of her final visits to Matapoisett, during which she fights in an air war with Luciente and sees the doctors who have operated on her brain in the enemy's ships, is ambiguously rendered. It may be a hallucination, or, as Luciente suggests, it may have taken place in another "continuum" (367), and/or it may retrospectively call into question the status of all the earlier visions. As Connie says, "Pues . . . never mind"; it doesn't matter anymore, as it once did to Connie, whether her visions are imaginary or real; the clarity of her moral purpose is inversely correlated with her concern for rationality. Similarly, the Handmaid stresses the precariousness of her hold on rationality and tells a story that is fragmented and imperfectly reconstructed, as she repeatedly says, because she does not know any version that is whole and original. From under her heavy, white, winged headdress, designed to keep her from seeing or being seen, she learns "to see the world in gasps" (40), and novelist and reader alike are positioned in such a way that they can only share her perspective.

Both women, then, see in much the same way as another figure, rare in imaginative fiction, a mother who tells her own story and tells it precisely as a partial, even impossible tale: Tillie Olsen's first-person protagonist in "As I Stand Here Ironing." This too is a story of a mother who might be viewed as "unfit" and her (partially) lost daughter who once was separated "for her own good" from her mother and whom the mother has not loved as well, she says, as she loved her later children. The daughter's potential is therefore, as the mother sees it, stunted: "all that is in her will not bloom" (20). It is "too late," in the present narrative time, for the love the mother would like to give, and the mother-narrator accepts this fact: "Let her be." Most saliently, the story is written as one that the mother will never tell to the teacher who asks for her help in "understanding" the daughter:

> Even if I came, what good would it do? You think because I am her mother I have a key, or that in some way you could use me as a key? She has lived for nineteen years. There is all that life that has happened outside of me, beyond me.
> And when is there time to remember, to sift, to weigh, to estimate, to total? I will start and there will be an interruption, and I will have to gather it all together again. Or I will become engulfed with all I did or did not do, with what should have been and what cannot be helped. (9)

Here Olsen suggests that the story of the missing daughter is a strained representation of what our culture finds so difficult to understand and negotiate, that most necessary, painful, disempowering, enabling aspect of mothering—the inevitable separation of the mother and child that begins at birth. In Piercy's Matapoisett, this ongoing process is embodied and celebrated, not repressed or psychoanalyzed, in a ritual ceremony called "end-of-mothering," when a child reaches adolescence and names herself or himself. This ceremony entails a rite of passage in which the child is left alone in the wilderness for a week, and Connie views this as cruel abandonment; but Luciente explains to Connie, "We set our children free" (116). Like Piercy and Atwood, moreover, Olsen explicitly challenges the basic assumption of virtually all the child-oriented theories of human development that our culture has depended on. As her mother-narrator says again at the end, "I will never total it all." Theories (like teachers, like social workers and doctors in *Woman on the Edge of Time*, like ideologues and academics in *The Handmaid's Tale*) are often assigned to choose, divide, set out limits, explain, "to sift, to weigh, to estimate, to total"; often that is what they conceive of their job as being. It is not the job, not the way, both narratives may suggest, of mothers or of novels.

Notes

1. I use the word "practice" with particular reference to Sara Ruddick's useful discussion of how to talk and think about what mothers do, in *Maternal Thinking*, esp. 13–27.

2. Some of the voices associated with the earlier emphasis on the opposition between feminism and motherhood—as a patriarchal institution, at least—include Shulamith Firestone, *The Dialectic of Sex: The Case for Feminist Revolution*, and, more ambiguously and with equal emphasis on the potential power of mothering, despite her critique of patriarchal arrangements, Adrienne Rich, *Of Woman Born: Motherhood as Experience and Institution*. New feminist attention to the privileged place of the mother and mothering was instigated by works like Rich's, Dorothy Dinnerstein's *The Mermaid and the Minotaur*, and Nancy Chodorow's *The Reproduction of Mothering*. Best known for their revaluation of the maternal as a site of discursive empowerment are French feminists Julia Kristeva, Helene Cixous, and Luce Irigaray; for bibliography and analysis, as well as one recent critique of this approach, see Domna C. Stanton, "Difference on Trial: A Critique of the Maternal Metaphor in Cixous, Irigaray, and Kristeva." The argument for maternal thinking as a resource for developing peace politics is Ruddick's in *Maternal Thinking*. For overview, development, and critique of the psychoanalytic approach to theorizing the maternal in particular, see Stanton as well as Carolyn Burke, "Rethinking the Maternal"; Mary Jacobus, "*Dora* and the Pregnant Madonna"; and Claire Kahane, "Questioning the Maternal Voice." Two essays that address the particular intersection of mothering and creative writing that I engage here are Nina Auerbach's "Artists and Mothers: A False Alliance," and Susan Rubin Suleiman's "Writing and Motherhood"; and a history of this issue in the nineteenth century is provided in Margaret Homans' *Bearing the Word: Language and Female Experience in Nineteenth-Century Women's Writing*. Marianne Hirsch's *The Mother/Daughter Plot* offers a recent full discussion of mothers, daughters, and narrative from the late eighteenth century to the present that begins with a consideration of the inadequacies of contemporary feminist writing on the maternal. To all of these and many other feminist thinkers about mothers and mothering and writing, this essay is indebted.

3. For example, see Suleiman, "Writing and Motherhood" (where her special interest in the autobiographical fact that a writer is a mother is made clear), and her continuation, "On Maternal Splitting: A Propos of Mary Gordon's *Men and Angels*." Kahane, performing the title of her essay, "Questioning the Maternal Voice," concludes her theoretical discussion of the idealization of the mother in recent feminist poetics by arguing that the task of feminist literary criticism is "to create optimal conditions for women writing" in which "an altered subject can evolve." Without specifying the sources of her hopeful assertion, Kahane suggests that "what seems to be emerging from the potential space of literary feminism at this point in history is the articulation of a powerful dream, of a lost but recoverable maternal voice that speaks especially to women." She does go on to sound a familiar warning that "dependence on the figure of the mother can perpetuate the repressive connection between matter, mater, and female subjectivity" (89–90). See the introduction to *The Mother/Daughter Plot* for Hirsch's articulation of why, in light of "the limitations of models and paradigms in the discussion of familial relationships," she turned to "the richness of individual literary texts as documents of personal interaction" (22).

4. In general it might be argued, as I suggest later, that Piercy valorizes the imaginative power of the mother's position in a way comparable to that of the French femi-

nists. However, I take Piercy as antithetical to the Kristevan position that the maternal is a site of constitutive splitting and radical otherness; for this view, see esp. Kristeva, "Herethique de l'amour."

5. Note that this is an act Connie has just imagined doing—when Geraldo breaks in, her hatred "gave her a flush in the nerves like speed coming on," and she imagines destroying his elegance in very creative ways that foreshadow her visionary capacity: "She dreamed of peeling off a slickly polished antiqued lizard high-heeled boot and pounding it down his lying throat" (13).

6. Later, in utopian Matapoisett at the end-of-mothering ritual, we learn tellingly that "aunts" (chosen, not biological) play an important role after naming, when the adolescent no longer goes to her mothers for advice, but to the aunts she selects as advisors for the next few years (116). Contrast Atwood's characterization of "the Aunts" in *The Handmaid's Tale*, an elite female Gestapo who brutally train and police other women and serve the interests of the antifeminist state.

7. Not only does Dolly, at Geraldo's insistence, have the abortion, but, in the few brief visits Connie has with her niece, we learn that Dolly, working harder than ever as a prostitute, is growing increasingly estranged from her own daughter Nita, who is cared for by her grandmother.

8. Here is Luciente's version of what happened: "It was part of women's long revolution. When we were breaking up all the old hierarchies. Finally there was that one thing we had to give up too, the only power we ever had, in return for no more power for anyone. The original production: the power to give birth. Cause as long as we were biologically enchained, we'd never be equal. And males never would be humanized to be loving and tender. So we all became mothers" (105).

9. Piercy's vision in the novel is usually taken to idealize androgyny, and she sometimes has been criticized for letting men into her utopia (see, for example, Peter Fitting, "For Men Only: A Guide to Reading Single-Sex Worlds").

10. In dystopian Gilead, this practice of naming a woman with an inflection of the patriarch's name serves, among other things, to make it impossible to sustain female alliances—once a Handmaid moves to another posting, for example, her identity is impossible to follow. Atwood cleverly suggests how this procedure in fact recoils and erases the identity of the patriarch, however, in the future time, when what survives is the Handmaid's tale itself: researchers speculate on which of two prominent Fredericks' might have been Offred's commander and cannot be absolutely certain which man she served.

11. For discussion of this interpretation, see Amin Malak, "Margaret Atwood's *The Handmaid's Tale* and the Dystopian Tradition."

12. In this passage she criticizes her lack of sympathy for another Handmaid, who has gone mad: "I look after her. Easy out, is what I think. I don't even feel sorry for her, although I should. I feel angry. I'm not proud of myself for this, or for any of it. But then, that's the point" (361). Leaving her readers to ask: the point of what? what's the point?

13. For a discussion of Atwood's relation to "postfeminism" in the novel preceding *The Handmaid's Tale*, a discussion with implications that I cannot explore here, see Hansen, "(Post)Feminism in Atwood's *Bodily Harm*."

14. It could even be argued that the Handmaid retrospectively highlights Connie's perhaps equally unsettling inability to give up the myth of individual and utter responsibility. While the women of Matapoisett apparently have done so, and share the work of mothering with a whole community (and then only until the child reaches adoles-

ence), Connie still embodies in her fairly standard brand of individual heroism itself another very ancient, long-lived, and romantic myth about good mothers: their willing and utter and lonely self-sacrifice.

15. This is one of the risks spoken about in Ruth Perry's interesting interview of Marea Gordett and Kathi Aguero, two writers with young children who say that they have written relatively little about their experiences of motherhood. Aguero says, "I find it a little hard to know how to write about it without being sentimental" (Perry, 30).

16. In Perry's interview, one contemporary mother/writer publicly states that her fiction is useful in exorcising her fears about her children. Gordett observes, "Well, when I was pregnant I was somewhat obsessed with the fear of having a child who had some handicap, and I wrote a story about it and it helped me tremendously" (Perry, 29). The mother's hatred of her child is rarely written about; but, for one interesting discussion of this problem (still from a child-centered point of view), see Janet Sayers, "Feminism and Mothering: A Kleinian Perspective."

Chapter 2

Mother Right/Write Revisited:
Beloved and *Dessa Rose* and the Construction
of Motherhood in Black Women's Fiction

Carole Boyce Davies

The historical construction of the Black Woman as the Great Mother—negatively embedded in the "mammy" figure of Euroamerican imagination and the more resonant definition of the Black Woman as first mother or primal mother of archaeological evidence—comes face to face with practical realities in recent black women's writing. As consumers of hegemonic popular and literary culture, we are recipients of these contradictory narratives of motherhood. But now, the selflessness of the "mammy" is positioned against or along with a series of deliberate self-constructions by black women. Motherhood and/or mothering thus become central and defining tropes in black female reconstruction. A conflicting set of possibilities have to be negotiated in reading African-American motherhood, and this is the source of the beautiful-ugliness[1] of its presentation in Toni Morrison's *Beloved* (1987). I propose to read *Beloved*, one of the most deliberate problematizings of motherhood that I have encountered, against Sherley Anne Williams' *Dessa Rose* (1986), which subverts many of the societal constructions embedded in *Beloved*.

The theoretical implications of mothering for black women are being advanced in a growing number of ways. Gloria Joseph's "Black Mothers and Daughters: Their Roles and Functions in American Society" and Patricia Hill Collins's "The Meaning of Motherhood in Black Culture and Black Mother-Daughter Relationships" move beyond the solitary biological imperative to a notion of shared responsibility for caring. Examinations of black womanhood have also pursued the meaning of motherhood. For example, Hazel Carby, in *Reconstructing Womanhood*, identifies how "within the discourse of the cult of true womanhood, wifehood and motherhood were glorified" (26). Sojourner Truth's "Ain't I a Woman" speech (1852) had asserted much earlier her specific experience of womanhood, which included a critique of the experience assumed for white women. Black women, defined in opposition to the terms of motherhood accorded white women, and with a different set of historical realities, developed their own discourse of womanhood. This is worked out, at a certain level, in black women's fiction. In "Mothering and Healing in Recent Black Women's Fiction" (1984), Boyce Davies identified a cluster of novels in which the mother construct seemed to be foregrounded and linked to the social and emotional reconstitution of black women in their communities. Further reflection on the literary history of black women writers—from Harriet Wilson's *Our Nig* (1859) to Alice Walker's *The Temple of My Familiar* (1989)—reveals that reconstructions of mothering have been continuous. For, when explored in relation to motherhood in African societies and when examined in materialist/feminist contexts which read-in the exploitative nature of motherhood in male-dominated societies, the rewriting of "mammy" offers its own theoretical excursions.

In a 1985 conversation with Gloria Naylor, Morrison identifies the project which has dominated her own imaginative world as bringing to life the "dead girl," the black girl that society has willed out of existence. For Morrison, this ongoing literary reconstruction of black female identity has been part excavation, part re-creation: "rescuing her from the grave of time and inattention . . . bringing her back into living life" (Naylor, "A Conversation," 593). Clearly, Morrison uses her creative writing as a way of engaging theoretical issues concerning mothering, including tensions between community and individuation. She says, for example, in discussing *Beloved*, that she was trying to find a channel for the negotiating which women have to do, between the imperatives of nurture/love for its own sake and the desire to be a complete individual. As well, she was looking at the ease with which women sabotage these efforts.[2]

Beloved, in my view, simultaneously critiques exclusive mother-love and asserts the necessity for black women to claim something as theirs. It is a work which resists single, unitary, laudatory readings. The text therefore speaks double-voicedly to those twin imperatives, each position continuously subverting the other. It speaks multiply, answering the meaning and practices of mothering; voicing the positions of daughters, grandmothers, fathers, male friends, neighbors, community, and, of course, the mother herself. Sethe's action is measured and weighed against numerous atrocities and destructions and the possible responses to them. The text, therefore, deliberately centers the historical fact that there were black women during slavery who suffocated their babies rather than allow them to be offered up to destruction by slavery. Morrison clearly does not bring a singular position to this issue; rather, she poses several arguments. In other words, the spectre of Beloved, the living embodiment of Sethe's mother-love and the painful past of enslavement she represents, never is really destroyed. That spectre is allowed to dissolve into the mythology and the history of the community. Read as Morrison's bringing to life of "the dead girl," then she will manifest herself elsewhere.

Issues of reading and writing in the making of the text are importantly implicated in *Beloved*. This work demands that the reader hold open a range of possibilities. An unquestioning endorsement of Sethe's action cannot reveal the text's complexity. My prototypical black woman reader (a friend, non-academic but aware, struggling alone with a difficult child after leaving an abusive marriage) was not empowered by reading *Beloved* at this juncture of her life. Contemplating it and her life, she felt herslef going into a spiral of depression, wondering if she should go back and offer her breast to her man, allowing "the responsibility for her breasts, at last, [to be] in somebody else's hands" (18), or find another man to affirm for her that she was her own "best thing" (273). At the same time, my academic feminist critic friends uniformly marveled at its narrative "mastery" and all the rich implications for literary analysis. In my reading of literary mothering, I hope to ally the spirits of both types of critical responses (academic/theoretical and personal/self-reflexive) and to suggest that each approach must interrupt the other. This reading of black motherhood and its representation speaks as well to the need for white feminists to racialize and historicize (their) motherhood. Questions of "maternal splitting" (Suleiman) and "maternal thinking" (Ruddick), and critiques of the "perfect mother" (Chodorow and Contratto) become empty and limited understandings if they do not configure the issues of race and history.

Marking, Captive Body, and "Abiku"[3]

Jeffner Allen, in "Motherhood: The Annihilation of Women," sees childbearing as a definite "marking" or "stamping." In this perspective, "the mark of motherhood" inscribes the domination of men into women's bodies: "Stamped, firmly imprinted on women's bodies, is the emblem that our bodies have been opened to the world of men: the shape of the pregnant woman's stomach. From conception to abortion, acts which are biologically different yet symbolically the same, our stomachs are marked MOTHER" (322). Hortense Spillers, in an essay appropriately titled "Mama's Baby, Papa's Maybe: An American Grammar Book," identifies the black female body as the site of a series of visible markings, mutilations, distortions, and violations during the period of slavery. Being an African at that historical juncture was to be marked for enslavement and physically lacerated against resistance. The enslaved African woman, with child, has to be seen then as both captured and multiply marked. It is important to make some distinction between "marking" and "naming" (re-marking) as used here. "Marking" is the product of abuse and is linked to societal inscriptions on the body of the Other. Naming (or re-marking) has to do with redefinition. In *Beloved* and in *Dessa Rose*, the visibility or invisibility of marking has multiple significances.

All of these multilayered markings of the black female body in *Beloved* create their own independent textualities. Sethe is physically marked, a marking which exudes blood and later keloiding. The evidence of physical brutality which is this marking is identified as a "chokecherry" tree by Amy Denver (79) and by Sethe herself (15); as the decorative work of an ironsmith too passionate for display, by Paul D (17); and as a revolting clump of scars, also by Paul D (21). Sethe, then, is a marked woman, marked physically by abuse, pregnancy, motherhood, and other societal inscriptions (by white female, by black male, and by the white male inflicter of the abuse which marks her initially). The marking which is re-identified as the branches of a tree ("chokecherry" itself resonates) and thus as life, with myriad reference points, when looked at differently becomes the signifier for captivity. The marking is also indicated, following Jeffner Allen, in the physicality of childbearing: a marking which similarly produces visible, physical result and bodily emissions. One correlative of racial marking, then, for people in racially stratified societies, is childbearing for women in male-dominated societies. Motherhood becomes, literally, embodiment — in both cases the body as *read* text. One has to read Sethe, as black woman, therefore, as the concentration of female identity, not as its aberration. Sethe is the convergence of these multiple bodily markings: "Sethe could not move. She couldn't lie on her stomach or her back, and to keep on her side meant pressure on her screaming feet" (79). The feet, for the slave the ultimate representation of flight, because of their swollen condition, caused by pregnancy, no longer function. Sethe's body is multiply captive. And, significantly, while she can flee slavery, she cannot flee the body that has been captured by the needs of her children.

That Morrison is using marking as a multiple signifier of captivity is indicated in an encounter that Sethe recalls between Sethe and the woman identified as her mother. Her mother, denied physical contact with her child because of the demands of slave labor, one day showed Sethe her "mark":

"'This is your ma'am. This,' and she pointed. 'I am the only one got this mark now. The rest dead. If something happens to me and you can't tell me by my face, you can know me by this mark.' . . . 'Yes, Ma'am,' I said. 'But how will you know me? . . . Mark me too,' I said. 'Mark the mark on me too.'" Sethe chuckled.
"Did she?" asked Denver.
"She slapped my face."
"What for?"
"I didn't understand it then. Not till I had a mark of my own."
"What happened to her?"
"Hung. By the time they cut her down nobody could tell whether she had a circle and a cross or not, least of all me and I did look." (61)

It is important that her self-identification is erased by the multilation of slavery. The most important referent of deliberate self-marking is African scarification. One thesis holds that African peoples, during the period of slave trafficking, deliberately inscribed ethnic identities on faces and bodies. In a version of this, Stamp Paid metaphorically stamps himself as having paid the ultimate price of enslavement and names himself with that self-identification. The notion of marking is carried over to the child Beloved and the way she is marked by Sethe. Like the legendary *abiku* children of Yoruba society of the *ogbanje* in Igbo culture, who die and are reborn repeatedly to plague their mothers and are marked so that they can be identified when they return, the marks of the saw on Beloved's neck (120) become the one visible sign to Denver and subsequently to Sethe that this is the physical manifestation of the dead child. Beloved then functions as an *abiku* to Sethe, and to author and reader as the "coming to life of the dead girl." The *abiku* concept provides another strategy for reading this text. Sethe's violent action becomes an attempt to hold on to the maternal right and function in a society where it defines the mother's existence. Sethe's persistent desire is to bring *her* milk to *her* children. In the face of that inability and the possibility of returning to that debased status, she says, "I stopped him . . . I took and put my babies where they'd be safe" (164). Sethe, as African-American mother, becomes the fictional embodiment of Spillers' theoretical assertion:

> The African-American woman, the mother, the daughter, becomes historically the powerful and shadowy evocation of a cultural synthesis long evaporated—the law of the Mother—[so that] . . . 1) motherhood as female bloodrite is outraged, is denied at the *very same time* that it becomes the founding term of a human and social enactment; 2) a dual fatherhood is set in motion, comprised of the African father's banished name and body and the captor father's mocking presence. In this play of paradox, only the female stands *in the flesh*, both mother and mother-dispossessed. (Spillers, 80)

The horror of Sethe's central act then resides within this social construction. Sethe is a marked daughter of a marked mother, who herself had appropriated the "law of the Mother" by deciding to let Sethe (the only child that was conceived with some aspect of participation) live. Sethe herself acquiesces in the only legality which the society paradoxically imposes. Both women, like Baby Suggs, stand as both "mother and mother-dispossessed." I am arguing that the African-American mother does not stand outside of traditional symbolics of gender, as Spillers concludes. Instead she becomes the most clarifying representation of society's expectations and contradictions surrounding motherhood.

So there is no abandonment of the tensions of gender identification in *Beloved*. Amy Denver's role in Sethe's difficult delivery of her child is representative of the paradoxical separations and commonalities among women. The child of an indentured servant and a victim of abuse attains a parallel dispossession. Her journey is in search of some softness, some velvet, the North (80). Had we not read Harriet Wilson's *Our Nig*, and the preliminary presentation of lowly Mag Smith, an outcast in the class-stratified Boston society, we could assume that Amy Denver's dream would be realized. There is an intertextual relationship between *Our Nig* and *Beloved*, in the construction of the white female without protection of the patriarchal power. Amy Denver massages Sethe's legs and reads and renames her marking so that it suggests life and not death, though the fact that Amy is not relieved of her racial baggage is seen in her casual acceptance of racial difference. Nevertheless, in a society stratified along race, class, and gender lines, the narrator asserts, there are a lot of "throw-away people," and, while a "slave and a barefoot whitewoman with unpinned hair" (85) may form a temporary alliance around the need to give birth, inevitably they take divergent paths to freedom.

Marking, re-marking, and their links to slavery and motherhood similarly inform Sherley Ann Williams's *Dessa Rose*. Here the tendency toward total immolation, seen in *Beloved*, is completely destabilized. In fact, the entire text articulates the subversive potential in each oppressive situation. Nehemiah sees "the darky's pregnancy as a stroke of luck" (29), allowing him increased access to information. Dessa uses her pregnancy to her benefit, to stay her impending execution and gain for her the space and time to defy all expectations. All of his attempts to *write* her existence are foiled. Instead, she persistently inserts her story: her child conceived out of her love for Kaine. Throughout, she offers her double-coded oral narratives, songs, gestures, and (re-)markings, which he cannot decipher:

> He and Hughes had heard upon approaching the cellar a humming or moaning. It was impossible to define it as one or the other. (29)

> She picked up a twig and began to mark in the dirt and to hum—not the same tune as the previous day, but one equally monotonous. (40–41)

Significantly, Dessa, with childbirth imminent, escapes through the coded messages in the song. Earlier she had rejected the idea that a pregnant female could not lead a slave rebellion. Marking, the physical scarring of the body, and the marking of childbirth are present but are renamed or erased at every turn. A variety of textual strategies of resistance and reversal organize this novel. For example, the erasure of Dessa's marking in this text is the point of final liberation. The old black woman called in to identify Dessa's scars (which would have ensured her return to enslavement) calls out: "I ain't seed nothing on this gal's butt. She ain't got a scar on her back" (231). Williams also permits Dessa a great deal of physical mobility. Deborah McDowell, in her study "Negotiating Between Tenses: Witnessing Slavery After Freedom — *Dessa Rose*", shows how the text destabilizes and resists a series of misnamings and representations. In fact, Dessa has "avoided public exposure as fiercely as she has hidden her bodily scars . . . Here, Dessa's body is her text and, owning it, she holds the rights to it" (154). McDowell also links this ownership of Dessa's body to Dessa's control of her own story and its writing.

Two distinct reconstructions are offered. Both novels are grounded in actual historical record: *Beloved* in the Margaret Garner story and *Dessa Rose* in the story of a woman who led a slave rebellion. But, in my view, *Beloved* is more in the tradition of the protest novel: recalling atrocities in order to challenge the viciousness of oppression and explain deviant behavior. Here I am using James Baldwin's critique of the protest novel for accepting white society's denial of humanity. The text essentially implies that slavery and racism wiped out resistance except at a very personal level. It offers a community which censures the mother after not coming to her aid. Baby Suggs, the mother-healer,[4] gives up all ability to resist and confines herself to bed in philosophical explorations of the meaning of color. A valid response, perhaps, but definitely not empowering.

The position on mothering in *Dessa Rose* validates Patricia Hill Collins' conception of motherhood as power in African-American communities ("The Meaning of Motherhood"), but it also resists it. The community is organized for its liberation. Since the entire text seems to be constructed to identify perpetual resistance to enslavement at personal and communal levels, then, within these boundaries, mothering is more liberatory. Still, it is necessary to hold open the other side of the contradiction and restate that mothering is not only power, it is also destruction for many women. Its very definition in patriarchal culture provides a complex mixture of meanings, ranging from annihilation to creation to changing given statuses. Audre Lorde, in "Man Child: A Black Lesbian Feminist Response," sees raising black children "in the mouth of a racist, sexist, suicidal dragon as perilous and chancy" (74). Yet mothers must teach children to love and to resist simultaneously. Mothering for Lorde is a cooperative venture which allows the formation of a variety of new and healthy responses to the world. Williams's rewriting of mothering is more in line with the Lorde formulation. A variety of reversals in the mothering function are effected. This strategy allows the conclusion that monolithic constructions of romanticized African-American motherhood close the door to an understanding of its multiple expressions in exploitative contexts.

Milk, Breasts, and Blood

Breastfeeding, as a reference to maternal identification and nurturing, is central in the two texts being examined here. True to its consistent subversion of the societal limitations of motherhood (as an institution), *Dessa Rose* reaches for a more definite alignment of biological motherhood (as experience) with nonbiological mothering. In a definite reversal of the arrangement in Euroamerican slave societies, where the black woman historically served as wet nurse, Rufel breastfeeds Dessa's baby along with hers: "The white woman, her shoulder still bare, the curly black head and brown face of a new baby nestled at her breast, faced her now" (88). Breastfeeding, as Williams poses it, is an expression of shared responsibility for raising the children. Dessa and Rufel consistently exchange maternal functions, depending on need. Rufel as white female, a more developed version of Amy Denver of *Beloved*, grows consistently in the process of her interactions with the marooned African-American community. It is a characterization, however, that is not without its contradictions. Rufel has to learn, for example, the true identity of the woman she identified as "Mammy"; "the comfortable, comforting image of Mammy" (147) which she held, had to be destroyed. The white woman, oblivious to her status as simultaneously privileged because of race and subordinate because of gender, has to recognize herself and others. Beyond that, the reified, monolithic, socially constructed "whitewoman" is dismantled by Dessa and the community in a series of symbolic acts. The structure of slave society, held in place by its characterization of the white woman, is decentered in a series of unmaskings which begin when Rufel breastfeeds Dessa's baby.

In this context, it is important to deromanticize the symbolics of milk in the construction of motherhood. Anna Davin, in "Imperialism and Motherhood" (1978),[5] shows how—in a series of manipulations of state apparatuses—white women were instructed in maternalism as a means of maintaining empire. Racist assumptions were allied to class and gender discourses on motherhood. Similarly, Spivak's translation of Mahasweta Devi's "Breast Giver" and Spivak's Marxist-feminist analysis of milk and motherhood in "A Literary Representation of the Subaltern: A Woman's Text from the Third World" help elucidate the textual emphasis on milk and breasts in the construction of motherhood. Inserting the "free/domestic" labor provided by women, Spivak argues: "The milk that is produced in one's own body for one's own children is a use-value. When there is a superfluity of use values, exchange values arise. That which cannot be used is exchanged. As soon as the (exchange) value of Jashoda's milk emerges it is appropriated" (248). She goes on to make a number of assertions about the idealization of the products of a woman's body and identifies how the erasure of gender in Marxist analyses allows this product of women's bodies to escape specific constructions of labor.

This allows us to problematize more definitively textual references to "milk" as a signifier for motherhood. Reaching for the complex economic and social meanings of "milk" and "breasts," Morrison offers a variety of associations with motherhood in exploitative contexts. The core response of Sethe in *Beloved* is to the appropriation of her milk and therefore to the reduction to animal status that is entailed in appropriated motherhood (clearly "schoolteacher's" intent in his research measurings). Sethe's assertion throughout the text is that she was trying to get her milk to her children and, paradoxically and uncritically, that she had milk for *all*:

> After I left you, those boys came in there and took my milk. That's what they came in there for. Held me down and took it. I told Mrs. Garner on 'em. She had that lump and couldn't speak but her eyes rolled out tears. Them boys found out I told on em. Schoolteacher made one open my back, and when it closed it made a tree. It grows here still."
> "They used cowhide on you?"
> "And they took my milk."
> "They beat you and you was pregnant?"
> "And they took my milk!" (16–17)

Paul D consistently misses the depth of Sethe's recounting, identifying primarily the physical abuse and not the violation which Sethe sees as primary and which lines up along with his own reduction to animal status by the bit in his mouth and the various collars used on the men. Angela Davis has identified the critical gaps in scholarship around the abuses of women in slavery:

> The designation of the black woman as a matriarch is a cruel misnomer. It is a misnomer because it implies stable kinship structures within which the mother exercises authority. It is cruel because it ignores the profound traumas the black woman must have experienced when she had to surrender her child-bearing to alien and predatory economic interests. (5)

So, it is around issues of milk, breasts, and bloodlines that Sethe is complexly caught. Her response to the exploitation of the material products of her body leads her to a process of holding on, which cannot allow cooperative care giving as it does in *Dessa Rose* or in the Lorde formulation.

This is where, in my estimation, a critique of the text's unfolding on the issue of maternity is valid. Morrison fails to overturn the symbolics of breasts.[6] The alignment of cows (with all the associations of milk giving) with women in *Beloved* speaks eloquently to this issue. In the absence of women, the narrator asserts, the Sweet Home men were "fucking cows," "taken to calves"

(10–11). Beginning when Sethe allows Paul D the responsibility for her breasts, Morrison fails to free them from their negative and exploitative representations. Morrison, it seems, in reaching for what Mary Helen Washington identifies as the "romantic text" and Deborah McDowell as the "family romance,"[7] shifts the responsibility for Sethe's final empowerment away from Sethe herself and her daughters and leaves it to Paul D to define in the final "Me? Me?" which Sethe is allowed in the text. Marianne Hirsch's reading in *The Mother/ Daughter Plot* sees the questions ("Me? Me?") as the beginnings of (or openings for) the construction of beyond her identity as a mother. In particular, Paul D, who knew her before she was so overdetermined by her status as mother, allows her to liberate her story. However, what is installed in the process is a heterosexual dominance, the woman operating without a certain clarity about her own subjectivity and about how she came to be so marked as mother.

The link of milk to blood to ink in both texts provides a series of associations that have to do with mothering, blood lines, and writing. Each text, in its way, engages with, affirms, subverts, challenges, or decenters the boundaries of motherhood which keep sex/gender or racial systems in place.

Braiding and Continuity: Writing/Mothering

Given the received, contradictory narratives of motherhood, then how do we read the self-constructions of mothering by African-American women, and of these two works in particular? On the issue of motherhood, *Beloved* has to be read intertextually with *Dessa Rose* and against continuing theoretical and literary reconstructions of mothering. Barbara Christian calls such reading a "special angle of seeing motherhood" ("An Angle," 211–52). Clearly, in this writing and righting of mothering, the tendency has been more to problematize the mother rather than to romanticize her. This problematizing has included a necessary removal of mothering from its biological mandates. Throughout, there is a need to affirm black motherhood and/or to construct an essentialized, "outraged"[8] mother as a strategic response to racist constructs. Strategically valid on some fronts, on others this affirmation becomes too defining and limiting of women. Even a radical suggestion in black mother theory that women mother cooperatively assumes that all African-American women want to participate in this activity.

The attempt to construct Sethe as resisting mother is highly charged but also problematic. We identify with her attempt to resist the appropriation of her body and its products for the salveholding class's benefit. We understand what it means for her to allow her daughter, Denver, to feed from her and take in the mixture of blood and milk at the point of her personal holocaust. We see the resistance to familial/community relationships when she resists Baby Suggs's attempts to take the child from her. But her mother-love is definitely "too thick," as Paul D says, because it too fully accepts the given paradigm of motherhood as exclusive responsibility of the biological mother. But how do we account for this "thickness" during a slave period designed to deny any family bonding? Spillers' position is legitimately recalled here. A slave mother is not supposed to demonstrate deep love for her children. Sethe defies that. Yet her heroic response to enslavement paradoxically becomes the kind of mother-love which the society enforces for women. Sethe shuttles back and forth between enslavements, exchanging one for the other, unable to be freed from both at once.

The unity of preservation, growth, and acceptability, posited in Ruddick's maternal thinking, is rejected in Sethe's action. She defines preservation as taking her children out of the reaches of the slave-holding system. But, paradoxically, in her situation this means that she has to function as their executioner, effecting the opposite of growth (unless one equates death with freedom, as was done in some of the sorrow songs). Growth and acceptability are unrealizable in such a context. But, as Stamp Paid notes, the community brings moral judgment on this act while itself erring in not being there as a supportive force in Sethe's hour of greatest need. Denver finally is able to break out of the narrowly-defined, self-destructive circle of family relationships of the house (124). One can read the entire narrative as Denver's take on Sethe's stifling mother-love. Denver moves back a generation, as she recalls her grandmother's (Baby Suggs's) voice and allows the community to participate in nurturing this family and dismantling exclusive motherhood. Importantly, Denver makes her link to the community through writing (the teacher who taught her to write) and reading (the notes left with the food.) Paul D, who knew Sethe before her maternal identity as well, establishes links with the community before he returns to help her put her traumatic experiences in place. He listens and affirms. Denver, as resisting daughter, writes herself out of this limiting construction.

In psychoanalytic readings[9] of *Beloved*, the spectre of the dead child actualizes theories of the child in the mirror stage. Although she is adult, Beloved's needs are for oral gratification and locking in of the mother's gaze. "Maternal splitting—i.e., both destructive and loving feelings—is demonstrated in Beloved's excessive needs. One can also read the Lacanian response—the desire of the Other (the father)—in her interaction with Paul D, which takes place in an overtly sexual though infantile need to appropriate the phallus: "You have to touch me. On the inside part. And you have to call me my name" (117). Sethe, for her part, in the stage when she is nurturing Beloved, is too heavily defined by guilt. Rather than understanding that mothering carries with it the conflict of guilt and selfishness, holding and letting go, her needs and the child's needs, she abandons the world and her life to the demands of nurturing a child exclusively. The child becomes a succubus: bloated, unhealthy, dangerous.

Any analysis of the novel *Beloved* ought to resist closure or definitiveness. Morrison sees it as an open text: "I was under the impression that I had written a third of it when I turned this book in . . . So I am not finished with these people and they are not finished with me" (75). In the interest of rewriting motherhood, we can see how desire drives the text. The women of that house wanted Beloved's presence as much as Beloved had to return, Morrison asserts. In a more discursive reading, the return of the ghost is Sethe and Denver's mother/daughter's reinventing of the Other, the absent. It is as well the *abiku*, willing itself rebirth in the perpetual torture of the mother. We can read *abiku*, alternatively, as the woman haunted by the societal demand to be a mother. In many ways, the physical manifestation of Beloved is a conjuring of that absence and rupture, pain and trauma, which Beloved represents. Thus the unified voices at the end, claiming Beloved, separately and collectively. Looked at another way, she is a necessary concentration of history, which has to be confronted and put in its place for wholeness to be regained. The forgotten languages and "different words" of Sethe's mother and Nan(ny) are recognized in Sethe's process of "rememory" which drives the narrative: "Holding the damp white sheets against her chest, she was picking meaning out of a code she no longer understood" (62). Perhaps this is why the line, "It was not a story to pass on" (274–75), is repeated in the text's final pages. In other words, the specific historical contexts which produce that kind of response have to be named and then released. The narrative becomes the ritualistic act which stays the returning of the *abiku*, the "return of the repressed." The African mythological pre-text may offer a more textured understanding, a sign of the mother possessed and dispossesed, than the vaporous context of the Western ghost. Beloved cannot be fully "re-membered" or brought into flesh and sustained in present form. In *abiku* mythology, the child eventually stays, when certain rituals and necessary passages have been accomplished.

Read as the act of writing motherhood, then Morrison may be subverting the terms of the protest novel:[10] "This is not a story to pass on" (275). Rather than adopting an open and single critique of a society which creates such violence, it also engages the internal narrative, the meanings which create specific responses: "I had to deal with this nurturing instinct that expressed itself in murder" (139). Tensions then exist around struggles to tell a difficult story, to place on record those things silenced or repressed, such as problematical responses to motherhood, to speak the unspeakable (she titles her essay "Unspeakable Things Unspoken"). The text in this way constructs multiple subject positions.

Providing a differently textured strand in this continuing discourse on mothering, though, *Dessa Rose* ends with *her* writing/righting her own story for her grandchildren, as she braids their hair—another nonscribal way of storytelling and maintaining history. She also ensures that the children know the story and that it is written down and then re-oralised.[11] Hers is definitely mother write/right, not mother-as-written. She foregrounds the need for some memory of a past of struggle and not of defeat. Nehemiah's text is erased: "Miz Lady was turning over the papers in her hand. 'And these is blank, sheriff,' she say" (232).

Dessa finally writes/rights her own story. Hers is a much more empowering gesture, with more human agency, than is Sethe's. The move from being the-mother-as-she-is-written to being the-mother-as-she-writes (Suleiman, 1985) is one of the text's most radical strategies. She becomes speaking subject, while the authorial or narrating "I" is submerged. The move is also one of re-oralising, which decenters the text's narrative control.

> This why I have it wrote down, why I has the child say it back. I never will forget Nemi trying to read me, knowing I had put myself in his hands. Well this the childrens have heard from our own lips. I hope they never have to pay what it cost us to own ourselfs. (236)

In the continuing discourse on motherhood and mothering which is being articulated in black women's fiction, there is a contest of interpretations. Any notion of an exclusivist, nativist, nationalistic articulation of an exoticized, reified, or romanticized black motherhood becomes limiting. Motherhood is both annihilation and empowerment; marking and renaming; the locus of change and growth but as well of pain and loss. Painful rememberings and liberating narratives seem necessarily to interrupt each other's dominance. All of these intersect at different points, as the narrative of the mother becomes more prominently articulated.

Notes

1. Contradictory descriptor taken from Barbadian oral discourse as reported in Marshall, "From the Poets in the Kitchen" 8.

2. Lecture at Cornell University, 10 May 1988.

3. The repeated manifestation of a single child in the life of a woman who loses infant children after they are born. Once this situation attains some repetitiveness,

the child has to be marked so that she is identified upon return. Idowu describes the *abiku* in *Olodumare: God in Yoruba Belief* (181; 196). Achebe's *Things Fall Apart* explores the Igbo version of this, the *ogbanje*: "one of those wicked children who, when they died, entered their mother's wombs to be born again" (70). Several anthropological texts make reference to this belief. To my knowledge, no African feminist scholar or writer has fully explored the social, theoretical, gendered implications of the *abiku* or *ogbanje* for African women.

4. It is significant that Morrison deflects the healing of Sethe away from Baby Suggs to Paul D. See Carole Boyce Davies, "Mothering and Healing in Recent Black Women's Fiction," 41–43, for fuller discussion of the mother-healer figure.

5. See also Ann Ferguson, "On Conceiving Motherhood and Sexuality," 153–182. Nancy Rose Hunt, in "Domesticity and Colonialism in Belgian Africa," shows how white women were constructed as mothers in the interest of Empire.

6. Morrison previously had identified a negative aspect of nursing, in her naming of Milkman in *Song of Solomon* and in Milkman's somewhat retarded social behavior, in part because of this oral need. One cannot view Sethe's obsession with nursing uncritically. In a gay reading supplied by a student, Vinnie Cuccia, the implications of the men "fucking cows" in the absence of women, belies the possibility of male relationships as it simultaneously reduces women to animals.

7. Notes taken at lecture at Syracuse University, Syracuse, New York, June 1986. McDowell, in a critique of African-American male responses to black women writers, offers the "family romance" as a guiding concept of the critics in question. See her "Reading Family Matters," 75–97. She uses the lines from *Beloved*: "They were a family somehow and he was not the head of it" to illustrate how black women writers redefine family relationships. My point is that, by the end of the novel, however one reads it, Morrison has disrupted the three-woman household and given Paul D the role of rescuer of Sethe.

8. The notion of the "outraged mother" is offered by Joanne Braxton in *Wild Women in the Whirlwind* (299–315).

9. See, e.g., Chodorow, *Reproduction of Mothering*; Suleiman, "Maternal Splitting."

10. See Baldwin, "Everybody's Protest Novel," in *Notes of A Native Son* (1955). I am indebted to members of the feminist research and writing group in Binghamton, N.Y.— Marilyn Desmond, Susan Sterrett, Elsa Barkley Brown, and Deborah Britzman—for their friendship, readings, and thoughtful comments on this and other issues in the paper.

11. See McDowell, "Negotiating Between Tenses," 156–57, for a similar argument which I came upon after having written this paper (presented at the NWSA Conference, Baltimore, Maryland, June 1989).

Chapter 3

Mothering an Autistic Child:
Reclaiming the Voice of the Mother

Jane Taylor McDonnell

Until I knew I had to bring
the world to you, I don't think
I knew or saw the world at all.
—Paul West, *Words for a Deaf Daughter*

Fortunately a case of autism
in the family concentrates the mind
wonderfully, as Dr. Johnson
said of impending hanging.
—Clara Claiborne Park

Autism, a severely incapacitating developmental disability, now recognized as neurological or physiological in origin,[1] for many years was attributed to cold, compulsive, and "overly" intellectual parents. In particular, the "refrigerator mother"[2] was thought to be the cause of her child's withdrawal from social contact and the failure to develop normally. Bruno Bettelheim, one of the chief "experts" on this baffling condition, argued that the child, in response to such a mother, became a heavily defended "Empty Fortress."

Comparing autistic children to prisoners in Nazi concentration camps, Bettelheim, in *The Empty Fortress: Infantile Autism and the Birth of the Self*, claimed that autism is a defense against a rejecting mother. This rejection may be deeply unconscious on the part of the mother, he argued, but nevertheless it can be sensed by the child, who then must erect barriers against the mother's feelings in order merely to survive. Deprived of the possibility of a healthy interaction with the mother, the child thus develops a set of autistic symptoms—fear of change, insistence on sameness in the environment, solitary and repetitive play, "pronominal reversals" (in which "you" is substituted for "I"), avoidance of eye contact, etc. But inside this "empty fortress" erected by autistic defenses against the world, there is no "ego," no core sense of self, nothing but emptiness.

Perhaps it is not altogether a surprise that this perplexing handicap at first seemed absolutely and by its very nature to confirm "maternal guilt": how else could one explain how a beautiful, well-grown, and seemingly intelligent child could disappear into blankly repetitive play with strings or spinning objects? If this were the case, however, autism would turn up at an increased rate in abused and neglected children, for example.[3] More recent evidence in fact suggests strongly that autism originates in neurological or physiological defects.[4]

In spite of evidence to the contrary, however, Bettelheim persisted in believing that the condition was created by maternal rejection, and for many years his influence and the Freudian paradigm on which his position was based were dominant both in professional circles and in popular culture. Thus Bettelheim—concentration camp survivor, author of an influential book on fairy tales, esteemed member of the psychoanalytic profession, voice from the intellectual Left—has been read far more widely than any mother who has written on autism. In fact, when the mothers of autistic children did begin to speak, they ran the risk of being discounted, "explained away," by the very theory which they sought to resist; as Bettelheim said, the mother hardly can be believed, nor should she be involved in a rehabilitative program with the child, since she is "the very person" who has "kept him from developing normally in the first place" (407). The example of autism is paradigmatic of mothering in general, as it has been viewed in much of twentieth-century psychological literature. This literature both silences the mother and assumes that she is all-powerful, capable of doing enormous harm to her child but incapable of understanding and addressing her child's condition (Ehrenreich and English).

This essay will deal with three issues posed by mothering an autistic child, issues which I consider central to a feminist reappraisal of the larger literature on mothering. I have already mentioned the implicit challenge to the "experts" and to the habitual silencing of mothers in twentieth-century psychological and childcare literature which the mother of the autistic child must undertake when she begins to write. This essay will seek to rehabilitate the mother, and in the process to confront some of our cultural beliefs about good mothering and the mother-child relationship. Second, such a mother tests and extends the insights of some feminist literature (such as that of Sara Ruddick), work which tends to be based on middle-class assumptions concerning childcare in optimal conditions and on predictable growth within a reliable "natural" and social order. In fact, Ruddick herself, recognizing that knowledge is socially constructed and that, of necessity, she must write out of her own privileged experience, calls for essays such as this one. The third and deepest challenge comes to the mother herself, in the way she must confront her own values and her least questioned assumptions about the nature of "reality" itself. The mother of the autistic child not only must challenge the experts; she also must reconstruct her subjectivity by reappraising some of her own deepest convictions. Like Dora talking back or the woman escaping both the "yellow wallpaper" *and* madness, these mothers escape appropriation by the experts, seize their own interpretive strategies, and record a reality which perhaps never has been recorded before.[5]

At the moment, the mother's narrative of raising a handicapped child exists in a kind of generic limbo, neither science nor literature, valuable neither for a psychology course nor a feminist course on the literature of motherhood. Claims have been made recently for the immense value of this material for clinical understanding of this particular disorder (Park), but no one yet has argued that it might be equally valuable for a feminist reconstruction of mothering. Focusing especially on Clara Claiborne Park's *The Siege: The First Eight Years of an Autistic Child* and drawing on my own experience raising a mildly autistic son, this essay will work at the boundaries of different discourses. It will deliberately blur the distinctions between genres and explore the intersection of "literature" with other forms of writing.

Clara Park begins her account of the first eight years of her autistic daughter's life by suggesting a profound dislocation in her own sense of reality. She notices that her young child "Elly" (whose real name is Jessy) does not imitate, nor explore her world, nor ask for anything. More simply, she doesn't even point, which Park notes is "to stretch out the self into the world" (6), in order to comment on an object, to direct attention to it, perhaps to desire it.*

This strangely beautiful, golden-haired child walks right past people on the beach, grazing them by a quarter of an inch, or sits on the floor contentedly snaking a chain up and down, watching it coil and uncoil for twenty minutes at a time, until someone comes and moves her. Her mother remarks with puzzlement, "Nothing had happened to her—no illness, no absence, no change in the environment. At that age, surely, the organism should be spontaneous" (8).

Surely the organism should be spontaneous, but apparently this one is not; Elly does not pass through the well-documented milestones of early childhood development, in fact she seems not even to follow the order of "nature." The profoundly "different," otherworldy quality of the child causes a friend to suggest that Elly is a fairy child, a changeling, one of the "Good People, who bear the human shape without the burden of the human heart" (5). This

---

* Quotations from *The Siege: The First Eight years of an Autistic Child* by Clara Claiborne Park, published by Little, Brown, and Company

old Irish story tells us that the "real" child was stolen from the cradle by the fairies, leaving behind a beautiful and healthy but blank and "inhuman" child. If such a child seems "cruel" in her indifference, "it is not real cruelty, only a certain remoteness, an inability to comprehend our desires, our needs, our warmth" (5).

Thus, at the very beginning, *The Siege* calls into question the basic assumptions of mothering and of that "maternal thinking," identified by Sara Ruddick, which is posited on the assured growth, development, and ultimate acceptability of the child. Ruddick's book, *Maternal Thinking*, is the first systematic account of mothering as a social practice characterized by distinctive kinds of thinking. She argues that maternal thinking arises in response to three demands in raising a child: preserving the life of a child, guiding its growth, and creating a socially acceptable adult who also meets with the mother's approval. But everything Ruddick says suggests that the mother merely guides her child gently through a set of predetermined, inborn stages of development. The givens of the situation in most cases of mothering thus start with what we choose to call the "humanity," the human condition of the child. We see ourselves responded to, our love for the child reflected back in myriad ways. Frequently it is the child who guides the mother, who sets the pace and indicates when she is ready to learn.

Park's experience with Elly, however, is profoundly different. "What is one to think, feel, and do when confronted by a two-year-old—one's own—who makes no exploration or approach, who expresses neither hostility nor anger, and who wants nothing?" (88).

What is one to think, indeed? Park concludes that she must mount a "siege" on her child. She must "beguile" her into the human condition, for the perfect equilibrium which her child has found blocks all possibility of growth. She uses the metaphor of a citadel, a castle, a fortress, but she uses it in a manner far different from Bettelheim's way. She suggests not that her child has walled herself off as protection from a threatening mother, but rather that she, the mother, must face the difficult imperative of intruding on, attacking, invading her child's self-imposed isolation. She doesn't have time to try to figure out the reasons for that isolation; provisional answers will come later. For now, this is all she knows, and this is the "terrible arrogance" with which she begins the book:

> The world we would tempt her into was the world of risk, failure, and frustration, of unfulfilled desire, of pain as well as activity and love . . . Confronted with a tiny child's refusal of life, all existential hesitations evaporate. We had no choice. We would use every stratagem we could invent to assail her fortress, to beguile, entice, seduce her into the human condition. (12)

Park's metaphors (the castle, the citadel, mounting a siege, seducing) are problematical in themselves, since they draw on militaristic and violent sexual imagery, and they become doubly problematical in the context of mothering a child. But the very violence of this imagery (which Park has taken from Donne's poem, "Batter my Heart, Three-Personed God") is, in a sense, appropriate; as she says, "I know no better description of the terrible imperative of the assault of love" (276).

This is maternal responsibility magnified a hundredfold—for how is Clara Park to know that the pleasures of growth will ever be her child's experience? It is the arrogance of all mothers to assume that the world of adult responsibility is the desired end of childhood, but most mothers can assume also that their children ultimately will be rewarded with adult understanding and competence, which will more than make up for the pain and stress of growing up. Park can assume no such reward for her child—or for herself.

What is this "siege" Park seeks to mount on her child? In four chapters— "Willed Weakness," Willed Blindness," "Willed Deafness," and "Willed Isolation"—Park describes the ways she taught her child to use a cup, to turn on a light switch, to turn on the water, to begin to see and to understand "reality" through pictorial representations of everyday objects. The tiny, the *minute* approaches she makes to her child hardly seem like an assault or a siege. She describes, for example, her efforts to help Elly learn to turn on an ordinary water faucet. Working with a series of delicate touches to Elly's limp wrist and fingers, she first turns the faucet on with her hand lightly placed over Elly's. Then, slowly, slowly, she removes the pressure of her own hand. She does this so gradually, so imperceptibly that, in the end, Elly *"goes on turning on the water"* (52). Through this long passage, we have the impression that hours have passed, that Park has scarcely drawn a breath, so intense is her concentration.

These chapters record in exhaustive detail such processes. But if that were all they did, the book might be of interest only to professionals and parents working with autistic children. In fact, however, Park also records her own mental processes, by which she seeks to understand her daughter, to understand a profoundly different way of being. And it is these mental processes of the mother which are so fascinating. Much of Park's reasoning is hypothetical, "as if" reasoning. "*As if*. Again and again we used this formulation, as we searched out explanations of our child's strange contradictions . . . We cannot help interpreting. The words *as if* must function to remind us that we can be sure of no interpretations" (46). Thus Elly stopped any activity that her mother made the mistake of noticing, *as if* she feared her mother would take advantage of her new skill, *as if* it would commit her to performing again. Perhaps we should say that Park does not "know" her daughter, she is wise enough not to "understand" her. Later, fifteen years later, in the post-script, she advances firmer and more theoretical explanations for her daughter's strange behavior, but she is astute enough to be a student rather than a teacher for many years.

There is another dimension to this experience of mothering—and a deeper pain—which Park touches on but does not explore in great depth. In many ways, Clara Park is very privileged, very secure, and the voice she speaks with at first is that of an unthreatened middle-class woman. As she says, she already has many of the things she wanted out of life—a good marriage, three bright, healthy, older children, a teaching job which gives her great satisfaction, many friends, enough money to hire a series of *au pairs* (mother's helpers or "Jessy-girls")—and, evidently, time enough to keep a detailed journal during all these years.

Nevertheless, there are intrusions on this secure world, and *The Siege* begins to confront and challenge many of the middle-class values which are standard in childcare books as well as in some feminist literature about mothering. Taking her child first to a big-city hospital for diagnostic testing, Park is asked to wait in a room with other mothers and other children. It is only slowly that she learns who these children are: noticing black eyes in faces "inconceivably thin," legs which are "frail sticks," she thinks first of "the starved and outraged children of Buchenwald and Auschwitz" (37). She wonders how any doctor's skill can "nourish such children back to health." Only slowly does the truth dawn on her: "The obtuseness of the fortunate is beyond belief. It was not until we had been three hours in that hospital that we found out where we were. Of course. This was the ward for terminal cancer cases" (37).

This is a disruptive new awareness. Not only does Elly herself disrupt her mother's secure world, but the child brings Park in touch with many experiences she otherwise would not have had. The sympathy Park experiences for these children and their parents is one of the things that keeps her from bitterness, that leads her towards a wisdom that seems unusual in the parent's narrative of raising a handicapped child. She reflects on her own "luck" up until this point in her life and realizes, "It is hard not to be proud of one's luck. Hubris is part of us." We think we deserve our luck, that we make it happen, yet "we deserve nothing, except to be human *comme les autres*." The instrument chosen to humble her, she notes, "had the exquisite appropriateness the Greeks noted in the operation of impersonal powers like Fate—or Biology" (40).

Such a mother of such a child, especially if she (like Park and myself) is a member of an academic community and herself a teacher or intellectual, is indeed humbled by an "exquisite appropriateness" of fate. She is injured in her pride of intellect. We all invest our personal ideals in our children; we also project our wishfulness onto them. They are our second chance at achievement, even our second chance at life. Thus, for a teacher or an intellectual mother to realize that her child is handicapped in understanding is to experience the death of her own deepest expectations. But it is also to be forced to reconsider her deepest values. An academic community is a place where pride of intellect is strong—and unexamined. Academics tend to identify intellect with virtue and with personal worth. But having a mentally handicapped child teaches us something far different—that intellect is a gift of nature, that it comes unbidden and through no merit or effort whatsoever of our own. Often even money that is inherited was once earned; intellect never is. This is the "slow lesson" that Park must learn, and this is the lesson which her book slowly unfolds for us.

Behind the imperative need to "mount an assault" on a child, to bring her into the human condition, lies a world of pain for her mother. First of all, such mothers feel the pain of loss, the complex and ambiguous grief of simultaneously having and not having a child, of being and not being a mother, since to be a "mother" is to encourage the growth of a developing human being. Helen Featherstone and others have written of the profound grief and guilt parents of handicapped children experience. Such a mother must mourn the loss of the child who might have been, while simultaneously struggling to care for the child who is. This mother feels that her "real" child is gone—dead or stolen away by the fairies—yet there is no clear and socially recognized occasion for grieving such a loss, no funeral, no ceremony, no outpouring of community sympathy and recognition that a kind of "death" has occurred.

With such a child, furthermore, there is no *time* to grieve these losses. Mothers of such children frequently are overwhelmed by the day-to-day struggles of keeping their children alive. Park mentions that Elly was once hit by a truck, yet never learned caution in crossing the street. No "mother's lesson" could teach where that experience itself failed to instruct. As she says, Elly did not learn to fear, for fear implies anticipation, the ability to generalize from past experience to a possible future. In more extreme cases, some autistic children have disturbances in the perception of pain and are liable to injure themselves without recognizing pain, to walk across the open flames of a stove without recognizing danger, or even to multilate themselves by biting their own arms or tongues or pulling out their hair.[6] These last are extreme examples (although not really unusual), but all such mothers are likely to put their own feelings on hold as they struggle to provide care for such a child in a close-to-impossible situation.

The beginning of *The Siege* points to another, even more profound onto-logical insecurity for parents. With such children, mothers are in the presence (the daily presence) of difference—of a different reality, a reality which is sometimes unnervingly "other" than our own. We may find that the very things which we take for granted as unquestionable in our assumption of humanness or "objectness" are often not assumed by older autistic children. For them, numbers may have mystical significance, dogs may straddle the boundary between human and nonhuman, machines may be permanent and indestructable, and objects may be dear old friends too exciting to see after a long absence.[7]

In her postscript to *The Siege*, for example, Park remarks how, for Elly (now called by her real name Jessy), some sounds are just too good, too meaningful. As a teenager, she must put her hands over her ears when a friend sews. For years, Jessy believed that there were "little imitation people" in household appliances that click or buzz or hum. Some numbers were so magic she could not say them, and radio dials, records players, railway crossings, electric blanket controls, quartz heaters all are intensely meaningful objects to her, even at the age of twenty-three (302).

My own son, at two, had a very typical autistic fascination with lights. He turned them off and on for hours each day. He knew where every light switch was in our house and the houses of our friends, and even in many of the stores downtown. Later he lived for screwdrivers, then fire hydrants, later still for power lines, grain elevators, then bell towers. For a long time it was pipes and plumbing; then scales and thermometers, or clocks and his watch. As he grew up, it became the weather and meteorology, again a very typical autistic fascination.

The point about all this is that each interest was exclusive, compelling, and *the* major organizing principle of his reality at the time. But as the mother of such a child, one is totally unprepared. I suppose none of us has ever seen before such narrowness of focus, such total concentration and dedication to task—or such oddity of interest in a child. For the parent of the autistic child, such difference can be profoundly unsettling. Mothering, we all know, is in many ways a very normative activity.

In addition to the need to "preserve the life and foster the growth of the child," Ruddick identifies a number of moral dilemmas in the "central challenge of mothering," which is that of training a child to become an acceptable adult. According to her, the mother must teach nonviolence together with self-defense, egalitarian ideals together with pride in personal achievement, orderliness but not too much order, etc. (104). She points out that, sooner or later, most mothers are forced to reflect on their own moral principles and to "place achievement in a human context" when they witness their children's failures. Yet the child she necessarily has in mind, given her own experience and that of most mothers, is "intact," the child who is not handicapped in some way, not blind, deaf, autistic, retarded, paraplegic, dyslexic, etc. When Ruddick discusses the two moral pitfalls of mothers—"inauthenticity" and "domination"—she has in mind the child who *can* learn, the mother who can feel pride in her child's growth and achievement in a fairly standard way.

The "inauthenticity" which Ruddick identifies as a potential failing of mothers, the loss of confidence in their own values and the loss of sympathy with their childrens' needs, is a far different thing—more benign, less threatening—than the temptations to inauthenticity which Park and other mothers of handicapped children have to face. Ruddick mentions the mothers' "susceptibility to the 'gaze' of others," the temptation to punish a child in public for small infractions of rules which would go unnoticed at home (111). She writes feelingly of the betrayal children feel when their mothers become a different person in public, when the confident mother they have learned to trust is "rendered confused and powerless by the gaze of others" (111).

If these are the temptations of mothering a normal child, what must they be for the mother of the autistic child who throws a tantrum in a public place because of some disturbing noise, who takes apart an unsuspecting neighbor's doorknobs and bicycles with a screwdriver, who screams when she hears the word "cricket?" What is a mother to do in the face of such bizarrely different behavior—behavior which can get in the way of the child's education, eventual employment, independence, or even simple social functioning? The "confused and powerless" mother in this case is not merely tempted to inauthenticity, to an "'abdication' of maternal authority," as Ruddick notes (111). She may be tempted to something far worse—a violent response to her child, total isolation of herself and her family from friends and neighbors, a complete loss of faith in herself which leads eventually to mental breakdown.

Autism thus seems at first to present an almost unresolvable contradiction for the mother. Park and other mothers of autistic children are immediately placed in a dilemma which most mothers never have to face. She can either struggle to normalize her child, to bring her into the "human condition," as she says, and attempt to make her into a socially acceptable adult. But if she does that too insistently or too strictly, the child quickly gets the message that she or he *isn't* all right. An intelligent, high-achieving autistic child can learn this way that he or she is somehow wrong, deeply flawed in ways that can't be understood or corrected.

On the other hand, such a mother can appreciate her child's difference, value it as an acceptable difference, in which case the dangers are just as great. Here she may run the risk of romanticizing her child's abnormalities, even of "giving up" on her child. I don't mean to claim that these are two absolute and mutually exclusive choices. A mother such as Clara Park somehow manages to push her child towards normality, while at the same time appreciating (but not patronizing) her differences. Nevertheless, within the highly normative activity of mothering, raising an autistic child poses problems of acceptance of socially "unacceptable" differences which go far beyond those encountered in raising nonhandicapped children. Many mothers of autistic children must have felt at times that it is best (as well as easiest) to leave a contented baby rocking for hours in a crib, or to allow an older child to tell tasteless jokes if telling such jokes is one of his few "social skills."

Park writes that, when her child did make progress, her oddities became more obvious:

> As she has improved her strangeness has acquired a much higher visibility. Now that she can "act out," she is no longer the silent child who took directions and caused no trouble, but a spring-tight, hyperactive little girl who uses her voice and her whole body to express the emotions . . . that are at length available to her. Newly at large in the world of feeling, she must learn to control it, and that without converting control into repression. (258–59)

There are no ready-made rules for the mother confronted with such a child, and there are no charts of development to be appealed to in guiding her through the complexities of such development. If the mother encourages her child to express and act on her new found emotions, the child may run the risk of discipline from her teachers and ostracism by other children. When Elly makes a clumsy approach to another child, the other child finds her frightening or bizarre and is likely to back away further. As Park says, "It is hard to build sociality on these fitful and easily discouraged advances" (258). But even more unthinkable is the idea of controlling all such advances; any clumsy advance towards other people, Park must feel, should be recognized, fostered, and built upon. No one wants an obedient child who is merely an automaton.

Once again, the challenges of this kind of mothering go far beyond those treated explicitly by Sara Ruddick in *Maternal Thinking*, although Ruddick recognizes the need for accounts of such experiences. Under the heading of "'Nature,' Normality, and Nurturance," in her chapter called "Fostering Growth," Ruddick appeals to the concept of a nature that is benign, the mother's ally in fostering the growth of a child; all children, she says, "naturally" go though relatively predictable stages, unpleasant as they may seem at the time. "When mothers excuse their children's behavior on the ground that it is 'natural' to their age, they also implicitly appeal to a beneficent nature . . . Nature offers a promise of healing; natural processes move toward health and integrity, despite their moments of undeniable ugliness and fear" (84).

For the mother of the autistic child, there is no such beneficent nature. Her child's development may not be guided by an inner clock which will go on working even in "the midst of social and personal disaster" (84). Most alarmingly, the autistic child's growth, as Park suggests at the beginning, at times must be forced. Later, when she has started to develop, Elly's development is socially unacceptable and brings adverse responses from others, even though it is following the "natural order" of that particular child's existence.

As we see at the beginning of *The Siege*, Clara Park must meet a number of challenges to the usual practice and construction of mothering. Responding to her child's difference, she must meet the exigencies of a very special situation. She cannot assume a "beneficent nature" which will guide her child's growth through a series of predictable developmental stages, and she is challenged to reassess her own deepest values as an intellectual who lives in an academic community and values the life of the mind. But Clara Park eventually is also confronted with the challenge of the experts, psychiatrists of "the Bettelheim school," who question her values—indeed, her personality and identity—in a very disturbing way.

In fact, Park and her husband themselves suggest a psychiatric evaluation of their child, despite the skepticism of their family doctor; as she remarks wryly, "I suppose he knew that the intellectual parents of a strange baby would not long be allowed to accept the irrelevance of psychiatry" (133). At this point in her life, Park first encounters the term "autism" in its earlier usage, signifying psychosis, a condition akin to or identical with schizophrenia, a mental illness thought to be caused, at least in part, by parents. She begins to question her own right to think differently about her child's curious handicap:

> Who are we to qualify this account of our responsibility . . . Bettelheim writes that parental rejection is an element in the genesis of every case of childhood schizophrenia he has seen. Beata Rank sets out as her "main hypothesis" that "the atypical child has suffered gross emotional deprivation," and adds that "the younger the child, the more necessary is it for us to modify the mother's personality." Even the wise and humane Erikson, though he remarks that the rejecting mother is the "occupational prejudice" of child psychiatrists, reiterates in the same study that a "history of maternal estrangement" may be found in *every* (italics mine) history of infantile schizophrenia." (125–26)

Park is soon to confront this model for understanding herself and her child, not just as general theory, but as embodied in the practice of psychiatrists the parents consult in a large research center, which Park calls simply "the Institute." After interminable delays, the Institute finally grants the couple an appointment, with three days' notice. The Parks learn, to their amazement, that they are not to bring Elly. Furthermore, mother and father are to be interviewed separately: "It was not their practice to interview parents together, where they could supplement, support, and correct each other" (135). Finally the Institute personnel do observe the child, and, after further delays of many months, they convey a three-sentence verbal report: (1) Elly needed psychotherapy; (2) she performed at age level on some parts of the test they gave her and therefore they thought she had no mental deficiency; and (3) "She has many fears" (139).

Park concludes that she has been naive about the purpose of the extensive interviews with herself and her husband. She had thought that the purpose of all the information the psychiatrists gathered was to offer a diagnosis of a child; she wonders later if the purpose had been to diagnose the parents instead.

In this chapter, Park confronts head-on the prejudiced views held by many psychiatrists at this time about parents of autistic children. Unusual because they were intellectuals and professionals, such parents were generally thought also to be unusually energetic and persistent and ultimately "a cold lot"— detached perfectionists without humor or social graces of any kind. "Kanner came to think of the group as 'refrigerator parents'—able to get together just long enough to produce a child" (127–28).

Park goes on to admit to a kind of shyness which can be interpreted as distance or detachment. She also admits to intelligence, energy, persistence, and self-control in herself and her husband. These qualities, she feels, had served them well. But now they see them converted into pathology. In other words, the very qualities which would be esteemed in professionals (including psychiatrists) — intelligence, energy, persistence, and self-control — are, in a parent, liabilities.

They are extreme liabilities in a mother. One of her "solicitous friends" lends her a book which gives a profile of the "typical" mother of an "atypical" child:

> On the surface these mothers may give the impression of being well-adjusted; not too rarely they are highly intellectual, prominent people. Close investigation reveals that the majority of them are immature and narcissistic with precarious social contact . . . who have struggled heroically to build and maintain the image they have created of a fine woman, wife, and mother. (Quoted 129, no source given)

This borrowed book goes on to speak of one such mother, someone very like Clara Park herself—a well-educated, energetic woman with many interests, someone with a graduate degree and success in a professional career. Yet once again, all these qualities are used against the mother; they are signs of a hidden pathology that manifests itself only secondarily in her child.

Park's experience here is paradigmatic of twentieth-century "mother-blaming" literature. The only person in existence who is supposed to have no life of her own, the ideal mother of much twentieth-century psychological literature is defined entirely in terms of the needs and desires of her child (see Garner, Kahane, and Sprengnether). If she does have an independent existence—if in fact she is well-educated and energetic, with numerous satisfying interests, a graduate degree, and a professional career—then she is a walking contradiction in terms. The more successful she appears to be, the more flawed in fact she is thought to be; self-assurance merely marks an "inner isolation."

A professionally successful woman cannot—by definition, it seems—be a successful mother. According to this conception, the job of mothering a child is so absorbing, so demanding of time and energy, so restrictive, that it would be impossible for a good mother also to be absorbed in any other work or interest. Hence the large body of literature on mentally handicapped children (with no clear physical symptoms) which attributes their handicaps to their mothers.[8] The arrogance of these professionals in presuming to "diagnose" the mothers of handicapped children stands in striking contrast to Park's own caution in taking on herself the right to intervene in her child's development, to decide what is best for her child, and in fact even to speak for her.

Various accounts have been given to explain why mothers have been so blamed. Some writers feel that those doing the blaming are motivated by "unprocessed" feelings left over from childhood (Chodorow and Contratto). Adult writers on the subject of mothering sometimes assume (as young children assume) that the mother is all-powerful and that she alone is responsible for the outcome of her mothering, even in a sexist, racist, classist, and otherwise corrupting society. The "fantasy of maternal perfectibility," as this attitude has been called, and the persistent tendency to idealize the "moral" mother (Block) have clearly done women (and society as a whole) a serious disservice. Such theories support the notion that mothers, in isolation from other adults (including fathers) and from the community as a whole, are responsible for most of the ills of society. The mother must provide a "haven in a heartless world" (Lasch), and, if she fails to do so, the argument runs, drug addiction, teenage pregnancies, delinquency, learning disabilities, asthma, autism, schizophrenia, and other disorders result.

I would like to suggest another explanation for the persistence of this belief in maternal deprivation as the cause of autism (and of schizophrenia and other mental or developmental disorders), despite accumulating evidence to the contrary. The myth of "maternal rejection" in general appeared as a controlling idea in twentieth-century thought after we lost other myths to explain "madness" or deviance. Earlier ways of explaining deviance—including demonic possession, original sin, delirium (which means literally "out of the furrow"), black bile, and melancholia—were all theories which were advanced at various times when people sought to explain madness in adults. For madness or "difference" in children, other explanatory stories were developed: the myth of feral children (children raised in the wild by wolves), the myth of changelings (children stolen away by the fairies), and the Enlightenment understanding of the conflict between "nature" and "civilization."

The loss of these myths left an enormous gap in our understanding of the causes of difference, especially difference in children. In much of the psychological literature of this century, the family configuration, and specifically maternal guilt, takes the place of these other explanatory models as a way of understanding the genesis of a condition which is baffling and virtually unknowable in its profound "otherness." As David Spiegel notes:

> In essence, the attribution of the causes of madness come closer and closer to home, starting with the devil or a variety of outside animal forces, passing through the body, and moving on to the individual's will and psyche, making the individual's psychological and family environment especially important. (96)

Unlike many other mothers of autistic children, however, Park has little trouble rejecting the myth of maternal rejection. Although it poses a far greater threat to her self-esteem than other myths (since the very qualities she prizes in herself are seen here as signs of "pathology"), in the end she simply places it alongside theosophists and clairvoyants, "aura" readings, crawl-therapy, and "the man in Philadelphia who prayed with the parents of abnormal children" (132). She comments that, although she is well-read in many fields, she never had read much psychology, and that she simply took every mother to be "her own Piaget," a position which allowed her to depend on the lore of other mothers, neighbors, and friends for advice about child-rearing. Park also reflects that, because she is the mother of three healthy, well-adjusted children, she need not feel guilt. She knows she has done a good job with them, and this awareness, together with a "certain natural skepticism," sustained her as she "read the formulations of the Bettelheims of this world" (131).

"No scientist's household, after all, can fail to be familiar with the great procession of plausible hypotheses that have yet proved incomplete and false" (131). Quoting Newton's *Principia* on the premature formation of hypotheses, Park continues to trust her own intelligence, persistence, energy, and experience: "Experience with three children had taught me that the mind-reading powers of babies are greatly exaggerated. I knew that Elly had never guessed that (like so many mothers of normal children) I had not really needed another baby" (131).

Nevertheless, in spite of her resilient good humor and wise skepticism (qualities which Ruddick singles out as the virtues of the mother), the wounds are felt. "It was only gradually that we began to feel angry and resentful, to react as intelligent adults, not as obedient children in the hands of those wiser than we" (141). She reflects, with justified sarcasm, that the doctors of "the Institute" were "wise to avoid" using the term autism, "it fitted them so closely." However, their "imperviousness" and their "terrible silence" undeniably have done harm.

As with the experience in the cancer ward, this personal harm is Park's gateway to empathy with other people. Instead of embittering her, her own hurt leads her to reflect on class privilege and on other ways in which people are dehumanized.

> Comfortable, well-educated members of the upper middle class ordinarily escape the experience of depersonalization, of utter helplessness in institutional hands, of reduction to the status of children to whom situations are mediated, not explained. Like so much that hurts, the experience is deeply educational. We know now in our skins that the most threatening of all attacks is the attack on personal worth, that the harshest of all deprivations is the deprivation of respect. We know now, I think, how the slum mother feels as the welfare worker comes round the corner. (143)

Later, in London, Park takes her child to the Anna Freud Institute and has a very different experience with professionals. The therapists there read her journals with absorption and admiration; they invite her, as the "real" expert, into a collaborative effort to teach Elly; and they themselves move cautiously, without set plans, playing it by ear, and learning from the child as they go. They also, she learns later, fear for *her*—Clara Park's—sanity, and feel that she, as the main teacher, therapist, and psychologist for her child, is at risk of a breakdown through exhaustion and lack of support, *not* because she was somehow flawed before she even became a mother.

This is a success story in many ways—Jessy can work outside her home, she has a number of social skills and many practical skills, and, more importantly, she has a remarkable artistic gift (indeed, her ability to draw and paint was her mother's way ultimately of reaching her). Even so, autism is, at least in these more "classic" cases, a lifetime handicap. Jessy never will be "normal" in the usual sense of that term.

We can now recognize that it was an act of enormous courage for Park to begin to tell this story. She spoke of the "terrible arrogance"—let us call it courage—of presuming to intrude on the serene isolation of her daughter, since she knew that enticing her into the human condition might bring her child more frustration than fulfillment and far more pain than pleasure.[9] She wrote movingly of the "arrogance" of taking on the experts of the time. Perhaps even more courageously, Park questioned her own middle-class assumptions and those of so much writing about childcare. I have discussed the demands made on Park's time and attention simply to preserve the life of her child; the struggle both to normalize her child and to appreciate her difference; and, finally, the fact that in fostering her child's growth, she cannot always appeal to the norms of "humanity" or to the concept of a beneficient and understandable "nature."

But there is a final arrogance (again let us call it courage) in this book. Clara Park must speak for someone else who is silenced, silenced even more profoundly than the mother of an autistic child. Park has the power to express her dauther's existence in a way which Jessy herself can never express or comprehend fully. She must enter into, create, the reality of a child who will never be able to do it for herself, at least not in this way. At the end of her book, in the postscript, she writes of how Jessy typed (without error) the complete Spanish translation of *The Siege*; yet she could not comprehend the meaning of this book about herself as we do.

Because she could not change her child, Park set out to change the world. And in some measure, she did just that. She helped to redefine autism and to advance professional knowledge of this strange handicap; she acted as an advocate for mental patients and their families and wrote a book on the subject (Park with Shapiro). Indeed, as you might expect, Park became a widely consulted expert herself. Her book has just been reprinted for the third time, twenty-three years after the first edition, and, although it is not read nearly so widely as Bettelheim's book, it can be found in most college libraries and many bookstores. She writes book reviews for the *Journal of Autism and Developmental Disorders* (renamed from the *Journal of Autism and Childhood Schizophrenia*), and she carries on an international correspondence on the subject of autism. In the spirit of Sara Ruddick's profoundest hope, she has recreated motherhood as a social activist position, turning her personal pain into the wisdom and courage to help others.

In *The Siege*, Clara Claiborne Park constructs a mother's identity, an identity-in-relationship which is also autonomous, not dependent on her children for self-esteem. As many people have pointed out, the creation of a mother's identity through the relationship with the child has not, until recently, been the focus of much writing. In Park's book we see a systematic exploration of the changes in a mother's life caused by the raising of a handicapped child, an exploration rare — almost unique — in literature. Because of the challenge of this child, Park grows in the understanding of her life as a mother. She discovers her deepest values, and in the process she creates a subjectivity we rarely glimpse in literature — that of the mother intimately engaged with her child. As she encourages her child to become a "self," Park herself becomes a deeper, more complex self. In other words, she tests and affirms those premises of so much feminist analysis — that knowledge is socially constructed, that mothering is a way of thinking (not merely an "instinctive" activity), that this way of thinking must be learned, and that the self is formed in the arena of interpersonal relationships and not in isolated meditation.

Notes

1. Autism has been called "the most severe behavior disorder of childhood." The condition seriously challenges parents and professionals because it represents not just a delay, but a severe disturbance, in the acquisition of physical, social, and language skills. Abnormal responses to sense impressions (sight, hearing, smell, taste, pain) are a hallmark of the disorder, and such children also relate abnormally to people, objects, and events. Autistic children fear change. They insist on sameness in their environment and attempt to cope with their handicap through a "rage for order": they frequently insist on the same food, the same clothes, doing things in the same sequence, rigidly lining up objects, etc. For more information, see, e.g., Sam B. Morgan.

2. The term is that of Leo Kanner, who later recanted and apologized for its use.

3. This is not to say, of course, that autistic children are never neglected or abused; in fact, like all handicapped children, they are at increased risk of abuse because they cause so much stress in parents, teachers, and others. Abuse and neglect, however, do not cause the disorder.

4. According to the National Society for Children and Adults with Autism, the symptoms are caused by physical disorders of the brain. Rubella in the mother during pregnancy; "Fragile X" syndrome: phenylketonuria; menningitis and other infections in the young child; and even, very occasionally, "cerebral allergies" to certain foods have been cited as possible causes of autism, and in certain autistics MRI (magnetic resonance imaging) brain scans have turned up abnormalities in the area of the cerebellum. Researchers are now exploring a possible genetic link in autism. The most recent and reliable sources of information are the *Journal of Autism and Developmental Disorders* and the *Autism Research Review International*.

5. See Lovell; Betts; Beavers, 1982; Morphett; Greenfeld, 1972, 1978, and 1989; and Callahan.

6. It is thought that such children are addicted to their own endorphins, a substance

naturally released into the brain to ease pain. See George Monaghan, "Saving Kenny from Himself," *Sunday Magazine, Minneapolis Star and Tribune*, 5 Mar. 1989.

7. There are now several first-person accounts written by autistic or "autistic-like" individuals which relate such experiences. See, e.g., Volkmar and Cohen; Simon Morphett, "I'm Simon!" in Morphett; and Grandin.

8. See, e.g., F. Bateson et al.; M.S. Mahler; T. Lidz, S. Fleck, and A.R. Cornelison; and R.D. Laing and A. Esterson. A good discussion of these and other works may be found in Spiegel.

9. This is true of high-achieving individuals with "infantile autism, residual state" or, as it is sometimes called, Asperger's Syndrome. See Volkmar and Cohen.

Chapter 4

Constructing the Mother:
Contemporary Psychoanalytic Theorists
and Women Autobiographers

Shirley Nelson Garner

For some time, I have been interested in the intersections of feminism and psychoanalysis. Feminism in the broadest sense has meant to me a way of seeing. It has meant putting the biologically female and the culturally feminine at the center of experience and looking from that perspective. Because I have found psychoanalytic theory and practice useful personally and also professionally as I interpret and teach literature, I have wanted to understand its biases: its exclusions, distortions, and impositions. Since the traditional subjects of psychoanalysis have been mainly white, middle-class heterosexuals, to what extent it *does* or *can* take into account the variety of women's experience, as feminism must, is a crucial question. Almost from its inception, many of the practitioners of psychoanalysis recognized that its understanding of women generally was inadequate — and perhaps simply wrong — despite the fact that the majority of the earliest patients were women. To his credit, Freud admitted that the psychology of women was a mystery to him, and Ernest Jones and Karen Horney, among his first disciples, almost immediately took exception to his theories pertaining to women.

I have been particularly interested in the responsiveness of psychoanalytic theory and practice to lesbians,[1] old women, and mothers. While it has persecuted lesbians and ignored or dismissed old women, it has seemed to "allow" mothers. In fact, one of its unstated — and even unrecognized — aims has been to socialize women for marriage and the family. In accepting her potential for motherhood, becoming a mother, a woman reached maturity — though this achievement could not be understood as a triumph but rather signified the acceptance of an essentially masochistic destiny. The way a woman supposedly finally overcame her penis envy was through gaining a man — a surrogate for her father — and having a baby, preferably a boy, which assured her, according to Freud, the most perfect of human relationships.

Though wife and mother were essentially the only roles that Freud imagined a woman playing, he paid relatively little attention to the mother. While assigning her a significant part in the oedipal drama and in the preoedipal period (particularly in the mother-daughter relationship), Freud more or less ignored her to focus on the oedipal crisis of the child, particularly of the son.

As psychoanalysts after Freud began to recognize the importance of the pre-oedipal period in the child's development, however, they began to emphasize the mother's significance. I want to chart briefly the directions this emphasis has taken, using several points of reference: D.W. Winnicott's essays, Nancy Chodorow's *Reproduction of Mothering*, and two recently published collections of essays—*Psychoanalysis and Women: Contemporary Reappraisals*, edited by Judith L. Alpert; and *Lesbian Psychologies*, edited by the Boston Lesbian Psychologies Collective.

Though object-relations theorists disagree with each other in various respects, they all concede that "an early, essential, and significant relationship between mother and child precedes and influences all other developmental phases" (Alpert, 185). From among these theorists—Michael and Alice Balint, Melanie Klein, D.W. Winnicott, Margaret Mahler, and W.R.D. Fairbairn—I use Winnicott because his notion of "good-enough mothering" has attained such prominence.

For Winnicott, woman's role as mother is social, not simply personal and individual. Because he sees the mother as laying down the foundations of her child's mental health, she contributes to the collective mental health of her community, which is essential to the "growth or perpetual rejuvenation" of the larger society (*Playing*, 140).[2] She is, first, to provide the infant with the opportunity initially for illusion and then for disillusionment. By adapting to the newborn's needs, she "gives the infant the *illusion* that there is an external reality that corresponds to the infant's own capacity to create" (*Playing*, 12). Her careful and gradual disillusionment of the child—her assertion of her own needs—allows the baby to separate from her, to begin to see her as having a reality of her own.

Second, the mother is to serve as a mirror for the baby. Because the mother's face reflects what she sees in the baby, the infant sees not the mother's face, according to Winnicott, but herself or himself. When the mother is distracted, depressed, or otherwise unable to give back what the infant offers, so that he or she sees only a face, the infant's "creative capacity begins to atrophy. . . . Perception take the place of apperception." What is cut off is "a two-way process in which self-enrichment alternates with the discovery of meaning in the world of seen things" (*Playing*, 112–13). Looking *at* replaces exchange and rapport.

Finally, the mother must be sufficiently present to prevent infant trauma. While Winnicott does not define the amount of time an infant can be deprived of its mother, he suggests that a mother's prolonged absence causes a "break in life's continuity." An infant's experience of such a break is, he suggests, equivalent to the experience of madness (*Playing*, 97).

By describing the mother who performs these tasks as "good enough," he intends to dissociate her from some idea of perfection, to make her human rather than ideal (*Playing*, 139). Yet his definition of the "good-enough" mother is heavy with expectation:

> The good-enough "mother" (not necessarily the infant's own mother) is one who makes active adaptation to the infant's needs, an active adaptation that gradually lessens, according to the infant's growing ability to account for failure of adaptation and to tolerate the results of frustration. Naturally, the infant's own mother is more likely to be good enough than some other person, since this active adaptation *demands an easy and unresented preoccupation with the one infant; in fact, success in infant care depends on the fact of devotion*, not on cleverness or intellectual enlightenment.
>
> The good-enough mother . . . starts off with an almost *complete adaptation* to her infant's needs. [italics mine] (*Playing*, 10)

Winnicott sees the human being from birth on as "concerned with the problem of the relationship between what is objectively perceived and what is subjectively conceived of." In solving this problem, he asserts, "there is no health for the human being who has not been started off well enough by the mother" (*Playing*, 11).

Repeatedly, Winnicott stresses the "naturalness" of the ability to mother. He is clearly wary of the efforts of doctors, nurses, and medical experts to control mothers and rob them of maternal authority. While he sees medical professionals as important in fostering the physical health of mother and child, he is suspicious of their interference in the relationship between mother and baby, which he likens to a "wound," an "insult," and even a "rape" (*Babies*, 64). He cautions doctors against giving advice about intimacy and insists that mothers need instead "an environmental provision which fosters the mother's belief in herself" (*Babies*, 27). He continually stresses the mother's "intuitive understanding" and insists that it comes naturally and cannot be taught. At times, he carries this idea very far:

> It is true that some mothers are able to get help of a limited kind from books, but it must be remembered that if a mother goes to a book or to someone for advice and tries to learn what she has to do we already wonder whether she is fitted for the job. She has to know about it from a deeper level and not necessarily from that part of the mind which has words for everything. The main things that a mother does with the baby cannot be done through words. (*Babies*, 61)

Here and there, in passing or occasionally in an introduction, Winnicott defines the womans' needs as mother apart from her natural ability and inclination to mother. They are: protection (which I will come back to), information, the best physical care medical science offers, a doctor and a nurse she knows and trusts, "the devotion of a husband and satisfying sexual experiences" (*Child*, 9). (I think we are meant to assume that the husband and the satisfying sexual experiences come together.) The ability to meet these needs implicitly assumes middle-class or substantial working-class incomes, and heterosexual aims are taken for granted.

Winnicott assumes that it is necessary for a good-enough mother to have a man, probably a husband, to support her financially and emotionally. He does not address himself to the working woman. He says, for example, that a woman will be ready to care for her child by the time of its birth "if properly cared for herself by her man or by the Welfare State or both" (*Babies*, 6). He does not deal with the widowed, divorced, deserted, single, or lesbian mother. He once raises the possibility: "Perhaps there is no father." But he drops the subject at once: "Ordinarily, however, the mother feels supported by her husband and so is free to be a mother properly" (*Babies*, 17).

Placing such great importance on the relationship between mother and infant, Winnicott insists on the need for "protection" of that relationship (*Playing*, 109). He means emotional protection, which he refers to with terms like "facilitating environment." He also means economic protection. In his system, it is mainly the father as husband who provides both kinds of protection. When Winnicott discusses good-enough mothering, he generally assumes the conditions necessary for it. At times, he divorces his system from economics altogether. He once remarks, "There are truly the haves and have-nots, and this has nothing to do with finance; it has to do with those who were started off well enough and those who were not started off well enough" (*Babies*, 251). At one point he says that child psychiatrists now "look at slums and poverty not only with horror, but also with an eye open to the possibility that for a baby or a small child a slum family may be more secure and 'good' as a facilitating environment than a family in a lovely house where there is an absence of the common persecutions" (*Playing*, 142). He defines these "persecutions" in a footnote as "overcrowding, starvation, infestation, the constant threat from physical disease and disaster and from the laws promulgated by a benevolent society." While good-enough mothering *may* occur in such circumstances, it is hardly likely to. Winnicott acknowledges that language is imprecise and theory is crude, and he expects us to take into account their inevitable reductiveness in describing and encapsulating the complexities of life. In other words, language and theory provide only outlines of a fuller text, skeletons of the body of life.

Winnicott's case studies reveal a generous, kind, tolerant analyst. But I suspect that confronting the disparity between what he felt was required and what was possible for the general population brought him to despair or absurd defenses. Can we really imagine that a mother who lives in an over-crowded (possibly rat-infested) space, who is often hungry, and who must worry continually about illness and other disasters could be anything other than depressed and distracted? While good-enough mothering in Winnicott's sense conceivably could occur in such circumstances, it would be rare indeed.

In Winnicott's system of thought, the mother has considerable power. Yet his image of the mother is only certainly available to a woman who accommodates herself to marriage and the family within a traditional white, middle-class patriarchal structure. In leaving her responsible for her child's mental health, he makes her responsible for her child's mental unhealth. Though it is not his intention, his system leaves the mother prone to anxiety and guilt. While Winnicott says that the good-enough mother does not need to be the biological mother, he does not suggest that the father can play this role. Winnicott's insistence on the "naturalness" and "intuitiveness" of the mother and his strong preference for breastfeeding suggest that he thinks women are biologically and psychologically suited for the role of mother. While he allows for imperfections and even considers a range of emotions and behaviors desirable in a mother, he continually emphasizes her capacity for nurturing, which he implies is innate and develops further as she experiences pregnancy and birth.

Winnicott clearly listens to what mothers tell him about their children and respects their wisdom. But he is interested in them mainly as they foster mental health or the lack of it in their children. In other words, he tends to look at them from the child's point of view. Through him we cannot know the mother's dreams, how she feels about the heavy responsibility that Winnicott sees resting on her, where mothering fits into the scheme of her life, whether her experiences of childrearing conflict with his, and so on. The mother is seen mainly through the effect that Winnicott sees her as having on her child. As a pediatrician and a child psychiatrist, he is interested only in limited aspects of her subjectivity.

After the mid 1970s, several American feminists published books that focus on women in their roles as mothers and childrearers. In 1976, Adrienne Rich's *Of Woman Born: Motherhood as Experience and Institution* and Dorothy Dinnerstein's *The Mermaid and the Minotaur* appeared, followed in 1978 by Nancy Chodorow's *The Reproduction of Mothering: Psychoanalysis and the Sociology of Gender*. All of these books are informed by psychoanalytic theory and, like Winnicott and the object-relations theorists, their authors concentrate on the preoedipal period and the child's early relationship with the mother. They see woman's femininity (patriarchally defined) and her capacity for nurturance as a consequence of her experience as society's exclusive childrearer. Reproducing these traits in her daughters, she passes on her strengths as well as those capacities that determine her subordinate position in society. Because Nancy Chodorow is more fully in dialogue with psychoanalytic theorists than Dinnerstein or Rich, and because her ideas have been taken up by psychoanalysts, feminists, and literary critics in the United States, I will concentrate on her work.

Chodorow's thesis, stated succinctly in her introduction, is that "women, as mother, produce daughters with mothering capacities and the desire to mother. These capacities and needs are built into and grow out of the mother-daughter relationship itself." Woman's role in mothering is responsible for "sexual asymmetry and inequality" (7). For the psychoanalytic underpinnings of her argument, Chodorow looks beyond Freud and his followers to "cultural school" psychoanalysts (such as Erich Fromm, Karen Horney, and Clara Thompson) as well as to object-relations theorists (such as Alice and Michael Balint, John Bowlby, and W.R.B. Fairbairn). She frequently refers to Winnicott. Her arguments concerning the reproduction of mothering are based on the persuasiveness of the object-relations theorists, who assert that the child's "social relational experience from earliest infancy is determining for psychological growth and personality formation" (47).

Chodorow is different from Winnicott in several important respects. She sees mothering as both psychologically and socially structured. Unlike Winnicott, she is interested in motherhood as an institution, as part of family and social structure as it is constituted within Western patriarchal society. While Winnicott obviously takes certain gender differences for granted, gender is not a category for consideration and discussion. For him, gender differences are assumed and submerged; in Chodorow, they are brought to the surface and highlighted. Chodorow stresses the differences in the girl's and the boy's preoedipal and oedipal experiences because of their relationship to the mother, who, except in rare instances, is the primary caretaker and child-rearer. Because mother and daughter are the same sex, there are two important consequences for the girl. Her preoedipal period is longer than the boy's, and the task of separation and individuation is more difficult and less complete. When the heterosexual girl resolves her oedipal conflict by turning from her mother to her father and men, she remains in an emotional triangle. Unlike the heterosexual boy, who turns to a woman, she does not turn to a person of the same sex as the mother, with whom she was in primary relationship:

> A girl does not turn absolutely from her mother to her father, but adds her father to her world of primary objects. She defines herself, as Deutsch says, in a relational triangle; this relational triangle is imposed upon another inner triangle involving a girl's preoccupation alternately with her internal oedipal and internal preoedipal mother. Most importantly, this means

that there is greater complexity in the feminine endopsychic object-world than in the masculine. It also means that although most women emerge from their oedipus complex erotically heterosexual—that is, oriented to their father and men as primary *erotic* objects (which the psychoanalysts seem not so sure of)—heterosexual love and emotional commitment are less exclusively established. Men tend to remain *emotionally* secondary, though this varies according to the mother-daughter relationship, the quality of the father's interaction with his daughter, and the mother-father relationship. (167)

According to Chodorow: "Girls in our society have normally remained externally and internally in relationships with their preoedipal mother and have been preoccupied with issues of separation, identification without merging, mitigation of dependency, freedom from ambivalence" (140).

The idea of the mother in Chodorow is inextricably bound up with the fact that she is a daughter, whose caretaker and primary childrearer was her own mother and a woman. Both the capacity and the desire to mother grow out of the mother-daughter relationship. The girl is more open to and preoccupied with those very relational issues that go into mothering. She does not identify with her mother or want to be like her; rather "they feel alike in fundamental ways" (110).

While Winnicott was occupied with the mother as she was responsible for her child's mental health and read her through her effect on her child, Chodorow is more interested in the mother herself. She sees the mother's relationship to a man as incomplete:

Given the triangular situation and emotional asymmetry of her own parenting, a woman's relation to a man *requires* on the level of psychic structure a third person, since it was originally established in a triangle. A man's relation to women does not. His relation to his mother was originally established first as an identity, then as a dual unity, then as a two-person relationship, before his father ever entered the picture.

On the level of psychic structure, then, a child completes the relational triangle for a woman. (201)

But the mother has a new place in the triangle—"a maternal place in relation to her own child" (201). Having a child also recreates a desired, exclusive mother-child relationship for a woman, while for a man it interrupts the exclusive relationship he had with her. "Women come to want and need primary relationships to children. These wants and needs result from wanting intense primary relationships, which men tend not to provide both because of their place in women's oedipal constellation and because of their difficulties with intimacy" (203).

Both Winnicott and Chodorow write what I have come to think of as psychoanalytic prose—flat, detached, tending toward abstraction, without affect. Despite the fact that reading Winnicott cannot help but make anyone who is a mother or who wishes to be one anxious, he conveys a sense of confidence and hope about mothering. At times, he speaks in the mother's voice with wonderful energy. For example, he imagines a situation in which an authority, a doctor or nurse, says to a woman, "You *must* breast-feed your baby." Winnicott comments, "If I were a woman this would be enough to put me off. I would say: 'Very well then I won't'" (*Babies*, 26). As a therapist, he often assumes a nurturing role with his patients—both adults and children— and describes occasionally needing to act as their "mother" in the interest of healing them.

While the mother, as Chodorow describes her, both has been raised and socialized to mother and tends to want and need children, Chodorow allows her considerable ambivalence about her role. She sees psychoanalysis as requiring the mother to be able to make particularly delicate assessments of her infant's needs and to be extremely selfless (84). She believes that psychoanalytic aims for mothers reproduce infant aims. Yet it is unclear whether Chodorow sees the extent to which the mother, as she describes her, must be unhappy. If heterosexual mothers never have their emotional needs met, both because of their place in the oedipal triangle and because men are so reared that they tend to find intimacy difficult, and therefore women must look to their children to satisfy their primary needs, surely this is a miserable circumstance. While the mother in Chodorow's system has enormous power over her children, particularly her daughters, the mother could hardly help but be a depressed or dispirited figure. She also may be in danger of misusing her children in a variety of ways.

Two recent collections of essays point to further movement in psychoanalytic thinking about the mother. The first, published in 1986, is *Psychoanalysis and Women: Contemporary Reappraisals*, edited by Judith L. Alpert. All the contributors to this collection are women, and they are all involved with psychotherapy of psychoanalysis as practitioners or teachers or both. Most of them hold Ph.D.s; only one is an M.D. Many of the contributors have read feminist texts, and there are frequent references to the work of Nancy Chodorow, Dorothy Dinnerstein, Evelyn Fox Keller, and Carol Gilligan. Though neither the mother nor mothering is given special attention in this book, two essays deal with issues that relate to psychoanalytic attitudes toward the mother. Both of the writers recognize the importance of gender and understand that the patterns that they are describing pertain to women in Western culture and that in other cultures and in different periods psychic structure would vary.

In "Autonomy: A Conflict for Women," Dorothy Litwin concludes that women in Western civilization are in a classic double-bind. On the one hand, autonomy is promoted as evidence of maturity and self-actualization; on the other, it is in opposition to the cultural expectation of women as caregivers. Litwin sees psychoanalytic thinking changing, so that "affiliation and attachment are regarded as progressive rather than regressive and maternal ties are considered to be positive and supportive rather than symptomatic of dependency and separation anxiety." She sees changes in self-awareness and in possibilities, so that women have more choices in terms of motherhood or careers or both; at this point in time, however, she does not believe that women can pursue a course easily "without superego constraints or identity conflicts" (210). More implicitly than directly, she suggests that the role of psychoanalysis is to help women deal with this conflict. In other words, women have this conflict almost inevitably and not because there is anything wrong with them.

Not surprisingly, Litwin herself may suffer from some of the ambivalence she sees in psychoanalytic theory and practice. At the end of her essay, she remarks, "Psychoanalysts can help resolve some of the conflict [between autonomy and relationship, having a career and being a mother] by enabling women to accept the necessity and the rewards of relationships" (211). I do not finally know whether, by emphasizing women's capacity to nurture and form relationships, she is taking a basically conservative stance or what might be a feminist stance and valuing something in women that is positive. It is significant that she does not suggest that psychoanalysts can resolve women's conflict by enabling them to accept the necessity and the rewards of meaningful work.

In "The Gendered Self: A Lost Maternal Legacy," Susan Spieler goes beyond Litwin to critique the concepts and terms that psychoanalytic theory has constructed to define its positions. Less optimistic than Litwin, she finds that the psychoanalytic community is "divided and constrained by a general adherence to dichotomous and linear theorizing." She asserts that theorists "have generally conceived of development as a linear progress from dependence to independence and have *either* focused on how people become able to relate to and love others . . . or on narcissistic development, self regulation, and the striving for individual fulfillment of 'creative/productive potential'" (33). She stresses that, while "the importance of attachment, cooperation, and interdependence — *all qualities that are often associated with female-ness* — is widely recognized, these qualities have found little place within psychoanalytic theory" (34).

Pointing out that the tendency of psychoanalytic theory to portray "separation" rather than "attachment and interdependency" as "a normal human striving is a limitation arising from linear thinking and a fuller representation of male concerns than of female concerns," she sees that tendency as "masculine." She emphasizes that *"both the structure and the content of psycho-developmental theory reflect the influence of 'male' thinking almost to the exclusion of 'female' thinking"* [italics hers]. She argues that psychoanalytic theory is fundamentally "androcentric." "'Female' thought," she comments, "tends to allow more of a commingling of boundaries between subject and object . . . in contrast to the linearity and dichotomous reasoning commonly associated with male thought. Female content is more likely to focus on relational issues than on separateness" (34). Spieler insists that "psychoanalytic tenets whose primary emphasis is on separation/individuation as a goal . . . signify the continued influence of androcentrism," and she observes that "usually the person from whom separation is to be achieved is female" (35–36).

Presenting the "female" and silenced voice of psychoanalysis, she describes its theories as neglecting

> both the human need to soften the experience of separateness through experiences of oneness and the self's need to reconcile the pursuit of its own fulfillment with the pleasure that is derived when one fosters the fulfillment of an other who is loved as separate from the self. In so doing, psychoanalytic theory has envisioned and perpetuated an unrealistic linearity and unnatural dichotomies between separateness and connectedness and between connectedness and self-fulfillment. . . . Mothers and femaleness have too exclusively come to represent attachment, while fathers and maleness have come too exclusively to represent separateness. Moreover, femaleness has become equated with self-abnegation and maleness with self-realization. (52–53)

Theory departs too much from life and is a male construction—whether men or women are constructing it. Spieler's criticisms touch the heart of psychoanalysis.

A second collection, published in 1987, is *Lesbian Psychologies: Explorations and Challenges*, edited by the Boston Lesbian Psychologies Collective. The contributors to this book tend to be psychotherapists and social workers; they do not describe themselves as psychoanalysts and are not connected with psychoanalytic institutions. The three essays included in the section "Family" all deal with the mother in one way or another. Several things struck me about these essays. There is no Mother; there are rather mothers. The writers are alert to race and class differences and to the need to define the specific group to whom their generalizations apply. Finally, these authors are sensitive to the ways in which the cultural milieu, and especially homophobia, affects lesbian mothers and their children.

These three essays have been very helpful to me in thinking about the kinds of considerations that are relevant to our understanding of mothers: Sally Crawford's "Lesbian Families: Psychosocial Stress and the Family-Building Process," which deals with lesbians as mothers and coparents; Sherry Zitter's "Coming Out to Mom: Theoretical Aspects of the Mother-Daughter Process," which in treating its particular topic describes many of the myths, expectations, and desires of heterosexual mothers; and Marjorie Hill's "Child-Rearing Attitudes of Black Lesbian Mothers," which compares black heterosexual and black lesbian mothers. All of these essays, even "Coming Out to Mom," focus more on mothers than on their children. The psychological is always viewed within a milieu that contains family, society, and culture. The implication, of course, is that these cannot be separated and that the psychological must be seen as one strand in a large and complex web.

Setting women autobiographers beside these therapists and theorists, I think of several who deal with mothers: Maxine Hong Kingston, Maya Angelou, Audre Lorde, and Kim Chernin. Published between 1975 and 1983, *The Woman Warrior, The Heart of a Woman, Zami,* and *In My Mother's House,* like the more recent theoretical works I have been describing, show the influence of the Women's Movement in their focus on mothers or mothers and daughters, who tend be less prominent in earlier autobiographies by women. Another feature these autobiographers have in common is that their mothers — and sometimes their fathers — are immigrants. This is not true, of course, of Maya Angelou's mother; coming from a poor, southern black family, however, she, like the immigrant mothers, is outside the dominant culture.

Though mother-daughter relationships are not so central in *The Heart of a Woman* or *Zami,* all of these stories attest to the power of the mother over her children. They are also stories about growing up and leaving home. For all of these writers, leaving home is both literal and metaphorical. In its metaphorical sense, it means separating from one's family, which tends to be only or mainly the mother. To the extent that psychoanalysis highlights the separation and individuation process, it provides a perspective on these texts. Each writer reveals her efforts to establish her difference from her mother, sometimes at a moment of painful confrontation; at the same time, we see each of them consciously or unconsciously incorporating or recognizing aspects of their mothers in themselves.

In most of these works, we see the mother, as we have so often seen her in psychoanalytic theory, through the eyes of her child. though all of these writers had children when they wrote their autobiographies, only two of them — Kim Chernin and Maya Angelou — write about themselves as mothers. For Chernin, this is a secondary and often submerged theme. There are some obvious reasons for these writers to exclude this part of their lives. To the extent that they have chosen to write a "growing up" story, their reaching maturity seems not to have anything to do with having children. Growing up has more to do with their coming to terms with their families, particularly their mothers. Another apparent motive for Kingston, Chernin, and to some extent Lorde, is to give voice and meaning to their mother's stories, which none of their mothers could write. Quite wonderfully, Chernin's mother asks her daughter to write her story. Chernin's response recalls what the psychoanalysts tell us: "I am torn by contradiction. I love this woman. She was my first great aching love. All my life I have wanted to do whatever she asked of me, in spite of our quarreling." "I'm afraid. I fear, as any daughter would, losing myself back into the mother." (12) Of course, it is probably easier to write about your mother than your children in autobiography, because it is easier to assume—even if it is not true—that your mother is less vulnerable than your children to anything hurtful you might say.

But more significantly, I think, it is harder to see yourself as a parent than to see someone else as a parent, especially if she is *your* parent. Finally, literature has not provided us with enough stories written from the mother's point of view to encourage us to write from this perspective. The absence of these stories leaves us with the special burden of creating our own forms and language for telling them, as well as suggests that they are not interesting or not the proper subject of literature. Literature, psychoanalysis, and even life have conspired to keep us from knowing our own feelings as mothers, much less telling our own stories. It is perhaps here that Muriel Rukeyser's notion—that if one woman told the truth of her life, the world would split open—awakens some of our greatest fears.

All of these writers in some sense make their mothers' cases, even while coming to terms with their own ambivalences toward their mothers. They do not write in the vein of Nancy Friday's *My Mother My Self*, a mother-blaming book. While confronting their mothers and their difficulties with these mothers, they also want to put those difficulties in a context such that they are understandable, to delineate the hardships of their mothers' lives as they see them. They also want to affirm their mothers' strengths, to validate their mothers' lives in a way the world at large does not. They are often making clear why their mothers are not nurturing, even valuing the sides of them that are not nurturing, even though as children they were hurt or puzzled by their mothers' responses to them and their actions.

The most important way these stories suggest the limitations of psychoanalytic theory in their portrayal of mothers is the way they place them in a social and cultural context. I want to look at Maya Angelou's *Heart of a Woman* to illustrate my point because she is the one of these writers who has written mainly from the point of view of a mother. Her position as a daughter and her depiction of her own mother are only secondary. Having already written autobiographies about her younger life, *I Know Why the Caged Bird Sings* (1970), *Gather Together in My Name* (1974), and *Singin' and Swingin' and Gettin' Merry Like Christmas* (1976), Angelou is present in *The Heart of a Woman* when she is in her thirties and is the mother of a fourteen-year-old son, who in the course of the book turns seventeen.

To begin with, she is an unmarried mother, made pregnant by a shockingly deliberate and almost arbitrary encounter on her part, described in *I Know Why the Caged Bird Sings.** She depicts herself as having an "immaculate pregnancy" without a man around, and she is proud of her independence. There are men who are significant for Angelou in the course of *The Heart of a Woman*, particularly the charismatic African Vus Make, whom she marries without legal ceremony, follows to Egypt to foster their mutual political aims, and finally leaves. But in her family of origin and in the family she makes with her son, she does not count on fathers or men as mates in child-rearing. Her reference to her mother's husbands is casual and dismissive: "My mother had married a few times, but she loved her maiden name. Married or not, she often identified herself as Vivian Baxter" (25). Angelou merely alludes to her own first marriage (which was not to her child's father) to explain something else.

When Angelou describes her mother, she, like Chernin, attests to the strength of the bond between them: "She smiled and I saw again that she was the most beautiful woman I had ever seen" (25). In her depiction of her mother, she makes her larger than life and retains a certain romanticism and idealization, but also draws her vulnerable and with frailties. As nurturer writ large, she is admirably tough. When they meet in Fresno in 1959 to spend the night at the Desert Hotel, where desegregation is a legal requirement but only that, the drama is very powerful. As Angelou walks through the lobby to the bar to meet her mother, she describes the scene: "The crowd made an aisle and I walked through the silence, knowing that before I reached the lounge door, a knife could be slipped in my back or a rope lassoed around my neck" (24). Sensing Angelou's fear, her mother tells her:

> Animals can sense fear. They feel it. Well, you know that human beings are animals, too. Never, never let a person know you're frightened. And a group of them . . . absolutely never. Fear brings out the worst thing in everybody. Now, in that lobby you were as scared as a rabbit. I knew it and all those white folks knew it. If I hadn't been there, they might have turned into a mob. But something about me told them, if they mess with either of us, they'd better start looking for some new asses, 'cause I'd blow away what their mammas gave them. (26)

---

* Quotations from *The Heart of a Woman* by Maya Angelou. Copyright © 1981 by Maya Angelou. Reprinted by permission of Random House, Inc.

Laughing, according to Angelou, "like a young girl," the mother tells her daughter to open her purse, where half-hidden under her wallet lies a German luger.

Yet, when this gun-wielding woman bids good-bye to her daughter, she reveals her vulnerability as she says to Angelou, "I hate to see the back of someone I love" (29). Later we see Vivian Baxter struggling to shore up her own marriage to an alcoholic man and to cope with loneliness, calling upon Angelou to be "the shrewd authority, the judicious one, the mother" to her (210). Angelou's mother is always there for financial support in an emergency, someone from whom Angelou can gather strength. In a crisis, when Angelou goes to visit her mother, she tells us, "I needed to see my mother. I needed to be told just one more time that life was what you make it, and that every tub ought to sit on its own bottom. I had to hear her say, 'They spell my name W-O-M-A-N, 'cause the difference between a female and a woman is the difference between shit and shinola'" (210). At the same time, this romanticism is undercut by the stark, harsh memory that Angelou's mother deserted her when she was a child. She recounts being sent with her brother, unescorted, when he was four and she was three, with wrist tags for identification, from Long Beach, California, to Stamps, Arkansas, the home of her grandmother.

As the story surrounding Angelou and her mother suggests, a mother in the world of this book cannot simply negotiate the domestic realm. She must be of the world and in it. As the Fresno episode reveals, Angelou's mother is continually showing her how to survive in a racist society and also as a woman alone. As Angelou goes into a Brooklyn bar for the first time, she follows her mother's advice and example in ordering a large drink, offering her largest bill, and inviting the bartender to take out enough for a drink for himself. "Vivian Baxter told me when I was seventeen and on my own that a strange woman alone in a bar could always count on protection if she had treated the bartender right" (98).

When Guy, through no fault of his own, runs into difficulties with the Savages, a gang at school, Angelou follows her mother's example. Borrowing a gun from a friend, she confronts the head of the gang and his girlfriend at the home of his girlfriend: "If the Savages so much as touch my son, I will then find your house and kill everything that moves, including the rats and cockroaches." After she shows the gang leader the borrowed pistol, he recovers his voice to reply: "O.K., I understand. But for a mother, I must say you're a mean motherfucker" (83–84). Angelou suggests that she is probably up to doing what she needs to do to survive, as is her son. While one could say that this is an example of woman as mother in her caretaking and protective role, since her interests and her son's are, after all, the same, I do not think this kind of action is contemplated by psychoanalytic descriptions of mother-child relationships or the mother as nurturer.

But let me turn to Angelou's actions that are not in her son's behalf or which may be, but may not be felt by him to be. Because Angelou recognizes her and her mother's ambivalences about each other, she understands the complexities of Guy's feelings toward her as well as her own toward him. At the heart of their relationship are three significant factors: their positions as members of a black minority in a predominantly white culture; their economic status, which fluctuates but often is very low; and the fact that Angelou is a single parent. Both Guy and Angelou are sensitive about the extent to which they have had to move around. Angelou recounts: "I followed the jobs, and against the advice of a pompous school psychologist, I had taken Guy along. The psychologist had been white, obviously educated and with those assets I know he was also well to do. How could he know what a young Negro boy needed in a racist world?" (29). By the time Guy is fourteen, he has developed a cynical response to Angelou's announcements that they are going to move yet once again: "Again? Okay. I can pack in twenty minutes. I've timed myself" (29).

This moving continues throughout the autobiography and is a source of Guy's hostility and weary resignation and a cause of Angelou's considerable maternal guilt. Yet she faces their situation head on and doesn't dwell on the guilt:

> My son expected warmth, food, housing, clothes and stability. He could be certain that no matter which way my fortune turned he would receive most of the things he desired. Stability, however, was not possible in my world; consequently it couldn't be possible in Guy's. Too often I had had to decline unplayable hands dealt to me by a capricious life, and take fresh cards just to remain in the game. My son could rely on my love, but never expect our lives to be unchanging. (123)

Angelou is talking here in part about economic necessity, but she is also talking about making a life for herself rather than having merely an existence. As her life proceeds, we see her finding work that is meaningful to her and important apart from the necessary income it provides; and some of her choices and her moves have to do with taking advantage of good opportunities.

She outlines some of the particular anxieties she feels as a black and single mother:

> The black mother perceives destruction at every door, ruination at each window, and even she herself is not beyond her own suspicion. She questions whether she loves her children enough—or more terribly, does she love them too much? Do her looks cause embarrassment—or even more terrifying, is she so attractive her sons begin to desire her and her daughters begin to hate her. If she is unmarried, the challenges are increased. Her

singleness indicates she has rejected, or has been rejected by her mates. Beyond her door, all authority is in the hands of people who do not look or think or act like her and her children. Teachers, doctors, sales clerks, librarians, policemen, welfare workers are white and exert control over her family's moods, conditions and personality; yet within the home, she must display a right to rule which at any moment, by a knock at the door, or a ring of the telephone can be exposed as false. In the faces of these contradictions, she must be a blanket of stability, which warms but does not suffocate, and she must tell her children the truth about the power of white power without suggesting that it cannot be challenged. (37)

Apart from the circumstances Angelou cannot escape, she makes choices as a single woman that affect her relationship with her son. Because she chooses to fulfill her sexual desires rather than deny them, she brings men and even "fathers" into Guy's life, inevitably causing emotional tumult for both of them. When Angelou settles down with a man, partly because she imagines he will be a good father to Guy and a good role model, the experience, though interesting, is a disaster in emotional terms. An African who is involved in politics and works for black rights internationally, Vus is a caricature of a sexist male. Angelou finds herself in conflict: "I wanted to be a wife and to create a beautiful home to make my man happy, but there was more to life than being a diligent maid with a permanent pussy" (143).

Vus begins to have affairs, which he justifies as his "right," spends money he doesn't have, and brings collectors and disgrace to Angelou and her son. He exerts or tries to exert control over Angelou and prevent her from working, even when they can't pay their bills. Enraged when he learns that she has taken a job as associate editor of the *Arab Observer*, he rages at her, "You took a job without consulting me? Are you a man?" (226). For a time, Guy, coming into adulthood, turns away from Angelou and begins to follow Vus's cues; to see her, in her words, as a "kind and competent family retainer." He begins to incorporate Vus's machismo more surely than his politics. Thus the experiment of marriage and the family fails for Angelou and finally for Guy.

The last image that Angelou evokes of herself as mother may seem contradictory. After Guy is in a very serious car accident, he lies before her unconscious:

> I looked at my son, my real life. He was born to me when I was seventeen. I had taken him away from my mother's house when he was two months old, and except for a year I spent in Europe without him, and a month when he was stolen by a deranged woman, we had spent our lives together. My grown life lay stretched before me, stiff as a pine board, in a strange country, blood caked on his face and clotted on his clothes. (263)

When he recovers and leaves for college, she comments, "My reaction was in direct contrast with his excitement. I was going to be alone, also, for the first time. I was in my mother's house at his birth, and we had been together ever since. Sometimes we lived with others or they lived with us, but he had always been the powerful axle of my life" (271). Yet, when he walks out the door, she describes something different from what we have been led to expect:

> I closed the door and held my breath. Waiting for the wave of emotion to surge over me, knock me down, take my breath away. Nothing happened. I didn't feel bereft or desolate. I didn't feel lonely or abandoned.
>
> I sat down, still waiting. The first thought that came to me, perfectly formed and promising, was "At last, I'll be able to eat the whole breast of a roast chicken by myself." (272)

This move from sadness to contemplated pleasure strikes me not as contradiction or ambivalence. It rather suggests the balance and complexity of feeling that exists where love and life are full, as both are when presented in Angelou's story. Angelou clearly struggled with maternal guilt as her son was growing up.[3] This feeling at times must have masked the kind of maternal rage that Adrienne Rich describes so powerfully in *Of Woman Born*. The close of the novel suggests further the way Angelou tends to sublimate that feeling in humor.

Angelou's image of herself as daughter and mother within a kind of matriarchal structure, an image that shows her chafing when she is brought within partriarchal bounds, simply falls outside Winnicott's system. While Chodorow's analysis of the relationships of mothers and daughters may not be entirely irrelevant, it is hard to squeeze this story into psychoanalytic theories. When Angelou and her mother have needed to or wanted to, they have been able to give up their roles as nurturers without disabling and overwhelming guilt or sadness. As for Chodorow's solution to what she views as an unfortunate entanglement of mothers and children, there are no men drawn in this story who are willing and capable participants as childrearers. The conflicts between autonomy and dependence that Dorothy Litwin describes seem for the most part a luxury in terms of this story. Autonomy is survival and is not something to be chosen or rejected. Susan Spieler's analysis is more to the point, for Angelou's portrait of herself and her mother subverts the categories of masculine and feminine. Because Angelou and her mother are heterosexual, the analysis in *Lesbian Psychologies* introduces issues that do not pertain to them. Yet the attention to class, race, and difference that those essays incorporate may alert us to the perspective we must bring to reading the mother in this autobiography.

To understand the roles, feelings, conflicts, and possibilities of mothers, we must turn to the fiction and autobiography of women writers, and to women's individual essays, and to collections of their writing. Psychoanalysts must learn to listen to mothers as well as to children and recollections of childhood. They must consider the limits of psychoanalytic understanding of class and race and reach for a broader perspective. They must sharpen the analysis of gender issues that some psychoanalysts have begun to elaborate. At this time, stories of mothers may enrich psychoanalytic theories more than these theories may aid us in interpreting mother's stories.

Notes

1. See Garner, "Feminism, Psychoanalysis, and the Heterosexual Imperative," 164–85.
2. See also Winnicott, *Babies*, 18–19, 24.
3. In "Singing the Black Mother: Maya Angelou and Autobiographical Continuity," Mary Jane Lupton discusses Angelou's expression of maternal guilt in autobiographical works written before *The Heart of a Woman*.

Chapter 5

Her Mother's Language

Cecilia Konchar Farr

In women there is always more or less
of the mother who makes everything
all right, who nourishes, and who
stands up against separation;
a force that will not be cut off but
will knock the wind out of the codes.
—Hélène Cixous

Since *Her Mothers* first appeared in 1975, Esther Broner's has been a prominent voice in the discussion of mothering in fiction. The publication in 1980
of *The Lost Tradition: Mothers and Daughters in Literature*, a collection of
essays that she edited with Cathy N. Davidson, made Broner's concern with
mothering even clearer. Her second novel, *A Weave of Women*, exploring the
relationship of Jewish women to their traditions, begins with a birth and
ends with an appeal to the Biblical mother Sarah, wife of Abraham, and to
"our mothers of the desert." Much of her recent short fiction continues in
this vein; motherhood is a recurring theme. In short, it would be difficult
to discuss mothering in fiction without considering Broner's important and
thoughtful contributions to recent American literature.

Broner's wise writing is never dull. As Denise Levertov said on the jacket
of *Her Mothers*, "People will read it, love it, hate it, scream about it, and talk
about it." This is not the sort of novel one forgets. Broner's experimental
style, lively prose, self-mocking irony, bitter nostalgia, and unfailing humor
make *Her Mothers* one of the most insightful novel written about this central feminist concern—our mothers.

In an interesting twist typical of Broner, *Her Mothers* uses mothering both
as the *impetus* for Beatrix Palmer's spiritual odyssey that is the central theme
of the novel (she is searching for her runaway daughter) and also as the *object*
of the quest (she is searching for women from the past who have mothered
her). Beatrix thus, like most of us, is both mother and daughter, and the novel
is richer for balancing what Maureen T. Reddy and Brenda O. Daly call, in

the introduction to this volume, the "daughter-centricity" of most contemporary studies of motherhood. This is the story of a mother *and* a daughter, of many mothers and many daughters; it's a life story of an individual and the history of a community of women. The way Broner intertwines these lives around one woman anticipates and illuminates the discoveries of gender-based psychological theories which were first published soon after Broner's first novel. *Her Mothers* is almost a textbook study of Carol Gilligan's "web of relationships," of Hélène Cixous's woman-affirming mother who "stands up against separation," and of Julia Kristeva's "immeasurable, unconfinable maternal body."[1] Because of this, its language has many of the characteristics of "l'écriture feminine," the language some French theorists say originates in the primary psychological ties with the mother.

Broner, in *Her Mothers*, asks questions about the pervasive psychological influence of the mother—the same questions twentieth-century feminist theorists were asking—and she seems to have been privy to similar insights into female psychology. To argue, as Cixous does in "Laugh of the Medusa," that in all of women's long tradition of writing, "with a few rare exceptions, there has not yet been any writing that inscribes femininity" seems to me egocentric (248). Though Cixous's ideas about "marked writing" are erudite and perceptive, it can hardly be assumed that no woman before her had made similar discoveries, especially if she is, as she claims, describing a basic psycholinguistic reality. Indeed, modern and contemporary women's writing resonates with the ideas of mother-language, anticipating or replicating French feminisms through rhythmic cadences, nonlinear structures, affirmation of women's creative power, and debunking of binary logic. Women novelists as well as theorists are going back to their mothers, both literal and preoedipal, not in reductive or essentialist ways, but to nourish, define, and empower themselves. The form of the novel itself, as Julia Kristeva has pointed out, obeys a law of multiplicity of forms, overturning the Law of the Father, the "law of one."[2]

I would not underestimate or oversimplify the rich theories of French feminists. I would, however, in a move Toril Moi would say is typical of the empirical American-feminist approach, take what is useful from them to understand better the practices of women writers, especially those on an introspective journey in search of their mothers and themselves. Broner certainly is one of these writers.

In order to explain more fully the affinities between Broner's novel and key points of French feminisms, I first shall build a context for the explanation by looking at the development of the theories. Western tradition, as feminists have pointed out repeatedly, contains cultural myths that situate women as objects of representation. Even if we don't believe in the myths, we are affected by them and must develop ways of dealing with them, because Western culture for so long has subscribed to and retold them. Within these male-centered myths, women cannot speak or write to represent themselves as subjects without revisionary or revolutionary linguistic tactics, tactics French feminists describe but, as I noted above, insist that they have rarely seen.

According to Lacan's formulation, which, though based on a male model, claims universality, children are born into "a dyadic relation with the mother in which they find themselves whole and unitary" (Eagleton, 166). This mother-infant relationship is prelinguistic, characterized by exchanges of body language and nonrepresentational sounds. Freud called this the preoedipal stage, in which everything is one to the child; everything is part of the unified mother-self. In Lacanian theory, this stage of psycholinguistic development is called the Imaginary Order, "in which there is no difference and no absence, only identity and presence" (Moi, 99).[3]

This stage ends when the child is about eighteen months old, when "two changes occur simultaneously: the child begins to acquire language, and . . . becomes aware of sexual difference." This stage "is the mythic equivalent" of the Freudian oedipal crisis, when the father "intervenes in the potentially incestuous dyad of mother and child" and forbids the child access to the mother's body. According to Lacan, because the father is marked by possession of the phallus, "the phallus becomes the mark of sexual difference, that is difference from the mother" (Homans, *Bearing*, 6). And because this awareness of difference generally corresponds with language acquisition (when the child discovers that everything is not self, that other things must be named), Lacan connects the two as marking the entrance into the Symbolic Order, when signs gain meaning only through the *absence* of the objects they signify.

The formulation of a subject-other polarity, then, becomes the foundation of the Symbolic Order and of Western language and thought. As Simone de Beauvoir explains, "The subject can be posed only in being opposed—he sets himself up as the essential, as opposed to the other, the inessential, the object" (45). And further, "[Woman] is defined and differentiated with reference to man and not he with reference to her; she is the incidental, the inessential as opposed to the essential. He is the Subject, he is the Absolute—she is the Other." She concludes, "Otherness is a fundamental category of human thought" (44). Hélène Cixous reiterates in "Sorties":

Activity/passivity,
Sun/Moon,
Culture/Nature,
Day/Night,

Father/Mother,
Head/heart,
Intelligible/sensitive,
Logos/Pathos

Thought has always worked by opposition . . . By dual, hierarchized oppositions. (90–91)[4]

Obviously the Freudian-Lacanian myth is a masculine model, a "hierarchiza-
tion" which "subjects the entire conceptual organization to man" (Cixous, 91).
As Margaret Homans points out, it is only males who "lack" the phallus,
because only males could have it in the first place. And only "those who
might once have had it . . . are privileged to substitute for it symbolic language; daughters lack this lack" (Bearing, 9). Chodorow suggests that, because the daughter does not experience sexual difference in the same way
as the son, she does not experience as completely as the male child the separation from the mother which would place the daughter in opposition to
the mother. In other words, she doesn't enter as completely into the Symbolic Order and, thus, is not as completely initiated into the male model of
the world as a set of polarities based on the concept of male self and female
other. She remains one with the mother, even while she reaches out to the
father—not because she covets his phallus and wants one of her own, but
because she covets his connection with the mother. Chodorow concludes
with a significant revision: "A girl's libidinal turning to her father is not at
the expense of, or a substitute for, her attachment to her mother." Instead,
she explains that "a girl develops important oedipal attachments to her mother
as well as to her father" (127).

Freud held that the female child's failure to separate completely from the
mother is a sign of her weakness, inferiority, and lack of successful psychological adjustment. It is incomplete individuation. Homans, however, claims
that this continued preoedipal attachment to the mother allows the daughter
to speak two "languages" at once—both the symbolic language and "the literal or presymbolic language that the son represses at the time of his renunciation of his mother" (Bearing, 13).

This revision of psycholinguistic theory has profound implications for
women's language. If the Lacanian model is "true" (and it is, to the extent that
it has been believed, repeated, and reinforced culturally), then our language
has been hostile to a female subject. Feminist thinkers since de Beauvoir
have, of course, repeated this assertion. They have attempted to overcome the
barriers in language to write themselves out of objectification. Chodorow's
revisionary female psychology (reinforced by similar studies by Gilligan,

Dorothy Dinnerstein, and Jessica Benjamin) and Homans' fascinating interpretation of it would open space in language for women beyond that which
has belonged exclusively to us—the presymbolic "language" of the infant-
mother dyad.[5]

This *l'écriture feminine*," "semiotic," or preoedipal literal language of the
mother, however, has been the center of French feminist thought.[6] In "Laugh
of the Medusa," Cixous explains the liberating effects of recovering this mother-
language: "[The woman] must write her self, because this is the invention
of a new insurgent writing which, when the moment of her liberation has
come, will allow her to carry out the indispensable ruptures and transforma-
tions in her history" (250). Likewise, Xavière Gauthier argues that *l'écriture
feminine* is the only avenue open to women who want to write: "As long as
women remain silent [signified], they will be outside the historical process.
But, if they begin to speak and write as men do, they will enter history subdued and alienated" (162–63). They will be forever relegated to the position
of signified other. In other words, as long as women attempt to write without
significantly altering phallocentric language, they will perpetuate their oppression, an oppression that is woven into the very fiber of our language.

Most French feminists argue against the possibility of women's combining
phallocentric language with their own, as Homans advocates. In *Les Guér-
rillères*, for example, Monique Wittig's women lament:

> Unhappy one, men have expelled you from the world of symbols and yet
> they have given you names, they have called you slave, you unhappy slave.
> Masters, they have exercised their right as master. They write, of their
> authority to accord names, that it goes back so far that the origin of lan-
> guage itself may be considered an act of authority emanating from those
> who dominate. . . . the language you speak is made up of words that are
> killing you. (112)

This psycholinguistic repression of the female is, for French feminists, the
crux of any discussion of women in Western culture. Political oppression
is secondary; it cannot be overcome until its foundations in language are
destroyed.

Anglo-American feminists, however, have opted out of this seemingly bleak
linguistic determinism, asserting that women *can* successfully unite two
worlds/words, the preoedipal *l'écriture feminine* and patriarchal language. By
treating Lacanian language acquisition theory as a cultural model, we escape
the oppression of its linguistic determinism and disrupt (and eventually
destroy) its phallocentric foundation. While Cixous insists that, with very
rare exceptions, "there has not yet been any writing that inscribes femininity,"

American feminists have demonstrated empirically that women writers *have* written as women, from a subject position, despite formidable cultural, psychological, and economic opposition. These theorists, such as Homans and Rachel Blau DuPlessis, uncover the strategies with which women writers have confronted phallocentrism. Women have written "in a different voice," a voice that, ironically, is best understood through the psycholinguistic descriptions of female language elaborated by French feminisms.

Broner's novel stands as a witness to the American feminist position—that women *have* found ways of speaking in their own voices even while using the language of the Fathers; that they *have* escaped the cultural relegation of women to Object; that they *have* valued the Subject position, modifying its phallic oneness to suit their multiple needs. I can find little in Broner which suggests collusion with patriarchal institutions or ideals.[7] In finding a language to describe adequately her *female* experience and accommodate her reunion with her mothers, Broner, in a sense, discovers *l'écriture feminine* by recovering her mother-language as she recovers her mothers. She not only works against patriarchy, deconstructing hierarchies, she also reconstructs unity in diversity, connecting characters and creating in *Her Mothers* a collective—significantly *maternal*—consciousness.

Beginning *Her Mothers* by invoking Virginia Woolf's statement that "a woman writing thinks back through her mothers," Broner sets the stage for what follows. *Her Mothers* is, ostensibly, Beatrix Palmer's thinking back through her mothers. In the winding progress of the novel, Beatrix reviews her life from childhood through high school and into adulthood and motherhood. She describes her high school reunion, her marriage to Harold, her sexual encounters (heterosexual and lesbian), and the loss and recovery of her daughter, Lena, who runs away from home. Laced with accounts of Bea's "real-life" events are accounts of the lives she lives through books and through her fictional mothers.

Bea progresses in *Her Mothers*; she matures and achieves a level of self-knowledge, not through individuation, a pulling away from her mother toward the Law of the Father, but through connection with women who nurture her—her biological mother; her high school friends; Emily Dickinson, Margaret Fuller, Louisa May Alcott, and Charlotte Forten; four Biblical matriarchs and wives of Hebrew patriarchs; her own daughter Lena; and, finally, herself. Gilligan explains that "for girls and women, issues of femininity or feminine identity do not depend on the achievement of separation from the mother or on the progress of individuation" (8). She adds: "While for men, identity precedes intimacy and generativity in the optimal cycle of human separation and attachment, for women these tasks seem instead to be fused. Intimacy goes along with identity, as the female comes to know herself as she is known, through her relationships with others" (12).

When Beatrix looks at her own picture in the high-school yearbook, for example, she sees it only in relation to other pictures: "She does not dimple like Shirley Panush. Her hair is not neat as Inez Muller's. She does not have lifted eyebrows and an amused smile like Marcia S. Liebowitz. She is not blonde, blue-eyed, frilly-bloused like Razel Schiller" (5). Later Broner uses Beatrix's strong identification with Louisa May Alcott to demonstrate how this attachment helps Bea to understand her own desire for and rejection of suicide. Broner juxtaposes their suicide attempts:

> How old was Mother Louisa when she looked into the river and thought of drowning herself? She stared down at the mill dam, at the running water below. Louisa was twenty-six. Her hair was thick and brown, her breasts full. No-one loosened her hair. No-one cupped his hands over her breasts. But, for practical Louisa, death is the final unemployment.
> "There is work for me," she says and scurries away.
> What artifacts did Miss Beatrix leave, typed on an electric typewriter? What last message to parents, Lena, to faraway Harold?
> . . . After the pills, Bea's head dropped onto the keyboard. Her hands pressed the whole alphabet. The borrowed machine buzzed. The keys pressed into Bea's face. She awoke, downed coffee, tea, and stimulants all night.
> "There is work for me," said Bea. (110)

When Beatrix reunites with her daughter Lena at the resolution of the novel, Broner continues this pattern of empathic attachment that is the basis of Bea's mothering relationships. Beatrix envisions Lena as "an obstinate shadow before her that will not move." When she steps to one side, so does the shadow. Then she looks "up into the eyes of a shadowed green sun hat, a bikini, a sneering smile, a daughter" (238). When they talk, Broner doesn't separate their voices:

> The night is full of: "Which of us is the kid?"
> "Your cowardice or is it disinterest?"
> "Answer me!"
> "Are you afraid?"
> "Who's your boyfriend this time?"
> Who is talking? Beatrix cannot always tell.
> "I still love you," Beatrix Palmer says to her daughter. (239)

The narrative voice reinforces this lack of differentiation among characters. It is almost always in a traditional omniscient third person, objectively looking on and dispassionately reporting the events of the story. But at one point, early in the novel, this voice breaks just long enough to make the reader suspect that this is Beatrix only *pretending* to speak in a third-person narrative voice. "My Spanish teacher joined the Navy and was torpedoed and killed," she reveals, picking up, in progress, the storyline of Beatrix Palmer's high-school reunion. She describes an early lesbian relationship with a high-school friend and reminisces rhythmically, "Janice and I talk and glide and slide from side to side." She recalls getting caught in bed with Janice by Janice's mother and concludes, "I was Dirty Bea, not allowed back in the house again. . . . It was more humiliating than when I was caught stealing *Peggy Goes to London* from S.S. Kresge's" (39). The confessional first-person ends after this single passage. It is absorbed into the third-person voice which dominates the novel, only now and again returning briefly to claim "my mothers."

The third-person voice, however, allows the narrator to enter as freely into the minds of Bea's mothers as into Bea's own consciousness. It details Janice's pain at being the dark stranger, "the daughter of a dainty mother but built like her muscular father" (40). It cites and quotes Margaret Fuller's letters, examining her similar pain at her unacceptably unfeminine appearance: "But, says Mother Margaret, 'When all things are blossoming, it seems so strange not to blossom too. I hate not to be beautiful, when all around is so.' (Mason Wade, *Margaret Fuller, Whetstone of Genius*, Viking Press, 1940, p. 80.)" (83). From an unfamiliar perspective, focused on the woman's emotions, this voice retells the familiar Biblical story of Sarah, who was barren and, in fear, "gave unto Avram her she-servant, an Egyptress." Then, "Sarai could not look upon Hagar . . . when Hagar's belly stretched and smoothed over" (151). In anger, she sends the pregnant handmaid from her tent.

Broner switches to a dialogue between the narrator and Beatrix to detail Beatrix's disgust with her appearance:

> Beatrix, undress. Look into the mirror. It is not obscene to be privately seen.
> What do you like? Can't you say even to yourself? Then, what do you hate about your appearance?
> Hair. All that hair, I hate. . . . My accordion-pleated navel I hate . . . My breasts I hate . . . Thighs, hate thighs. . . .
> Legs too full, shoulders too wide, neck too long. Eyes are becoming smaller, elbows wrinkled (81).

This narrative reveals, observes, accuses, and questions. The voice is sympathetic, demanding, and angry by turns. It is Janice and it is Bea. It is Margaret Fuller and Sarah. This is a narrative voice to accommodate the multiplicity of female psychology, a multiplicity Cixous connects with the female body:

"A woman's body, with its thousand and one thresholds of ardor . . . will make the old single-grooved mother-tongue reverberate with more than one language" (256).

Female multiplicity also reveals itself in a diversity of forms. Just when the narrative seems on the verge of becoming a traditional chronological storyline, Broner shifts from storyteller to poet, filmmaker, diarist, singer, comedian, or Talmudic scholar. At one point she even gives the *TV Guide* listings for a day of television viewing. Her most frequent device, however, is a series of call-and-response interjections throughout the novel. These ask an all-knowing mother for common-sense answers — and sometimes a bit of humor. Almost always the daughter is pregnant with a baby girl (abbreviated sometimes to "p. with a b.g."), and the baby girl has the same problems as the characters whom Beatrix is seeking as mothers. For example, Broner writes:

> "Mother, I'm pregnant with a baby girl and she's dreaming."
> "Don't let her tell anyone."
> "Her dreams are betrayed!"
> "She told someone." (33)

Broner then picks up her story of the high-school friends with Shirley Panush, who trusted her lover but was abandoned by him. When she writes of Janice's failed marriage, she inserts:

> "Mama, I'm pregnant with a baby girl."
> "What does she want to know?"
> "Will she be happy in marriage?"
> "Let her stay in the womb, for once she is out of it, she could marry a baby boy who would crouch in *her* womb and refuse ever to leave." (49)

At one point, while Beatrix is examing the lives of her literary foremothers, the daughter voice announces, "Mother, I'm pregnant with a book." The mother replies, "Hard or soft cover?" (73). One of the best examples of this oracular, lyrical intrusion combines humor with a conscious (pre–*Madwoman in the Attic*) revision of Freudian psychology:

> "M., I'm p. with a b.g. and she wants to be a writer."
> "That's penis envy."
> "But she wants to write cookbooks."
> "Then that's an acceptable degree of penis envy."
> "But her doctor wants to write cookbooks with her."
> "That's womb envy." (60–61)

The mother also tells the daughter that an abortionist and a psychiatrist are the same thing. "They both look into your womb. The abortionist sees the fetus there, the psychiatrist your mind" (12).

This constant reference to childbirth is also significant, especially as it relates to Cixous's theory of marked writing. "By writing her self," Cixous theorizes, "woman will return to the body which has been more than confiscated from her, which has been turned into the uncanny stranger on display . . . Write your self. Your body must be heard. Only then will the immense resources of the unconscious spring forth" ("Laugh," 250). In *Her Mothers*, Broner acknowledges "the body which has been more than confiscated," as well as the connection between the body and the unconscious. The passage above, for example, in which Beatrix enumerates the things she hates about her body, is subtitled "CARTOGRAPHY OF BEA," as if she is exploring territory heretofore unknown. The final thing she names is her womb. "My womb, my womb. I hate my womb," she says (82). Clearly this is not a physical characteristic, nor something as apparent as hair, thighs, or navel. It *is* apparent, however, in that it makes her female. And, Broner notes, our culture teaches us to loathe the female body:

> Beatrix has her monthly, her cycle, her bad time, her period, her exclamation and question marks, her curse, her ovulation, her menstruation.
> Professor Stone is horrified. He releases her arm.
> "There are certain taboos that are signposts to mankind," he says. "Incest is one. Menstruation is the other."
> He gags. His lips become white and his firm hands shaky. His blue eyes milk over.
> "Blood," he says bloodlessly.
> She is at the back of the cave. She is Rahel sitting on the totem of her father Lavan, and he will not enter his daughter's tent because of her filth. She is every chicken cut open, every entrail, liver and heart lifted, leaving dark blood spots. She is the Blood Woman, Blood Worm, Blood Blister, Vampire. (199)

But Beatrix, in reclaiming her mothers, reclaims their female bodies. Biological birth, in fact, serves as a metaphor for the spiritual rebirth of women through other women. It is this insight, I believe, that leads Broner back to what Lacan called the Imaginary Order, that mother-centered realm the echoes of which are found in marked writing. As Broner pulls together biological and psychological mothering, as she has Beatrix return to her mothers to understand herself, she takes her writing beyond (or behind) the experimental linguistic games of other postmodernists. She catches the cadences and echoes the themes of *l'écriture féminine*.

Woman images abound in *Her Mothers*—the "concave," the "receptacle," which Cixous elucidates in "Sorties" (90). Women are gourds, shells, wells, containers, caves, and cavities. In a passage very suggestive of Cixous's dictum to "write the body," Broner writes: "With fortune, Bea's heart, hand, ENT, vagina walls opened. She bestowed love, generosity, attention, and the clasp of her womb on those who needed one or all from her. It is the final generosity to embrace one's mother" (116).

The orality and the mirroring which characterize the prelinguistic oneness with the mother that is part of the Imaginary Order also appear in Broner's story. The touching moment of Beatrix's reunion with her biological mother, when Bea tells her she loves her, is characterized by an orality the father can't understand:

> he left, looking amazed at the cannibalistic scene behind him: the mother chewing Bea's hair, her ears (without their wax), nibbling her nose (no more sinus trouble), kissing the lips with Hungarian Mira's nonallergenic lipstick, her neck, with anti-crepey neck on it, her shoulders. Bea's mother did *"Miesele, Meisele,"* little mouse, little mice, to each finger, tickling up Bea's inner arm.
>
> Bea was in her mother's oven—baked, basted, fluffed, stuffed. (116)

After Bea feels a mystical connection with the ghosts of her mothers, she sees "two monarch butterflies" mirroring each other. "They couple with double sets of wings, on the patio stones. They hold tight, leaping together onto the glass top of the wrought-iron table" (140). Bea often sees herself in mirrors, mirrored in the faces of others or, once, "in [a] horizontal row of tiny mirrors, a bit of an eye, an arch of brow; next row, the nose; two rows down, the mouth. . . . She is faceted like *The Fly"* (178).

Also characteristic of the presence, the lack of differentiation, of the Imaginary Order is the absence of a hierarchical sense of time. The novel, replicating this, moves effortlessly through past and present, mingling them and never valuing one over the other. When Janice runs away from home, for example, the all-knowing mother-voice advises, "Hire a detective or don't hire a detective." Broner/Beatrix adds, "Which Janice's family did, and which I did not do years later" (45). And then it's back to Janice's story again. While Broner describes Charlotte Forten's response to the Fugitive Slave Law, she observes, "Mother Louisa is watching the scene. Mother Louisa is Sweet Twenty-Three. Mother Margaret is not watching. . . . She set sail to America, suffered shipwreck and death on July 19, 1850. Mother Margaret has not been watching for four years. Mother Emily is Sweet Twenty-Four. She is afraid to watch" (128).

Central to the task of *l'éctriture feminine* is overthrowing the Law of the Father, which demands the female's complete initiation into the Symbolic

Order and the consequent rejection of the mother. Cixous writes that she will "blow up the Law" ("Laugh," 257). Broner undertakes a similar destruction. She begins by blasting Beatrix's academic, intellectual assistant editor, who studies the porno film as "an historical reality," from "Brigitte Bardot and her towel, through *I am Curious (Yellow)*, Warhol's *The Couch*, quickie nudies, the transvestite Cockettes." (His book, we learn, "will be academic—all but the book jacket" (18).) She then blows up Shirley Panush's rabbi father, who would practice the law of ritual slaughter on Shirley. She then takes aim at Beatrix's sexually manipulative husband, Harold. She completely undermines Bronson Alcott for his self-centered monopolization of Louisa, responding with vehemence to a critic, Earl Schenck Miers, who wrote, "To know Louisa May Alcott . . . one must also know the father whose compassionate, indestructible nature was the warm kiss shining in her eyes." Wrong. "Men become characters because women have built their characters," Broner (Beatrix?) writes. "Who made Bronson Alcott? Who were his mothers?" (107). Through Louisa May Alcott, Broner reaffirms Virginia Woolf's contention that the father's life would end the daughter's:

> "Mother, I'm pregnant with a baby girl."
> "What is she doing?"
> "She is praising her father."
> "How is she praising him?"
> "She is longing to see him first among lecturers, kindly spoken of and inquired about."
> "She is not praising him. She is writing his obituary."
> "Why?"
> "So she can live." (133)

Perhaps Broner's most devastating strike at the Law, however, is her attack on the traditional novel via metafiction. She clarifies the lack of linear plot development, the absence of a singular individuated heroic figure, and the loss of a disinterested narrative voice, by setting *Her Mothers* off in relief against Beatrix's work-in-progress, *Unafraid Women*—which is, debatably, *Her Mothers*. Broner casts off her authorial authority, granted in literary collusion with the Law of the Fathers, by calling attention to the act of writing. Beatrix brainstorms over her novel: "Perhaps her heroic women, her unafraid females will sing instead of talk. . . . She has an inspiration for the book: *Singing Mothers*. Beatrix stops. She turns off the tape. She puts down her pen" (113). Broner casts off her authority and, in doing so, breaks its spell. She breaks the Law.

She also makes it clear that those who don't break the Law aren't doing themselves any favors. It is impossible for a woman to live under the Law of her Father. The daughters who "bear their father's dreams," who fulfill what the fathers want for them, are disinherited because they are not at home reflecting the father's glory. Fathers need objects against which to define their subjectivity, their centrality. "Fathers are always disappointed in us," one daughter says (171).[8]

And for all the celebration of motherhood that is the psychological reality of the novel, actual mothering in *Her Mothers* is also extremely problematic. The mothers are, often, as disappointed and disappointing as the fathers. They collude with and often outdo the fathers in their betrayal of their daughters. Romanian Lois's mother, for example, fawns on her son. "His mother smooths his hair, touches his collar, kisses him. He tweaks her. The father nods proudly from his armchair in the living room" (24). But when Lois asks her pharmicist father for help in getting into the high-school Chemistry Club (for which she is eminently qualified except by gender), she gets no sympathy, no help, only a dance. The mother undermines even this meager attempt at fatherly aid by belittling Lois's pain and by being jealous of the father's show of affection: "'Sarah Heartburn,' says the mother." And "'I rather thought I was your partner,' says the mother" (24–25).

Broner avoids simple-minded valorization of the mother, reflecting honestly some of the anger feminists feel toward our mothers. Beatrix storms:

> Mothers, what have you taught me? . . . Mothers, you have taught me that a woman is as good as her womb. If she bears, her sons will place a standing marker where she has died. And if she is barren, she is not part of the Old Testicle.
> Mothers! Sarai! Rivka! Lea! Rahel! You have taught your daughters that women fight for the penis of a man. . . .
> Who named *you* my mothers? Who names *this* a matriarchy? (168)

The practical mother-narrator warns: "Beatrix, choose carefully, for we can pick and choose not only our mothers but among their qualities!" (79).

So Bea chooses women who can mother her, women who can mother the qualities she wants to develop. She replaces the pictures of men on her walls — Gene Kelly, Gregory Peck, Eugene V. Debs — with pictures of her mothers — Margaret and Emily, Doris Lessing, Mary Ann Evans, Anaïs Nin. "Why does Bea frame these photographs, these engravings, copies from paintings? Because the women are not looking at or thinking about men" (91). Clearly, Broner is replacing the old order. She is taking Beatrix back to the Imaginary Order, to the realm of the mother, to reclaim her self. She reaches back to the preoedipal mother to nourish Beatrix, "to make everything right" again. It is this reaching back that enables Bea to "stand up against separation," to be reunited with the part of herself that never abandoned the Imaginary Order, the part that maintained significant ties with the mother. The rediscovered mother also empowers Beatrix to "knock the wind out of the codes," to confront phallocentrism without fear. While, at the beginning of the novel, "Beatrix is taking years with *Unafraid Women*" because "she is afraid of them," at the conclusion of the novel, one woman, ostensibly Beatrix Palmer, steps forward from among a group of women, ascends a podium, and celebrates birth and womanhood (63). "Birth me, Mothers," Broner writes. "Carry me in the brine of your belly and your tears. Let us sit on each others' laps, daughters and mothers." The narrative voice returns to Bea: "We have hired our own hall. We hold hands. Our engagement rings do not scratch. Our wedding bands do not disband us." She repeats the call-and-response refrain:

"Mother, I'm pregnant with a baby girl."
"What is she doing?"
"She is singing."
"Why is she singing?"
"Because she's unafraid." (241)

The power of *Her Mothers* is this power to overcome fear of our phallocentric culture, to free ourselves from enthrallment to the Law; it is the power to value and celebrate our selves by reclaiming mother-centrism and our mothers themselves, in all their/our diversity and flaws, in all our femaleness, in all our strength.

Notes

1. I don't mean to imply that these three theorists are in any way interchangeable. Gilligan's psychological theoretical work is empirical, sociological, and very much in the American feminist tradition. Cixous's linguistic work, Derridean in origin, is often denigrated on this side of the Atlantic for being "essentialist," because, like the theories of other French feminists quoted in this paper, it calls on biological difference to liberate women from linguistic repression. Kristeva's comments on the mother, taken from "Stabat Mater," are one small aspect of a comprehensive linguistic and psychological theory which rejects characterization of "male" and "female" except in speaking of motherhood (and even then Kristeva makes distinctions only with great caution): "If it is not possible to say of a *woman* what she is (without running the risk of abolishing her difference), would it perhaps be different concerning the *mother*, since that is the only function of the 'other sex' to which we can definitely attribute existence?" (161). All three theorists address aspects of motherhood and mother-language in ways I find useful for this study; however, it is impossible to hold that all three are "true" without running into numerous contradictions—contradictions, I might add, which have kept the dialogue among feminists (French, American, and others) lively and

exciting. How I resolve or revel in these contradictions will, I hope, become evident as my analysis of *Her Mothers* progresses.

2. In this citation from "Word, Dialogue and Novel," Kristeva is elaborating on the theories of Mikhail Bakhtin. She is not speaking of a specifically female novelistic tradition.

3. For clarity, these citations and the ones which follow call on Margaret Homans, Toril Moi, and Terry Eagleton and their concise, abbreviated versions of obscure primary material.

4. This binary opposition is also the basis of Susan Griffin's fascinating study of pornography in her *Pornography and Silence: Culture's Revenge Against Nature*.

5. It is not entirely accurate to call the infant-mother exchanges of the Imaginary Order a language *per se*, since they are, again, presymbolic. For lack of a substitute for the word *language*, I call attention to the special use of it with quotation marks.

6. The term *semiotic* belongs, of course, to Julia Kristeva's linguistic theories, which, though tied to the Imaginary Order and the mother's body, are not defined as gender-distinct. *L'écriture féminine*, however, as Cixous explains, is biologically female: "I maintain unequivocally that there is such a thing as marked writing" ("Laugh," 249). I address the two together because of their similar origins in the presymbolic stage of development, though, clearly, the theories of Kristeva and Cixous should not be conflated under a single label of "French feminism."

7. Except, of course, in her use of phallocentric language itself.

8. These references to fathering address fatherhood symbolically, as representative of the patriarchal Law of the Fathers. I don't mean to imply that *all* fathering is necessarily unsuccessful.

Part II

Mothers
Mapping Boundaries

Chapter 6

Facing the Gorgon:
Good and Bad Mothers in the Late Novels
of Margaret Drabble

Mary Jane Elkins

Margaret Drabble's eleven novels, read in sequence, constitute a fictional history of the lives of women, specifically mothers, in late twentieth-century England. These works focus on various types of women, in a chronological sequence that moves from young mothers in their early twenties through mature, successful, and worldly women (who also happen to be mothers) in their fifties. Motherhood—as it defines, restricts, and also enables and empowers women—is a consistently central theme throughout Drabble's work. Her late novels (*The Realms of Gold, The Ice Age, The Middle Ground, The Radiant Way,* and *A Natural Curiosity*) differ from their predecessors in apparently shifting attention away from the immediate domestic problems of motherhood and family to the larger concerns of society and the problems (and joys) of women who have reached middle age and are finding greater opportunities for creative lives outside the home. On the surface, these women seem to be refuting the claims of some feminists concerning the crippling effects of the institution of motherhood. They have it all: good, emotionally healthy children, warm friends and lovers, and interesting and socially valuable careers. Patriarchal society and its demands on mothers seem to have left them largely unscathed.

In these later novels, social criticism is increasingly foregrounded, as children and husbands slip into the background. Drabble seems to be implying that, for some women at least, the problems entailed in mothering are less pressing than in the past, and that women have taken their rightful places in the world and now can turn their attention to other issues. A closer reading, however, reveals that society's expectations remain—these women are the nurturers, the caretakers of personal relationships, the self-sacrificers. And however glamorous their work, they remain on the periphery of the larger power structure.

Kate Armstrong, Frances Wingate, Liz Headleand, and Alix Bowen, the central female characters of these novels, have much in common. They enjoy successful and prestigious careers, a goodly amount of luck, and an enviable degree of self-confidence. In this sense, they bear little resemblance to their Drabble predecessors or to many of the other women who people these novels.

Frances is an archaeologist, Kate a successful writer, Liz a psychiatrist, Alix a social worker, and Esther an art historian. They are all liked and respected by men, and they are all women who are "greedy"—voracious eaters, drinkers, lovers, choosers of life.

The women in these novels who are managing less successfully tend to be overthin, perfectionist, tightly drawn. They expect too much and insist on a recognizable order to life; they are the ones without the capacity to accept the accidental. The central character in *The Ice Age* is a man, Anthony Keating. But the most prominent woman in the novel, Alison, fits neatly into this category and suffers accordingly.

In other words, these novels (with the important exception of *The Ice Age*) offer us a picture of women who can turn their creative energies in useful directions and live happy, productive lives, despite the possibilities for misery that exist around them. Each of these novels ends in a moment of serene acceptance, even joy. What could be wrong with this picture?

For one thing, these women are clearly the exceptions rather than the rule in the novels they inhabit. Moreover, there seems to be very little "middle ground"; there are these few survivors, and then there are the ghastly failures, the wretched mothers. There is an extraordinary number of "bad" mothers in these late novels. In *The Middle Ground*, we hear of Kate Armstrong's mother, an overweight agoraphobic who embarrassed her children. *The Realms of Gold* presents Beata, whose *anorexia nervosa* prevents her from mothering her baby, and Frances' own mother, a gynecologist and outspoken proponent of abortion, whose cold charm provokes Frances into comparisons with a snake. In *The Radiant Way*, we find casual mention of Hilda Stark, actress and would-be infanticide, and, featured more centrally, Rita Ablewhite, mother of Liz and Shirley, who is mad, isolated, unaffectionate, and unloved by her daughters to the point that they wish for her death. Finally, in *A Natural Curiosity*, there is Angela, the ironically-named monster-mother of a mass murderer, the Horror of Harrow.

These mothers catch and hold our attention, partly by their sheer numbers, partly by the outrageousness of their behavior, and partly because they are the mothers in these novels who have a relationship, however terrible, with their children. By contrast, the central women of these novels have perfect children who cause them little or no anxiety and who, interestingly, seem to have become healthy and happy largely on their own. To their credit, these mothers usually do not take too much credit for this success, and occasionally they congratulate themselves on not having done anything to ruin their children's lives (a possibility they recognize). They, their fellow characters, and the narrator generally credit these maternal successes to their usual good fortune. But good fortune does not begin to describe it. How is

it possible in a fictional world that posits, as Drabble's does, inescapable genetic destiny, that Liz, Kate, and Frances—all of whom had dreadful unloving
and unloved mothers—should be such remarkably successful mothers themselves? How did they learn their roles as mothers if not from their own
mothers? For the most part, Drabble presents the good mothering of these
women as a given and proceeds from there. This has a fairy-tale quality,
however, and we tend to find more credibility in the bad mothers or in the
struggling mothers, such as Janet in *The Realms of Gold*, whose low self-
esteem and whose own ineffectual mother keep her from completely trusting her own nurturing instincts, or Alison in *The Ice Age*, whose two daughters
present her with overwhelming problems. Occasionally Drabble suggests
that neglect, at least in the form of physical and psychic space, is what has
produced such healthy children; their mothers were so vitally involved in life
that they did not have time to be overprotective, hovering, oppressive mothers.
The successful mothers travel and are away from home a great deal; this too
seems to account for much of their success with children. Frances is the
prime example of this. As an archaeologist, she often is away from home for
long periods of time.

The opposite of travel is enclosure, even imprisonment. The unhappy
mothers usually are surrounded by images of entrapment. Alison Murray consciously wishes for such enclosure, away from the harsh and hostile world.
And Liz Headleand thinks of her mother—initially confined within her own
home, apparently by choice—as now terminally imprisoned: "A pupa, a chrys-
alis, it had been to her and to Shirley, but to her mother a tomb. Her mother
would never emerge again" (*The Radiant Way*, 121). Images of agoraphobia
abound in these novels.

But, successful or unsuccessful, mothering is the primary business of women
in these novels. Further, the late novels take up in earnest the questions (and
the implications of these questions) that boundaries pose for mothers. These
works deal with self-created and self-imposed boundaries, societally imposed
ones, and, most important, the relations between the two. The earlier novels
deal with these things, too, of course, but the later works suggest as well
some possible strategies, however formidable, by which mothers can leap
over or break down some of these boundaries.

In the novels of early and late middle age, Drabble's heroines are in the process of finding other outlets for their mothering impulses and having some
trouble doing so. Frances Wingate wonders if her bouts of depression have
any relationship to the octopus' refusal to take nourishment and subsequent
death, once it has finished reproducing. This is, of course, not a serious question for Frances, who is as vital a character as any in fiction; even her depres-
sions are on an heroic scale. However, she does not question the ideas that

motherhood is nature's intention for women and that creative activity in other spheres is a substitution or, more accurately, a redirection of the energies nature intended for childbearing and nurturing. The narrator tells us that Frances gave birth to four children, for a variety of reasons. One reason was defiance of her mother, a fierce advocate of birth control and abortion. (Drabble, interestingly, connects these positions with Lady Ollerenshaw's snakelike coldness and her presumed sexual frigidity. Frances has a "deep dislike" of birth control; no Drabble heroine takes conventionally feminist positions on this issue.) Frances also took pleasure in the physical condition of pregnancy; she had children "partly (no not partly, all, of course all) because she loved children, and would have wanted more and more, loving each one as it arrived" (82). Frances, noting the signs of aging, thinks that she and Karel should have had a child together.

In total agreement with Frances is Kate Armstrong, about whom the narrator says, "Maternity had been her passion, her primary passion in life" (230). Kate, finding herself at age forty unexpectedly pregnant by the husband of a good friend, had decided, after agonized consideration, not to have a abortion but to have the child and raise it alone as a single mother. Then she learns that the baby will be born with *spina bifida*, and she decides that she must have the abortion. But it is not a decision she is comfortable with. In fact, it takes the course of the novel for Kate to come to terms with what she has done and to forgive herself. She believes that she has gone against her nature and therefore deserves her emotional suffering.

Drabble does not, of course, leave Kate in the state described above. Her novel ends with acceptance and affirmation, gained, as usual, through a journey in time and space, a clearer understanding of one's relation to one's own childhood, and a willingness to accept the accidental. But there is no suggestion that Kate might be overreacting here; Drabble accepts the idea of the mothering role as "natural" for women, and her characters are restless and miserable when they find no outlet for this impulse or when, like Kate, they are forced to work against "nature." The men in her novels never are as spiritually whole, never as in tune with the universe, the natural life forces, as the women are. And her women characters achieve a kind of peace by supplementing rather than by replacing their roles as mothers.[1]

This is not to say that Drabble is complacent about mothers and their roles in society. She has harsh words for society and its definitions of mothering, its contempt for what it should value and assist. In *The Realms of Gold*, Frances' cousin Janet, a sympathetic character and a loving mother, is almost defeated in her attempts to be a good mother by her bullying husband and the unsolicited, arrogant advice of others concerning childrearing.

There is no support for Janet until she meets Frances. Prior to that, everyone patronizes her and adds to her feelings of inadequacy. She thinks, "Vicars and doctors were all the same, they told one it was *natural* to suffer from headaches and misery at puberty, to dread marriage, to feel ill and get cystitis when newly married, to dread pregnancy and feel ill and cry a lot when pregnant, to cry a lot with post-natal depression. It was *all so natural*" (126; italics mine). Janet understands, as does Drabble, how society's authorities use the concept of the natural to oppress and confine women. The true "natural" manifests itself in Janet's deep abiding care for her son. This would seem to be what Drabble consistently calls a "passion for maternity." It manifests itself instinctively in doing the right thing, despite criticism and advice, well-meaning or otherwise, and apparently, and paradoxically, it results in the benign neglect that otherwise would seem the opposite of "passion."

However, in these late novels, there is one stunning example of a good and "natural" mother whose embracing of maternity dooms her. Alison Murray is not the central character of *The Ice Age*; Anthony Keating is, but she is a very important one, and she is the one whose situation provides the last and the bleakest words in this bleakest of Drabble novels. Alison, divorced from her husband, is the mother of two daughters with very real problems. These are not the healthy, happy children of Kate, Frances, and the others. One of her children—the younger, Molly—suffers from cerebral palsy, and, at her birth, we are told, Alison "had retired from her profession, she had ceased forever to compete, had ceased to contend, had withdrawn herself and put herself away" (80). The wording here suggests that, like Kate, she somehow feels that she deserves this suffering, that she has penance to do. She devoted all her energies to caring for Molly, keeping her out of institutions, taking full responsibility for her life. She is, of course, widely admired by her acquaintances, who see her as the "perfect" mother. Only Anthony can see the folly in aspiring to perfection and the price it exacts. Alison's older daughter, perhaps neglected (neglect is not benign and beneficial if it is the result of obsessive attention to another child), perhaps only feeling herself so, turned in defiance from her mother and, as the novel begins, has fallen into serious trouble. She has been involved in a car accident in a fictional East European country and is imprisoned there.

Alison's capacity for guilt is enormous. Not only does she feel guilty about the unhappiness of her older child, but she feels guilty about herself as well; with no work of value—that is, work that comes to something, that feels like an accomplishment—she sees herself as little more than a "clotheshorse" (161). And, at times, she even suspects her own motives in her sacrifice; resenting Anthony's returning health and independence, wishing a bit for a return to the days when he needed her help.

It is Alison's sufferings that are at the center of this novel. Whatever might have been the crucial points in her history, the moments when she could have taken a different turn, Alison now is imprisoned in her cell of mothering, laboring at her impossible task, finally alone without even Anthony. Alison stands at the end of this novel and throughout the subsequent novels as a gloss on her more fortunate successors. She is an attractive, intelligent, nurturing woman who has had been dealt a very bad hand. Although she is a perfectionist of sorts, circumstances rather than character seem to account for the difference. She is, as Anthony says, "unhappy, *unlucky* lovely Alison" (63; italics mine).

Drabble often uses the word "mad" to describe many of her "bad" mothers, and, as we come to the later novels, instances of true madness become more prevalent. So many characters exhibit madness, in fact, that we and the main characters begin to take mental illness as an inescapable fact, an occupational hazard of life in the late twentieth century. Madness is far and away a property of women more than of men, the same overly-thin perfectionist women mentioned earlier (this thinness finds its logical conclusion in Beata in *The Realms of Gold,* who suffers from anorexia and who must be coaxed by her husband to eat anything at all during her pregnancy).

Mrs. Sondersheim in *The Middle Ground* is typical of these thin, mad women. Kate meets her at a dinner party at which Mrs. Sondersheim, unlike Kate, barely touches her food. Eventually she launches into a hysterical recounting of a dreadful incident from her past and finally leaves the table and locks herself in the bathroom, refusing to be coaxed out. She is not an important character and plays no further role in the novel. She is a counterpoint, a *memento mori.* Once she is gone, the narrator tells us, "They ate and drank, the survivors, excited, exhilarated, their lease on life renewed by the precarious tenure of others" (50). In the two most recent novels, madness moves from parenthetical incident to center stage. Liz Headleand is a psychiatrist and Alix Bowen a social worker; between them, they come in contact with large numbers of people, again mostly women, who are at some stage of serious deterioration.

The most profoundly mad of any character in these novels is Paul Whitmore, the Horror of Harrow, who has murdered an indeterminate number of women by severing their heads. The central action of *A Natural Curiosity* is Alix's "adoption" of Paul. She visits him in prison, talks with him, brings him gifts, tries to intercede on his behalf with his estranged biological parents. Alix's family and friends all see her current behavior as unprofessional at best, obsessive and dangerous at worst, increasingly crazy in its single-mindedness.

Alix's madness is temporary, though real enough, and, by implication, necessary for her human survival. There is an interesting parallel in this same novel with Shirley Harper, Liz's sister, who runs away from home following her discovery of her husband's suicide and behaves in a way that she, as well as others, see as a temporary insanity. No longer is it possible in this latest novel for a central character to survive by witnessing another's madness, as it was for Kate in *The Middle Ground*. More and more, an immersion in the darkness is something not to be avoided, but something to be embraced as healing. Consequently, the descriptions of crucial moments of madness and healing in these late novels come cloaked in the language of myth and ritual.

Most of Drabble's novels, and in particular the latest ones, emphasize a circularity in human life. Her central characters go back into their childhoods to find themselves as adults. Each of these characters—Kate, Frances, Liz—takes a journey, literal as well as figurative, to her old childhood home and relives, this time with new insight, central defining moments on the way to accepting who she is now and how she fits into the world.

However, *A Natural Curiosity* goes a step further. It does what no previous novel has done. It forgives bad mothers, specifically Liz and Shirley's mother, Rita Ablewhite, and Paul's mother, Angela. At the end of this novel, we learn that Rita had a richer life than her daughters knew, a sadder life, a reason for her crabbed and unhappy behavior. She is offered up to the reader for sympathy. We learn too that Paul's mother, whom Alix chooses to believe (the skepticism of the other characters and the narrator notwithstanding) is the prime mover behind Paul's homicidal insanity, had her own tragedies, her own unbearable burdens. And so, as the novel ends and the three central characters rehash events, they redefine Angela as suffering woman rather than monster. Interestingly, the women in these novels free themselves by recognizing that these women had individual lives, apart from their being mothers (most feminist theorists see the lack of such recognition as central to the oppression of women). Drabble seems to be implying that the madnesses result from the suppression of the mother's self and her own life, and that this "mad" condition, however overdrawn here, is more common than not among mothers and that her successful characters are the exceptions. By having lives of their own, by working and traveling and living in the world, they have kept madness and unsuccessful mothering at bay.

A Natural Curiosity, like its predecessors, ends on an upbeat note. However, images remain which undercut the optimism and render the ending a bit problematical. Drabble's narrative strategies encourage us in another direction. As illustration, I would like to look at several crucial scenes from two of these novels, *The Realms of Gold* and *A Natural Curiosity*. Each of these novels ends in true Drabble fashion, with an idyllic, peaceful closure. But before they do, Drabble gives us traumatic scenes of conflict and climax whose dramatic and emotional impact is far greater than the scenes which follow them.

In *The Realms of Gold,* Frances learns that a great-aunt, Constance Olleren-shaw, whom she scarcely knew, has died of starvation alone in her remote cottage. This event brings Frances home and creates the opportunity for a meeting between Frances and her cousin Janet. Janet, as it happens, is the last person to have seen Constance alive and the only member of the family who attempted any communication with her. Janet recalls having taken the baby and a box of candy as a gift for Con on her one visit. As she approaches Constances's cottage, the journey takes on a mythic and somewhat frighten-ing quality. The pathway is overgrown, rendering the cottage almost inacces-sible, and indicating how long it has been since anyone made this journey.

Intimidated, Janet almost turns back, but, like any hero on a quest, she steels herself and goes on. Eventually she is "rewarded" by suddenly coming upon the fortress-cottage and by seeing the face of Aunt Con at her window. Con is described as looking like a witch, with her white hair, hooked nose, and threatening demeanor. Janet can hear a dog and understands that Aunt Con is threatening her with the dog. Janet identifies herself and places the offering, the box of chocolates, at the windowsill. Feeling that she has done her part, she is about to bolt, when the old lady begins to rap at the window. Eventually Janet understands that the old lady wants to see the baby:

> What did she want with the baby? Did she want to see it? It would be ill luck, surely, to let her set eyes on the baby, she might wish it evil, she might cast a spell. Janet thought of those cracked gray shells in the snails' graveyard. Sacrifices, on a small altar. Witches in the old days sucked the blood of infants and pounded their bones in mortars, pounded them into paste. (278)

The ritual language continues, with its emphasis on magic, on sacrifice, and on looking into the eyes of the witch. But Janet reminds herself that Con is no witch and holds the baby up for her to see. Con, satisfied, dismisses Janet and turns her attention to the chocolates. Janet leaves believing that "she had placated an ancient spirit" (279).

Later, with Con's body safely removed, Frances makes this same ritual trip. She too must fight her way through the bushes and sees the landscape as looking "like Sleeping Beauty's terrain" (292) and the cottage itself as "ancient, decayed, dank, dark, beautiful" (292). Frances, the archaeologist, enters the cottage respectfully and, as an archaeologist would, explores and investigates, piecing together a picture of human life from remaining artifacts. What Frances discovers among the remnants is evidence of a love affair and of a child, illegitimate and dead at eighteen months. The humanizing of Con, pointing back to Janet's holding up of her baby, establishes an almost holy connection for Frances, who begins to feel completely at home in this cottage.

Frances is in her role of primitive and timeless earth mother, absorbing her family history into herself. All of the ritual behavior, her coming to terms with the "monster" in her den, and her subsequent understanding of the mother in the monster culminate in this point.

In *The Radiant Way*, this imagery recurs with respect to Liz, whose task, which she avoids assiduously, is to come to terms with her "monster-mother." We are told that "sometime soon, when she had a free moment, she would make her way North and brave her mother, her gross mother, swelling and aging in her traumatic den" (226). When this meeting finally takes place, the monstrous imagery remains, and the identification begins:

> Liz stared at the heap of flesh that was her mother. Shirley was right, she had put on weight, mountainously. Four stone, over the past six years. Monstrous. . . . The flesh twitched. One side of the face was paralysed: it sagged, lopsided. This is nothing to do with me, thought Liz, and yet it is myself. Dry eyed she stared. . . . Liz felt her own face twitch, drily. (304)

The ritual confrontation with the monster of family relationships and resemblances is clearly the confrontation with self. The argument that, in Drabble's novels, one finds one's personal identity through a recognition of one's membership in a family, with all its foibles and apparent contradictions, is made, of course, by many of Drabble's critics and most extensively by Mary Hurley Moran in *Margaret Drabble: Existing Within Structures*. My argument here centers on the characters' recognition of their membership in the family of mothers. Acceptance is waiting there, but the imagery is so dramatic and powerful that the negative aspects, the destructive aspects, of the mother remain unexorcised.

The ritual encounter with the monster in *A Natural Curiosity* is even more pronounced and dramatic than the preceding ones. Alix Bowen, adoptive mother, and Angela Malkin, biological mother of the Horror of Harrow, meet in combat, and this moment seems to bring together all of the forces that have been building in the previous novels. Moreover, Alix does not come on this battle as accidentally or as spontaneously as her predecessors. She has, as part of her preparations, become something of a witch herself.

Alix pays a visit to Paul's father, a butcher. William Whitmore's butcher shop is now closed, presumably because of the bad publicity surrounding his notorious son (who incidentally is a vegetarian and always refused to work in the butcher shop), but Alix looks through the window and sees the butcher block stained with old blood. The meeting is both ordinary and appropriately sinister. He provides Alix with the address of Paul's mother, Angela Malkin.

Drabble plays on the ironic aspects of Angela's name and foreshadows the final battle when she has Alix speculate that William "seems to be attracted, now, by the idea of Alix and his wife in confrontation: Alix, the avenging angel with unwelcome news" (138).

Next, Alix makes a preliminary "reconnaissance trip" to meet Angela. Although the trip is unnerving for her, the scenery also recalls, unbidden, childhood rural memories. The memories are pleasant, but Alix feels ill and frightened. On arrival, she is overwhelmed by the smell of dogs; Angela, once a hairdresser, now works as a dog breeder. When Angela opens the door, she is described in terms that suggest a Medusa: "She had a hairstyle of arranged carved red solid waves rising from her square brow" (197). The dogs are frightening to Alix; they are bull mastiffs, hounds of Hell. On a tour of the house, Alix sees "a room containing a huge wooden butcher's slab with cleavers. A bunch of unskinned rabbits dangled from a hook" (199).

There is no question that Alix is in Hell: "Another sporadic burst of barking and howling broke out somewhere in the nether regions" (200). Alix half-expects to be chopped up and fed to the hounds, to disappear forever, leaving not a trace. Impatient to be rid of this visitor from the other world, the Medusa orders Alix to leave and, like Aunt Con, threatens to let the dogs loose.

This visit is followed by a dream clearly designed to prepare Alix for the forthcoming battle. She dreams of a dog that is her responsibility. She has taken him to a veterinarian whose brutal, bullying assistant inexplicably cuts off the dog's tail. In the dream, Alix "began to shout abuse and condemnation at the *monster woman* on behalf of the silent, quivering, maimed dog" (208; italics mine).

Only one step remains in the preparations for battle: Alix has her hair done, an act unusual for her and clearly an attempt to absorb Angela into herself. She deliberately goes to a cheap hairdresser and speculates on what Angela's salon might have been like.

The final confrontation is brought on by Angela herself, who, believing that Alix has continued to snoop around, has sent her a threatening note which Alix has taken as a challenge. This time, as Alix approaches the house, she finds it boarded and overgrown with weeds. About to leave, she hears the dogs barking, but in a qualitatively different way than before. Alix goes around to the back and looks through a window. The ensuing description brings together all of the imagery of previous mutilations and suffering:

> Hanging from the ceiling, suspended from a beam, where earlier had hung a bunch of unskinned rabbits, is a horse's head. Beneath the horse's head lies a heap of dead and dying dogs. Some of them are dead, dead surely, skeletal, starved, collapsed, caved in, their ribs standing out, their lips

drawn back in the grin of death. Others are still alive, still just alive, just stirring. One of them, hearing her, seeing her, sensing her, makes a dreadful effort, and rears itself up from the heap of corpses, only to collapse silently once more.(283)

These tortured animals are the victims of Angela; they are the dog in Alix's dream and, of course, Paul. She feels that she has "vindicated her theory about Paul Whitmore. He had been mothered by a mad woman, a fury, a harpy, a gorgon" (287). Alix is throwing food in through the window to the one surviving dog, having smashed the window and released a hellish stench, when Angela arrives. In the fight that ensues, Alix falls through the door that has imprisoned the dogs and gets up covered with dogfood and slime. The momentum, however, shifts permanently to Alix (whose name recalls Ajax), and she takes control of the terms of battle. She has become the champion of every suffering animal. In a very real sense, too, Alix has become Angela, her alter ego. She is the avenging angel the defender of Angela's dogs; and, in calling Angela a "bitch," she uses the same term that Angela used for her. She has taken on her language, her appearance, her madness.

Having subdued Angela, Alix gets in her car and goes to report her to the authorities. But first she must clean up. Her bath in the river is described in ritualistic terms. While bathing, she sees a kingfisher and feels blessed. She dresses herself after her bath in clothes she has found in her car—a lace blouse and sequined evening skirt that she had intended to give away. She sticks a flower behind her ear and returns to her car. An old man appears out of nowhere, smiles upon her, and opens the gate for her to pass through.

Magic everywhere. Benediction everywhere. The madness Alix has taken on to fight this battle now falls from her shoulders; the monster-mother has been vanquished.

Clearly, Drabble intends these ritual confrontations—whether comparatively benign, as with Aunt Con; shockingly evil, as in this case; or somewhere in-between, as in Liz's meeting with her mother—to be confrontations with the self, with the monster-mother inside all mothers. To defeat Angela, Alix has had to take on the qualities of her opponent, to recognize the human connection, the monster-mother inside herself. Earlier in this novel, Liz speculates on something a friend had suggested to her: "We pursue the known unknown, on and on, beyond the limits of the known world. What was that phrase Stephen had used? The fatal curiosity? When we see the Gorgon face to face, we die" (212). But clearly, one can look upon the Gorgon and not die if one prepares adequately and if one brings to the endeavor not a "fatal curiosity" but a "natural curiosity," one in search of the natural connection, the universality within the monster.

That these epic confrontations with the monster-mother must be made by the most successful mothers in these novels is significant. It indicates a certain ironic stance taken by Drabble toward this very success. It undermines the self-congratulation of these characters, at the same time that it demonstrates their unusual imaginative capacity for overcoming this crippling self-congratulatory dimension of mothering.

The identification of Alix and Angela is obvious, but, looking back over the novels, it is easy to see that Drabble intends us to see the connections between good and bad mothers throughout. Her narrative style underlines this sisterhood of mothers. Drabble, as many critics have noted, employs an omniscient, even Victorian, narrator who oversees the action and offers comments on the characters' behavior and on possible reader responses. One effect of this narrative decision is to maintain some distance between the narrator and the characters and to set up obstacles to the reader's too-narrow identification with characters or to our willingness to accept at face value the character's self-evaluation. The suspicions that we feel concerning these "good mothers" are planted there by the narrator, who sees the bigger picture and eventually makes us see unlikely connections between pairs of characters.

One of Drabble's favorite narrative tricks is to juxtapose characters against each other. Before the cousins, Frances and Janet, have ever met, Drabble has prepared us for their meeting by placing them in narrative proximity. Frances and Janet are, of course, related, so perhaps this juxtaposition is not so unusual, but the device is not limited to these characters. As we get to the last two novels, the tendency to draw emphatic connections between very different women becomes even more pronounced. One of Liz Headland's patients in *The Radiant Way*, a Mrs. Hood, dissatisfied with her own performance as a mother, tells Liz that she always thought that she would be a better mother than she is. She goes on to criticize her adoptive mother and to tell Liz about the way she always fantasized about her real mother. Her fantasies parallel those of Liz, who had always pretended that her real mother was spirited away and Rita left in her place. These fantasies, of course, always ended in a glorious and well-deserved rescue.

Drabble demonstrates that, no matter how dissimilar these women are, their childhood fantasies about their mothers are startlingly similar. Liz and Mrs. Hood are spiritual sisters, a fact which is reemphasized when Liz finally visits her mother in the hospital. That scene recapitulates the scene described to her by Mrs. Hood at this same session. Mrs. Hood has told Liz that she has been visiting her mother in the hospital:

> "The nurses say she's getting more confused. I don't think she wants to see me."

"If she doesn't recognize you, how can she want not to see you?"
"If she doesn't recognize me, who am I?" Liz does not answer. She does not
know. (137)

Ultimately, all of Drabble's mothers are forced to look for the answer to the
question "Who am I?" in the same place, in the den of the monster-mother.

For Drabble, mothering remains a central theme and most definitively a
"good." It is not too much of an exaggeration to say that her women, however
successful at other endeavors, are happiest as mothers, or even that their success in life generally seems to be connected to nurturing skills. Even the few
men who seem humanly successful in these novels are the ones who have
some nurturing qualities, and in her men these qualities cannot seem to co-
exist with worldly ways. But as we have seen, however "natural" mothering
may be, it meets obstacles at every turn, and more women fail at it than succeed. It is worth considering the nature of some of these obstacles.

The unsuccessful mothers in Drabble's novels tend to be isolated, without
support, and, even more disastrous, subject to criticism and blame. Rita
Ablewhite is driven into seclusion, for herself and her children, by the double
disgrace of having borne an illegitimate child and having married a man who
turned out to be a child molester. She responds to her terror of society's condemnation and retribution by a form of self-protection that in fact constitutes self-imprisonment. The good, conscientious mother, locked in shame
and deprived of support, turns in on herself.

In most cases in these novels, we look back at last and learn from the past:
what catastrophes have befallen these women that transformed them into
monsters? In the case of Janet Ollerenshaw in *The Realms of Gold*, we are
invited to witness the forces of oppression at work. At a dinner party she is
giving for friends of her husband, childless people she finds glamorous and
intimidating, her baby begins to cry. Her own anxiety makes the situation
worse, and the scene culminates in her husband's smiling ominously at her
and asking, "Are you going upstairs to throttle that baby, or shall I?" (157).
The dinner party continues in this vein, with her husband treating her as
a particularly dull servant, sneering at her attempts at conversation, and the
guests treating her with a combination of pity and condescension. When it
finally ends, she blames herself. With no support anywhere, Janet would
seem to be heading for the inward-turning madness of the monster-mothers,
but the ending of the novel seems to suggest that she will escape. For this,
we have her meeting with her cousin Frances to thank; perhaps some of
Frances' very good luck will transfer to her cousin.

Every successful woman in these novels has rich support from friends:
Kate has Evelyn; Frances has countless friends; and Liz, Alix, and Esther have

each other. This support, in addition to society's approval of their outside work, provides them with the self-confidence to face their critics, for there are plenty of those.

As mentioned before, these later novels differ from the earlier ones in that they offer a more serious critique of society at large. England, in the last quarter of the twentieth century, appears as an increasingly dehumanized and deteriorating place. At the center of *The Ice Age* is an architectural scandal which involves a collapse of the property market, bankruptcy, and jail terms. The scandal is a microcosm and metaphor for the despondency and corruption throughout the society.

Although *The Ice Age* offers the direst picture of the age, nothing in the subsequent books substantially refutes this position. Labor problems and financial instability persist, and the implication remains that this state of things is a self-inflicted wound brought on by greed and loss of perspective, the perspective that comes from an understanding of the past. Significantly, Drabble's women play societal roles which place them at some distance from the political power, and consequently, the social ills of the day; the women of these novels are writers, psychiatrists, art historians, social workers, and archeologists, all of them in search of the human, probers into the cultural, individual, personal past. This aloofness is, on the one hand, very good; who would wish responsibility for this mess? On the other hand, it underlines women's traditional societal function: nurturing. The mothering role is still exclusively female; the sexual division of labor is intact; women are not bringing those nurturing and humanistic qualities to bear in shaping the larger social sphere. In fact, they unwittingly contribute to the system that victimizes them, and the boundaries remain for mothers in general. Their "success" is largely irrelevant. The peace attained by the women at the end of these novels is by and large a separate peace. As long as this is so, mothers still eventually will have to meet the Gorgon face to face, and only the imaginative (and the lucky) will survive.

Note

1. Like Drabble, her critics tend to take this mothering role as a given in the body of her work. Few of them have examined it in detail or questioned the values being posited by the novels. Representative is Carey Kaplan's essay, "A Vision of Power in Margaret Drabble's *The Realms of Gold*." Kaplan regularly refers to Frances Wingate in the essay as "the monolithic matriarch" and "earth mother" (135).

Chapter 7

The Mother's Part:
Incest and Maternal Deprivation
in Woolf and Morrison

Paula Bennett

For Deborah

Had I not killed her
she would have killed me.
—Virginia Woolf

Incest is a violation of boundaries—specifically, of those boundaries which define sexual behavior appropriate among family members. By the victim, it is experienced as exploitation, even when, as can happen, it feels pleasurable at the same time. For the perpetrator, it involves the imposition of one's desire and will on a subject who is smaller and less powerful than oneself. The presence of incestuous desire, as Alice Miller remarks, can be indicated by nothing more obvious than the look in a parent's eye (123). But whether so confined or not, incest is destructive. Insofar as it is enabled by the victim's inability to protect her or his boundaries from invasion—or to find protection elsewhere in the family—incest is also a family affair.[1]

In this essay, I wish to look at the works of two women novelists—one of whom was the victim of incest, the other of whom writes about it explicitly—which dramatically illustrate the relationship between incest and the deprivation many daughters experience as their share of the mother-daughter bond. While the incestuously-functioning families which Woolf and Morrison depict in *To the Lighthouse* and *The Bluest Eye* stand worlds apart socially, economically, and educationally, the fates of the daughters—in life and in literature—are strikingly similar. Given both authors' focus on the mother's failure to protect either her daughter or herself from invasion, also similar is the way in which the mother-daughter bond renders the daughter vulnerable in each work. Both these novels are written from the daughter's perspective. But, as I hope to show, both encourage us to reconceive essential aspects of the mother's role, based on the knowledge that the daughter has won at such terrible cost.

Research into mother-daughter relationships over the past twenty years (Dinnerstein, Rich, Chodorow, Gilligan) makes clear that, given the power arrangements in our society, the great strength of the mother-daughter bond

is also its point of greatest vulnerability. "The nurture of daughters in patriarchy," Adrienne Rich declares, "calls for a strong sense of *self*-nurture in
the mother" (*Of Woman Born*, 245). But this "strong sense of self-nurture"
is precisely what oppression (whether "patriarchal," racial, or economic) undermines. Far from endowing her daughter with strength, the mother's close
identification with her, the fluidity (as it is usually called) of the ego boundaries between them, too often becomes the point through which the mother
transfers her own sense of deprivation and helplessness. Where the mother
compounds the problem by identifying with the oppressor—that is, where
she accepts "his" version of reality, she also will seek to impose this reality
on her daughter. Unable to nurture or protect herself, such a mother cannot
nurture or protect her daughter. Nor, equally important, will she encourage
her daughter to learn how to nurture or protect herself.

In families where the mother has assumed the traditional role of caretaker—
the kind of archetypically "patriarchal" family Virginia Woolf depicts in *To
the Lighthouse*—the mother's commitment to bourgeois ideology results
not only in the mother's self-deprivation, but in her depriving her daughter
as well. The dynamic which informs this deprivation has been analyzed at
length by feminist psychotherapists Luise Eichenbaum and Susie Orbach. In
Understanding Women, they offer the following explanation for the impact
deprivation has on the daughter's psychological development, an impact
which makes it impossible for the daughter to break out of the cycle of failed
nurturance which dominates her mother's as well as her own life, and which
leaves her prey to the exploitation of those more empowered socially than
herself:

> Unconsciously mother gives the message to the daughter: "Don't be emo-
> tionally dependent; don't expect the emotional care and attention you
> want. . . . don't expect a life much different from mine; learn to accom-
> modate."
> . . . the mother's unconscious identification makes her annoyed with
> the child for displaying her needs and for not controlling them as she her-
> self does. At these times mother is unconsciously driven to respond to
> her daughter with resentment and disapproval, thus transmitting the mes-
> sage that there is something wrong with her daughter, something wrong
> with her desires. . . . Unwittingly, mother provides her daughter with her
> first lesson in emotional deprivation. (43–44)

Instead of meeting their daughters' needs, Eichenbaum and Orbach claim,
such mothers, both by example and by admonition, encourage their daughters
to learn, like themselves, to put others' needs first. As the daughter matures,
she discovers that she must suppress various aspects of her "little-girl" self
(44), her "childish" wants and desires, if she wishes to gain her parents' ap-

proval, and she begins to seek in men the care and attention her mother deprived her of. She learns, in short, to capitulate to the system, becoming the "dutiful daughter," the "good girl," the self-sacrificing mother, that her mother and her society wish her to be. But, Eichenbaum and Orbach conclude, "Even though a daughter comes to look toward men, she still yearns for mother's support and care. From girlhood to womanhood women live with the experience of having lost these aspects of maternal nurturance. This nurturance is never replaced. Women look to men to mother them but remain bereft" (52).

While there are many literary portraits of the potentially destructive elements within the bourgeois construction of the mother-daughter bond (what Eichenbaum and Orbach call its "push-pull" dynamic [92]), none is more thoroughgoing in its revelations than Virginia Woolf's semi-autobiographical *To the Lighthouse*. Given Woolf's powerfully ambivalent feelings toward her mother, Julia Duckworth Stephen, and given her own personal situation as the victim of brother-sister incest, none is more poignant. As Louise DeSalvo observes in her recent study of the effects of child sexual abuse in Woolf's writing, the Stephen family conforms to the profile of the incestuous family with appalling exactitude (8–9; see also Herman, 50–95). Whether consciously or not, in depicting the Ramsays, her surrogate family in *To The Lighthouse*, Woolf was exploring the role her mother played in her daughter's victimization. In doing so, Woolf reveals the strategic role which the mother-daughter bond plays in helping lay the groundwork for the daughter's abuse.[2]

Although she presumably loves her four daughters as much as she loves her four sons, Mrs. Ramsay, the novel's mother-figure, treats her children in a painfully lopsided and stereotypical manner. "[F]or reasons she could not explain," we are told quite early, Mrs. Ramsay has taken "the whole of the other sex under her protection" (13). And she expects her daughters to do likewise: "[W]oe betide the girl—pray Heaven it was none of her daughters!— who did not feel the worth of it [that is, male neediness], and all that it implied, to the marrow of her bones!" (13). Mrs. Ramsay's concern with protecting men is so great that she relentlessly subordinates herself to their needs, real or imagined. Indeed, she is not above inventing needs for them in order to give herself and other women something to do (*vide* her conviction that Mr. Bankes is "pitiable" and in want of a wife [127–28]). Mrs. Ramsay knows that her constant emotional giving is draining her. "[S]he often felt she was nothing but a sponge sopped full of human emotions," the narrator tells us after one of Mrs. Ramsay's frequent altercations with her husband (51). But, worn and harried as she is, her sense of depletion does not prevent her from continuing to put out. Nor does it prevent her from urging her daughters to do likewise. Ever the angel in the house, she will always sit in the draught. Ever the matchmaker, she expects her daughters, biological and "adopted" (Lily and Minta as well as Prue and Cam), to join her there: "An unmarried woman (she lightly took [Lily's] hand for a moment), an unmarried woman has missed the best of life" (77). There is no suggestion that Mrs. Ramsay ever tries to look at things from an unmarried woman's point of view. "[T]hat was true of Mrs Ramsay—she pitied men always as if they lacked something—women never, as if they had something" (129). What women "have" is their capacity to nurture men. Presumably they do not require anything else, since it is on this quality that their suitableness for marriage—"the best of life"—is based.

As the abundant critical literature written in her praise attests, Mrs. Ramsay is an enormously seductive figure.[3] Who of us, male or female, does not long to be loved and nurtured in such a compellingly single-minded way, to have a mother this beautiful, this caring, this provocatively withholding? Because the other side of the coin, of course, is that Mrs. Ramsay cannot admit to needs of her own. That would spoil the game. With the exception of the wily poet Carmichael, who appears to prefer opium to mothering, virtually every character in the novel falls under her spell. However much or little they receive—whether *Boeuf en Daube* with Mr. Bankes or constant solicitude with James—they long for her love. And for it, the majority of them end up giving themselves, becoming what she wants them to be: the boys "men," the girls, "women."

Thus Andrew, the Ramsays' oldest son, goes off to war and gets killed. His sister, Prue, gets married, becomes pregnant, and dies giving birth. James follows in his father's wake to the bare, sterile lighthouse. Cam retires to the dream world her mother first concocted for her, a dream world that—like Mrs. Ramsay's shawl—helps her deny the reality of the terrors she feels: the pig's bare, horned skull branching in her bedroom, the lighthouse to which her father is taking her and to which she does not want to go.[4]

Whether or not Woolf consciously meant to suggest this, it appears clear that the sexual arrangements which control the Ramsay household—and which Mrs. Ramsay in particular seems determined to perpetuate (she, after all, not her husband, is the incessant matchmaker)—are directly responsible for the literal and/or figurative deaths of her children, boys and girls alike. They are also responsible for a good deal of unhappiness elsewhere, e.g., the Rayleys' unsuccessful marriage.

As a number of critics have noted, Lily Briscoe, the artist who is Woolf's principal alter ego in the text, does not succumb in the end. At the conclusion of the novel, we leave Lily on the terrace with poet Carmichael. Her painting is completed at long last, and she has not married Mr. Bankes (a safe bank: a shore or a holding place?) as Mrs. Ramsay wanted her to do. She has stuck bravely to her profession, her art. But, although I sympathize with those feminist critics who wish to see in Lily a resolution of the issues raised by the text, I do not think that the resolution is that easy.[5]

Lily may complete her picture, but she is hardly a complete human being. Far from it. In her own eyes, she is little more than a monster, a freak. Even at the end of the text, Lily still believes that "real" women look after and succor men, no matter how much she detests such behavior. She still longs for Mrs. Ramsay's love and approval—to the point that she feels obliged to nurture Mr. Ramsay in the dead woman's stead. And she still seesaws back and forth between loving and rejecting both "parents," all the while convinced that she is unworthy in their eyes. That is, the novel replicates the situation which obtained in the Stephen household when Woolf was growing up. Like thirteen-year-old Virginia, Lily is not attractive enough to be her beautiful "mother's" ideal daughter, nor is she nurturing enough to replace her "father's" dead wife.

The result is that, although Lily finishes her picture, which she could not do while Mrs. Ramsay was alive, she still has no real faith in herself, her work: "It would be hung in the attics, she thought; it would be destroyed. But what did that matter?" (309–310). I would answer, it matters a great deal. "With her little Chinese eyes and her puckered-up face" (29), her self-negating, spinsterish ways, Lily is not an appealing heroine, despite her moments of rebellion and vision.[6] She is a deprived child. It is clear that she is deprived. However courageously she sticks to her outcast status, this is not a price that one should have to pay for the independence that secures art. Her loss is too huge. She seems all but swallowed up in it. Her longing for Mrs. Ramsay, legitimate and poignantly expressed, undermines the whole. In particular, it undermines the joy and fullness a truly positive sense of self would bring. Like the women Eichenbaum and Orbach describe, who have never been able to separate completely from mothers who nurtured them inadequately, Lily still has not separated from her "mother" at the end of the novel. She still accepts Mrs. Ramsay's judgment of her work. (Apparently sharing Tansley's opinion that women cannot paint or write, Mrs. Ramsay rejects Lily's painting early in the novel as inconsequential.) And Lily still feels the need to nurture Mr. Ramsay, even though he is now well out to sea. She is, in short, still trying to be her mother's "good girl."

Like Cam, Woolf's other alter ego in the text (their names may be a split reference to the Camas lily), Lily does not have a secure place in this family. Nor does she feel a secure member of the human community. Her awareness of her own deprivation is simply too great. So is her knowledge that her "mother" will not protect her. For, just as wrapping something in a shawl does not make it go away, "wrapping" male domination up in marriage does not make it any the less destructive to women. In pushing Lily toward marriage rather than supporting her rejection of it, Mrs. Ramsay comes down on the side of male right just as she does in the nursery when she prefers James's needs over Cam's in the matter of the pig's skull. In paralleling one instance with the other, Woolf is laying at her mother's door, responsibility for both the vulnerability of her womanhood, which made her insecure in respect to male power, and her vulnerability as a child to her half-brother's unwanted advances. (According to DeSalvo, Woolf consistently associated George Duckworth with pigs, which he raised [159].)

As an artist, Lily Briscoe does find a way, as Jane Lilienfeld observes, to "move beyond" Mrs. Ramsay and "her mother's limiting example" (in Davidson and Broner, 172). In doing so, she at least partially heals herself and compensates for her loss. In her painting, if not in life, she can give herself the mother she never had and, not coincidentally, revenge herself on the mother she did have. In her moment of "vision," the steps to the house are—finally—empty of Mrs. Ramsay's ghost. And Lily is able to draw the all-important "line" that presumably secures her from further invasion.[7] But the sequence of events in Virginia Woolf's own life suggests that this victory was fragile at best. And the victimized Cam, who has been encouraged by her mother to use autistic fantasy to escape—or deny—the reality of her fears, is the artist's real-life fate. As she approaches the lighthouse where her father and brother will leap out to have their "extraordinary adventure," Cam, staring backward toward the island from which they came, drifts to sleep on her mother's words: "All those paths and terraces and bedrooms were fading and disappearing, and nothing was left but a pale blue censer swinging rhythmically this way and that across her mind. It was a hanging garden; it was a valley, full of birds, and flowers, and antelopes" (303). In its erasure of all lines, all boundaries, all differences between this and that, gardens and valleys, dreams and realities, "it" was, in fact, madness and death.

Insofar as it represents a white, middle-class ideal, Woolf's image of motherhood, her "Angel in the House," is essentially irrelevant to most black mother-daughter relationships—as black critics are quick to point out of this mother image as a whole (Wade-Gayles, 11–12; Collins, "Meaning of Motherhood," 3–4; Joseph and Lewis, 75–126). But this does not mean that the bond between African-American mothers and daughters is not susceptible to analogous problems, as some of this literature also seems to imply.[8] On the contrary. Even as the white mother passes on to her daughter her own deprivation and vulnerability to oppression, so the bond between black mothers and daughters can become equally dangerous to the daughter if the mother is unable to keep her faith in herself—her blackness as well as her power—

alive. In Toni Morrison's *The Bluest Eye*, the incest implicit in Woolf's *To the Lighthouse*, where it is rendered metaphorically in the pig's skull episode, is made the explicit subject of the text; and in the differing fates of Claudia MacTeer, the artist-narrator, and Pecola Breedlove, the victim, Morrison plays out in black terms the difference separating Lily from Cam.

The Bluest Eye is a novel about two daughters who could have been—but are not—one. Both are girls on the brink of adolescence. Both live in the same poor black community in Lorain, Ohio. Both go to the same school, play with the same children, buy candy at the same store. Claudia, the narrator, and Pecola, the victim whose story Claudia tells, are explicitly separated only by the difference in their families. While the MacTeers are hardly the white middle-class "ideal" alluded to in Morrison's epigraphic reference to *Dick and Jane*, they are, to use Winnicott's designation, "good-enough" parents.[9] Pecola's are not.

It is within Claudia's memories of her own childhood that Morrison sets Pecola's story, beginning with Claudia's recall of the harsh but nurturant treatment she received at her mother's hands: the hot flannel and Vicks vapor rub for colds, the impatience and concern, the "love, thick and dark as Alaga syrup," (14). Claudia can see her mother's limitations: the hardness, the distance, the delight in gossip; but always there are crucial compensations. The blue-eyed baby dolls Claudia receives for Christmas are balanced by the blues songs her mother sings and by the warmth and security of her abundant kitchen. If the former speaks to the mother's absorption of some of the white values of the culture at large, the latter attests to her ability nevertheless to retain her own sense of a positive black identity, and to pass this on to the daughter she loves. For Claudia, as Michael Awkward observes, quoting Morrison, childhood is finally "characterized by 'a productive and fructifying pain' . . . filled with the . . . love of a mother 'who does not want me to die'" (59). Not so, for Pauline Breedlove and her daughter Pecola.

If Pauline Breedlove is not Winnicott's "good-enough" mother—nor the "ideal" mother of white middle-class fantasy—what she is instead, with almost bruising irony, is that fantasy's "ideal servant." Bred in poverty and lamed by a childhood accident, Pauline is ninth of eleven children and the most severely deprived. The one satisfaction she learns to take in life is in "housekeeping," which, Morrison tells us, she not only was good at but also "enjoyed" (90). In caring for other peoples' things, first in her own family of origin, then in the homes of wealthy whites, Pauline is able to bring order into her life and gain a sense of accomplishment. And in caring for the fine, beautiful things of white families, in particular, she is able to possess all that she could never have in her own right:

> She looked at their houses, smelled their linen, touched their silk drap-
> eries, and loved all of it. The child's pink nightie, the stacks of white pillow
> slips edged with embroidery, the sheets with top hems picked out with
> blue cornflowers. She became what is known as an ideal servant, for such
> a role filled practically all of her needs. (100)

But the greater the satisfaction Pauline feels in caring for what belongs
to her white employers, the less she is able to care for herself, her own things,
or, above all, her daughter, whom she sees as the epitome of all she loathes
most in herself, the qualities which make her—to her way of thinking—the
deprived person she is: her "ugliness," her blackness, her poverty, her dis-
empowerment. "When," Morrison continues, "she bathed the little Fisher
girl, it was in a porcelain tub with silvery taps running infinite quantities
of hot, clear water. She dried her in fluffy white towels and put her in cuddly
night clothes. Then she brushed the yellow hair, enjoying the roll and slip
of it between her fingers" (100–101). For Pauline's own daughter, Pecola, there
are only a zinc tub, water heated on a wood-burining stove, "flaky, stiff, gray-
ish towels washed in a kitchen sink," and "tangled black puffs of rough wool
to comb" (101).

Forced to choose between Pecola and her employers' child, as she is in one
scene, Pauline not surprisingly opts for the latter. In one of the most harrowing moments in this harrowing text, she comforts her white "baby" while
sending her own child, who has just been burned by hot blueberry cobbler,
out of the house with harsh words and a blow. Pauline's need for the "power,
praise, and luxury" (101) that, given her circumstances, she can possess only
by being an "ideal servant"—and thus a legitimate part of an "ideal" (white)
family—blinds her to the very real but competing claims of her own child.
It does not occur to this poor woman to put Pecola's well-being—in effect,
her own well-being—first. Indeed, the lesson given to her by white society
is that she must not or she will risk losing her job (95–96).[10]

As Morrison makes clear, the perversion of Pauline's nurturing impulses—
her willingness to sacrifice her child for the sake of another woman's baby—
is a direct consequence of her economic deprivation and of the racism which
lies at its root. But the net effect is that, like Mrs. Ramsay, who would sacrifice Lily to the "pitiable" Mr. Bankes and Cam to James, Pauline absorbs the
values which determine her socially disempowered role, and this absorption
leads her to abandon the daughter (so like herself) who depends upon her.
"Like the traditional foot-bound Chinese woman," Adrienne Rich writes, in
an analogy which the black critic Joyce Pettis also applies to Morrison's story
(28), "[the mother] passes on her own affliction. The mother's self-hatred and
low expectations are the binding-rags for the psyche of the daughter" (Of
Woman Born, 243). They are binding rags that not only make it impossible

for a mother such as Pauline to protect her daughter, but they also make it impossible for the daughter, who has absorbed her mother's acceptance of victimization, to defend herself:

> Dandelions. A dart of affection leaps out from [Pecola] to them. But they do not look at her and do not send love back. She thinks, "They *are* ugly. They *are* weeds." Preoccupied with that revelation, she trips on the sidewalk crack. Anger stirs and wakes in her; it opens its mouth, and like a hot-mouthed puppy, laps up the dredges of her shame.
>   Anger is better. *There is a sense of being in anger. A reality and presence. An awareness of worth.* [My emphasis.] It is lovely surging. Her thoughts fall back to Mr. Yacobowski's eyes, his phlegmy voice. The anger will not hold; the puppy is too easily surfeited. Its thirst too quickly quenched, it sleeps. The shame wells up again, its muddy rivulets seeping into her eyes. (43)

Pecola's inability to hold onto her anger is a direct result of Pauline's similar inability.[11] The art of protecting oneself against intrusion, of knowing how and when to say "no," is not, after all, something an "ideal servant," anymore than an "ideal" wife or mother, does well to learn. Indeed, how can there be anger when, as in the *Dick and Jane* readers, everyone is "nice"? But if the mother cannot say "no," she cannot defend herself or her daughter. For both, anger will be dissipated in feelings of shame and low self-worth. The mother will not protect the child. The child will grow up knowing she is unprotected and that, therefore, she must capitulate in order to survive. At this point, the bond between mother and daughter becomes actively detrimental to the daughter's well-being.

As a number of critics (Awkward, Christian, Pettis) have observed, Morrison has specifically given to Claudia the resources and strengths which Pecola lacks. Mrs. and Mr. MacTeer are poor. Their house is old and cold, and rags stuff the window cracks; but at least it is theirs. And a sense of solidity and pride is theirs' also, sufficient pride to allow them to protect their boundaries and keep themselves and their children intact. Insofar as it is within their power, they do not permit themselves to be abused. Thus, when the boarder, Mr. Henry, "messes" briefly with Claudia's sister, Frieda, Mr. and Mrs. MacTeer kick the man out of the house, Mrs. MacTeer using her broom at one point to make the message clear. Nor, as so often happens in such cases, is Frieda blamed for what Mr. Henry tried to do. In the seriocomic aftermath of the incident, which Frieda relates, it is upon the neighbor Miss Dunion that Mrs. MacTeer's wrath falls, for suggesting that Frieda might be "ruined" (80–81).

By Claudia's own admission, both sisters are later contaminated by the self-hatred and "fraudulent love" (22) which, Morrison seems to suggest, is virtually unavoidable for blacks living in a white-dominated culture.[12] But their mother and father have placed a floor, as it were, beneath their daughters' oppression, giving them permission, in effect, to fight back. Even after she is seduced into "loving" Shirley Temple, Claudia can still remember a time when, with "pristine sadism," she destroyed white baby dolls and tormented "little white girls" (22). Like Lily drawing her "line," Claudia has, as a result, the wherewithal to establish a boundary against invasion. Unlike Pecola, who has neither witnessed nor experienced rage in her own defense, Claudia will reject "shame" and survive. Pecola does not.

As poverty grinds the Breedloves down, husband and wife split apart in bitter acrimony. The son runs away; but Pecola, unable to separate from the mother she never had, stays to become the scapegoat of her father Cholly's self-hatred and despair. He rapes her in their storefront kitchen:

> The rigidness of her shocked body, the silence of her stunned throat, was better than Pauline's easy laughter had been. . . .when the child regained consciousness, she was lying on the kitchen floor under a heavy quilt, try-ing to connect the pain between her legs with the face of her mother loom-ing over her. (128 and 129)

The connection which Pecola seeks between the pain between her legs and her mother's face is made for us by the author. It is part of Morrison's genius in this text, that when the reader has finished it, there is no way to blame one parent more than the other for Pecola's fate, or indeed to blame them at all. Both Pauline Breedlove and her husband Cholly are victims of social institutions and ways of being that raped them, figuratively if not literally. In the way of such things, they have passed their victimization on to their child. In Pecola's silence at the moment of her rape lies a world of words. Don't, the mother's message reads, get angry at those who abuse you, "don't expect a life much different from mine." There is no small amount of irony in the fact that this is the message both racism and traditional modes of mothering instill in their victims—or in the fact that Pecola's subsequent fictional life mirrors in its madness and disorganization the path Virginia Woolf's life actually took. For both, the mother's failure to protect (that is, to insist upon the integrity of the self, whether self as woman or self as black) is a necessary precondition for the daughter's destruction.

Particularly since the publication of Carol Gilligan's *In A Different Voice*, there has been a tendency among white middle-class American feminists to romanticize women's so-called connectedness to others and to treat it as an essential and positive quality differentiating women from men. This essen-tialist tendency has been reinforced in literary criticism by the emphasis which French theorists place on *femininité*. Like connectedness, *femininité* defines women in terms of their capacity to lose themselves in others. In both schools of thought, weak ego-boundaries are seen as a plus while separation and autonomy (the qualities which allow us, in effect, to establish boundaries, to say "no"), are devalued as psychological goals for female development.[13] They are identified with "male" behavior—and with everything that is presumably wrong with men: failure of "intimacy," tendency to objectify the other, aggressiveness, and so on. "Male identity," Jessica Benjamin writes, citing Chodorow, "emphasizes only one side of the balance of differentiation—difference over sharing, separation over connection, boundaries over communion, self-sufficiency over dependency" (76). In their desire to hear women's "voice," many feminists have stressed or, perhaps, overstressed the other side. In doing so, ironically, they have refueled the fantasy of the ideal mother, which feminism originally sought to challenge: the mother who always puts herself, her needs, and therefore her boundaries last.[14]

But theory is one thing and the reality of women's lives is another. For incest victims, there is little to choose between the aggressiveness of the "father"—or brother—perpetrator and the mother who, because she has been taught "connection" *at the expense of self*, is unable to prevent, or, indeed, even to speak out against, her daughter's violation. Ultimately, from the daughter's point of view, both parents are responsible for her fate. Hence the rage which so many incest victims direct toward their mothers, often greater than that which they feel toward the perpetrators themselves (Herman, 82; Renvoize, 114).

When mothers cannot confront effectively the men who violate their daughters' sexual boundaries, they are, I would argue, only passing their own victimization as women on. Like Mrs. Ramsay and Pauline Breedlove, the women whom Eichenbaum and Orbach see in their everyday practice as working psychotherapists suffer enormously from their inability to act in an independent manner—to see themselves, in Benjamin's terms, as separate subjects. Whether as wives or servants or both, and whether or not out of economic necessity, they have lived their lives in terms of others' values and in terms of reigning social ideologies. In learning how to subordinate their own desires, however, they have failed to develop a sense of separate self, the kind of self which would make connections *between* subjects possible.

As a result, they have lived with deprivation as a way of life, and, in the cyclical way of such things, they have passed their deprivation—their sense of inner worthlessness and vulnerability—on to their daughters. The full growth and creative development of both mother and daughter are effectively aborted thereby. At best, the daughter learns that her worth lies not in herself but in how she relates to and takes care of those around her: the phenomenon

Jean Baker Miller describes in *Toward a New Psychology of Women*.[15] At worst, as in the Breedlove family, the mother's sense of inadequacy, projected onto her child, leads the daughter—like Pecola—into a passivity (a silence) that will make her destruction inevitable. In either case, the daughter's ability to act in her own defense is mutilated beyond recognition. "The complement to the male refusal to recognize the other," Benjamin writes, "is *woman's own acceptance of her lack of subjectivity,* her willingness to offer recognition without expecting it in return. (The classic maternal ideal of motherhood—a paragon of self-abnegation—is only a beautification of this lack)" (78; my emphasis). Without this subjectivity, Benjamin argues, women are susceptible to the masochism which insures their victim status. Where racism is involved, this lack of subjectivity will also insure that the victim will internalize the oppressor's view of her presumed lack of worth. Like Pauline and her daughter, she will silently acquiesce in society's and her father's rape.

The mother-daughter bond is unquestionably a bond of tremendous strength, but as long as mothers participate in and help perpetuate the social and sexual arrangements that abuse them, this very strength will make it dangerous to their daughters. As *To the Lighthouse* and *The Bluest Eye* make clear, both Mr. *and* Mrs. Ramsay, Cholly *and* Pauline Breedlove, represent poles of personality development which, given the power inequities of our society, are mutually destructive to one another and to the children bred of their parents' loins. In advocating connectedness without stressing at the same time the need for autonomy and separation (that is, the need for boundaries), feminists risk serving the very institutions they wish to change, and true connection (connection *between* subjects, whether husband and wife, parent and child, brother and sister, or, for that matter, black and white) will remain wanting. "Good-enough" mothering—that establishes boundaries while offering nurturance—will also remain, like the difference between Claudia and Pecola, a matter of luck.

Notes

1. I am studying mothering in relation to incest in order to highlight what I see as potentially pathological elements in what is usually deemed "normal" female development (i.e., "weak" ego boundaries). Following Renvoize, however, I view incest itself as a product of family dysfunction (89–90). As my wording indicates, I also agree with her that our thinking on incest should not be limited to female victims and male perpetrators. Recent studies indicate that there is far more father-son and mother-child incest than was previously acknowledged (Renvoize, 136; Lew); and this has important theoretical implications for the study of incest. Unfortunately, however, these implications go well beyond the scope of this essay.

2. DeSalvo's large claims for Woolf's awareness of the impact incest had upon her are highly problematical; but I concur with the critic in viewing the incest itself as the formative experience in Woolf's life and as central to her writing. Also see Alice (Miller, 124–26). Consistent with her overall thesis that the suppression of knowledge damages more than the act itself, Miller relates Woolf's psychosis to the repression which her feelings surrounding the incest experience underwent in her own mind and in the family.

3. Prefeminist interpretations of *To the Lighthouse* tend to center on thematic issues such as time, death, and loss, taking Mrs. Ramsay as Woolf's primary spokesperson for these ideas. See, for example, Eric Auerbach's classic study of the novel in *Mimesis* (463–88). Also see Naremone, Ruotolo, and Fleishman, among others. Although feminist critics are more prepared to recognize Mrs. Ramsay's limitations, (in my opinion) they have treated her with undue politeness. See Phyllis Rose; DiBattista; Lilienfeld, "The Deceptiveness of Beauty"; Lilienfeld, "Reentering Paradise"; and Dash, Kushner, and Moore, "How Light a *Lighthouse*."

4. Read against the history of brother-sister incest in the Stephens' household, the episode of the pig's skull, which DeSalvo also discusses (177), puts Mrs. Ramsay's treatment of Cam in a very dark light. Cam sees the pig's horns "branching at her all over the room" (172), in precisely the same way that Woolf, one suspects, felt that her half-brother George Duckworth was invading her bedroom—and self. (Cam's brother, James, is, after all, the one who insists on keeping the skull in the room.)

The only defense the mother offers against this invasion is "denial." She wraps the skull in her shawl in order to hide it and then tells Cam lovely stories to make her forget her fears (to put her to sleep). While this may seem innocent, it is not. "Hiding" was the way the Stephen family seems to have dealt with most messy family issues, from Woolf's insanity to her niece Angelica's true paternity, and it was destructive in every instance (Quentin Bell, 2:18; Garnett, 37–38; DeSalvo, 48 and *passim*). It also replicates the denial pattern found in incest families generally (Renvoize, 101–4; Alice Miller). Using "fantasy" as an "escape" from unpleasant reality is what psychotics do.

I should note here that DeSalvo and I arrived at our interpretations of the pig's skull episode independently of each other. DeSalvo does not link the episode with Cam's later reponse to the lighthouse (a linkage which Woolf herself makes through the repetition of the mother's words). The phallic symbolism of the lighthouse is implied by James's reaction to it: "It was a stark tower on a bare rock. It satisfied him. It confirmed some obscure feeling of his about his own character." It leads him, the narrator goes on to say, to identify with his father, in a "knowledge" they "shared" (301–302). Immediately after this passage, Cam has her own, very different mother-centered revery.

5. See, in particular, Lilienfeld, "Reentering Paradise," (172); and "The Deceptiveness of Beauty" (346–47, 360–66). Phyllis Rose, on the other hand, is considerably more cautious and, I think, on the mark, when she notes that Lily's (and Woolf's) ambivalence in the book is never completely resolved (166–73).

6. This point was brought home to me by my students, who consistently refused to see Lily as heroic, no matter what I said in her defense. I finally concluded that they were right. Withdrawn as she is, she is not a heroine with whom anyone in the process of developing themselves would want to identify.

7. Drawing lines, or rather the failure to draw lines, is one of the most striking features of the Duckworth-Stephen-Bloomsbury ensemble, whether those lines would have established family roles, gender roles, sexual roles, or merely the limits of any one particular household grouping. The obliteration of lines is, of course, one of the

defining elements of incest (as well as psychosis). It is tempting to speculate that Woolf's open and fluid style (which permits subtle shifts from one character's thoughts to another's, often with no notice at all), partially at least, reflects her family situation. Certainly, I do not think it an accident that Lily's final gesture, the one that brings her painting to a satisfactory conclusion, is the drawing of a line.

8. Where black daughters tend to fault their mothers, it is usually on the score of lack of affection, but this quality is attributed to the mother's hard life and to her emphasis on survival. Passivity and weak ego-boundaries in black mothers are explicitly denied (see, for example, Wade-Gayles, 8–12; Joseph, 18–19; Collins, "Meaning of Motherhood," 7; and Joseph and Lewis, 94–106). Interestingly enough, in the work of African writers, mother-daughter relationships appear, more than African-American relationships, to be fraught with the kinds of difficulties and tensions which typify their white Anglo-American counterparts (see Davies, "Wrapping," 11–19; Christian, Black Feminist Criticism, 211–48).

9. Winnicott's notion of the "average expectable environment" has been widely influential, especially among family therapists, in formulating concepts of "normal family development" (Nichols, 183–205). However, I am not sure that this "average" is as frequently achieved as Winnicott's terminology would suggest. That is, Winnicott's "good-enough" mothering also may be something of an ideal.

10. Pauline learns this lesson on a previous job, where she is given the choice of breaking up with Cholly or losing her position. When she refuses to leave him, she loses not only the job but eleven dollars in pay her employer withholds. This is not the sort of lesson she would be likely to forget, especially when she is working for employees like the Fishers, whom she truly likes and who (in their own way) truly seem to like her.

11. I have discussed the role of anger as a liberating agent in Bennett, My Life a Loaded Gun (260–67).

12. While black critics emphasize Claudia's capacity for survival, they also note the damage done by her absorption of white values. See in particular Christian, Black Women Novelists, 138–53, and Awkward, 58–62. For all her obvious virtues, Mrs. MacTeer models this damage for her daughter. Not only is she implicated in the purchase of the "big, blue-eyed Baby Doll[s]" Claudia loathes, but also and perhaps more important, she joins "good" black society in condemning Pecola, who stands symbolically for all that Claudia finds hardest to accept in her own black identity (see Bluest Eye, 19–23, 158–60). Both these positions leave Claudia vulnerable on the score of self-love, as Claudia herself is the first to recognize (19–21). And, of course, it is this vulnerability that makes Claudia so exquisitely sensitive to Pecola's plight. In effect, she seems to be saying, "There but for the grace of God—and some good mothering and fathering—go I."

13. The points of similarity between French and American thought on motherhood and weak ego-boundaries have been discussed by Hirsch, "Mothers and Daughters," and Stanton, among others.

14. Chodorow and Contratto have discussed this re-idealization from a somewhat different perspective, in "The Fantasy of the Perfect Mother." Their discussion, published in 1982, was written prior to the publication of In a Different Voice.

15. Part of the difficulty with Jean Baker Miller's thesis is that the psychological qualities which she asks us to value most in women (connectedness, caring, concern for others) are also, she argues, the products of their social subordination. What would happen to women's "psychology," one wonders, if women had ready access to power? This is a question Miller does not answer, but it lurks on the margins of her text, as of Gilligan's, which ignores social issues altogether.

Chapter 8

The Diaries of Jane Somers: Doris Lessing, Feminism, and the Mother

Gayle Greene

Like it or not, Doris Lessing is still our most extraordinary woman writer and still in some sense our foremost feminist novelist. Though she has disavowed feminism, *The Golden Notebook*, first published in 1962, is unsurpassed for its depiction of "the position of women in our time" (579) and for its influence on a generation of readers. Margaret Drabble expressed the feeling of many when she hailed it as "a document in the history of liberation" (quoted in Showalter, 311), though others have seen it as "alienated 'from the authentic female perspective'" (Ellen Morgan, 63; Showalter, 311). In the three decades of her career, Lessing has continued to write fiction that centers on women, while also continuing to distance herself from the Women's Movement; and critics have continued to respond variously and contradictorily to her, some placing her in the tradition of "feminine sensibility" (Brooks, 104, 106; Rapping, 39), others finding in her novels "an aversion to the feminine sensibility" (Markos, 88; Sukenick, 99; Stimpson, 194; Gubar, 51).

I think that such divergent responses have their basis in Lessing's own ambivalence about female identity, an ambivalence that originates in her vexed relationship with her mother. I will use the Jane Somers novels as a way of looking back through Lessing's earlier fiction with a veiw to examining her attitudes toward female identity, the mother, and feminism. To be sure, Lessing has reasons besides her mother for dissociating herself from feminism— as she says in the introduction to *The Golden Notebook*, "the cataclysms we are living through" make "the aims of Women's Liberation look very small and quaint" (viii–ix). As her recent fiction indicates, she has despaired of the efficacy of political action generally. Still, the matrophobia expressed by many of Lessing's protagonists and her own disavowal of feminism can hardly be unrelated. My discussion raises further issues—the extent to which Lessing views the self as socially constructed or innate, and the evolution of her narrative forms.

With her revelation in the *New York Times* on 23 September 1984 that she had published two novels under the name "Jane Somers," Lessing blew the cover off one of the most fascinating literary hoaxes of recent years. The main reason she gave for this "little experiment" was her desire to make a point about the literary marketplace; she wished — as she said — "to highlight that whole dreadful process in book publishing that 'nothing succeeds like success'" (Goodman, 3). In the preface to the novels (published together as *The Diaries of Jane Somers* shortly after she came out as their author), she said that she wished to be "reviewed on merit, as a new writer, without the benefit of a 'name,'" suggesting that this would "cheer up young writers, who often have such a hard time of it." In this preface Lessing gave reasons more closely related to her own writing: she hoped that the pseudonym might set her "free of that cage of associations and labels that every established writer has to learn to live inside," "free to write in ways [she] had not used before." Most important for the purposes of this paper, she associates Jane Somers with her mother, suggesting that "reflections about what my mother would be like if she lived now: practical, efficient, energetic . . . conservative . . . a little sentimental . . . though always kind"—went into the creation of this protagonist and persona (xvii–xviii).[1] Though this suggestion comes as something of a surprise to those of us who quailed, as younger readers, at the terrifying Mrs. Quest, it is consistent with Lessing's reminiscences about her own mother in recent talks and interviews.[2]

Lessing's mother must have been on her mind in other ways, for, besides influencing her characterization of the protagonist Jane, the mother seems also to have been behind the ninety-two-year-old woman Jane befriends, Maudie. Not only is Maudie old enough to be Jane's (and Lessing's) mother; her name also happens to be the diminutive of the name Lessing's mother went by, "Maud." Lessing's mother was named "Emily Maud," but, as Lessing tells us in a recent autobiographical essay in *Granta*, she preferred "Maud" to "Emily" (59) — perhaps because "Emily" was the name of her own mother, a redundancy that must have reinforced Lessing's horror of "the direct line of matriarchy" (the term Martha Quest uses when she gives birth to a girl [PM, 151]).[3] If thoughts of her mother influenced her characterization of both Jane and Maudie, what *The Diary of a Good Neighbor* depicts, in a veiled way, is the situation of the daughter becoming mother to the mother and "delivering" her from life.

Lessing has only recently begun to speak and write about her mother. Though she has had much to say about her father,[4] her first personal statements about her mother occur in the 1984 *Granta* essay, "My Mother's Life," in which she admits, "Writing about my mother is difficult. I keep coming up against barriers, and they are not much different now from what they were [years ago]" (68). Yet, from the beginning, the mother has loomed large in her novels. Mrs. Quest in *The Children of Violence* is the prototypical "bad mother" of contemporary women's fiction and one of the most memorable mothers in all fiction. Given the autobiographical nature of Lessing's work, it is impossible not to associate her with Lessing's own mother, but Mrs. Quest is more than a personal failure; she is "the nightmare repetition" (PM, 77, 95), both victim and representative of recurring cycles of behavior—biological, psychological, social, historical—that threaten to entrap Martha, a nightmare of pain and guilt passed from one generation to the next. Lessing returns to the mother-daughter relationship more than twenty years later and again attempts to understand its personal and general significances, in *The Memoirs of a Survivor* (1974), which she calls "an attempt at autobiography" (dust jacket, 1974 edition). In *Memoirs*, a young girl—named "Emily"—who has been damaged by her relationship with a bad mother who has in turn been damaged by *her* bad mother, is given to the keeping of the narrator, a nameless "I"; the narrator, by becoming a surrogate mother to Emily and coming to understand the historical processes that have damaged them all, develops powers that "deliver" her and her world from the nightmare of history into the timeless realm of myth. This liberation requires, however, a framework of fantasy, for Lessing does not conceive of a way of breaking the chain of misery or "cutting the cycle" (PM, 95) within this world or the social realism that expresses it. Here, as in *The Four-Gated City*, the attainment of "something new" requires the move to "another order of world altogether" (*Memoirs*, 217) and to a reconceptualization of the self not as socially constructed but as innate and in touch with a transcendent reality.

In the Jane Somers novels, a decade after *Memoirs*, Lessing returns to the subject of the mother, distanced and deflected this time by a surrogate relationship *and* a pseudonym, and again attempts to confront this relationship, but from within the framework of social realism. I shall argue that Lessing's use of the pseudonym allowed her to deal with matters she could not confront as Doris Lessing—still-cathected matters related to the mother.

Lessing has always had a strong sense of what Nancy Chodorow calls woman's "tendency . . . toward boundary confusion." Like Chodorow, Lessing sees this tendency as originating in the mother-daughter relationship. Whereas the male engages "in a more emphatic individuation and a more defensive firming of . . . ego boundaries," the female "experiences herself . . . as a continuation or extension of . . . her mother in particular, and later of the world in general" and so tends "toward boundary confusion and a lack of separateness from the world" (Chodorow, 102, 110, 166–67, 112). This lack of separation or differentiation from the mother and then from others creates—according to Chodorow—boundary problems for women. But Lessing has always been ambivalent about what she thinks of this issue, seeing female boundary confusion at times as an advantage and at other times as a disadvantage.

In her first novel, *The Grass is Singing*, where the protagonist relives her mother's life and dies for it, Lessing's matrophobia is unequivocal—and the term "matrophobia" was coined in an essay on Lessing (Sukenick, 102). But the more autobiographical *Children of Violence* evokes a more complex response. Martha declares her determination "*not* [to] be . . . like her mother" (MQ, 10)—"I won't give in, I won't; though it would have been hard for her to define what it was she fought" (MQ, 19)—and reaches (as she later says) "for anything as a weapon in the fight for survival," banishing pity as "an enemy" which "could have destroyed her" (FGC, 218, 222), naming her "weapons" as "sexuality" and "intelligence," and identifying her intelligence as "masculine" (FGC, 230). But Martha also experiences the longing for fusion which is expressed in her mystical moments on the veld, the appeal of "the eternal mother, holding sleep and death in her twin hands, like a sweet and poisonous cloud of forgetfulness" (MQ, 24)—what Ellen I. Rosen describes as "a continued need for symbiotic attachment" (56) traceable to her mother's coldness. The guardedness that is Martha's most pronounced quality is a defense against her mother, as is the *persona* she develops, "Matty"—hard, cheerful, chatty, amusing. In *A Proper Marriage*, Lessing describes the "bastions of defence behind which she [Martha] sheltered" as a

> building whose shape had first been sketched so far back in her childhood she could no longer remember how it then looked. With every year it had become more complicated, more ramified; it was as if she, Martha, were a variety of soft, shell-less creature whose survival lay in the strength of those walls. (94)

But her efforts to defend herself against what Lessing calls a "female compliance," a "need to . . . melt into situations," leave her "locked into herself" (LL, 14); and, since they conflict with strong urges to merge with others, they leave her divided against herself, locked into the "cycles of guilt and defiance" (PM, 201) which govern her behavior with her mother, husband, and daughter.

In *Landlocked*, the fourth novel in *The Children of Violence*, Martha breaks these cycles by ruthlessly separating herself from those closest to her and learning to say "no." A recurrent dream instructs her to "keep separate" (14) the rooms of her house or parts of her life—separate from one another and separate from *herself*: "Keeping separate meant defeating, or at least, holding at bay, what was best in her . . . the need to say yes, to comply, to melt into situations" (15). She heeds the instruction of the dream by saying "no" to various men who attempt to control her: to her employer Mr. Robinson, who tries to persuade her to take a job she does not want; to Magistrate Maynard, who tries to bully her about Maisie; to her husband Anton, who wishes to keep her as his wife. But above all, she must separate herself from the pain of her parents and refuse even pity for them, lest they "get her, drag her down into this nightmare house like a maze where there could be only one end" (76), a nightmare house where people "sat around waiting for an old man to die" (197–98). Martha withdraws from the "physical awfulness" of her father's long illness and from the pain of her mother, of which she has occasional glimpses too intolerable to sustain: "Martha allowed herself to think, for a few short moments, of her mother's life, the brutal painfulness of it—but could not afford to think for long. It made her want to run away now, this minute—out of the house and away, before 'it' could get her, destroy her" (76). Lessing, of course, has a compassion for the mother beyond what Martha is capable of, as is clear from the poignant "Victory Day" section narrated from Mrs. Quest's viewpoint. But it may be that, behind Jane Somers's atonement for her failure to enter into her mother's painful experience—her mother's nursing of her mother, her death by cancer—is some personal regret on the part of Lessing for withdrawing from the pain of a mother whose life was one long round of tending the ill, whose "roses" (in the image from Mrs. Quest's nightmare; *LL*, 63) all turned to a medicine bottle.

Saying "no" becomes "a matter of self-preservation" and "self-definition" for the protagonist of *The Summer Before the Dark*, which, published nearly a decade after *Landlocked*, takes a similarly defensive view, though this time from the mother's perspective. Kate Brown is appalled at her "adaptability to others," at "not being able say no": "Her need to love and give made her call herself a dog, or a slave" (18, 65, 42). Her "midlife crisis" is in large part a revulsion at the very qualities she has had to develop as a mother: "Looking back it seemed as if she had been at everybody's beck and call, always available, always criticized, always being bled to feed these—monsters" (89). These repudiations are somewhat qualified as Kate comes to realize that she herself has been sustained by the process of feeding others, that "the invisible fluid or emanation" (45) emitted by women to make social relations work has also supported her—that "all her life she had been held upright by an invisible fluid, the notice of other people" (180). Nevertheless, her most important lesson is to say "no," to estalish ego-boundaries and separate self from others—a statement that is made in her hair: "what she hoped were now strengths, were concentrated here—that she would walk into her home with her hair undressed . . . now it was . . . a matter of self-preservation, that she should be able to make a statement, that she should be understood . . . now she was saying *no*: no, no, no, NO" (244).

Lessing's major works, *The Golden Notebook* and *The Four-Gated City*, offer more positive evaluations of female identity. In *The Golden Notebook*, Anna Wulf's boundary confusions become the source of strength and integration, whereas the bounded, defended selves of the males leave them divided and destructive. In this novel, Lessing articulates differences between men and women—"Because we aren't the same. That is the point" (44)—to women's advantage (as I have argued in *The (M)other Tongue*; see also Abel, 102–105). Though Anna deplores "women's need to placate, to submit" (484) and is threatened by "crack-up" because her conditioning as a woman has left her without resources to deal with "the end of the affair," her very vulnerability becomes a means to change. Rather than saying "no" and closing off, as the male characters do, she keeps herself "open for something," and her openness becomes a means to new creation—a "gap" which allows "the future . . . in a different shape" (473). Entering into the experience of the men she becomes involved with, taking on their sickness and pain, she learns to participate imaginatively in the lives of others and to wrest "out of the chaos, a new kind of strength" (467). It is significant that Lessing risks so positive a view of female identity in a novel from which mothers are absent. Anna's mother, dimly recollected as "somebody strong and dominating, whom Anna had to fight" (42), died when she was a child, and her surrogate mother, "Mother Sugar," is a Jungian analyst who supports her on her journey. Besides, Anna's own experience of motherhood has given her a sense of "everything in a sort of continuous creative stream" (269), a sense that enhances her capacity for compassion and extending the boundaries of the self.

In *The Four-Gated City*, Lessing implies a view of boundary fluidity, like that suggested in *The Golden Notebook*, as the source of strength and salvation. Though Lynda eludes the socially-prescribed female roles of wife and mother, her telepathic powers may be seen as an extreme form of female empathy, an ability to enter into experiences beyond her own, and the powers she and Martha develop in their "work" together predict the Catastrophe and assure "a future for our race" (643). As Christine Sizemore suggests, Martha "develops an ability to feel comfortable with fluid ego boundaries" and "to cross Lynda's ego boundaries" (178–79). Martha develops intuitive and telephatic powers like Lynda's by becoming a surrogate mother to someone else's children, for it is by assuming responsibility for Mark's family that she learns to read peoples' thoughts and tune in on their "wavelengths." But, again, Lessing suggests this possibility in relation to characters who do not have to contend with biological mothers; Lynda's mother died when Lynda was a child, and Martha's mother disappears midway through the novel.

However, Martha's relationship with Mrs. Quest—and this is the mother-daughter relationship that most nearly resembles Lessing's relationship with her own mother—remains one of several "loose ends" in the novel (586). Made frantic by Mrs. Quest's impending visit to London, Martha realizes that the pain she has repressed with regard to her mother has caused her to lose parts of her past and her self, and she sets about "digging out" (to use her term in RS, 85) cathected portions of her past, turning to Dr. Lamb "to give her back pity" (232) — the pity she had banished as an adolescent. But though she does retrieve her past and the feeling of pity, she never learns how to *act* on this pity, and Mrs. Quest's presence leaves her incapacitated, as it always has. Martha never does bring herself to embrace the repulsive aged body of her mother (285), and mother and daughter never communicate, except in the "look of ironic desperation" they exchange just before Mrs. Quest returns to Africa, and in their brief, unsatisfactory dialogue — "Then, as she vanished from her daughter's life forever, Mrs. Quest gave a small tight smile and said: 'Well, I wonder what all that was about really?' 'Yes,' said Martha, 'so do I'" (286–87). All Martha's nurturing is directed to the future — to Mark's children and then to the "new children" on the island, after the move to fantasy, at the end. But the mother-daughter relationship is failed, thwarted, dropped rather than resolved — or postponed until Lessing can return to it in another guise.

Lessing again portrays female empathy and compassion as the source of strength and salvation — though again in the absence of blood ties — in *Memoirs of a Survivor*, where the protagonist's compassionate receptivity becomes the power that frees her and her world from the nightmare of history. Though the protagonist does little more than observe and enter imaginatively into the experiences she observes, it is her sympathetic imagination that gives her the capacity to move beyond the wall into "another order of world altogether" (217), the fluidity of her personality corresponding to the thinness of the wall between this and the other world. Lee R. Edwards describes a "metaphysics of femininity" in this novel which sustains the protagonist's quest for "a new order, a new species of earthly communitas," and he sees the novel as the culmination of a movement "from fictions fascinated by the need for daughters to escape their crippled and crippling mothers . . . to tales concerned with figures who are themselves both mother and daughter" (236, 283, 240–41).[5] It would be nice to think that Lessing was becoming more generally optimistic about the powers of female identity. However, that *Memoirs* (1974) was published close in time to the bleak *Summer Before the Dark* (1973), and that *Summer* was published after *The Golden Notebook* and *The Four-Gated City*, with their optimistic assessments, make it impossible to trace a clear line of development. Lessing seems, rather, to remain ambivalent throughout, and critics who emphasize different sides of her attitudes are responding to real ambivalences.

In this context, we can see the Jane Somers novels as Lessing's return to the unresolved mother-daughter relationship and as an attempt to replay that relationship in a different key. In *The Diary of a Good Neighbor*, Lessing constructs a fictional situation which enables the protagonist to enter the perspective of a mother figure, to love and tend her and *act* on pity in the way Martha could not. As Jane learns to enter into Maudie's experience — and, by extension, to participate imaginatively in the lives of other old people — she is released from her bounded self and learns the intimacy that she risks in the next novel, *If the Old Could*, with Jill, Kate, and especially Richard. As in *The Four-Gated City* and *Memoirs*, by becoming a "good mother," the protagonist "delivers" or "gives birth to" herself — but in this novel, Lessing does not leave this world and social realism for the fantasy of another world.

Though at first glance the Jane Somers novels are — as Ellen Cronan Rose calls them — "a good read, densely realistic," with nothing of "the epistemological gymnastics of *The Golden Notebook*" (7), they are actually more complicated than they first appear. They include the stories of several women: besides Jane, there is Jane's sister Georgie, who, unlike career-woman Jane, has become a housewife and raised two daughters, Jill and Kate; Jane's friend and coworker, Joyce, torn between staying and working for the magazine *Lilith* and following her husband to America; Jane's younger coworker Phyllis, who marries her incompetent boss, Charlie; and the old women Jane befriends — Maudie Fowler, Annie Reeves, Eliza Bates. We learn about the past histories of these women and about their present lives, their families, husbands, children, and work. Their stories are interwoven, so that they comment on one another and comment on such subjects as youth and age, living with others and living alone, responsibility, commitment, work; and they raise such questions as the value of families, motherhood, marriage, male-female relationships, and female friendships; and the value of a life — "how do we value ourselves" (25), what *use* are we? *The Diary of a Good Neighbor* also investigates, in an unobtrusive way, some questions similar to those addressed by *The Golden Notebook*, as Jane ponders how to express Maudie's story, what literary modes best express it, and problems of memory, language, and style.

These novels concern the processes by which youth turns into middle age and middle age into old age. They include young people (Kate's nieces, Jill and Kate; Phyllis; the children of Richard, the man Jane falls in love with in *If the Old Could*) and old people (Maudie, Annie, Eliza). Jane is in the middle, in middle age, aware of the processes by which each stage becomes the next, able to remember herself at an earlier age and to imagine herself at a later. Jane watches younger women watching older women "for signs of processes that would lead to their being replaced" (46); she is able to imagine the steps by which Maudie let herself go (55); and, when her own back gives out, she is incapacitated in a way that makes her understand Maudie's helplessness. But whereas in *The Children of Violence*, Lessing's sense of life as process reduced everything to a meaningless repetition, in the Jane Somers novels, it makes life more meaningful, enhancing the value of what passes so quickly. Jane understands that merely "a bone the size of a chicken's rib" separates her from the helplessness of Maudie, and this sense of fragility makes her appreciate life as "a miracle": "I love—all of it. And the more so because I know how very precarious it is" (166). Lessing describes the Jane Somers *persona* as freeing her from "a kind of dryness, like a conscience, that monitors Doris Lessing whatever she writes": (*Diaries*, viii), and these novels do show more geniality and generosity than one is accustomed to finding in her fiction.

These novels are celebrations of life, of London, of its people. London is rendered in loving detail; its parks, streets, pubs, food, seasons, weather are registered with "wonder" and "admiration" (237), a "feast of possibilities" (165): "Oh, the good humor of this city, the pleasantness, the friendliness!" (198). "If the young knew," the unstated other half of the proverb from which the title *If the Old Could* is taken, is as important as the stated half of the proverb, for both novels concern what the young do *not* know: "I was thinking of them all [the young] as possessors of some treasure, but they disregarded it; a marvelous inheritance, but they did not know it; though warnings enough reach them of the vast deserts" (491–92). What the young do not know is what the old *do* know—to love that well which must be left ere long—though Lessing also suggests that neither the young nor the old know how to enter imaginatively into the experience of the other, and one of her central concerns is the failure of sympathy that fixes people within the limits of the self.

Most remarkably, the Jane Somers novels are celebrations of old people. *The Diary of a Good Neighbor* breaks what de Beauvoir calls "the conspiracy of silence" (2) surrounding old age and celebrates age in a way unprecedented in fiction: "Once I was so afraid of old age, of death, that I refused to let myself see old people in the streets—they did not exist for me. Now, I sit for hours . . . and watch and marvel and wonder and admire" (237).[6] Jane comes to know the value of life from the aged: "I could learn real slow full enjoyment from the very old, who sit on a bench and watch people passing, watch a leaf balancing on the kerb's edge . . . I love sitting on a bench by some old person, for now I no longer fear the old, but wait for when they trust me enough to tell me their tales, so full of history" (166). In fact, the same sense of life as process that in Lessing's earlier fiction reduced people to cliched expressions of what has "been done and said before" (PM, 34), in these novels humanizes people: "One day we will be old" may be (as Jane suggests) "a cliche so obvious, so boring" (21, 24); but it is our denial of this commonplace that reduces old people to "other" and so excuses our indifference and cruelty (as Simone de Beauvoir observes), whereas it is the recognition that "one day we will be old" that allows us to understand the aged as ourselves at a later stage.

This new empathy for the old is related to Lessing's reevaluation of her mother. Her reassessment of her mother in the preface—as practical, efficient, energetic, conservative, sentimental, kind—is paralleled by her protagonist's reassessment of her mother within the novel. Jane comes to admire her mother and even at one point wishes to be like her: "The doctors could not talk to me about what was happening to my husband, but they could talk straight to my mother about what was happening to her. *Because of what she was.* It was the first time in my life I wanted to be like her" (7). Jane's befriending of Maudie is an atonement for her withdrawal from her mother and grandmother (as Jill says, Maudie is "a substitute for Granny, you weren't nice to her, so you are making it up with Maudie Fowler" [23]) and from her husband's death by cancer, events which she had "not taken in," against which she "had armoured" herself (67). When her mother became ill, she tried to "take it in," but she still "couldn't do it"; "I hate physical awfulness"; "I couldn't touch her, not really . . . I could hardly make myself meet her eyes"; "I couldn't think of anything to say" (7–8). Her sister Georgie was capable of the physical and emotional intimacy she could not manage; their mother "held Georgie's hand. The point was, Georgie's was the right kind of hand," and their talk "was interesting. Because they were so involved in it" (9).

Jane's withdrawal from her mother leaves her feeling unreal, without "substance": "It must have seemed to her that there was nothing much there—I mean, as if *I* was nothing much" (8). Though she attributes her failures to who she is—"I had let Freddie down and had let my mother down *and that was what I was like*"—and though she says, "It is not a question of will, but of what you are," she *wills* herself to become something different and sets about changing, deciding "to learn something else" (11). Jane has always been "real" at work, at the magazine *Lilith*, where her life centers; there she is "the one" person she knows how to look for in any organization—the one who takes responsibility and makes things happen (45, 56). Entering into a relationship with Maudie, she sets about becoming that "one" in a friendship—learning to be present, substantial, and to have, like sister Georgie, "the right kind of hand" for holding.

Though Jane panics at committing herself to a relationship with someone whose need is so boundless, she enters it nevertheless, accepting the responsibility and adhering to the "promise" it entails (70). She learns to be capable of physical contact by washing Maudie and "lifting" her in response to her desire to be held, and she learns to listen to Maudie's stories, to participate imaginatively in her life, to *see* old people who were formerly invisible to her, to understand "the interest of their lives, the gaiety" (148). Through Maudie, she enters perspectives once closed to her and becomes capable of the sympathetic imagination that allows her to transcend the limitations of her former self. The punchline Jane attributes to Maudie in the story she tells of her just after her funeral—"You've helped me, and now I'll help you" (252)—suggests an attitude toward relationships generally. Jane counters the story Maudie's family tells of a Maudie who returned one cherry for one strawberry—a story which confirms their image of her as calculating and mean-spirited—with a story of Maudie as someone who, having found a coin in the street in answer to a prayer, returns to the church box the change left over from buying food, saying, "You've helped me, and now I'll help you." This line resonates beyond the immediate context to suggest a right relationship between youth and age, an exchange based on reciprocity which Jane comes to understand and fulfill.

This sort of entering into relationships with strangers in order to repair the ravages inflicted by family occurs frequently in Lessing's novels. In *The Four-Gated City*, Martha Quest "pays debts" to surrogate children which she has incurred by her earlier failures as a mother; and in *The Summer Before the Dark*, Kate Brown becomes surrogate mother to a young woman in a way that enables her to work through some of her problems as a mother. By means of such surrogate relationships, Lessing deals with a central ambivalence—her attraction to and fear of intimacy. On the one hand, she always portrays the nuclear family as stifling and destructive—as she does in the Jane Somers novels—and prefers to remain in her own life an "outsider on principle" (as Mona Knapp calls her, 2). On the other hand, she has a strong sense that life is rich and interesting only insofar as our connections with others are rich and interesting. As she puts it, "The only thing that really matters in life is not wealth or poverty, pleasure or hardship, but the nature of the human beings with whom one is thrown into contact, and one's relation with them" (SPV, 120). This tension leads her to explore, in her fiction, relationships which are chosen rather than inherited. One might see such surrogate relationships as providing radical alternatives to the nuclear family, as Rachel Blau DuPlessis (especially chapters 10 and 11) describes alternative familial arrangements functioning in twentieth-century women's fiction. A less optimistic reading would suggest that chosen relationships are simply safer than familial ones, since they are voluntary and have built-in limits. (It seems significant in this respect that nearly all the great loves of Lessing's protagonists—Richard in *If The Old Could*, Thomas Stern in *Landlocked*, Michael/Paul in *The Golden Notebook*—are safely married to someone else.)

In *The Diary of a Good Neighbor*, as in *The Children of Violence* and *Summer Before the Dark*, the protagonist enters into a surrogate relationship in order to set right a failed mother-daughter relationship. But Jane learns to say "yes" where Kate Brown had to say "no," as the very intimacy that once threatened the self now becomes the source of the self's substantiality or reality. And the surrogate relationship Jane Somers enters into with Maudie is more complex than most in Lessing's earlier novels, in that Jane becomes mother to the mother, and in "delivering" her from life, delivers herself from the isolation of the bounded self to feeling and relationship. Moreover, the relationship between Maudie and Jane resonates with a meaning that is more than personal: their exchange, with its return of kindness for kindness— "You've helped me and now I'll help you"—reverses the nightmare repetition, with its return of pain for pain, and establishes a right relationship between the generations.

In the second Jane Somers novel, as in the first, the protagonist similarly atones for an earlier guardedness—though, in *Diary of a Good Neighbor*, Jane atones for a failure of compassion, while in *If the Old Could*, she atones for a failure of passion, expiating failures with Freddie by enduring torment-ing and unfulfilled desires for Richard. Jane regrets "the girl I was once," "that cold girl, negotiating allowances of emotion, of sex" (277), and recognizes her former self in the guarded young women around her, especially in her niece Jill—"myself, at her age" (195)—but also in Phyllis, who can no more be asked for help than Jane could at her age. She wants to warn Jill against "locking up" such "treasures" (292) and weeps that she herself was so foolish (323). But the romantic relationship between Jane and Richard is less convincing than the central relationship of the first novel, between Jane and Maudie, which has the force of Lessing's regret and atonement for her mother behind it. Though Lessing seems to have intended the sequel to show the effects of Jane's "rebirth," she does not persuade with this recuperation of the romantic love she has so thoroughly repudiated elsewhere; it may be that she simply did not have sufficient material left to make a second Jane Somers novel.

Concurrent with the recuperation of romance is a reevaluation of other matters which earlier Lessing protagonists repudiated—romantic fictions, glamour magazines, and nostalgia itself. Whereas Martha Quest and Anna Wulf condemned romantic and nostalgic distortions in their pursuit of the truth, Jane Somers—who not only works on a glamour magazine, *Lilith*, but also writes romance novels in her spare time—welcomes romance because "the truth is intolerable" (151) and people need "escape" (140). Jane's enthu-siasm for romance, however, is qualified by Lessing's use of a graphic realism, and the qualification makes for an interesting complexity, a self-reflexiveness analogous to—though less elaborate than—that of *The Golden Notebook*.

Just after Jane meets Maudie and sees the squalor she lives in, she feels ashamed of working on *Lilith*, but she soon realizes that Maudie loves this sort of magazine, just as she loves her beautiful clothes; and she defends her romantic novel, *The Milliners of Marleybone*, on the grounds that "Maudie would love her life, as reconstructed by me" (244). In this "reconstruction," the powerful males in Maudie's life "value" and "cherish" her (244); the fantasy of this novel, as of romances generally, is that men behave gallantly and respectfully toward women, rather than exploiting and discarding them as has been the case in Maudie's life. Similarly, Jane's delight in the stories by which Maudie reconstructs her past implies an acceptance of the "lying nostalgia" repudiated in *The Children of Violence* and *The Golden Notebook*. The "coy, simpering" *persona* constructed by Annie Reeves (172–73) recalls the "humorous and gay" facade of Mrs. Quest (PM, 97) which so infuriated Martha, but this sort of fabrication is tolerated here, just as Annie's cliches (168, 171), the sort condemned as "lies, evasions, compromises" in *Martha Quest* (MQ, 7, 168, 171), are accepted as the way a mind deals with experience and approved of as softening intolerable truths: "I know very well what I heard from Eliza about her life is not at all the truth, probably nothing like it; and I commend her as I would the writer of a tale well-told" (153). "Lovely things . . . to think about" (112) are all old people have.

Although these novels contain an *apologia* for romantic novels, they are not themselves romantic novels. Of the two kinds of writing that Jane tries out as ways of representing Maudie's life, she may approve of the romantic — "I know only too well why we need our history prettied up. It would be intolerable to have the long heavy *weight* of the truth there, all grim and painful" (141) — but she uses a realistic record of facts and events to render that grim and painful truth, to render even the "unprettied," unadorned "freezing smelly lavatory" which Jane claims will *not* be on Maudie's mind as she lies dying (141). In the process, she contemplates questions like Anna Wulf's — "I wrote Maudie's day because I want to understand. I *do* understand a lot more about her, but is it true?" — and comes to the realization that she cannot transcend her own point of view (126) or put herself "into the place of another" (233). She wonders whether even her straightforward account may be a way of "presenting" for an "observing eye" (64), and she is bewildered by the shifts of liking, anger, and irritation, "the grit and grind of a meeting" (31), that make it so difficult to capture the quality of her time with Maudie. Though Jane defends romantic rewritings of reality, she undertakes in her diaries the "grit and grind" necessary to the hard task of understanding.

Elsewhere, however, the juxtaposition of perspectives makes for contradiction rather than complexity. These novels celebrate women — women's relationships, women's work, older women — while also denigrating "women's lib"; and these perspectives do not qualify one another but remain simply incongruous.

These are novels in which "Chloe likes Olivia," a world whose "emotional center of gravity"—as Rose aptly puts it—is women. In fact the only real love in *Diary of a Good Neighbor* exists between women—between Jane and Joyce, Jane and Maudie. Jane's friendship with Joyce is based on their work together, on a kind of wordless communication—"Joyce is the only person I have talked to in my life. And yet for the most part we talk in smiles, silences, signals, music without words"(64)—and on laughter: "those sudden fits of laughing, music without words, that are among the best things in this friendship of ours" (67). Jane also communicates wordlessly with Vera, in a "shorthand" that similarly grows out of shared work (105). Maudie's happiest memories are of working with women—at the hotel in Brighton (32–33) and at the milliner's workshop, "singing and larking and telling stories," all while she is being exploited by a lecherous boss and roughed about by her "man" (90–93). Yet when Joyce feels that she has "no choice" but to sacrifice her life to a husband who does not particularly want her, to leave everything and follow him to America, Jane thinks, "Well, women's lib . . . what do you have to say to that? What, in your little manifestoes, your slamming of doors in men's faces, your rhetoric, have you *ever* said that touches this? As far as I am concerned, nothing. . . . of—whatever the power men have that makes Joyce say, I have no choice" (69), "women's lib thoughts" "aren't the point; they never were the point, not for me, not for Joyce" (66).

This seems perversely obtuse, for, as Lessing doubtless knows, "women's lib" "manifestoes" are concerned precisely with "the power men have" that makes Joyce feel she has "no choice." But in these novels Lessing attributes the ills and inequities of the world to innate human nature and "the human condition" (223).[7] Just as the sisters Kate and Jill are inexplicably different, so Joyce has no choice simply because of *what she is*—"It is not a question of will, but of what you are" (11).

This analysis is contradicted by the central experience of the protagonist, who, not liking what she is, sets about changing. It is also belied by social structures depicted in the novel that explain "the power men have." Jane's interest in the way things "work"—"what is developing inside a structure, what to look for, *how things work*" (75)—leads her to observe, again and again, that it is women who do the work of the world, while men are given the credit and authority. Women run *Lilith*, while pretending that their incompetent male bosses do—first Jane and Joyce defer to Boris; then Phyllis, to Charlie. In the caring professions, "female" qualities of giving and empathy provide the "real structure" on which everything depends. The "home help" hold together their own homes as well as the homes they are paid to help. In the hospital, "it is the nurses who monitor the changes of need, of mood, of the patients, and the doctors who appear from time to time, issuing commands" (241–43). What Jane calls a "freemasonry of women" with their "humble" "multifarious" activities "keep[s] things together . . . [and] underpin[s] our important engagements" (199). Women working, "doing the same kind of thing at home as . . . at work" (249) — this forms the fabric of caring that knits society together.

Women do the work while men have the power, and "the power men have" is not gently wielded, but is a "stick they beat you with" (110), as Maudie asserts, who nevertheless clings throughout her life to a pitiful notion of "her man": "Such is the power of—?—that Maudie refers to that awful husband of hers, even now, as My man" (110). As both novels suggest, men have this power because women give it to them, acting against their own best interests by overrating "romance" and underrating their real ties to other women and to work. Following "her man," Maudie gave up the chance to work in Paris as a milliner, at a job she would have loved (92), just as, following her husband to America, Joyce leaves behind work, friends, and home — choices which both women live to regret. Similarly, Phyllis's marriage to Charlie takes her away from work she loves to raise a family she does not particularly want. (Against these errors, Jane's decision to stay and work at *Lilith* rather than follow Richard to Canada is right.) But part of the reason women cooperate in their oppression must surely be the enormous influence of romance novels and glamour magazines. In a moment of rare insight, Jane admits that magazines like *Lilith* actually help *produce* the situation which necessitates the escape which they then provide: "At this very moment a million girls tapping away at their typewriters . . . are dreaming . . . not of women's lib and emancipation — but of *I love you* and a wedding dress. . . . Why? For one thing, because of the efforts of *Lilith* and her sisters" (454). This suggestion is not followed through in these novels, however. The novels would support a feminist analysis, but Lessing does not bring the various strands of her thought together, and their celebration of women, disconnected from a larger perspective, remains a kind of female chauvinism rather than feminism.

Similarly, there is a discrepancy between Jane's analysis of aging as part of an inevitable "human condition" (223) and the suggestion that old age is at least to some extent socially constructed. What Jane observes of society's dehumanization of the aged — that *Lilith*'s "images of women" exclude old women, that old people are invisible on the streets — supports a view of aging like de Beauvoir's, that old age "is not solely a biological, but also a cultural fact" (de Beauvoir, 13, 10). Jane's insights — that Maudie ought to be allowed to die surrounded by family (222), that if Annie Reeves were with people it would ease the anguish of her "unused vitality" (424), that old people were better off in workhouses than in "homes" where "they die or go mad of boredom" (227) — suggest that age is made worse by the loneliness, isolation, and inactivity imposed on old people in this society. There is a flash of the old

Lessing when Jane expresses indignation at being thought "neurotic" for taking an interest in Maudie: "What has happened that, for someone like me, well off, middle class, and in possession of my faculties, to undertake such tasks without any necessity for it means that I am wrong-headed? Sometimes I look at the thing one way, and sometimes another: first, that I am mad, and then that the society we live in is" (221). But, unlike Lessing's earlier protagonists, Jane does not really see the world as "mad"; she is not really outraged that what she spends on hot water could transform Maudie's life.

There is also the question of Kate, Jane's loser of a niece. Kate is supposedly "innately" different from her winner of a sister Jill, who succeeds so spectacularly where Kate fails. Yet Lessing has analyzed the disaffection of the young in social terms in *Four-Gated City* and *Shikasta*, accounting for it in terms of a world so absurd and brutalizing that it offers young people nothing to connect to. In *If the Old Could*, young Kate and old Annie are both burdens on Jane, and the author of *The Golden Notebook*, who insisted that we see things in relationship to one another, would have seen them as related symptoms of a larger cause, as victims of a system that values young and old alike in terms of production and damages both by making them "redundant." An earlier Lessing would have agreed with de Beauvoir that "old age exposes the failure of our entire civilization. It is the whole man that must be re-made, it is the whole relationship between man and man that must be recast ... It is the whole system that is at issue and our claim cannot be otherwise than radical—change life itself" (543). But the Lessing who is Jane Somers no longer sees life whole or as capable of being changed.

The Jane Somers *persona* does release Lessing from "a kind of dryness" and allow for a geniality not customary in her fiction, a mellowness related in part to the reconciliation worked out with her mother and in part to her own age. These works are informed by a mood of acceptance and forgiveness like that of Shakespeare's late romances, a calm after storm. But one senses in this mellowness the "nostalgia" an earlier Lessing repudiated. Nostalgia is a prerogative of age, but it is also a forgetting (as Lessing once knew), and Lessing has done some forgetting—of the social structures that shape people and the connections between personal and political. (Forgetting was what I heard in her remarks at UCLA in 1983, when her dismissal of causes she had once passionately cared for—"The Communist Party has always been a pretty ghastly organization"—simply eradicated her own earlier commitments and selves.[8]) Jane Somers grows in sensitivity, but it is as though this intensification of feeling occurs at the expense of a broader perspective. In more ways than one, Lessing may have become her own mother, for the terms she applies to her, "conservative" and "sentimental," apply as well to herself: "sentimental" in the emphasis on personal sentiment at the expense of political analysis, "conservative" in the retreat from the political.

I read these novels knowing they were by Doris Lessing. I wish I had not known who wrote them, for this meant that I brought certain expectations to them, expectations that were disappointed. Lessing has made a point about how readers's expectations become writers' "cages," and I admit to being one who would put her back into the cage formed by my expectations. That cage, however, was paradoxically a larger space than the place she would escape to. I miss not only the political dimension and the intimations of relationship, but also the cosmic significance that is customary in her fiction. Unlike almost everything else she has written, these novels do not open on transcendence. Underlying their mellowness is resignation, even a despair, a sense that reality is both intolerable and unchangeable. Having accustomed us to wide horizons, Lessing pushes us back into the "terrible dark blind pit" of life (to use Martha's phrase in *Four-Gated City*), depriving us of all sense of "lit space," "light and thinned space," bright promise or "marvelous sweetness" from a place beyond (FGC, 41, 643). Though Lessing's fiction has always insisted that we (as she puts it) make "the effort of imagination necessary to become what we are capable of being" (SPV, 9), that we imagine a better world, the Jane Somers novels do not. However moving they are, they are actually as bleak as her other recent fiction—*The Good Terrorist* both dismisses all possibility of political action and mocks the efficacy of female nurturance, and *The Fifth Child* forfeits all sense of the shaping structures of society and asserts the innateness of self with a vengeance.

Notes

1. Lessing suggests that there may have been another personal factor behind *Diary of a Good Neighbor* when, in the afterword to *The Making of the Representative for Planet 8*, the fourth novel in the Canopus series, she accounts for her interest in the freezing planet in terms of her lifelong fascination with the Antarctic expeditions of Robert Falcon Scott—an interest she shared with her mother. She adds, almost as an afterthought, "Or perhaps something else was going on. I finished writing [*Making*] the day after the death of someone I had known a long time; though it did not occur to me to make a connection until then. It took her a long cold time to die, and she was hungry too, for she was refusing to eat and drink, so as to hurry things along. She was ninety-two" (144–45).

2. In Bernd Dietz and Fernando Galvan, "*Entrevista:* A Conversation with Doris Lessing," Lessing describes her mother as "in her way a feminist; in a talk at UCLA (10 April 1984), she called her "a kind of early feminist."

3. PM is *A Proper Marriage*, MQ is *Martha Quest*, RS is *A Ripple from the Storm*, LL is *Landlocked*, FGC is *The Four-Gated City*, and SPV is *A Small Personal Voice*.

4. The essay "My Father" first appeared in the London *Sunday Telegraph*, was reprinted in *Vogue*, and then appeared in *A Small Personal Voice* and *The Norton Reader*; and *Shikasta* is dedicated to her father.

5. Marianne Hirsch similarly describes a "double-voiced" mother-daughter discourse as an ideal: "The story of female development, both in fiction and theory, needs to be written in the voice of mothers as well as in that of daughters . . . Only in combining both voices, in finding a double voice that would yield a multiple female consciousness, can we begin to envision ways to 'live afresh'" (*Mother/Daughter Plot*, 161).

6. However, though Lessing shows the triumph of the old, "the interest of their lives, their gaiety" (DGN, 148), she nevertheless shows aging as a narrowing and a regression, a petulance and a paranoia. She does not show any of the old people in the novel attaining the greater compassion and generosity that she herself has.

7. Ingrid Holmquist discusses the development of this idea of the innate self in Lessing's fiction.

8. Eva Bertelsen's interview with Lessing, "The Persistent Personal Voice," shows Lessing rewriting her history with regard to politics, as I have suggested she does with regard to her mother. Ellen Rose suggests that the Jane Somers novels are "tinged with 'lying nostalgia'" (8).

Chapter 9

"This Is Not For You":
The Sexuality of Mothering

Judith Roof

"This is not for you": the daughter's paradox of the sexual mother, the punch line of her narrative of identity and differentiation. "This," the mother's desire, "is" for a moment within your grasp, knowledge, experience, but passes on, over you, is "not for you." Knowing it, you cannot have it. The story of your own desire generates theories of a barely-remembered fusionary peace—preverbal, preoedipal, utopic, innocent—the paradoxical sexuality of genderless innocence swathing the threatened incestuous homosexuality of the mother-daughter bond. In the sanctity of remembered beginnings, in their representation which is all we can ever know, "This is not for you" becomes "This was once for you," a way of admitting and denying the loss of the mother's desire, of living on with her, of fulfilling a continued wish with imagined traces of "already was" in the perpetual, impossible, illusive circularity of origins.

But "This is not for you" also begets a lesbian story: the tale of desire for desire. Here "this" is, but you cannot have it; "this" is directed elsewhere. Its presence proclaims and defers the loss that generates desire; its persistent denial provokes the desire that would be extinguished by its fulfillment. The paradox of "This is not" is the wish fulfilled by its nonfulfillment. While the wish for the mother is unfilled, the wish for an unfulfilled desire— the desire for desire—is sustained. Instead of evoking memories of Edenic joinder, the second explication of "This is not for you" casts the daughter's dilemma as a perpetually present absence.

These two parables are stories of desire I distilled from heterosexual and lesbian narratives of mother-daughter relationships. In this paper, I want to trace these stories of desire through their sources, first through presumably heterosexually-based analyses of mothering: Nancy Chodorow's *The Reproduction of Mothering* and Julia Kristeva's various accounts of the psychosocial operation of the mother, and then through two typical lesbian novels, Jane Rule's *This Is Not For You* and Rita Mae Brown's *Rubyfruit Jungle*. The purpose of this examination is to see, insofar as desire is imbricated in narrative, whether there is a difference between female heterosexual and lesbian narratives of the mother, what that difference is, and how that difference might help characterize representations of female heterosexual and lesbian desire.

To arrive at these parables of desire, I am making certain assumptions and choices. I am perplexed by what I see as a paradoxical relation between mothering theory as represented by Chodorow and Kristeva and the absence of the mother in lesbian novels; to understand this contradiction, however, means that I must compare the dissimilar forms of argumentative analysis and fiction. When I make that comparison, I assume that, despite their differences in purpose and style, both genres provide symptomatic narratives that reveal something about how the combination of the mother-daughter relation, desire, and sexual preference is represented. Even though Chodorow's and Kristeva's analyses are attempts to identify and explain broad cultural representations of the mother, they are also narrative depictions of the maternal phenomenon they are analyzing. Similarly, while portraying lesbian experience, Brown's and Rule's novels are also representations of a mother-daughter relation, though the mother is most often missing. Since narrative inscribes desire (another assumption) and since these narratives also overtly describe desire, these four works are double inscriptions of desire: the desire that shapes the narrative and the desire described by the narrative. I also assume that this narrative desire reflects sexual preference, though desire and sexuality are not coterminous. By comparing different inflections of desire as they operate in these two strains of narrative, we might understand why lesbian and heterosexual versions of mother-daughter history seem incongruous, what kinds of desire and self-perception are embedded in these two versions of mother-daughter history, and how that understanding might help define the relation, if any, between sexual preference and narrative.

The Sexuality of Mothering

Nancy Chodorow and Julia Kristeva confront and circumscribe the image of the mother in order to understand the mother's psychic and social functions. Starting from the imagined experience of the infant daughter, both Chodorow and Kristeva return to origins—to the infant's preoedipal maternal origin and to their own syllogistic source in Sigmund Freud's theories of infantile sexuality. Freud's hypothesis of an infantile sexuality eroticizes the mother-infant relationship, and, like Freud, Chodorow and Kristeva both assert and deny this sexuality. Described by Freud as fragmented autoeroticism, infantile sexuality is aimed toward a self not yet formed, toward disconnected sites—oral and "sadistic-anal"—that are not yet "'masculine' or 'feminine'"

("Three Essays on the Theory of Sexuality," 198). But this autoeroticism is not a solo performance: the mother (in Western culture at least) is the primary source of the stimuli that produce infantile sexual excitation. The paradox of this infant sexuality, however, is that it develops before both identity formation and the infant's recognition of sexual difference; therefore, for the infant this is a kind of asexual sexuality, while the mother of the pair is a gendered, sexual being. For Freud, who views from the perspective of the male child, the mother's entry into the infant's fragmented world establishes around her the primal paths of adult sexuality. For Chodorow and Kristeva, who see from the mother's perspective, the lack of differentiation, sexual and not, is the safe place before the trouble starts.

The trouble is sexual difference, associated with the infant's growing capacity to differentiate itself. Sexual difference sexualizes sexuality, outlaws the incestuous mother/child duo, and begins to organize the infant's scattered autoerotic drives. It is at this point of differentiation that Chodorow and Kristeva both diverge from Freud — at the point, not-so-coincidentally, of what Jacques Lacan terms "the mirror stage," the phase in an infant's development when it is able to begin to perceive its own illusory future mastery or integrated wholeness. In Lacan's formulation, this period not only presages a concept of a separate self, it also initiates the child into history, constituting the place where history begins — the child's, Freud's trajectory of human sexual development, Chodorow's theory of the circular reproduction of gender roles, and Kristeva's psycho-semiotic investigations of motherhood.

This mirror-stage point of beginning — a second origin — is actually in the middle of a chronology, though it is the point from which we are able to see the first origin. The mirror stage thus defies chronology and becomes the source of the origin. Operating in a temporal dialectic, the infant anticipates a future wholeness which enables a recognition of a previous chaos and fragmentation *as* chaos and fragmentation. The celebrated preoedipal lack of differentiation is actually a perceptual product of differentiation, both sexual and individual.[1] The chaos — only recognized by virtue of the passage through the mirror stage, with its concomitant introductions to both sexual difference and castration/loss — is the same as the utopic, nostalgic lack of differentiation seen by Chodorow as essentially feminine, clinging to the female throughout her adult life, and seen by Kristeva as outside language — the chora, the semiotic. Both Chodorow's and Kristeva's accounts of mothering, then, have the understandable but impossible impetus of a desire to return to a pre–mirror-stage, preoedipal, pregendered world. Caught, as they inevitably and paradoxically are, in a post–mirror-stage world, their ancient histories actually are generated from the misrecognitions of an inescapably gendered grid. While language and thought can only come from the point of the mirror stage forward, the third contradiction—that the origin of the origin is not original—inevitably and retrospectively revises representations of preoedipal chaos which become paradoxically and problematically gendered after the fact.

That the preoedipal is transformed by the "trouble" of sexual difference generates the heterosexual structures that make the sexualized mother and the reproduction of mothering a problem. Chodorow, interested in the psychic effects of the mother's representations, explores how the mother herself represents gender and mothering to her daughter, thereby reproducing attitudes about gender and inculcating mothering roles in the daughter. These gender messages and the mother's differing perspective towards sons and daughters operate asymmetrically on infants, producing in the son the "masculine" characteristics of independence, and creating a longer-lasting, more ambivalent bond with the daughter, thus reproducing exactly the gender ideologies of the culture. And for Chodorow, gender is clearly the primary factor influencing both psychological and social development: "Because they are the same gender as their daughters and have been girls, mothers of daughters tend not to experience these infant daughters as separate from them in the same way as do mothers of infant sons" (109).

Chodorow's mother, as agent of gender, quite literally reiterates the mirror-stage retrospective gendering of the preoedipal. Via the mother, the infant is always already gendered, its psychological trajectory determined primarily by the fact of this gendering. Chodorow assumes that infants will automatically internalize their mother's gendering of them, even before they can perceive themselves as differentiated from her. This "always already" gendered self helps Chodorow account for the asymmetries in male/female development via the oedipus complex, which for "girls is characterized by the continuation of preoedipal attachments and preoccupations, sexual oscillation in an oedipal triangle, and the lack of either absolute change of love object or absolute oedipal resolution" (133–34).

In her reading of the oedipus complex, Chodorow introduces the issue of sexuality, occulting, however, all sexual variations except heterosexuality as the inevitable culmination of the daughter's "oscillations." On the one hand, mother-daughter sexuality, suggested as one side of this oscillation, is dangerous, leading to a threatening incest: "given the organization of parenting, mother-son and mother-*daughter* incest are the major threats to the formation of new families . . . and not, equivalently, mother-son and *father*-daughter incest. Mother-daughter incest may be the most 'socially regressive,' in the sense of a basic threat to species survival" (132). On the other hand, because she assumes that mothering—conceiving a child—is the act of a heterosexual woman (or the heterosexual act of a woman), she limits her examination of mother-daughter relations only to the reproduction of heterosexual daughters. She is concerned "with the kind of social and intrapsychic relational situation in which . . . heterosexuality and . . . identifications get constituted" (113). The effect of this limitation, of course, is the creation of another circular reproduction of the reproduction she is exposing.

And the dangerous spot in this, the blind spot of Chodorow's "dream of symmetry," is the implied homosexuality of the mother-daughter bond, an implication she symptomatically ignores. The lesbian daughter is the one example which does not prove her case, and yet the lesbian daughter would seem to be an obvious result of the psychosocial structure she elaborates. Because, in her model, the mother injects gender into her relationships with her children, any sexuality between mother and child shifts from the auto-eroticism of Freud's undifferentiated infant to the potentially incestuous relation between two gendered beings. In the case of the daughter, Chodorow describes these erotic investments as "bisexual," and further avoids any lesbian implications by defining this bisexuality as the daughter's "emotional, if not erotic, bisexual oscillation between mother and father—between preoccupation with 'mother-child' issues [presumably the homosexual side] and 'male-female' issues" (168).[2] The few times Chodorow raises the issue of the mother as a primary love object for the daughter, her elaborations follow Freud's tortuous path to the father, the vagina, and "normal" heterosexuality. The daughter's path is triangulated through the father; her love for mother co-exists with, and is made safe by, a competing love for the father. What is dangerous in Chodorow's account, and what she studiously avoids, is not so much mother-daughter incest, but the possibility of its exclusivity, the possibility that such exclusivity might prevent the reproduction of mothering.

In fact, Chodorow deliberately has very little to say about those who escape being reproduced as heterosexual women. In her account, mother-daughter sexuality is clearly part of the path toward heterosexuality. She discounts that both mothers and daughters may not be heterosexual, confessing in a note that she ignores the possible effects of a lesbian mother, since her scenario is completely dependent on the "fact" of heterosexuality—"part of what I am talking about also presumes a different kind of cathexis of daughter and son deriving from her [the mother's] heterosexuality" (110n). She rarely acknowledges that lesbian daughters are generated in this heterosexual paradigm, a fact which might bring the whole model into question, or at least her insistence on a heterosexual effect.[3] The only time she uses the term "lesbian," she dismisses the relationship with an evasive reference to social pressure:

> Deep affective relationships to women are hard to come by on a routine, daily, ongoing basis for many women. Lesbian relationships do tend to

> recreate mother-daughter emotions and connections, but most women are
> heterosexual. This heterosexual preference and taboos against homosexual-
> ity, in addition to objective economic dependence on men, make the op-
> tion of primary sexual bonds with other women unlikely—though more
> prevalent in recent years. (200)

Though her reference to a specific "cathexis" deriving from the mother's
heterosexuality suggests that there may be other possible cathexes that ob-
tain from a mother with a different sexuality, Chodorow's conception of
mothers assumes a dominant heterosexual notion of maternity that necessarily takes place within clearly patriarchal organizations. For Chodorow, the
term mother refers to father, even if father is absent and even if mother has
no relation to him. Maternity is unquestionably the site of the merging of
sexual differences, even if that merging occurs only as an exchange of genetic
material. In this patriarchal scenario, heterosexuality (conflated with heterogeneity) creates maternity, which is then the effect of a paternal cause. If,
however, the mother were not predefined as heterosexual, if her maternity
were not necessarily created by paternity, then the cycle by which heterosexual
maternity is endlessly reproduced might be stopped. If we detach maternity
from heterosexuality, it also is disengaged from the strictly familiar versions
of the oedipal complex, leaving not chaos but a repositioning of maternity
outside the nuclear, familial, patriarchal organization with which it has inevitably been associated, and by which it has been defined as a position and
a relation more than as an activity. Conceiving mothering as an activity
makes it a function rather than the fate of a gender. And if it is a function,
then mothers can be (and are) lesbian, adoptive, unmarried, celibate, sterile,
grandmothers, aunts, hired nannies, or males. In any case, heterosexuality
may well reproduce the mother, rather than the other way around.

Like Chodorow, Julia Kristeva is interested in representations of mothering, but, while Chodorow's mother is an active messenger to the preoedipal,
conveying gender codes to an as-yet-undifferentiated infant, Kristeva's mother
is a turning point, embodying the mirror-stage paradox of plenitude and loss,
love and death. In *Revolution in Poetic Language*, Julia Kristeva essentially
reiterates the temporal contradictions of the preoedipal stage by postulating
two points of origin—the preoedipal and post–mirror-stage conceptions of history—as two coexisting, inseparable, metaphorical modalities. The first is
the semiotic "chora," a concept borrowed from Plato, connected to the maternal body, and characterized by the same motifs of fragmentation and lack of
differentiation attributed to the preoedipal. Kristeva describes the chora "as
rupture and articulations (rhythm), preced[ing] evidence, verisimilitude, spa-
tiality, and temporality" (26). The other modality, the "symbolic," chronologically succeeds the semiotic, but, like the mirror stage, precedes all represen-

tation, including representations of the semiotic. Connected to law, syntax, and language, the symbolic "is a social effect of the relation to the other, established through the objective constraints of biological (including sexual) differences and concrete historical family structures" (29). Simply, the chora is preoedipal and prelinguistic, but like pre–mirror-stage chaos, can be recognized only after the ideas of separation and wholeness have been imagined in a relation to the other. The chora reiterates the representational paradox of the preoedipal: it cannot be until it cannot be, yet, according to Kristeva, it still is. Wanting to sustain the chora and its maternal matrix, Kristeva posits the simultaneous survival of both modalities, made possible by the chora's continued amorphous atemporality. The chora can have a place within the symbolic, because, by definition, it is placeless.

Like Freud in his formulations of infantile sexuality, Kristeva connects this preoedipal phase with the mother and, via the mother, links the semiotic and the symbolic. The mother is the undifferentiated other around whom are organized the primitive paths of sexual excitation. But in Kristeva's description, where the mother meets the chora, there is a footnote which veils that which "situates" the mother "in space": the phallus. The transition point between semiotic and symbolic is achieved in metaphorically gendered terms; the mother becomes the phallic mother in an apparent gender paradox symptomatic of the symbolic's rendering of the chora. This phallic mother is posed against the surviving non- or not-yet-phallic mother, who also is associated with the chora and the preoedipal. For Kristeva, the mother, phallic and not, and her body which "mediates the symbolic law" (27) become *the* location of the mirror-stage temporal paradox, containing within motherhood more than one mother, extending her oscillating matrices from pre-oedipal to post-mirror stage, and becoming the other of the mirror, who ultimately injects sexual difference retrospectively back into representations of the semiotic. While the phallus can be construed as power rather than as a signifier of gender (or as both at the same time), Kristeva tends to slip into the terminology of sexual difference at this transitional point in the maternal matrix.[4]

Kristeva's regenderment of the semiotic takes place in her essay, "Motherhood According to Bellini," where she rereads the semio-symbolic functions of the mother in sociocultural terms, as expressed in Italian Renaissance paintings of Madonna and child. Prefiguring Kristeva's own path to the mystical conflation of psychoanalysis, religion, and the maternal, which culminates in her 1987 collection of essays, *In the Beginning Was Love: Psychoanalysis and Faith*, Kristeva's notion of motherhood in "Bellini" turns out to be mother as "a thoroughfare, a threshold where 'nature' confronts 'culture'" (238). At this threshold—this turning point—the "so-called 'Phallic' mother" is posed against that other "choric" motherhood which is "impelled *also* by a nonsymbolic, nonpaternal causality," a "spasm" of "pre-linguistic, unrepresentable memory" (239). What happens in this text is that this "spasm of memory" becomes gendered, becomes feminine, homosexual, lesbian:

> Such an excursion to the limits of primal regression can be phantasmatically experienced as the reunion of a woman-mother with the body of *her* mother. The body of her mother is always the same Master-Mother of instinctual drive, a ruler over psychosis, a subject of biology, but also, one toward which women aspire all the more passionately simply because it lacks a penis: that body cannot penetrate her as can a man when possessing his wife. By giving birth, the woman enters into contact with her mother; she becomes, she is her own mother; they are the same continuity differentiating itself. She thus actualizes the homosexual facet of motherhood, through which a woman is simultaneously closer to her instinctual memory, more open to her own psychosis, and consequently, more negatory of the social, symbolic bond. (239).

After her heterosexual marking, the "woman-mother" regresses into a homosexual facet, which, like the chora, is "a complete absence of meaning and seeing; it is feeling, displacement, rhythm, sound, flashes, and fantasied clinging to the maternal body as a screen against the plunge" (239–40). Though she admits this "homosexual facet," Kristeva envisions maternity as the effect of an encounter with sexual difference. For her, the only functional, differentiated mother is a heterosexual mother; the lesbian mother, a contradiction in Kristevan terms, disappears in "a complete absence of meaning."

In "Stabat Mater" Kristeva makes the mother-daughter relation even more rigid, limited, and, paradoxically, mystical. A final unarticulated shift to the side of the symbolic—signified in her sidebar choric lyric of the birth of a son—creates problems for the daughter. Only able to achieve singularity through maternity, women, unless they acquiesce to the masculine, are entangled in the group indistinguishability of the semiotic. The daughter's story is thus omitted:

> Among things left out of the virginal myth there is the war between mother and daughter, a war masterfully but too quickly settled by promoting Mary as universal and particular, but never singular—as "alone of her sex." . . . a woman seldom (*although not necessarily*) experiences her passion (love and hatred) for another woman without having taken her own mother's place—without having herself become a mother, and especially without slowly learning to differentiate between same beings—as being face to face with her daughter forces her to do. (261; emphasis added)

Though Kristeva leaves a slim opening in her parenthetical "not necessarily," the daughter generally cannot be separate or singular except as she is able to identify with the mother as same, *as* a mother. Sameness cannot be recognized unless the woman has encountered the difference intrinsic to maternity—the heterosexual encounter with masculinity. Thus armed, she can face off against other women and depart from the undifferentiated semiotic.

The woman who "repudiates" "the other sex (the masculine)" is the woman relegated to undifferentiated sameness where she cannot recognize an "other woman as such." Like the pre–mirror-stage infant who cannot recognize chaos *per se*, without maternity the woman either is destined to a kind of figurative autoeroticism or is subject to the symbolic, linguistic mark of the phallus. Among women:

> women doubtless reproduce among themselves the strange gamut of forgotten body relationships with their mothers. Complicity in the unspoken, connivance of the inexpressible, of a wink, a tone of voice, a gesture, a tinge, a scent. We are in it, set free of our identification papers and names, a computerization of the unnameable. No communication between individuals but connections between atoms, molecules, wisps of words, droplets of sentences. The community of women is a community of dolphins. (257)

If Kristeva's woman should see differences among women—see difference as not necessarily the category of gender—she is marked with a gender difference that removes her from the community: "If the woman aspires to singularity—she is condemned, by other women—as masculine" ("Stabat," 258). Does this not doom the woman who wishes to be singular among women, to recognize other women as such, and to accede to the subjectivity that enables a nonautoerotic sexuality? Kristeva's use of the term *masculine* is tricky in this context; if *masculine* means a representational rather than a literal masculine, then she is insightfully observing the representational politics for the depiction of lesbians, as her second use of the term suggests. But her first meaning of *masculine*, as the sex repudiated, implies not representation but biological difference. The woman-to-woman relation is erased in the transition from biology to representation.

A creature of representation, Kristeva's fulcral mother denies this third—this lesbian—possibility, resting as she does on gendered oppositions and differences that coalesce in the figure of the mother—the meeting ground of the sexes. The only way to individuation is through the mother—the figurative mirror stage. For the woman to pass through the mother, she must accept the Law of the Father—maternity, heterosexuality—or be condemned to a "countercathexis in strong values, in strong *equivalents of power*," to psychosis, to a "disturbance of the libidinal relation to reality" (Stabat," 261).

The circle of paradox is complete: biology becomes representation becomes a psychotic lack of relation between biology and representation. The homosexual woman refuses to relate properly—heterosexually—to the maternal (hence patriarchal) system; therefore, her libidinal relation to reality is disturbed. She is mad. Discarded, she is omitted from the story. What is not, then, for the reader of Kristeva is the lesbian's story.

What kinds of desire reside in these circular and paradoxical narratives? Both Kristeva and Chodorow set up contradictory, inter-reliant wishes: a desire for differentiation enabled by encounters with sexual difference, and a nostalgic wish for preoedipal unity with the mother. The coexistence of these wishes, like the coexistence of the semiotic and the symbolic, enables the illusion of a potential wholeness and fulfillment dependent upon an oscillation between preoedipal memory—the dream of the mother—and sexual differentiation—becoming a mother. Nostalgia for the mother becomes an unfulfillable desire which nonetheless is fulfillable via memory and representation—through Kristeva's chora. This fulfillable unfulfillable wish is displaced into a fulfillable wish—the desire for a child. And this wish for maternity encapsulates the mirror-stage paradox: by becoming a mother, the daughter can simultaneously identify—rejoin—with her mother, enjoy the differentiation endowed by her patriarchal marking, and enjoy a placental unity with her own child. Maternity has it all. Or does it?

Desire here is a circular wish that is desired, then fulfilled, then desired, then fulfilled in a cycle of deprivation and illusory gratification. Kristeva celebrates this cycle, but Chodorow critiques it, seeing it as an imprisoning desire generated by the mother. In her doubts about mother-daughter interdependence, Chodorow seems to want to remove the unfulfillable wish for the mother and replace it completely with maternity itself, as the site of daughterly independence and the place of the fulfillable wish. Denying the desire for desire in favor of an illusory dream of heterosexual fulfillment, Chodorow fixes finally on the father instead of the mother. She wants to break the cycle of the reproduction of mothering by redefining mothering as parenting—by inserting the father into the frustrating, desire-generating mother-daughter duo. With this solution, Chodorow displaces the nostalgic "demand for love" and its unfulfillable desire for the mother entirely into marriage, making both disappear into a heterosexuality that promises the illusion of fulfillment. But as she is unable to get rid of the sum of the daughter's desire, that desire, repressed, returns in her constant celebrations of the preoedipal moment. While her analysis places the mother-daughter preoedipal relation as the source of the reproduction of mothering, it also constantly returns nostalgically to this moment as one of peace and harmony. For Chodorow, as for Kristeva, the memory of the mother stands in the place of desire.

The Absent Mother, or the Desire for Desire

If heterosexual scenarios of maternity play on an illusion of maternal ful-fillment, many lesbian novels focus on the unfulfillability of desire — on the desire for desire. In a number of lesbian novels, the lesbian protagonist has no mother nor is she likely to be a mother. The absence of a biological mother in a remarkable number of lesbian novels (for example, Rita Mae Brown's *Six of One*, Jane Rule's *The Desert of the Heart*, Colette's *Claudine* novels, Isabel Miller's *Patience and Sarah*, Alice Walker's *The Color Purple*) denies from the start the nostalgic wish and maternal fulfillment of Kristeva's and Chodorow's stories, since from the very beginning there has been no mother. Lack of mother means lack of origins and vice versa. Beginning, instead, *in media res*, after mirror-stage differentiation, lesbian novels avoid a mirror-stage tem-poral paradox in favor of confounding post–mirror-stage history itself, by deny-ing the importance of origins, even as the protagonists seem to return to them.[5]

This Is Not For You (1970) and *Rubyfruit Jungle* (1973) are prototypical les-bian novels, characteristic of a genre which typically recounts, more or less realistically, fictional histories of the development of a lesbian protagonist or the course of lesbian relationships. *This is Not For You* is a chronicle of the relationship between the first-person narrator, Kate George, and her be-loved but difficult friend, Esther Woolf. Borrowing from the literary conven-tions of autobiography and epistolary novel, *This Is Not For You* is a retrospec-tive account of why a romantic, sexual relationship between Kate and Esther never occurs. Kate explains the failure as the triumph of her own self-denial and her unwillingness to take advantage of the compliant but naïve Esther. After Esther has cloistered herself in a convent, Kate begins to recount their fifteen-year friendship, from the start of their association as college room-mates, ostensibly because she likes "to remember" (4). The ensuing narrative does more than merely reiterate history; while recording the relationship be-tween Kate and Esther, it also reveals the fruitlessness of looking to the past for answers to questions of character and motivation. Only in the most lim-ited sense are either character's antecedents — Kate's mixed white and Native American ancestry and Esther's wealthy lapsed-Jewishness — relevant to the aesthetics of self-denial that rule the novel.

Rubyfruit Jungle is a *bildungsroman*, the first-person history of the life of Molly Bolt, who, like Kate George, is an illegitimate child of mixed ancestry (French and American), living with adoptive parents. The chronicle of a les-bian's gradual self-discovery, *Rubyfruit* follows Molly through childhood moves from Pennsylvania to Florida, her first high-school loves, her truncated Flor-ida college career, her adventures in New York City, and her final return to Florida to film her adoptive mother. While the narrative leads away from and back to Molly's origins, like *This Is Not For You*, *Rubyfruit* ultimately reveals their meaninglessness as explanation for anything other than Molly's physical attributes. Instead, the novel focuses on the exploits of the assertive, inventive Molly, whose personality is a given rather than something to be analyzed.

In both novels, the paradox of the lesbian story begins with the representation of the lesbian protagonist as an orphan, as illegitimate, as of mixed parentage, as lacking an original relationship with a biological mother, and as having no link to a patriarchally-blessed beginning. Because lesbian novels are cast as histories or *bildungsromans*, it seems that the initial focus on lack of origins, signified by the protagonist's orphan status, would make the solution of the mystery of those origins a partial explanation of the character, as it does in *Jane Eyre* or *Bleak House*. But in both *This Is Not For You* and *Rubyfruit Jungle*, genetic origins at first seem to be important but in fact turn out to be irrelevant. The lesbian narrative severs the connection between present and past and eliminates the past—the origin—as a useful explanation for the present. Sexual preference is detached from origins, either biological or psychological; no implicit or explicit connection is ever made between the lack of biological mother and the protagonist's sexual preference, except by Molly's adoptive mother. Lesbian fictional histories, thus, exist in a paradoxical relation to any notion of history; with origin denied or useless, the lesbian novel traces a history with no beginning, its writing urged on by a desire for a total picture—a desire already defined as unfulfillable. The fact that origins fail to answer the questions of history in lesbian novels suggests that origins themselves are lures away from the "key" or solution to the character which exists somewhere else—perhaps always already there. On the one hand, the novels trace history; on the other, they declare that history finally cannot explain either character or sexuality.

The uselessness of—and ambivalence about—origins threads its way through both novels. In Rule's story, Kate's particular brand of self-denying self-sufficiency might be read psychologically as her response to her lack of origins, though Kate claims that her origins were made irrelevant:

> I had my own stories to tell, being the illegitimate child of an Indian woman and a white man, a half-breed, adopted by an Episcopal minister and his wife who had already raised their own daughter. . . . My background was never mentioned to me by my adopted parents on the theory that I was to be made to feel no separation from them. And I half forgot it myself, growing up in the world given to me. (11)

Only half-forgotten by the "half-breed" Kate, this anonymous and illegitimate background might seem to incite Kate to an overcompensatory solitude, as if her background exists to make her feel separation rather than no separation at all. She almost but never quite hints that it is a factor in her behavior. In the end, Kate does not link her background or lack thereof to her lesbianism or to her moral choices or to the particular quirk in her personality that enables her to delight in an unfulfilled wish.

Molly Bolt also tantalizes us with a suspiciously nonchalant attitude about her lack of parents. She begins the novel in an apparently defensive analysis of the importance of origins: "No one remembers her beginnings. Mothers and aunts tell us about infancy and early childhood, hoping we won't forget the past when they had total control over our lives and secretly praying that because of it, we'll include them in our future. I didn't know anything about my own beginnings until I was seven years old" (3). Her cynical denial of memory is suspect, especially since the novel traces Molly from childhood to adulthood, when she returns home in what appears to be a quest for her own history.

This paradox of history in lesbian novels is related to, and perhaps creates and sustains, a similarly paradoxical structure of desire that typifies lesbian accounts. While the drive of conventional history is to know, lesbian fictional histories frustrate the possibility of total knowledge and from the start define the desire for mastery as unfulfillable. Not fulfilling the desire to know sustains desire, continues it, so that desire, like history, is a paradox: to desire is to desire not to have a desire fulfilled; it is the desire for an unfulfilled desire.

This Is Not For You is replete with paradoxes of this kind: the paradoxical desire for an unfulfilled desire, the protagonist's desire for Esther, and the protagonist's depiction and sustenance of desire in her writing. As the history of an unfulfilled relationship (as opposed, for example, to the story of unrequited love), Kate's account embodies a desire for Esther that is never explicit but is assumed almost from the beginning. This desire is textual, created and sustained by a narrative shaped in the quest to understand this desire which is not directly depicted. The connection among the desire to know, the desire to see, and the desire of the text is embodied in the title, which operates as a paradox on all of these levels. "This" refers to the text itself, to the explanation offered the reader, to the lesbian love felt by Kate, to the manner in which Kate has decided to live this love. In all, what is offered both is and is not; the text is not for Esther, the lesbian love Kate has for Esther is not for Esther to share, Kate's self-denial is not the way Esther should live, the history provides the reader with few answers, the desire it embodies is not named or described; yet in each case the opposite is equally true. The paradox "This is not for you" is the paradox of a desire fulfilled by its unfulfillment, by remaining a desire, a question. Paradoxically, then, in its nonfulfillment, the desire for desire is fulfilled.

Like Kate George, self-sufficient Molly Bolt has a series of lovers, all of whom are rejected, either because of Molly's career or because of her personal morality. Unlike Kate, Molly has no single love like Esther to catalyze her desire for an unfulfilled wish. She quickly loses interest in the lovers she does have; when her desire is fulfilled, it fades as desire. Instead, Molly's dream is for a career as a film-director, a singular impossibility that remains as her unfulfilled wish at the end of the novel. In her final summation—a wish-list—Molly says, "I wished I could get up in the morning and look at the day the way I used to when I was a child. I wished I could walk down the streets and not hear those constant, abrasive sounds from the mouths of the opposite sex. Damn, I wished the world would let me be myself. But I knew better on all counts. I wish I could make my films. That wish I can work for" (246). While Molly accepts the impossibility of going back, of returning to origins, signified by her use of the past tense "wished," her unfulfilled desire remains in the present, potentially fulfillable, and important because it is a desire that is presently unfulfilled. In this way Molly sustains desire. Both Kate and Molly are self-sufficient women who place careers ahead of love but who are left with a wish for a wish, a "this is not for you" that is a future rather than a past they know they cannot return to.

Structured around a desire for a desire, both novels lead to an absence: in *This Is Not For You*, the absence is Esther, who signifies Kate's desire. In *Rubyfruit*, Molly's desired film-making career stands for absence in two ways: not only is she unlikely to achieve it, but making film has already led her back to the mother and the story of her origins: the place of absence. Both novels begin with this absence, a lack in the place of the mother, and the importance of this originary lack is consistently denied. Their descriptions of the maternal reveal this structuring absence located in the place of the mother. Kate describes her adoptive mother as "old enough to be my grandmother" and as knowing "too little about the world to discover the promises to exact" (9). Though this mother is depicted as distant and kind, for most of the novel she is suffering from the effects of strokes and quite literally is not all there. And in *This Is Not For You*, no memory of a biological mother is evoked to fill the space. In *Rubyfruit*, Molly's adoptive mother constantly reminds Molly that she is not in fact her mother, and complains to her husband, "I'll never know what it's like to be a real mother" (40). And even at the end of the novel, when Molly returns to reclaim her origin, she finds that her biological mother, Ruby, looked and was nothing like her: "You don't look a whit like Ruby except you got her voice, exactly" (235). With nothing but voice from her mother, Molly's presence, bravado, athleticism, and artistic fervor all come from her father, a French Olympian. Even though Molly makes peace with her adoptive mother, the resolution constitutes the film that begins Molly's career and ends her childhood. When the film is shown, it is greeted with silence.

But while the protagonists have no memories of their biological mothers, and though the antecedents provided by the identities of these mothers are only superficial ones relating to their daughter's physical attributes, in both novels, the daughters are either told or know the rudimentary facts of their birth-mothers' circumstances. Kate's and Molly's biological mothers are both heterosexual outlaws; Kate's Indian mother bears a child begotten with a white man, and Molly's mother, an unruly, rebellious girl, conceives Molly out of wedlock with a "foreigner." In each case, the mother's sexuality is suspect; indubitably heterosexual, these mothers break patriarchal rules of propriety. The disappearance of these overly-sexed mothers and the absence and distance of adoptive mothers does break any cycle by which mothering (and heterosexuality) is reproduced. Not as causes of their daughters' lesbian sexuality but rather as reasons for their motherlessness, the mothers' active sexuality and patriarchal transgressions are remote precursors of their daughters' lesbian desire.

The insistent appeal to maternal absence in these novels suggests the real importance of the missing mother as the original model for unfulfilled desire, as hovering behind the characters' denials of their desire and of their beginnings. If we see the relationship to the mother as one of lack instead of as the plenitude suggested by Chodorow and Kristeva—if these lesbian stories privilege the moment of separation from the mother rather than the time of unity with her—we can see the genesis of a hysterical (defined by Freud as woman desiring woman) desire, as opposed to the nostalgic desire that characterizes heterosexual accounts of mothering. Whereas the heterosexual accounts privilege the illusion of a desire fulfillable via maternity, lesbian stories situate desire as fulfillable only by desire itself. These different emphases reflect not radically different structures of desire, but different positions within the same structure. The difference in position between heterosexual and lesbian accounts has to do with their different placement of the mirror stage and the ensuing problem of individual and sexual differentiation. Kristeva and Chodorow reproduce a mirror-stage dialectic, seeking a pre-differentiated state from a post–mirror-stage position. The lesbian accounts erase the preoedipal and focus instead on an already differentiated and very independent protagonist daughter, where the lack represented by the absent mother is displaced into the lack constituting desire itself. The heterosexual accounts' oscillations around the mirror stage result in a notion of difference defined as sexual difference; woman are different from men, but not from one another, because in those stories femaleness is located before the mirror stage, in the place of sameness, and maleness is located after the mirror stage, in the world of differentiation. Lesbians' post–mirror-stage conception of difference situates difference between individuals, male or female, rather than privileging sexual difference as the primary difference.

The differing shapes of female heterosexual and lesbian desire suggest that the differences in the narratives and their interpretations have to do with differing perceptions of the locations of the sexualities in relation to one another. While clearly the two are not in fact completely separate, in heterosexual scenarios, lesbianism is depicted as immature—as a stage, as pre-oedipal, as undifferentiated and therefore unsatisfiable—while heterosexual relations are seen as mature, with potential for fulfillment. In this convention, lesbians are portrayed often as crazy, self-destructive, unfulfilled, and/or travesties of masculinity. Lesbian narratives portray lesbianism as the act of a completely independent, self-defined, but marginal woman whose fulfillment comes in the understanding that there is no such thing as fulfillment, that desire perpetuates desire. These same narratives depict heterosexuality as a difficult deception that ends in a fairly peaceful acquiescence to a *status quo* of nonfulfillment or death.

These differing depictions of desire have to do, finally, with questions of the operation of desire in narrative. If, as Teresa de Lauretis observes in *Alice Doesn't*, narrative is shaped by an oedipal desire for completion and mastery, only female heterosexual narratives would come close to fulfilling that narrative desire, while lesbian narratives would thwart it. But just as humans rarely exhibit purely heterosexual or homosexual desires, so narratives might inscribe conflicting and incongruent desires. The mixture of heterosexual and lesbian desire in many novels by women may account in part for the kind of unresolvable tension in women's writing that prevents it from easily conforming to oedipal expectations. Instead of reflecting "pure" theoretical trajectories derived from heterosexual or homosexual texts, these narratives present a confused mixture which reproduces not only the varied tensions of desire/fulfillment or desire for desire, but also a tension among these two and the variants that fall between them. The interplay of these desires in such novels as Virginia Woolf's *Mrs. Dalloway*, Gloria Naylor's *The Women of Brewster Place*, Djuna Barnes's *Nightwood*, and Toni Morrison's *Sula* may help account both for their fascination and for the difficulties we encounter in characterizing them as they mix different patterns of desire or different stages in the same pattern.

It is also true that not all lesbians nor all heterosexuals will operate within the parameters of one or another desire; cross-desire identification permits a wider, more dynamic interplay of desire and narrative than the models imply. If desire is shaped differently according to gender and sexual orientation, then it may differ in respect to other criteria as well. As the terms multiply, so do the varieties of operations of desire. This possibility complicates any simple correlations among gender, sexuality, reading identifications, and either characters or trajectories of desire. The reader's desire in relation to the desires that shape the narrative also complicates economies of desire as they weave through text and reader, producing, rather than harmony, a discordant tension between reader and text that produces yet another level of desire—the reader's desire for the text and the reader's desire to change the shape of the narrative to reflect or inscribe other desire.

All of this suggests that, insofar as narrative is driven by desire, the idea of a standard, monolithic oedipal narrative is too narrow for an adequate understanding of narrative. Given the possibility that there are many different shapes of desire, the fact that the oedipal trajectory is so often dominant—the only one recognized—reveals the cultural hegemony of the heterosexual and the patriarchal. We need to recognize the multiple shapes of desire that drive and shape narrative in order to read differences themselves; and, by reading those differences, we may escape from the oedipal to new scenarios of desire.

Notes

1. In *Reading Lacan*, Jane Gallop explicates the mirror stage in this way, emphasizing the mirror stage's role in relation to individual conceptions of history and subjectivity.

2. Jacqueline Rose observes in her "Introduction" to Lacan, *Feminine Sexuality*, that Chodorow displaces "concepts of the unconscious and bisexuality in favour of a notion of gender imprinting. . . . The book sets itself to question sexual *roles*, but only within the limits of an assumed sexual *identity*" (37, note 4). Rose's analysis is another way of accounting for Chodorow's omission of the factor of sexual orientation, if in fact that orientation is a product of the unconscious. In Chodorow's account, lesbianism cannot exist because it cannot be created.

3. Adrienne Rich, in "Compulsory Heterosexuality," questions Chodorow's assertion about the changing prevalence of lesbian relationships: "Is she saying that lesbian existence has become more visible in recent years (under capitalism, socialism, or both?) and that consequently more women are rejecting the heterosexual 'choice'?" (636). See also Shirley Nelson Garner's discussion of the relationship between heterosexuality and the use of psychoanalytic paradigms in "Feminism, Psychoanalysis, and the Heterosexual Imperative."

4. Jane Gallop discusses Kristeva's adoption of the phallic mother at length in her essay, "The Phallic Mother: Fraudian Analysis," in *The Daughter's Seduction*.

5. While it is true that many novels written by women depict the protagonist as an orphan, the difference between contemporary lesbian novels and other women's novels lies in the way the lesbian novels make this originary lack irrelevant rather than making the discovery of origins the way to matrimony and maternity. The orphan pattern in contemporary lesbian novels may also represent the daughter's story; fiction by or about lesbian mothers may present a different paradigm of desire. The specific problems, perspectives, and politics of lesbian motherhood is matter for a different essay.

Chapter 10

Adoptive Mothers and Thrown-Away Children in the Novels of Louise Erdrich

Hertha D. Wong

Native American Feminism, Contemporary Theories of Mothering, and Chippewa Identity

For many years now, women of color have insisted that their experiences and concerns differ from those articulated by "mainstream" feminism, which generally focuses on white, middle-class women. "If women are typically muted within their own culture even when they constitute a demographic majority," points out Roberta Rubenstein, "then women of ethnic minority groups are doubly muted. Both gender and ethnic status render them 'speech-less' in patriarchy" (8). In fact, though, many American Indian women reject a feminism that they perceive as irrelevant to the realities of Native American female experience. Many indigenous women "cannot afford the luxury of feminist goals because they must devote their energies to keeping families intact, getting jobs, and fighting the political battles of their people" (Bataille and Sands, 129). Perhaps, according to Sioux anthropologist Bea Medicine, "Indian women do not need liberation . . . they have always been liberated within their tribal structures" (Bataille and Sands, vii). Indeed, many anthropologists have speculated that native women have had a less traumatic transition than men under colonialism, because their routines, duties, and consequent self-images have been less drastically altered than those of males. Beginning in the late nineteenth century, men were forbidden to hunt or to perform religious ceremonials and thus were forced to change their fundamental activities, while women continued to feed and care for their families (Lurie, 101), or at least what remained of their families. Furthermore, Native American women long have been associated with the continuance of tribal tradition, both through childbearing and through transmission of cultural values in stories. Native American feminists like Beth Brant challenge the "romantic fantasies" of indigenous women as "earth mother" or helpess "victim." "We are organizers," she says, "we are freedom fighters, we are feminists, we are healers. This is not anything new. For centuries it has been so" (12–13).[1]

In *The Sacred Hoop*, Paula Gunn Allen presents a historical consideration of Native American spiritual and cultural notions of the female. Allen goes so far as to insist that sexism was imposed on often matriarchal Native American cultures by Euroamericans who brought their patriarchy along with Christianity, whiskey, and smallpox. In fact, contrary to many ethnographic reports, in pre-Columbian times indigenous women held important and honored roles in many tribes—as political leaders, warriors, healers, and mothers. In addition, Allen reclaims the understanding that, as she says: "Woman is the sun and the earth; she is grandmother; she is mother; she is Thought, Wisdom, Dream, Reason, Tradition, Memory, Deity, and Life itself" (268). Allen is referring specifically to Keres tradition, but many other tribes believed in the power of woman-mother-earth as well.

Unlike these Native American notions of female roles, contemporary theories of mothering, generally based on Western assumptions, emphasize how gender roles are constructed biologically and socially. Nancy Chodorow notes that girls feel more empathy for and more connection to other people than do boys—that is they have a greater "relational potential" (166–67). In other words, "the basic feminine sense of self is connected to the world, the basic masculine sense of self is separate" (169). Because women are "almost universally in charge of infant and early child care," argues Dorothy Dinnerstein, gender-role differentiation is a direct response to the mother (26). For instance, as each child gains a distinctly individual identity, he or she becomes conscious of being separate from mother. A male child, however, identifies increasingly with his father and correspondingly less with his mother, while a female child continues to identify with her mother. While the daughter recognizes *herself* in her mother, the son recognizes an-*other*. The result, according to Chodorow, is a "greater ambivalence and confusion over ego boundaries" for females, and thus "girls come to define themselves more in relation to others" (93).

This may be true for Western cultures, but what about Native American cultures, which, from a Euroamerican perspective, appear to be female-centered because they value interconnections rather than ruptures, cooperation rather than individualism? Of course, it is simplistic, not to mention ethnocentric, to claim that any culture has a gender affiliation, since such an assertion assumes a particular cultural understanding of gender. Certainly cultures vary in their notions of what appropriate gender characteristics might be.[2] My point is only that there are correspondences between what feminists have discussed as distinctly "female" and what Native Americans have described as "Indian." For example, for a Native American male or female, defining oneself "in relation to others" is not "confusion over ego boundaries," but rather a realistic notion of the intricate interrelatedness of each individual with others. Images of the finely woven web spun from Grandmother Spider and the sacred hoop of the people attest to this.

Thus, one key distinction between Euroamerican and Native-American women is that the former often define themselves primarily by gender, whereas the latter, says Paula Gunn Allen, are "primarily defined by . . . tribal identity" (43). Not surprisingly, then, inheritance and kinship are the foci of "many novels by ethnic women" (Dearborn, 32). In fact, for many American Indian women poets, notes Dexter Fisher, "Feminism is synonymous with heritage, a search for one yields a concern with the other" (13). Other scholars have pointed out that, while Euroamerican women tend to write about struggles of will and identity between mother and daughter, Native American women seem to focus on harmonious relations between and among female family members. Among Anglo women, notes Patricia Clark Smith, it seems "common for daughter to regard mother, mother to regard daughter, as some sort of stranger—unreachable, unknowable, and threatening to her identity" (113). While Euroamerican mother-daughter relationships mirror Chodorow's model, this is less true in the works of Native American women poets. In fact, says Smith, "The image of a woman relative as an alien being simply does not appear in American Indian women's poetry" (114). Instead, the Native American writers "see personal discord between women as a matter of cultural alienation" (114), arising from the conflict between traditional family values and the cold facts of contemporary life. The native woman knows that her grandmother, maybe her mother, is a link to an older tribal heritage. A disrupted relationship with a mother ruptures the daughter's bond with her people; a broken relation with a daughter severs the mother's connection to the future (both cultural and personal).

The breakdown of tribal social structures (such as family and clan relationships) is a reality for indigenous people—the result, in part, of a sustained assault on tribal integrity by the United States government. Thus, despite claims that Native American women poets present positive relationships among female relatives, there are numerous instances of troubled mothering relationships in novels by Indian women.[3] In fact, "in the twentieth century," claims Judith A. Antell, "the loving Indian mother as a significant literary character disappears" (216). Such strained mothering relationships are central to Louise Erdrich's novels.

The novels of Louise Erdrich, who is of German-American and Turtle Mountain Chippewa descent, highlight the complex and strained family and community relationships in both Chippewa and Anglo cultures. *Love Medicine*, *The Beet Queen*,, and *Tracks*, three novels of a planned tetralogy, tell the multivoiced story of several generations of Chippewa[4] and white relatives in North Dakota. Mothers—both Native American and Euroamerican, individual and collective—are central throughout. The proliferation of mothers in Erdrich's novels—absent mothers, all-too-present mothers, abusive mothers, silent mothers—reflects the Chippewa emphasis on the family as "the basic political and economic unit in the woodland and the primary source of personal identity" (Vizenor, ix). Basil Johnston elaborates on what he sees as the fundamental Chippewa sense of identity and its source in extended family (totem groups) and community: "Men and women preferred to regard themselves as members of a totem and then a community. Strangers, when they met, always asked one another, 'Waenaesh k'dodaem?' (What is your totem?); only afterwards did they ask, 'Waenaesh keen?' (Who are you?)" (59). Most Chippewa communities, then, "consisted of extended family members united by a common totem"; a "totem animal [served as] each person's family mark" (8, 78). According to ethnographers, even the Chippewa understanding of personal identity is "more inclusive" than the Euroamerican notion, since it encompasses "both human and 'other-than-human' persons" (e.g., spirits, humans, animals, and inanimate objects) (Overholt and Callicott 143). "Society," they conclude, "is cosmic in scope" (143). Feeling "at home," in a traditional sense, is sensing one's relationship to one's social, geographic, and cosmic networks, as well as to one's immediate and extended family. Mother is not merely one's biological parent; she is all one's relations (male and female, human and animal, individual and tribal); and she is connected to the earth. Erdrich, however, is not a "traditional Chippewa," and, with one or two exceptions, neither are her characters. Having had their totem/family identities destroyed by Euroamerican domination, these characters must reformulate notions of self, family, and community. In Erdrich's novels, women, and mothers in particular, feel the tremendous responsibility of family/clan relationsips which, although often troubled, sustain both individual and community.

Love Medicine

"We had been in one body then, yet she was a stranger."

Love Medicine (1984) tells the story of several Chippewa families on and near a reservation in North Dakota (see figures 1 and 2). Multiple points of view and voices provide an achronological, multidimensional account covering fifty years, 1934–84. Assorted narrators in The Beet Queen (1986) tell a somewhat parallel series of personal stories from the period 1932–72, focusing on the lives of several white and mixed-blood Indian characters in Argus, a small town in North Dakota. In Erdrich's most recent novel, Tracks (1988), only two individuals, Nanapush and Pauline, relate the history of several Chippewa family members from 1912 to 1924. Community and family relationships, particularly mothering relationships, predominate. Family his-

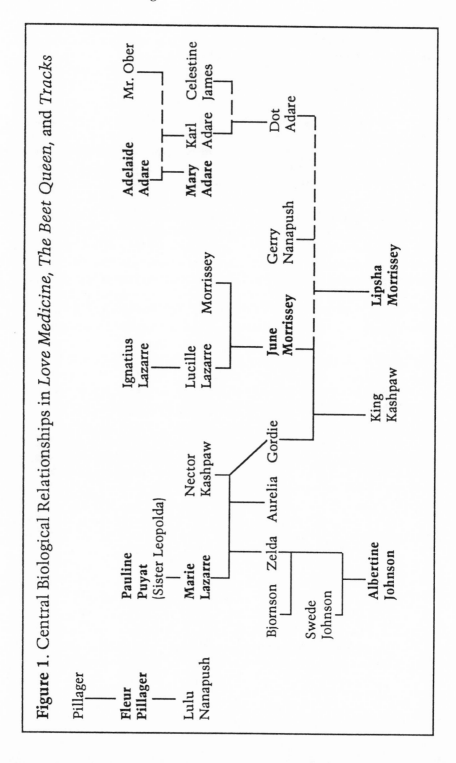

Figure 1. Central Biological Relationships in *Love Medicine, The Beet Queen,* and *Tracks*

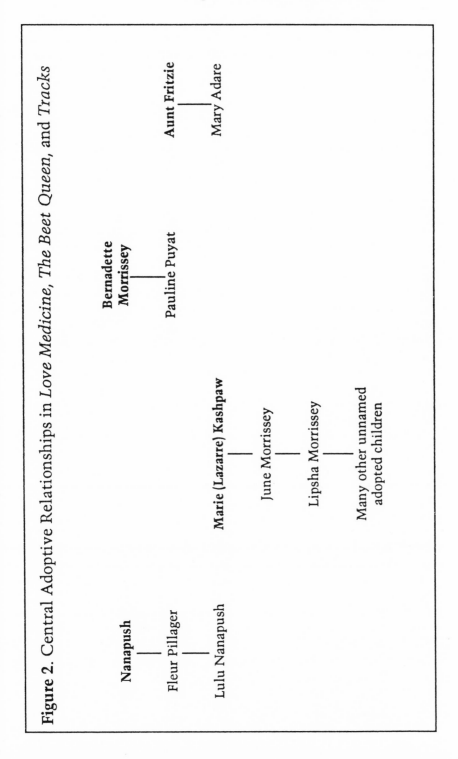

Figure 2. Central Adoptive Relationships in *Love Medicine*, *The Beet Queen*, and *Tracks*

tory is narrated over generations from multiple points of view, highlighting changes in "mothering" throughout the generations, as women meet challenges to their personal, ethnic, and cultural identities.

Erdrich's novels are filled with orphans, thrown-away children, adoptive (by choice or circumstance rather than by law) mothers, and quests for or denials of one's mother. With the exception of Lulu, whose eight sons adore her, the central women in *Love Medicine* are all troubled by strained mothering relationships. Albertine, a mixed-blood and her mother Zelda have contemporary tensions that mirror those described by Euroamerican women. At the age of fourteen, Albertine ran away to escape life in a small town near the reservation. Now she goes to nursing school in the Twin Cities. As she reads a chapter in her textbook entitled "Patient Abuse," she thinks of her mother: "There were two ways you could think of that title," she explains. "One was obvious to a nursing student, and the other was obvious to a Kashpaw. Between my mother and myself the abuse was slow and tedious, requiring long periods of dormancy, living in the blood like hepatitis" (7). Such a metaphor of disease highlights the symptoms of their simmering relationship—cyclical, inflammatory, debilitating, and possibly deadly. Even so, Albertine returns to her mother's house for a family reunion after her Aunt June's death. In her mother's kitchen, she joins her Chippewa mother, aunt, and grandmother, who bake pies, tell stories, and affirm female community.[5] Later, though, King Kashpaw, June's son, violates this female domain as he tries to drown his Anglo wife in the cold dishwater, in the process upsetting knives, spoons, and bowls and smashing the pies. Albertine works diligently to piece the pies back together, but, like family relationships, "once they smash there is no way to put them right" (39).

Albertine and Zelda have minor problems compared to those evident in the other key mothering relationships in *Love Medicine*. June (whose presence permeates all of the book, although she dies on page six) gives up her out-of-wedlock son, Lipsha, to be raised by her own adoptive mother, Marie Kashpaw. Grandma Kashpaw, as the boy calls his new "mother," never tells him the identity of his biological mother, preferring to tell him that his "blood mother wanted to tie a rock around [his] neck and throw [him] in the slough" (242). This fabrication insures Marie of Lipsha's gratitude and hence his obedience and love. But "gratitude gets old" (189), notes Lipsha, especially when his half-brother, King Kashpaw, takes every chance to remind him that he is not one of "the *real* children" (249). It is Lulu, Marie's rival and Lipsha's genetic grandmother on his father's side, who finally tells him about his biological mother, explaining: "You never knew who you were. . . . I thought it was a knowledge that could make or break you" (245).

Armed with this unsettling information, Lipsha sets off to "get down to the bottom of [his] heritage" (248). In a poker game with his half-brother and his heretofore unknown father, he deals himself "a perfect family" (264) (precisely what he has been lacking throughout the novel, as Cynthia Taylor notes) and wins the jackpot: the car King purchased with their mother's life insurance. Lipsha discovers that "belonging was a matter of deciding to," that he was "a real kid now" (255). Knowledge of his biological parents frees Lipsha to place himself in the reassuring context of family and community, from which he had felt alienated. With his sense of self clarified—not apart from but a part of—Lipsha thinks fondly of Grandma Kashpaw, his adopted mother, and heads for home. This "brings the novel full circle," since *Love Medicine* begins with June's death as she tries to walk home to the reservation during a spring snowstorm and ends with "her son returning to the reservation to 'bring her home'" (Taylor, 3).

Both Albertine and Lipsha describe, from a daughter/son perspective, how they feel about the insufficiency or absence of their mothers. Marie provides a mother's point of view as well. More than any other character, Marie is both biological and adoptive mother. Ironically, though, Marie Lazarre (Lipsha's "Grandma Kashpaw") never intended to be a mother. Responding to her "mail-order Catholic soul," the fourteen-year-old Marie made a pilgrimage "up the hill to Sacred Heart Convent" (41), where she yearned to "sit on the altar as a saint" (45). There she wrestles with the sadistic would-be saint, Sister Leopolda, who pours a kettle of scalding water on Marie's back to burn the "'wild cold dark lust'" (49) out of her soul. Earlier Sister Leopolda had warned Marie that she had "two choices": "One, you can marry a no-good Indian, bear his brats, die like a dog. Or two, you can give yourself to God" (45). Since giving herself to God meant surrendering to Sister Leopolda and her cruel ministrations, Marie runs away. But before she is even out of eyesight of the convent, she runs into Nector Kashpaw, who assaults her. Despite, or perhaps because of, Sister Leopolda's warnings, Marie marries Nector, has children, and takes in countless orphans.

Lipsha is only one of the many abandoned, given up, or thrown-away children Marie cares for. Many years before she takes in Lipsha, Marie cares for Lipsha's mother, June. At first, Marie does not want the nine-year-old girl: "I didn't want her because I had so many mouths I couldn't feed. I didn't want her because I had to pile the children in a cot at night. One of the babies slept in a drawer to the dresser. I didn't want June" (63). Already, babies, which seem to appear out of nowhere, crowd her couch, her drawers, and her bed. Babies are abundant; money is scarce. Marie softens, however, when she learns the circumstances of June's life, how her mother (Marie's sister) died in the woods, leaving June to survive by eating pine sap. Soon she offers June not only shelter, but motherly love. "It was a mother she couldn't trust," however, "after what happened in the woods" (70), explains Marie. So when Marie offers: "'You can be my girl and live here'" (69), June responds with indifference, preferring Uncle Eli, a Chippewa who lives the old way of life. Marie understands that, like June, Eli is from the woods. Associated with Chippewa tradition, he sings "wild unholy songs," "songs used to attract deer or women" (69). He hunts, traps, and is linked to earth, the giver and sustainer of life, the mother of all. At this point, Eli takes over mothering or, more precisely, parenting June.[6]

After twenty-three years of complicated mothering, Marie goes back up the hill to the convent to see Sister Leopolda, drawn by an invisible pull to the crazed, dying, failed saint. This time she takes her daughter Zelda. Again the electric antagonism between the two women is astounding. Marie feels that she "had come full circle to that rough girl, again, for one last fight with Leopolda before she swirled off and was nothing" (121). This time they wrestle for the black spoon which Leopolda tries to bring down on Marie's head. After an exhausting struggle, both are spent. Marie sits with Leopolda in silence, realizing that Leopolda will die soon. "There was nothing I could do after hating her all these years" (122), muses Marie. What Marie does not know, and what readers do not know until they read *Tracks*, is that Leopolda is the former Pauline Puyat, Marie's blood mother. With this information, the irony of the chapter's title, "Flesh and Blood," becomes clear. Her lifetime struggle with Sister Leopolda is a fight not only with an all-consuming Catholicism, but an almost predetermined, Chodorow-like battle between daughter and mother, a continual seeking on the part of the daughter for the dispensation of grace and acceptance from the mother, the same blessing Leopolda seeks from her Christ-husband. Not surprisingly, both women are disappointed. Due to the breakdown of traditional Chippewa structures, both Marie and Leopolda must create an identity in isolation. Leopolda seeks escape in solitude and isolation, while Marie attempts to reconstruct family and community. Estranged from both mother and community, Marie attempts to provide both for numerous abandoned children.

On the walk away from the Sacred Heart convent and her biological mother, Marie reminisces lovingly about her daughter Zelda: "I remembered the year I carried her. It was summer. I sat under the clothesline, breathing quiet so she would move, feeling the hand or foot knock just beneath my heart. We had been in one body then, yet she was a stranger. We were not as close now, yet perhaps I knew her better" (122). It is the daughter who chases down Nector, as she has done many times before, when he abandons Marie for Lulu. Just a few pages later, Marie contrasts her connection to her daughter to her estrangement from her son, Gordie: "I thought to myself, he wouldn't go after Nector and bring him home. . . . even though, like with Zelda, there was a time we had been in the same body. He wouldn't go, even though I had nursed him. We were closer when I carried him, when we never knew each other, I thought now. I did not trust him" (127). Both of Marie's visits to the convent trigger new levels of awareness and new commitments to family and community. In the passages above, Marie endorses Chodorow's model of psychological development from a mother's perspective; a daughter identifies with her mother and a son against her. As a biological mother, she experiences a distinct contrast between the intimacy of her child in the womb and the growing separation between them as her child develops into an autonomous individual. Like many mothers before her, Marie learns that she cannot maintain continual intimacy with her children. Indeed, she notes that they "were closer when I carried [them], when we never knew each other." If to mother is to be the bountiful dispenser of grace, first through a mother's milk and later through a mother's care, mothering is bound to disappoint both child and mother. A mother's milk dries up; a child's dependency disappears.

While the relationships between Zelda and Albertine; June and Lipsha; and Marie and June, Lipsha, Zelda, and Gordie suggest the realistic diversity of mother-daughter and mother-son relationships, they are united by the common act of abandonment. For these women, mothering a child is frustrated by personal and cultural alienation. While Zelda does not leave her daughter (in fact, it is Albertine who runs away from her mother), Albertine feels her mother was not "there" for her. Abandoning her son, June, the "long-legged Chippewa woman" (1), attempts to leave reservation life and an abusive husband behind, only to lose herself in a series of men in oil boomtowns, hoping each time that this one "could be different" (3). In contrast to the insufficiency of Zelda's and June's mothering, Marie mothers everyone. Having been forsaken by her mother and having unknowingly rejected her, Marie mothers her biological children, her taken-in children, and her irresponsible child-husband. Rising above the "massive cultural breakdown" (Allen, 182) of her people, Marie fights against tribal, family, and personal disintegration. She does so by taking on the traditional female role of insuring cultural continuity, adopting those who are left behind and helping them find a place within the family and the community.

Tracks

"The one you will not call mother."

Tracks also focuses on contrasting but parallel stories of mothers and community. From the alternating narratives told by Nanapush and Pauline to

Lulu, we learn about the full-blood Chippewa, Fleur Pillager, and the mixed-blood Pauline Puyat. Fleur, "the last Pillager" (2), is an independent, strong, daring woman who "dresse[s] like a man" (12) and lives alone in the woods,[7] while the anemic-looking Pauline tries to emulate white ways in town. Fleur knows and maintains the Pillager clan (totem) markers, her sense of community, even though she lives deep in the woods, while Pauline belongs to the Puyats, who were "mixed-bloods, skinners in the clan for which the name was lost," and outsiders (14). Pauline refuses to speak her native language; she refuses to bead, to do quillwork, or to tan hides. Although her father allows her to leave for the white folks' town, he warns her: "You won't be an Indian once you return" (14). Both Fleur and Pauline are orphaned; both give birth to daughters. Fleur pampers her daughter Lulu, but Pauline gives up her daughter at birth. Fleur has a home on her ancestral land; Pauline has no land. Even though she may be the brunt of gossip, Fleur has a place in the community; Pauline is an outsider, part of a "clan for which the name was lost," and is, like a white person, generally ignored. Fleur has connections to Chippewa tradition and to the earth; Pauline rejects Chippewa tradition for self-imposed Catholic martyrdom and resists any connection to the earth. Fleur is an actor; Pauline, in part due to her invisibility, is an observer. Fleur delights in sensuality; Pauline abhors it.

When Pauline discovers she is pregnant, she thinks, "Since I had already betrothed myself to God, I tried to force it out of me, to punish, to drive it from my womb" (131). She tries all kinds of violent means to abort the baby, but her mother-mentor figure, Bernadette Morrissey, insists that she deliver the child secretly. When the time comes to deliver, however, Pauline resists childbirth, reducing herself "to something tight, round, and very black clenched around [her] child so that she could not escape," "no taint of original sin on her unless she breathed air" (135). Baby Marie is finally wrenched into the world, forced from her unwilling mother with homemade forceps made from black iron cooking spoons, similar to the black spoon her mother would try to brain her with in *Love Medicine*. Not unexpectedly, Pauline refuses to breastfeed Marie. Instead, she joins the convent, where she cultivates her fanatical suffering—wearing her shoes on the wrong feet, fastening pins in her nun's headpiece, wearing underwear made from scratchy potato sacks, and restricting urination to twice a day.

Pauline's rejection of her child is simply a continuation of her self-rejection, brought on, in great measure, by her mixed-blood status and her cultural alienation. At the convent she conceives herself anew, gives birth to herself as she believes God has directed her to do: "He said that I was not whom I had supposed. I was an orphan and my parents had died in grace, and also, despite my deceptive features, I was not one speck of Indian but wholly white" (137). Since the order "would admit no Indian girls" (138), to be a nun meant to be non-Indian. Now, Pauline calls Indians "them," not "us" (138), and plans to "fetch more" Chippewa souls to Christ. To gain entry into the white, Judeo-Christian world, Pauline must renounce herself—her name, her Indian-ness, her family, her female body, and her daughter. She even imagines that her blue-eyed, male God (an apt conjunction of Euroamerican patriarchy) tells her: "I was forgiven of my daughter. I should forget her" (137). Soon after, Pauline remembers one of Nanapush's stories about how the animals on the plains understood their forthcoming destruction:

> He said that when the smoke cleared and hulks lay scattered everywhere, a day's worth of shooting for only the tongues and hides, the beasts that survived grew strange and unusual. They lost their minds. They bucked, screamed and stamped, tossed the carcasses and grazed on flesh. They tried their best to cripple one another, to fall or die. They tried suicide. They tried to do away with their young. They knew they were going, saw their end. (140)

Such images suggest the parallel destruction of Indian people, who were dying of influenza, consumption, and self-destructive ways that sprang from despair. This passage also provides a vivid vision of Pauline's madness. In a world that condemned even her small amount of Chippewa blood, she tries "to cripple" herself, to commit suicide, and "to do away with [her] young." Pauline's madness is to recognize her female Chippewa self as Other, even as she tries to destroy it.

Fleur also abandons her daughter, but for entirely different reasons. Because the Pillager land is being taken away by the lumbermill, because the old way of life is impossible to live anymore, because there is no safety for her daughter on the reservation, Fleur decides to send Lulu to a government school. While tribal breakdown does not destroy Fleur's personal integrity, it annihilates her ability to mother her daughter. She has no home, no land, no economic security to offer Lulu. For her part, Lulu resents Fleur, "the one [she] will not call mother" (2). By the time Nanapush rescues her from the boarding school, she has rejected her mother's earthy ways in favor of red lipstick, permed hair, and tall high heels. By the end of the novel, however, Lulu has returned to the reservation to live with Nanapush, who tells her the story of her mother.

In fact, it is Nanapush, the elderly man who gives Lulu his name, who "mothers" most consistently throughout the novel. He is the one who discovers an almost dead Fleur and nurses her back to health during the influenza epidemic, taking care of her like a daughter. He is the one who cares for Fleur's daughter Lulu. When Lulu runs through the frozen night to get help for the birth of Fleur's second child, she gets lost. Nanapush finds her. As he nurses Lulu's frostbitten feet, Nanapush remembers losing his wife and children to the flu epidemic. In the process, he ponders a woman's perspective:

> Many times in my life, as my children were born, I wondered what it was like to be a woman, able to invent a human from the extra materials of her own body. In the terrible times, the evils I do not speak of, when the earth swallowed back all it had given me to love, I gave birth in loss. I was like a woman in my suffering, but my children were all delivered into death. It was contrary, backward, but now I had a chance to put things into a proper order. (167)

Due to the cultural and economic oppression of the Chippewa, Nanapush's "children were all delivered into death." Now, like a mother, Nanapush delivers Lulu into life. In so doing, he restores the natural order and eases his earlier loss. "We don't have as much to do with our young as we think," he ponders. "They do not come from us. They just appear, as if they broke through a net of vines" (169). Later, he tells Lulu about his words of comfort to Fleur while she mourned the death of her second child: "We lose our children in different ways. They turn their faces to the white towns . . . or they become so full of what they see in the mirror there is no reasoning with them anymore, like you. Worst of all is the true loss, unbearable, and yet it must be borne" (170). Fleur suffers "the true loss" when her second child dies. Yet Fleur does not really abandon Lulu, she simply loses her in a different way. She cannot prepare her daughter for a world which is so different from what she knows. Sending Lulu to the government school seems like the last option to prepare her for life in the Anglo-dominated world: the world that has felled the forests around Fleur's cabin; the world that has silenced Misshepeshu, the water monster; the world that has turned Chippewa against Chippewa as relatives steal land allotments from one another. Both Fleur and Pauline suffer cultural alienation which makes mothering almost impossible. If the resourceful, resilient Fleur cannot protect her daughter in such a tumultuous world, how can the ill-equipped Pauline, who has always been an outsider to both Indian and white communities, be expected to nurture Marie? Under such circumstances, abandoning one's child is not an act of selfishness; it is an act of despair or an act of desperate mercy.

The Beet Queen

"I try to be the mother that I never had, to the daughter I never was."

The Beet Queen focuses primarily on German-Americans in Argus, North Dakota. Like Chippewa mothers in the other novels, the Euroamerican Adelaide abandons her children. After her married lover dies, Adelaide discovers she is pregnant with his third child. Of course, everything she has disappears overnight, because she has no legal claim to his support. She and her children, Mary and Karl, are left destitute. One night shortly after the birth of her second brother, eleven-year-old Mary Adare sits beside her mother's bed, cradling the baby in her arms. She overhears her mother mumble: "I should let it die. . . . I could bury it out back" (9). Mary tries to awaken her mother, telling her that the baby is hungry. "But," explains Mary, "Adelaide rolled over and turned her face to the wall" (9). The undernourished Adelaide does get milk and does breastfeed her baby. But while she does not ignore the newborn, "she refuse[s] to name him" (9), underscoring her emotional distance and his lack of family identity. Burdened by lack of economic and emotional support, Adelaide cannot endure another child.

Soon after this incident, the family attends "The Orphans' Picnic," where the children are orphaned indeed, when Adelaide flies off into the sky with "THE GREAT OMAR," AERONAUGHT EXTRAORDINAIRE" (11). The intentional misspelling of "aero*naught*" underscores the irony of Omar's "greatness." Soon the plane "blended into the pale sky and vanished" (12). When the baby Jude is taken away by a soft-spoken, sad-faced man, Mary and Karl are left alone. After a quick trip to their apartment, the two children jump into a boxcar, bound for Aunt Fritzie in Argus, North Dakota, where, covered by their mother's quilt, they "curled tight, with [their] heads on the suitcase and [Adelaide's] blue velvet box between [them]" (15).

As they travel through the winter night, Mary dreams of her mother "flying close to the pulsing stars" (16). She envisions Omar running low on fuel and chucking her mother out of the plane, where she falls "through the awful cold" (16). "My heart froze," explains Mary. "I had no love for her. That is why, by morning, I allowed her to hit the earth" (16). Fearing another abandonment, Mary goes to work to make herself indispensable to her new family. "I planned to be essential to them all," she says, "so depended upon that they could never send me off" (19). Her plan works so well that several years later, Aunt Fritzie, unaccustomd to showing emotions, uneasily shows Mary a postcard her mother had sent from Florida. Her mother writes: "I am living down here. I think about the children every day. How are they? Adelaide" (56). The next few moments between Mary and Aunt Fritzie are tense and tender, as, without words, they share the pain and anger of Adelaide's abandonment and their fear of losing each other. When Mary finally finds words, she assures Fritzie: "'You're more a mother to me'" (57). Several weeks later, Mary selects a postcard, "*Aerial View of Argus, North Dakota*" (58). On it the abandoned daughter forges a perfect imitation of Aunt Fritzie's handwriting: "All three of your children starved dead" (58).

Mary never marries and never has children, but she competes to mother the daughter of her best friend, half-Chippewa Celestine James. Celestine's daughter, in fact, is Mary's niece, the daughter of her brother Karl. When Mary moves in with Celestine and her daughter, Dot, for a few weeks, Celestine becomes concerned about how Mary tries to "weasel her way into Dot's affection" (219). "I'm the one who has to be strict and tell Dot to do her homework," she complains. "Mary is the one who keeps her up late, having fun . . . I'm the one who tries to make Dot eat lima beans and wash her neck. . . . I ached for a mother because I never had one. . . . But Dot had always had me there no matter what. I've been steady but unexciting" (219–20). Throughout the novel, Mary, Celestine, and "Uncle" Wallace Pfef compete by doting on Dot, who treats them all equally dreadfully.

In the final chapter, the only one narrated by Dot, we hear a daughter's perspective. When Dot learns that her "Uncle" Wallace has rigged the votes so that she will be crowned Beet Queen at the Sugar Beet Festival, she is furious and humiliated. As she sits on the queen's platform in the drought-cursed field with the scorching sun glaring down, she recognizes a connection to her family: "There is a thread beginning with my grandmother Adelaide," she muses, "and traveling through my father and arriving at me. That thread is flight" (335). She decides, like her grandmother before her, to jump into a nearby plane, intended to skywrite the queen's name, and disappear. When she returns to earth an hour later, the grandstand has been vacated. Only one person is waiting. "It is my mother," she says. "In her eyes I see the force of her love. It is bulky and hard to carry, like a package that keeps untying. It is like this dress that no excuse accounts for. It is embarrassing. I walk to her, drawn to her, unable to help myself" (337). Like Mary and Aunt Fritzie, this mother and daughter don't articulate their feelings. In typical Erdrich fashion, the reader is set up for an emotional scene which is undercut, in this case by Celestine's words: "Let's get going" (337). Intense feeling, repressed, is only that much stronger.

At home later that night, Celestine prepares a meal for her daughter and, as she sits at the table, Dot thinks of her mother in a new way: "I want to lean into her the way wheat leans into wind, but instead I walk upstairs and lie down in my bed alone" (339). She continues:

I watch the ceiling for a long while, letting the night deepen around me, letting all the distant sounds of cars and people cease, letting myself go forward on a piece of whirling bark until I'm almost asleep. And then it begins. Low at first, ticking faintly against the leaves, then steadier, stronger on the roof, rattling in the gutters, the wind comes. It flows through the screens, slams doors, fills the curtains like sails, floods the dark house with the smell of dirt and water, the smell of rain. I breathe it in, and I think of her lying in the next room, her covers thrown back too, eyes wide open, waiting. (338)

With her new, more mature understanding and appreciation of her mother, Dot feels united to, and so strengthened by, that relationship. This harmony, noted by many American Indian women poets, is reflected in the natural world, by the rain which relieves the long Argus drought.

Anglo and mixed-blood Chippewa mothers and daughters are not so different from one another in *The Beet Queen*, perhaps because (with the exception of Adelaide), Fritzie, Mary, Celestine, and Dot all are part of the small-town comunity of Argus. Adelaide flies off from her children; her son, Karl runs away from his daughter. Dot tries to fly away from her mother. But when she does, she comes to understand the "hugeness" of flying into the sky, "the flat world tipping, no end to sky and earth" (336), and the fear of feeling "unconnected" (336). She returns to earth, where she now understands the wonder and security of feeling "connected" to her mother. Mothering, and its inherent interconnectedness, is central to female identity in this novel.

Reweaving the Narrative Design of Family and Community

Throughout *Love Medicine, The Beet Queen,* and *Tracks,* a complex assemblage of mothers—Chippewa, mixed-blood, and Anglo—struggle with their children and their communities. Often, like June, Fleur, Pauline, and Adelaide, mothers abandon their children and their community. As a result, these women wander "unconnected." June seeks fulfillment with a series of oil-town cowboys; Fleur travels the countryside, selling rags and trinkets; Pauline actively pursues a saint's matyrdom; and Adelaide succumbs to bouts of breaking every piece of glass in her husband's house, standing on the floor, "her feet smeared with blood" (232). The rage and despair of all these women certainly is personal, but, for the Chippewas June and Fleur, and to a certain extent for the mixed-blood Pauline, it is also cultural. As a result of the "breakup of ancient orders of life" (Allen, 182) which locate identity in family and community, June, Fleur, and Pauline are cut off from their people and from themselves. Their inability to mother reflects such cultural alienation.

June and Fleur no longer can live the old ways of life in the woods; Pauline lives on the boundaries of two cultures. Erdrich's emphasis, though, is on those left behind—the adoptive mothers and the thrown-away children they take in. Marie mothers everyone but feels the erosion of self which accompanies that responsibility. Aunt Fritzie takes in Mary but loses her own daughter. Fathers often are altogether absent, physically and emotionally. When biological fathers are present, they are abusive like King; replacement fathers, like Nanapush and Eli, tend to be more nurturant. The forsaken children, including Lipsha and Mary, narrate their rigorous struggles to become family and community members and thereby to create, affirm, and sustain a personal identity.

Such fractured families reflect two things. One is the continuance of the traditional sharing of mothering by many members of the tribe. Sisters, aunts, grandmothers, and, less frequently, older uncles and grandfathers shared in rearing a child. In fact, mothering is not merely an activity but an orientation to the world—a recognition of and responsibility to the interrelatedness of all beings. Second, amid the strains of contemporary reservation and/or town life, family and clan relationships no longer are clearly defined. Young people like Lulu run off to the city to find a livelihood, a glimmering promise, but too often end up finding poverty and alienation. Often, they return to the reservation to find skepticism and doubt about their Indianness.[8] On the reservation there may be alienation from a biological mother, but there is always a relative to take over as an extended mother, someone to weave the individual back into the web of community. Off the reservation, there is no such support, but only alienation from both family and community, a central loss of identity for a Native American.

Such alienation also acutely plagues mixed-bloods, as Erdrich notes in an interview with Joseph Bruchac: "One characteristic of being a mixed blood is searching. You look back and say, 'Who am I from?'" ("Whatever Is Really Yours," 83) Who is my clan? Who is my family? These are particularly crucial questions for those whose ethnicity is in doubt. Having grown up in a small community "where you were who you were in relation to the community," explains Erdrich in another interview, "you knew that whatever you did there were really ripples from it" ("An Interview," 205). Such ripples resonate throughout Erdrich's novels. In fact, says Kathleen Mullen Sands, the root of Erdrich's "storytelling technique is the secular anecdotal process of community gossip" (15). Such a network of family histories, rewoven repeatedly by community tellers, is essential for Erdrich's characters, who, in order fully to find their identities, must be woven into the narrative design of family, totem, clan, and community.

It is simplistic to make too many claims for distinctions between Indian and Anglo mothering in Erdrich's novels, especially when the writer, by blood and education, is both. Similarly, to claim that Erdrich's novelistic style is "Indian" and "female" because it is nonchronological, polyvocal, and interiorized, and to contrast this style to a putative Western, male, chronological, univocal, and external narrative is problematical. What makes a novel "Indian" or "female" is still being debated. Unfortunately, the debates usually ignore each other. While the multiple narrative voices indeed may be an extension of a Chippewa or a female oral tradition, those alone are not sufficient explanations. Erdrich points out that, as well as her Chippewa mother's stories, her German-American "father's stories are just indelible" ("An Interview," 204). In addition, such a narrative technique derives as much from Faulkner and other Euroamerican canonical writers. "I had a literary education," explains Erdrich, "so the entire literary canon is a background" ("An Interview," 203).

Even Erdrich's method of writing confounds feminist expectations, since she and her husband, Michael Dorris, collaborate. Collaboration is common to both Native-American and female artistic traditions, but those who insist that "autonomy [is] essential to the practice of any art" (Miles, 21) are suspicious of collaboration. While Erdrich's collaboration is certainly communal, it is also individual, mirroring the community of distinct voices in the novel and replicating the positive role of mothers as creators of identity and producers of meaning. If, as feminist scholars have suggested, "the traditional order of much fiction is the tension between the ambitious text (traditionally male) and the erotic text (traditionally female)," Erdrich, suggests Susan Jaret McKinstry, "makes the division more creative," since the "individual stories become a history of revisions of the erotic and the ambitious text," balancing the need for community and autonomy by creating "community history" (5–6). Erdrich's novels, then, transcend easy categories of gender and ethnicity, reflect both Native American and Euroamerican influences, and extend Western notions of mothering. Mothering can indeed be a painful process of separation; it might be the necessarily insufficient dispensation of grace. But mothering can also be a communal responsibility for creating and maintaining personal identity. Shared responsibility for mothering emphasizes the Chippewa-female sense of the interconnectedness of all life, the responsibility of each person to care for others. That this is not an easy task, especially for a community threatened by cultural extinction, is accentuated by those mothers who flee to the white towns or to the Catholic God, leaving behind their culture and their children. It remains for those left behind, the adoptive mothers and thrown-away youngsters, to reweave the broken strands of family, totem, and community into a harmonious wholeness.

Notes

Completion of this essay was aided by a California State University Research Award granted by California State University, Chico.

1. See also Domna Stanton, who warns against "the essentialist traps of Romantic fictions" (176).

2. The Western dualistic insistence on being *either* male or female is challenged by the *berdache*, "the term used by anthropologists for those American Indians . . . whose lifestyles bridged men's and women's social roles" (Roscoe, 127). For a discussion of how the berdache suggests a "third gender" (or a spectrum of genders), see Paula Gunn Allen, Walter L. Williams, and Will Roscoe.

3. One might question whether there is some reason for the different presentations of female relationships in the two genres.

4. Throughout this paper, I will use Chippewa, the tribal name used by Erdrich. According to Gerald Vizenor, Chippewa and Ojibway (or Ojibwa) are names imposed by Euro-Americans. "In the language of the tribal past," he explains, "the families of the woodland spoke of themselves as the *anishinabe*" (ix). See also William W. Warren, 35–36, 56.

5. See Ruth Landes for a discussion of traditional Ojibway women, who "live in a world of values all their own, a world closed to the men" (11).

6. According to Ann Dally, "Fathers can be as influential as mothers, can act as mothers and can be maternal" (246).

7. See Landes for a discussion of traditional Chippewa women's "hermaphroditic tasks."

8. For a discussion of how, in Euroamerican novels, "whites keep leaving home," while, in Native-American novels, Native Americans keep "coming home" (581–82), see William Bevis.

Quotations are from *Love Medicine* (Holt, Rinehart, and Winston, 1984), *Tracks* (Henry Holt & Co., 1988) and *The Beet Queen* (Henry Holt & Co., 1986). Reprinted by permission of Henry Holt and Company, Inc.

Part III

Mothers
Transforming Practices

Chapter 11

Truth in Mothering:
Grace Paley's Stories

Judith Arcana

In her definitive work on maternity, *Of Woman Born*, Adrienne Rich identified the twentieth-century Western patriarchal *institution* of motherhood,
defining it in juxtaposition and antipathy to women's *experience* of mothering. Rich discussed the ways in which the idea of mother, and of the ideal
mother, are fantasies born of male fears, desires, and needs, featuring the demand for unconditional love, absolute forgiveness, and unhesitating self-
abnegation on the part of all women, even those who are not actually mothers.
She analyzed the history, structure, and maintenance of the institution and
offered the results of her extensive research in conjunction with memoir and
commentary drawn from her own mothering. She explained that, as she
studied what turned out to be a construct and practice designed by men, she
sought the truth of mothering beyond the motherhood institution; the constant question in her mind was, *"But what was it like for women?"* (16). Grace
Paley's stories, in their depiction of the lived experience of women and children, however specific to the time and place of her characters, offer an answer
to that question and, in doing so, reveal the distortion and falsity of the
motherhood institution.

Grace Paley has chosen not merely to acknowledge but to emphasize mothers
and children in her work—a choice that distinguishes her from many of her
peers, the majority of postmodern writers of short fiction, whose interests
preclude the use of such subject matter in any depth. Annie Dillard has described, with some distaste and much regret, the common practice of fiction
out here at the end of the twentieth century, which she calls "contemporary
modernism": "Characters are not interested in society at all. Their sphere of
activity is the text" (39), and they "are no longer fiction's center" (40). Most
contemporary writers have moved "fiction's arena from the material world to
consciousness itself" and thus "stress modern *self*-consciousness" (43–44).
Nonetheless, sounding a lot like Grace Paley, Dillard insists that "fiction
[still] keeps its audience by retaining the world as its subject matter. People
like the world. Many people actually prefer it to art and spend their days by
choice in the thick of it" (78).

The world is with us, late and soon, in Grace Paley's stories, which insist that material considerations are inseparable from the "private" facts of individual lives. In "Ruthy and Edie," when the women gather to celebrate Ruthy's fiftieth birthday, her wish on the candles of her cake is "that this world wouldn't end. This world, this world, Ruth said softly," whispering the chorus of Malvina Reynolds' song "Love It Like a Fool" (LSD, 124).[1] Grace Paley's fiction, evolving within the conflicting aesthetics and politics of the postmodern era, demonstrates the structural and linguistic influence of its time. The texts are spare, the language honed; first-person narration predominates, the voice—and intimate presence—of the narrator/author is never really outside of the story, and metafictionality is both an issue and a delightful game. But Paley rejects the cool postmodern embrace of language for its own sake, and offers a warm maternal embrace instead.

Even her earliest stories, written in the 1950s—long before their author became a conscious feminist—are distinctly radical in their placement of women and children at the center. Her characterization of mothers is especially notable; they are obviously struggling with the disparity Rich has described, between the patriarchal institution of motherhood and their own lived experience. For these women, the palpable essence of motherhood—in their bodies and the bodies of their children, in their rejection of sacrificial martyrdom and their willingness to give by choice, in their clear intellection of the tasks of mothering— is in constant opposition to the role men have created for women to play as mothers. Generally excluded from canonized literature or depicted entirely in terms of their connections to fathers, sons, male lovers, or husbands, mothers and children are remarkable in Grace Paley's fiction for the fact that they appear in stories about their own lives. These stories, in their consistently frank portrayal of the conflicts and contradictions of the experience of maternity, both offer a consistent refutation of the idealized and oppressive institution of motherhood and present strongly drawn alternative models for mothering.

In Paley's work, motherhood is fundamental: of forty-five collected stories in three volumes, twenty-two have motherhood at the center, and at least eight others include motherhood as a major issue. Some stories exercise the theme of motherhood almost musically, as a backbeat, or as a reminder. In "Come On, Ye Sons of Art" (ECLM), after the whole story has focused on Jerry Cook's grief over his inability to be a sufficiently "crooked" capitalist, his lover Kitty's pregnancy is revealed, and the mood changes with the subject; the story suddenly is focused on the feeding and raising of small children and the warm pleasures of family life on Sunday mornings. And very early in "The Story Hearer" (LSD), Faith—who is Paley's most autobiographical central character—explains that Jack's mother's disappearance in his childhood is the weapon he uses against her (Faith) whenever she has made "some strong adversary point in public"—foreshadowing much of the rest of the text, by drawing the lines in the battle of the sexes in terms of definitions of mothering.

Many of Grace Paley's stories simply include motherhood as a fact of life, as in the natural anxiety of "The Burdened Man's" neighbor at the tearing of her son's new corduroy pants (ECLM)—which is neither played for laughs nor wrung with sentimentality. Such simple inclusion, ordinary as it may seem, is in fact unusual in a male-centered literary world, where mothering generally is presented in terms of romanticized service and hostile blame, or simply erased. But there are fewer than half a dozen stories by Grace Paley in which the mother/child relationship—as idea, theme, plot element, or major focal point—does not figure notably.[2]

In Paley stories, women talk about mothering, and they talk about children. Ordinary issues that affect mothers and children, such as milk supplies, school policies, playground fences, and the carefree charm of irresponsible fathers, all figure in the daily conversation of the women who have to contend with them, and in the commentary of narrators who, more often than not, are within the circle of mothers. Adulthood doesn't remove their children from consideration: Dolly Raftery brags about her son John's exemplary behavior, even as she accepts the duplicity of his extramarital affair; Faith describes in detail even the less-than-lovable behavior of her two boys as they grow from childhood into their late teens and early twenties; Ruth Larsen worries about her daughter Rachel, an underground revolutionary.[3] In "Listening," written in the early 1980s, the military consumption of mothers' sons is commented on merely in passing, registering the author's understanding of numberless centuries of mothers' raising children to kill and die for the state (LSD, 200).

Tenement windowsills, butcher shops, city sidewalks, and the halls of public schools are the simple props and sets for the stage on which the considerably less simple daily lives of mothers and children are played out in these stories. Children are kidnapped. They are raped. They become addicts and die far away from home. Marriage is forever fractured, despite heterosexual attempts at love and romance. Friendship is a source of sustenance, nurturance, inspiration—and sometimes grief—for women. But mothering is basic in most women's lives, even though the patriarchal nuclear family is under fire from all sides. Paley is a writer who understands the world in politically ecological terms, as one entity made up of inextricably related and interdependent, though variously exploitive and supportive, elements. To a world of undeniable pain, Grace Paley's stories offer babies and children as a source of love and delight, regeneration and healing. In both metaphor and plot, the stories repeatedly present us with mother-child relationships which offer relief and salvation to a beleaguered world.

For instance, Paley brings issues of racism and inclusiveness into the maternal sphere in her several stories in which babies are born to parents of different colors, or are being raised by a mother whose skin doesn't match theirs; in each, the babies bring not only pleasure and contentment, but also higher consciousness to the adults around them. In "Northeast Playground," one of the characters is Leni, a young white Jewish street whore whose baby's skin is brown (ECLM). Becoming Claude's mother has pulled Leni off the streets and into the playground, where she is more than happy to raise her son on ADC. "At That Time, or The History of a Joke" (LSD) offers a young woman who receives a transplanted uterus in which a foetus is already implanted and growing. When the young woman gives birth and the child is revealed, the baby, black and female, is hailed as a messiah — a miracle-child. The infant — a virgin birth — is regarded as a saviour around the globe, and her birth taken as a sign of redemption by much of humanity; but her skin color would hardly be notable if her "mother" were not white.[4]

In "Zagrowsky Tells," Paley presents Emmanuel, the five-year-old son of white Cissy Zagrowsky and a black gardener who worked at the mental hospital in which she had been a patient. Emmanuel is "a little boy brown like a coffee bean," a "brown baby. An intermediate color," his grandfather says, just a little lighter than a chocolate popsicle (LSD, 159, 170, 173). His name — insisted upon hysterically by his mother — means "messiah" in Hebrew, and he is indeed the harbinger and catalyst for Izzy Zagrowsky, whose garden-variety racism has receded considerably since his grandson's birth. That change in his grandpa demonstrates the fact that Emmanuel serves to heal the grief and misery in his family, embodying a bond which holds the generations together; like the unnamed little girl in "Joke," this messiah-baby signifies a hope for peace and justice in the wider family of the world.

Similarly, in "Ruthy and Edie" (LSD), Sara, the daughter of Ruth (who is probably Jewish and is married to Joe Larsen, who probably is not), is married to Tomas, whose name suggests that he is Latino. Letty, their daughter, is her grandma's darling. The child Letty also embodies two aspects of this theme: not only is she a child of her parents' own rainbow coalition — and thus represents hope for an end to racism — but, as a little child in need of both freedom and safety to grow up, she represents the urgent necessity for adults to save the world for her sake, for the future of humankind. As Letty squirms out of her grandma's arms, the narrator notes that this adorable rosy baby is "already falling . . . onto the hard floor of man-made time" (LSD, 126).

The passage about Letty exemplifies many found in Paley stories published after the early 1970s, in which she not only offers tales of mothers and children, but also expands mothering into a mode, a metaphor, a way of being in the world that—in contrast to the ego-nursing and unconditional support featured in the motherhood institution—is caring, nurturant, healing, and radically opposed to the patriarchal militarism and rapacious profiteering that dominate our planet. In "Listening," for instance, she asserts a relationship between the world itself, lovingly described in its natural beauty and urban richness, and the young people who must be taught to care for it despite, or because of, its clear and present terrible danger. Faith explains that "in order to encourage the young whom we have, after all, brought into the world. . . . We must . . . continue pointing out . . . what is good or beautiful so as not to have a gloomy face when you meet some youngster who has begun to guess" (LSD, 204).

In the same collection, Faith, speaking as first-person narrator claiming authorship, concludes the story "Friends" by justifying herself as a writer of fiction—"I was right to invent for my friends and our children a report on . . . the condition of our lifelong attachments" (LSD, 89)—and does so in response to her son Tonto's political criticism: "Anthony's world—poor, dense, defenseless thing—rolls round and round. Living and dying are fastened to its surface and stuffed into its softer parts. He was right to call my attention to its suffering and danger. He was right to harass my responsible nature." This repeated emphasis on the indissoluble connection between "the world" and the mother-child relationship is rooted in Grace Paley's nurturant consciousness, her preoccupation with the global need for taking care, for mothering-in-the-world, which is reflected in the preponderance of her stories that focus on mothers and motherhood issues.

Paley says that she always wanted to be a mother; she never considered a life without children and thought about having them as soon as she married, at the age of nineteen.[5] She considers her attitude "part of my general optimism" and views the bearing and raising of children not only as a natural outcome of love between women and men, but as a commitment to human life. Her literary concern with mothering, however, is not based in her own motherhood, for it has developed through a lifetime of work as a radical activist. The author is a woman for whom motherhood is an extension and manifestation of nurturant sensibilities which dictate fierce pacifism and stubborn, intense personal and political attachments.

Sybil Claiborne, a longtime friend, neighbor, and colleague in the writing and political work of their lives, says that we must speak of Grace Paley

as a nurturer rather than a mother, because that [meaning] spills over into so much of the world—like her concern about the environment—everything goes beyond her being the mother of two children. You have to be careful with a word like "motherhood," because it can be so restrictive and so self-ish. Being a mother was what rooted her in her community, and pushed her into a certain kind of activity at a certain time in her life. Grace says, "Your politics is where your life is"[6]

Understandably, then, her politics are where her fiction is. Grace Paley insists upon truth in fiction; in this era of "the text," she still speaks of "art" and "literature," and even corrects herself when she says "a work of art"—saying that she means, rather, "a work of truth." Quintessentially candid, her stated intent is to demystify; she is determined to reveal what has been hidden. She speaks of the writer's "job" as the task of shining light where there has been no light, revealing what is not yet known and what has been buried, what cannot be understood because it has been obscured. When Paley began to write fiction in 1952, the lives of women and children were hidden subjects in literature; where they did appear, they were generally sentimentalized, trivialized, or denigrated. She herself was embarrassed by her subject matter and used to tell interviewers that she was surprised at her success, because she didn't think that "anybody else would be interested in this crap"—by which term she meant the daily lives of women and children. Her first book, *The Little Disturbances of Man*, published in 1959, reflected her reticence and contained only four stories in which motherhood was the central issue; but her second book, published in 1974, contained eleven—its author influenced and encouraged by her success in those years of the beginning of the second wave of the North American Women's Movement.

Her characters willingly accept the real burdens of mothering. They complain, of course—they are that much like real mothers—but they eschew the patriarchally-conceived traps of masochistic martyrdom and idealized mother-love. They even enjoy sex and manage to take their sexual pleasure without guilt and without bringing shame to their children. This has always been true in Paley's stories. The young Anna in "The Pale Pink Roast" (written in the mid-1950s), who goes to bed with her ex-husband "for love," while their daughter plays in the park, is not so different from the middle-aged Faith of "The Expensive Moment" (written in the early 1980s), who visits her lover Nick in his office on weekday afternoons for delicious conversation and the pleasures of sex on "his narrow daybed" which opens "to a comfortable three-quarter width." Questioned by her friend Ruth—"Are you lovers?"—Faith explains the double excitement of her affair: It's "the fun of talking, Ruthy. What about that? It's as good as fucking lots of times, isn't it?" (LSD, 184, 180).

The psychoanalytic perspective is absent from this writer's work, rendered useless by her insistence upon social, economic, and historical causes and motives. Leni, for instance, in "Northeast Playground," has given up turning tricks because one of her johns, unable to pay, brought her the infant Claude—

his own son—as compensation,[7] and now she spends her time mothering. In "Enormous Changes at the Last Minute," Alexandra, a social worker who becomes pregnant for the first time in her forties, chooses to keep and mother her baby in concert with several of her adolescent clients, who are also new mothers; she rejects the offer of her young lover, who wants to move in with her.

These latter stories present situations that are charmingly unlikely, but Paley often is sharply realistic. In "Living," the narrator and central character Faith is hemorrhaging from an abortion or miscarriage[8] and believes she might be dying:

> I was bleeding. The doctor said, "You can't bleed forever. . . . No one bleeds forever." It seemed *I* was going to bleed forever. . . . I was frightened. . . . I could hardly take my mind off this blood. Its hurry to leave me was draining the red out from under my eyelids and the sunburn off my cheeks. It was all rising from my cold toes to find the quickest way out. . . . My sister took the kids for a while so I could stay home quietly making hemoglobin, red corpuscles, etc., with no interruptions. I was in such first-class shape by New Year's, I nearly got knocked up again. (ECLM, 60–61)

That wisecracking conclusion underlines the fear and pain of the foregoing passage. When her friend Ellen dies in that same story, Faith considers adopting Billy, Ellen's son, even though she hasn't the resources to raise him. She has no idea, she confesses to the reader, "where the money, the room, another ten minutes of good nights, where they would all come from. . . . He would soon need a good encyclopedia, a chemistry set" (ECLM, 61). Irony is frequently Grace Paley's tool in her most realistic depictions of the difficult and unremitting responsibilities of motherhood.

By the time she wrote "Living," Paley already had delineated exquisitely—excruciatingly—the mother's point of view in the following passage of one of her earliest stories, "A Subject of Childhood," a text which defined both the essence of maternal conflict and the literary genre required to treat that conflict. As rare in fiction as clear descriptions of menstruation and contraception, this mother-child dialogue illuminates the painful tension of the motherhood experience:

> 'Now listen to me. I want you to get out of here. Go on down and play. I need ten minutes all alone. Anthony, I might kill you if you stay up here.' . . .
> 'O.K., Faith. Kill me.' . . . 'Please,' I said gently, 'go out with your brother. I have to think, Tonto.' 'I don't wanna. I don't have to go anyplace I don't wanna,' he said. 'I want to stay right here with you.' 'Oh, please, Tonto, I have to clean the house.' . . . 'I don't care,' he said. 'I want to stay here with you. I want to stay right next to you.' 'O.K., Tonto, O.K. I'll tell you what, go to your room for a couple of minutes, honey, go ahead.' 'No,' he said,

climbing onto my lap. 'I want to be a baby and stay right next to you every minute.' 'Oh, Tonto,' I said, 'please, Tonto.' I tried to pry him loose, but he put his arm around my neck and curled up right there in my lap, thumb in mouth, to be my baby. 'Oh, Tonto,' I said, despairing of one solitary minute. . . . 'No,' he said, 'I don't care if Richard goes away, or Clifford. They can go do whatever they wanna do. I don't even care. I'm never gonna go away. I'm gonna stay right next to you forever, Faith. . . . I love you, Mama,' he said. 'Love,' I said. 'Oh love, Anthony, I know.' (LDM, 144–45)

That is the penultimate passage in "A Subject of Childhood"; the story concludes with an extraordinary metaphor that displays the author's insistence upon telling the truth about mothering: "I held him so and rocked him. I cradled him. I closed my eyes and leaned on his dark head. But the sun in its course emerged from among the water towers of downtown office buildings and suddenly shone white and bright on me. Then through the short fat fingers of my son, interred forever, like a black and white barred king in Alcatraz, my heart lit up in stripes" (LDM, 145).

Grace Paley not only denies masochism and unconditional love in mothering, but also rejects mother-blame. Even her long struggle to work out her relationship with her own mother (left out of or minimized in several earlier stories, strongly and positively portrayed in her third collection[9]), did not foster the kind of anti-mother stance we find in so much post–World War II fiction, including work by women.[10] In 1975, Paley published "Mom," in which the I-narrator makes a statement on the proliferation of mother-blaming in the culture:

Science and literature had turned against her [the mother]. What use was my accumulating affection when the brains of the opposition included her son the doctor and her son the novelist? . . . What is wrong with the world? the growing person might have asked. The year was 1932 or perhaps 1942. Despite the worldwide fame of those years, the chief investigator into human pain is looking into his own book of awful prognoses. He looks up. Your mother probably, he says. As for me . . . I missed the mocking campaign. (85)

Mothers are never mocked in Grace Paley's fiction, though some of her mothers are not always what they should be. (And who—almost any Paley character would immediately ask—who is?) None is measured against the hopelessly impossible romantic ideal of the patriarchal motherhood institution; all are judged within the contexts of their lives, in terms of what is possible for them. The first-person narrator in "Mom" understands this, and says of her mother, "Her life is a known closed form" (86). So the harried working-class Catholic mother in dialogue with a teacher-nun in "Gloomy Tune"

(ECLM), a woman whose many children are ill-behaved at best, delinquent and dangerous at worst, is not blamed for the facts of her socioeconomic and cultural matrix. The causes of her children's frustration and unhappiness — and her own — are unmistakable.

The mothers of Mickey and Abby, adolescents who left home for madness and addiction, are described with sympathy and empathy, the historical facts of their mothering time — the impassioned 1960s — recounted in a way that precludes kneejerk blame ("Friends," LSD). And the mother of Lavinia not only is unable to save her daughter from the fate of ordinariness, the terrible drowning of her gifts in the soapy water of domesticity, but also is enraged by her daughter's falling away from her own bright possibilities. When the mother realizes that the young woman has become "just a mother" and apparently has failed — just as she herself had failed — to fulfill the promise of her gifts, "I let out a curse. . . . I cry out loud . . . Damn you, Lavinia — for my heart is busted in a minute — damn you, Lavinia, ain't nothing gonna come of you neither" ("Lavinia," LSD, 67–68).

Grace Paley always has understood that mothers cannot help but be ignorant of the private lives and distant actions of their children: "Their mothers never know where they are," says a woman watching the dangerously cavorting boys on the subway in "Samuel" (ECLM, 104). But the mother of Samuel, the boy who falls beneath the wheels of a subway train, clearly is not to blame for his death. That story, impressively loaded with information about the masculinity training of young boys, is a textual rendition of a mother's worst nightmare: when children go out into the world of trucks, subway trains, and grownups who aren't their parents and don't especially love them, even the most careful mother cannot protect them.

From 1975, when Grace Paley first published "Mom," to the present, the developing figure of the mother in her stories — especially when contrasted with the previously blameless figure of the father — reveals a changing consciousness in the author's written voice. After criticizing in "Mom" what she recognized as a "mocking campaign" against mothers by male writers, she gradually made her own motherwomen more seriously critical of men. Even the new young fathers, with their babies in backpacks and their acceptance of childcare responsibilities, are criticized for the notable gap between their acceptance of those responsibilities and the growth of emotional responses requisite to fulfill them. So the curly-haired young father whose ego takes precedence over his little daughter's innocent silliness is chastened by the watching I-narrator in "Anxiety" (LSD), warned by a character who strongly resembles the author herself, about the danger of his incomplete assumption of mothering.

Grace Paley's fictional mothers, like real mothers, live in the heart of the motherhood institution but, through the insistent optimism of their author, are not destroyed by it. Truth plus hope is Paley's formula, and part of the truth of her portrayal of mothers is that their relationships with their children, however absorbing or exhausting, do not constitute their entire lives. On the contrary, their motherhood is a catalyst and a resource; mothers take action to save the world, and to make the world safe for their children; this is their hope. Political activism grows out of the responsibility of motherhood in these stories; motherhood is a source of consciousness-raising.

Grace Paley's children, now grown, explain that dynamic in their mother's own life. Nora Paley says that, in her childhood, "All the [important political] action was always taken by the mothers." And Danny Paley realized, even in his boyhood, that, "As a mother she wanted to help make the world safe, help make a world that would still exist when her children grew up."[11] In "Politics," the author describes some of that important action, displaying the accuracy of Nora's analysis with hilarity in a story about those mothers Danny describes, working to make the world safe for their children:

> A group of mothers from our neighborhood went down-town to the Board of Estimate Hearing and sang a song. . . . [The soloist's lyrics and the "recitative," which all the attendant mothers deliver in chorus, request the construction of a fence for their local playground to keep out "the bums and tramps," the "old men wagging their cricked pricks," the "junkies," "Commies," and other assorted "creeps."] No one on the Board of Estimate, including the mayor, was unimpressed. . . . all the officials said so. . . . The comptroller . . . said, 'Yes yes yes, in this case yes. . . . why not . . . ' Then and there, he picked up the phone and called Parks, Traffic and Child Welfare. . . . By noon the next day, the fence was up. (ECLM, 139–41)

Even in the relatively early story, "Living," written and published when the author was still reticent about including overt political involvement in her fiction,[12] one sentence reveals that the young mothers have taken action; they "pasted white doves on blue posters and prayed on Eighth Street for peace" (ECLM, 61). The collected version of "Faith in a Tree," a story which describes a political pivot in the life of the autobiographical Faith Darwin Asbury, concludes when her elder son's passionate response to an antiwar demonstration effects a life-changing decision in his mother. The disappointment and disillusionment of our children are powerful consciousness-raisers, as Faith explains after Richard condemns her and her friends. When a police officer tries to silence the demonstrators, Richard responds explosively to his mother's passive acceptance; he screams, "I hate you. I hate your stupid friends. Why didn't they just stand up to that stupid cop and say fuck you. They should of just stood up and hit him" (ECLM, 99). Richard then takes action himself, as a graffiti sloganeer. His mother says, "That is exactly when events turned me around, changing my hairdo, my job uptown, my style of living and telling. . . . I thought more and more and every day about the world" (ECLM, 99–100).

Unlike writers who—like Sue Miller in *The Good Mother*—present individual mothers as relatively solitary, isolated in their mothering, Grace Paley presents mothering both as the task of individual mothers and as the shared business of women whose children spend their hours and days in the same neighborhood, park, and schoolyard. A mother who remains aloof in the park is defined by her rejection of the maternal community: "She never grabs another mother's kid when he falls and cries" (ECLM, 79). Motherhood in Grace Paley's fiction is practiced collaboratively and is a source of bonding and longterm friendship. In "Friends," a woman in her fifties muses, "I remember Ann's eyes and the hat she wore the day we first looked at each other. Our babies had just stepped howling out of the sandbox on their new walking legs. We picked them up. Over their sandy heads we smiled. I think a bond was sealed then, at least as useful as the vow we'd all sworn with husbands to whom we're no longer married" (LSD, 89).

These women are a community—including some who are not themselves mothers—which, in concert with the children and men in the collected stories, forms the core of the Paley story cycle. Her stories are clearly connected, in much the same way that Faulkner's Yoknapatawpha County tales are, or so many of Eudora Welty's stories; and all of these loosely-constructed cycles resemble the more overtly unified classic collection Sherwood Anderson published as *Winesburg, Ohio*. Paley's cycle, as regionally defined as those of Faulkner, Welty, and Anderson, contains a central set of characters who—like their author—have mostly come out of the Bronx but now live in or around the Village in lower Manhattan and have been aging and changing together through the past four decades. The cycle itself is a community of stories, mirroring its community of characters.

Though each of Paley's stories is complete in itself and may readily be understood alone (many are, of course, anthologized individually), almost all are part of the cycle. Characters appear in each other's stories, are discussed across texts, or are casually mentioned in passing. For instance, the narrator tells us that Kitty, who plays a major role as Faith's friend in "Faith in a Tree," snuggles down into a patchwork quilt made by her friend Faith's grandmother in "Come On, Ye Sons of Art" though neither Faith nor her grandmother appears in that text (ECLM, 72). Two stories published years apart, "An Interest in Life" and "Distance," offer many of the same events and most of the same characters but are told from two different women's points of view. Three stories, "The Contest," "Faith in a Tree," and "Love," all discuss, feature, or refer to the character Dotty Wasserman, who thus links the three stories, the three collections in which they appear, and the characters who interact with her or discuss her; in "Love," she is even discussed by Faith and Jack *as a fictional character*.[13]

Throughout the ongoing cycle, Grace Paley writes of ongoing mothering, delineating the changes that occur as both children and mothers age and mature. As their children grow out of childhood dependency, we realize that the women always have been independent, working for money to live, active within their community; they no longer need to take up the kind of hands-on mothering tasks they accepted when their children were young. Having determined that she has spent enough time "lying down or standing and staring," Faith leaves her sons ("It was near the time for parting anyway") with her neighbor Dolly Raftery and becomes a long-distance runner. She hollers to them as she walks out the door; they are all—the boys and Mrs. Raftery—lying in front of the television set, engrossed in a newscast. They are oblivious to the momentous separation, and Faith knows it. She takes—appropriately enough—the Independent subway line to Brighton Beach, where she changes her clothes and begins to run (ECLM, 180–81). Despite their understanding that the role of mother is a lifelong assignment, Grace Paley's mothers do not define their lives in terms of that role.

Within the core group of Paley characters in the story cycle, the mothers' relationships with each other have grown more and more important over time. They develop individually and as a group, recalling personal histories which have been recorded in other, earlier stories and exchanging memories while they look into the future together. These women actively support and further each other's lives, critically but lovingly providing each other with a network of knowledge and wisdom. Eventually, in the cycle of characters who've been appearing in Paley stories for nearly forty years, the continuing text offers a realization to this community of middle-aged heterosexual women: they not only have come to value their friendships with each other as much as or more than those with lovers and spouses, but also have come to value their children more highly than the men in their lives. When Xie Feng visits from China, she and Faith acknowledge this: "Ah, the woman said, do you notice that in time you love the children more and the man less? Faith said, Yes! but as soon as she said it, she wanted to run home and find Jack and kiss his pink ears and his 243 last hairs, to call out, Old friend, don't worry, you are loved" (LSD, 194).[14]

This extraordinary revelation—albeit accompanied by tender remorse and a surge of affection for the man who is her longtime lover and sometime husband—defines the essential centrality of the mother bond in Paley's canon, even as it opens the circle to bring China into the neighborhood. These stories forcefully deny the power of the patriarchal motherhood institution

Adrienne Rich identified; they displace adult men and situate the mother-child community at the center of everyday life, offering a fictional representation of the actual experience of mothers and children.

Philosopher Sara Ruddick recently has suggested that those who mother are "committed to meeting [the demands of mothering] by works of preservative love, nurturance, and training" (17). She goes on to argue that these same "works" are necessary in the promotion and maintenance of a "politics of peace." She quotes Paley's character Faith in "Midrash on Happiness," explaining that "work is a requirement for happiness and that 'work' includes training children."[15] Ruddick offers, ultimately, a description "of peacemaking [that] is a description of mothering" (244) and writes that, in this world of possible perspectives, a "feminist maternal peace politics is one story" (251). Grace Paley is telling that story; from her earliest fiction written in the fifties through poems, essays, and yet more stories, Grace Paley depicts mothering in ever-broadening terms. In her work, maternal nurturance is necessary on a global scale; the planet and all its inhabitants require the same cooperative shared mothering practiced by the community of women and children in her stories.

Notes

1. References to Paley collections will be noted by initials: *The Little Disturbances of Man: Stories of Women and Men at Love* (LDM); *Enormous Changes at the Last Minute* (ECLM); *Later the Same Day* (LSD).

2. Even commentators whose interest is not particularly aroused by this issue find themselves focusing on it. Anne Tyler, for instance, in her *New Republic* review of Paley's third story collection, *Later the Same Day*, discusses the stories' politics and the author's unique narrative voice, giving motherhood just a brief comment in her text, but the piece nonetheless is titled "Mothers in the City."

3. All of these characters appear in more than one story; their concerns, too, are repeated.

4. Her race/color is not described, but only assumed—Grace Paley is not immune to the ingrained white narrative assumption of a character's being white by default, black only when so labeled.

5. Interviews with Grace Paley, 1985–89, taken by Judith Arcana, transcripts unpublished.

6. Interviews with Sybil Claiborne, 1985–88, taken by Judith Arcana, transcripts unpublished.

7. This story, written in the middle 1960s—prefeminist consciousness for its author—is about motherhood, yet it presents the notion that a child belongs to its father and can simply be taken from the woman who gives birth to it. There is no commentary on this from any character or from the strongly autobiographical narrator.

8. In the original manuscript, the author's repeated changes—written in and scratched out in both pencil and ink over typescript—indicate that at least one version was a

miscarriage, and one version an abortion. The published version does not specify; readers interpret the cause of Faith's bleeding.

9. Drawn from manuscript of Arcana, *Cultural Dreamer: Grace Paley's Life Stories*, in progress.

10. Unfortunately, mother-blaming in women's writing has been supported and encouraged by the work of contemporary writers like Nancy Friday and even apparently feminist theorists like Dorothy Dinnerstein and Nancy Chodorow, all of whom believe that the raising of children almost exclusively by women has caused gender-connected emotional, social, and political problems.

11. Interviews with Sybil Claiborne, Nora Paley, and Danny Paley, 1985–88, taken by Judith Arcana, transcripts unpublished.

12. For many years, following the New Critical rule that art could not sustain an affiliation with politics, Paley was reticent about mentioning activism in her stories. With the exception of "Politics," only a few stories included even a line or two that could be construed as "political content." She wrote nonfiction for movement publications, maintaining an artificial separation which belied the integrated quality of her life work.

13. Much of Paley's work, especially in the past fifteen years, is notable for its metafictionality; she has written stories in which language is discussed as language, in which the writing of poems and stories is the subject at hand, in which characters are described by narrators as if the (also fictional) speaker had in fact created them, and so forth.

14. Actually, there are signs of this phenomenon even in earlier stories: Faith dumps her boyfriend Clifford because he does not understand or appreciate her mothering, in "A Subject of Childhood" (LDM, written in the mid-1950s); in "An Interest in Life" (LDM, same period), Ginny takes John as a lover for the sake of her children, though she neither loves nor desires him; Lucia's grandmother in "Debts" (ECLM, written in the late sixties) took her common-law husband for several reasons, but most are directly concerned with the welfare of her children.

15. "By work to do she included the important work of raising children righteously up. By righteously she meant that along with being useful and speaking truth to the community, they must do no harm. By harm she meant not only personal injury to the friend the lover the coworker the parent (the city the nation) but also the stranger in all her or his difference, who, because we were strangers in Egypt, deserves special goodness for life or at least until the end of strangeness" (Ruddick, 104, quoting Grace Paley's "Midrash on Happiness," *The Writer in Our World*, ed. Reginald Gibbons [Boston: Atlantic Monthly Press, 1986], 151– 53).

Chapter 12

Mary Gordon's Mothers

Ruth Perry

An odd lacuna in the representations of women's consciousness was perceived some years ago by feminist critics. Where, we asked one another, was the voice of the mother in literary discourse? What was it like to negotiate the world as a mother? Where could one hear from Mrs. Ramsey herself? And then, as if the critics had conjured them — but really as the crest of the same impulse — some novels began to appear in which the protagonist was a mother: Sue Miller's *The Good Mother*, Margaret Atwood's *The Handmaid's Tale*, Toni Morrison's *Beloved*, and Mary Gordon's *Men and Angels*. All were laced with the complicated mixtures of pride, guilt, joy, and fury that comprise motherhood as we know it.[1]

The family has a peculiar position in contemporary Anglo-American culture: isolated generationally, disempowered politically, often (especially in big cities) disconnected from local communities, the family nevertheless is expected to make good the psychic losses of the impersonal marketplace. This configuration makes of motherhood, that most humdrum of occupations, both a linchpin of the system and a role that needs to be created anew in every generation. In contemporary fiction, for example, white middle-class mothers lack ordinary role models and have to keep reinventing motherhood for themselves. Mothers are themselves, so to speak, motherless.

Black mothers in African-American fiction, struggling against great odds to sustain life itself rather than simply to reproduce middle-class behavior, rarely have the luxury of this anxiety about whether they are doing it right.[2] Nor are they always represented in isolation from their communities. In Gloria Naylor's *Mama Day*, for example, the mother figures are magically powerful, operating at the center of a coherent, idealized community which recognizes their place in it without question.

But the lonely mothers of Anglo-American fiction often feel intense guilt as a central feature of their experience — not surprising in an endeavor with such enormous but indefinite expectations and such minimal support. Guilt bubbles up in these narratives in peculiar and unexpected ways: in unpleasant characters, punitive events, and horrible coincidences. In *The Good Mother*, for instance, the protagonist mother is literally found guilty — by the court of law in which she loses custody of her child. Legally as well as psychologically, the plot pits the mother's sexuality against her maternity, and makes the reader ask whether or not the mother, despite her good intentions, has exposed her daughter to more adult sexuality than was good for her.

Susan Suleiman, in a pioneering article on the subject, "Writing and Motherhood," has explored a particular form of this mother-guilt in artistic production. She has described the mother-guilt that artist mothers feel when they take time "away from" mothering to pursue their art. (361–66, 373–77). This heightened consciousness of a select group of women who write or paint—who work—voluntarily, for love of it, is a more specialized form of mother-guilt than what concerns me here. Nor am I referring exclusively to the guilt of working women who must earn their own bread while entrusting their children to others or leaving them alone. Rather, I wish to call attention to the freefloating mother-guilt felt by nearly all mothers in Anglo-American culture, independent of their individual circumstances—a guilt ready to attach itself to any phenomenon, a nagging feeling that we never do enough for our children or do it quite right, never properly protect them from danger and disappointment in the world, and are never quite sure that we have always acted in their best interest.

Toni Morrison's *Beloved*, which, like her *Song of Solomon*, demonstrates the immense power of the mother to give and to take away life, can also be read as a parable about the mother's guilt over this power. Mother-guilt is figured in "Beloved" herself, the full-grown ghost of the girl Sethe killed as a baby. Although "Beloved" haunted 124 Bluestone Road as a disembodied spirit from the time of her unnatural death, her literal incarnation is simultaneously a delight and a reproach to her mesmerized mother. The way she battens on the mother, growing fat as Sethe grows thin, figures the insatiability of mother-guilt. Again, I am speaking of a generalized experience of motherhood, even in this case, for Morrison depicts conditions extreme enough to make the single limited act of infanticide morally defensible, paradoxically, as an act of protection. The "returned" child represents—among other things—the freefloating guilt all mothers feel because their children suffer and because they are unable to protect them. Sethe's guilt, figured in her returned ghost child, is guilt for all her inevitable inadequacies—her impatience, her anger, her own needs, her inability to create and protect domestic life. Not coincidentally, the guilt takes hold and flourishes in the absence of community, and the ghostly reminder of mother-guilt finally is exorcised with the help of the community mobilized by Sethe's daughter, Denver.

Mary Gordon's *Men and Angels* explores these issues—maternal power and mother-guilt, friendship and community, sexuality and family—in the context of a story about the contented mother of two, who finds her way back to the intellectual work she adores. Gordon's novel figures mother-guilt in the babysitter Laura, a schizophrenic young woman who epitomizes the failure of the mother and who stands in sharp contrast to Anne Foster, the novel's good mother. Anne hires Laura to take care of her children so that she can work on her biographical essay on the painter Caroline Watson for an exhibition catalogue. Rejected by her family of origin—and most of all by her mother—Laura embodies the psychic crippling that results from a mother's failure to love her child adequately. There are other significant victims of the breakdown of maternal love in this novel as well: Stephen, Caroline Watson's own son, who died at twenty-eight of lifelong maternal neglect, and the children of the minor character, "Betty the Basher," who now tyrannize over their mother because she once beat them. But Laura, whose interior monologues alternate with Anne's, is the most significant of these victims. She has been damaged beyond reach by her mother's hostility toward her. Hallucinating a Spirit who will love her unconditionally, she is blank and unknowable to the family she works for, to the reader, and quite possibly to the author.

Laura's alien presence in this otherwise familiar, academic, bourgeois, two-child family, is like a time bomb that Anne Foster has unwittingly brought into her home so that she can work. When and how it will explode are the questions that provide the narrative tension in the novel; we turn the pages anxiously awaiting the denoument, which we know will be bloody. Laura is fanatically evangelical, scarred by a series of encounters with exploitative religious charlatans, from a lower-class family with no pretensions to culture. These qualities—her class and her frightening religious beliefs—are the marks of Laura's otherness, her difference from her employer. When the explosion comes and Anne fires Laura for letting the children walk on thin ice, we are relieved that Laura kills only herself, that she removes only her own inarticulate, superfluous, lumpish presence from a world in which she has always been a servant and never—despite the first-person passages—a subject.

This, then, is the allegory: in hiring a babysitter, in putting her work first, Anne, the fostering mother, jeopardizes the welfare of her children. The danger to which she subjects them is unpredictable, unknowable—like the dynamic by which Laura's mother and Caroline Watson are estranged from their own offspring. That dangerous and terrifying ground remains unexplored—how a mother develops an antipathy toward her child—as opaque, finally, as Laura herself. Three times in *Men and Angels*, Mary Gordon intones the cardinal rule of motherhood: "You did not hurt your children. You kept them from harm. That was what you did in the world if you were a mother" (129; see also 69, 228). Yet the choice to work and to hire childcare is undeniably dangerous. Laura's stubbornly indigestible presence in the narrative figures the guilt of the working mother: whether that of Anne Foster, Caroline Watson, or even Mary Gordon herself.

Susan Suleiman puts this text at the center of her second brilliant paper exploring the psychological dimensions of motherhood, "On Maternal Splitting." She reads Gordon's novel as a study in the psychological mechanism of splitting, a mechanism used to maintain our fantasies of maternal omnipotence—which fantasies, Suleiman argues, appear to be necessary to our psychic balance as mothers. Suleiman's analysis focuses on the multiple combinations of good and bad mothers in *Men and Angels*, good and bad children, and mother-figures who are themselves children. She argues that splitting off the bad from the good preserves the fantasy of the omnipotent mother. It makes possible a belief in a mother who is all goodness and provides a similarly unambivalent target for blame in the all-bad mother. According to her reading, Laura and Anne are "structural twins," two sides of one coin, with Laura the "split-off projection—of Anne herself," a projection whose separate existence guarantees the unmixed goodness of the Anne mother. Although as women and as mothers we (and I include Mary Gordon here) are frightened by the responsibility of motherhood, according to Suleiman, we are not willing to give up our belief that mothers are all-important to the health and happiness of their children. Somewhere in the history of any psychically healthy human being, we imagine that there had to have been a good, nurturing mother figure—whether a birth mother or surrogate—and, conversely, that psychological breakdown is attributable to the absence of such a figure.

Yet I would argue that Anne's power as a mother is more present in this novel as fear and guilt than as positive capacity—whether insight, knowledge, or competence. Not that mother-guilt is independent of fantasies of omnipotence. On the contrary, mother-guilt is the inevitable corollary, the other side, of fantasies of maternal omnipotence. If, as mothers, we believe that we are all-important in the lives of our children, that our effects are all-determining and all-powerful, it is inevitable that, as our children grow up unhappy and imperfect—buffeted by life—we will feel guilt in proportion to our presumption. Where Suleiman argues that Laura symbolizes the danger and unknowability of all caregivers but the primary mother—thus corroborating the fantasy of the omnipotent mother—I would urge that the novel is more explicitly concerned with the inexplicability of maternal failure, externalized and scapegoated in the figure of Laura, but explored too in the various mothers who are themselves doubled and split—good-enough mothers for one of their children but lethal for the other. Caroline Watson, for one, is represented as a failed mother to her son Stephen but as a mother made in heaven for her daughter-in-law Jane; schizophrenic Laura's mother loved her second daughter, Debbie, after her own fashion, and raised her healthy and whole; Anne's own mother consistently takes the part of Beth, Anne's younger sister, and abandons Anne, who is her father's favorite.

These doubled mothers hedge the issue of maternal responsibility and emphasize what all mothers recognize as the truth: that we operate in the dark, and that, as Mary Gordon puts it on the penultimate page of this novel, no one knows what kills or saves. Indeed, the conscious message of this epilogue is that mother love is complicated and unpredictable, that its effects on children are similarly inexplicable, and that, this being so, thank God that there is more to a woman's life than her children!

> And there was the other part of mother love: it was not all of life. And that was wonderful; it was a tremendous mercy. For there was so little you could do for them, even if you spent every moment with them, gave them every waking thought, there wasn't much that you could do. You gave them life, you loved them, then you opened them out to the world. You could never protect them; so you left them to themselves. That was the mercy, that you could turn from them to something else, something they couldn't touch or be a part of. You could turn, sometimes, from the sight of them, making their way in the world, so dangerous, so treacherous; you could put down the burden of that mother love, could swim up from it, passing the exhilarating sights, the colorful quick fish, the shining rocks and bubbles. (239)*

Gordon seems to be telling us here that writing—art—relieves the anxiety of motherhood by giving a woman something else to pay attention to. The text redeems the mother: the act of writing, of analyzing and creating in another sphere, refreshes and replenishes the mother—and makes possible the intensity of her life with her children. Turning her attention from her small fry to the world around her, Gordon's amphibious mother gives birth to herself, swimming up out of the protective womb of motherhood.

Still, one wants to know, what causes such anxiety in motherlove that requires rational exposition to allay it? Why does Gordon feel called upon to write this epilogue to soothe our fears? Child mortality rates—at least in the white middle-class families that Mary Gordon writes about—are lower than they ever have been in history. Food, clothing, medicine—these can be taken for granted.

Perhaps it is because the physical health of the planet in which our children will have to live has never been so precarious. Surely the pervasive fearfulness about the safety and future of children that is displayed in much con-

---

* Quotations for *Men and Angels* by Mary Gordon. Copyright © 1985 by Mary Gordon. Reprinted by permission of Random House Inc.

temporary fiction written by women must be understood as a reaction to this current critical state of affairs. Worries about children also must be read as a reponse to the squandering of fossil fuels, the dumping of hazardous wastes, and the ruthless contamination of our very air and water by irresponsible corporate leaders. But it is also true that American society does not make it easy to be a mother, for all the hysteria in recent years about fetuses' "right to life." The last industrialized country in the world to ignore its citizens' needs for subsidized childcare, the United States also pays the women in its workforce considerably less than its men. Motherhood must be undertaken at one's own risk in the United States. It is even considered a punishment by some opponents of legal abortion, the just consequence of women's sexual activity. There are enormous strains for women in the way our society constructs motherhood.

Fittingly, Suleiman ends "On Maternal Splitting," her article about *Men and Angels*, by observing how bad daycare arrangements are in America, a material condition that exacerbates the guilt of working mothers immeasurably—as well as the fantasies of omnipotence that are the other side of that guilt. Small wonder that a country that would poison its own wells, with a callous disregard for the future, would also neglect to make provision for the care of its children. How then, one wants to know, did the author of this novel, born and raised in America, experience the institution of daycare, as a child and as a mother? How might our cultural arrangements be said to have affected her construction of these issues of maternal power and maternal guilt in her novel? Beyond the usual interest in the life of any artist whose work touches us, in the case of a *woman* artist—as Gordon herself observes—one always wants to know "the grossest facts: Whom did they sleep with? Did they have any babies? Were their fathers kind to them, cruel to them? did they obey or go against their mothers? Infantile questions, yet one felt one had to know" (Gordon, *Men and Angels*, 50). One wants to know how other women have managed to live a life both of the body and of the mind. As Gordon explains: "One wanted to believe that the price was not impossible for these accomplished women, that there were fathers, husbands, babies, beautifully flourishing beside the beautiful work" (50).

To the extent that the material conditions out of which art is produced affect that art, Mary Gordon's involvement in daycare arrangements is relevant here. For the fact is, she has had a kind of genius for them. As a young woman, she cared for the children of one of her college professors, whom she adopted as a kind of mother. Her own extremely powerful mother, a disabled woman in a wheelchair, worked all her life to support the family. Gordon, an only child, was entrusted to a series of caretakers, including her father, David Gordon, a writer of uncertain employment, a Jew converted to Catholicism, a "maternal" man who fostered her imagination (Gordon, "David"). Later, miraculously, she was discovered by Margaret Drabble, who "mothered" her career. When she grew up and had her own children, she hired as adolescents the very children she had cared for as a college girl, to babysit her own small children so that she could write.

Thus Mary Gordon participated in the daycare process at every level: she received daycare as a child; she provided daycare as a young woman; and she hired daycare for her own children as a young mother. Yet the crudest level of plot in this book would seem to warn that lapses in attention to one's children could prove dangerous. Surely Suleiman is right to understand this book as a culturally specific artifact expressive of a collective American attitude about the centrality of the mother to the psychic as well as bodily health of the child. "Why is it" she asks, "that mothers—even enlightened, creative, feminist mothers—in the United States today find it so difficult to acknowledge, in their deepest fantasies about their children, the possibility that they are not the only ones on whom the child's welfare, the child's whole life and self, depend?" ("On Maternal Splitting," 39).

It is because Gordon's book is a profound meditation on the relations between motherhood and work that Suleiman is led to ask her questions. *Men and Angels* configures and reconfigures motherhood and intellectual work, compulsively trying them out in this combination and that, fascinated by both processes, concerned simultaneously with the lives of children and the creation of art. What is so satisfying and uniquely relevant about this novel is that it imaginatively portrays a life centrally concerned with the complicated interplay between work and motherhood—how they feed and reinforce rather than thwart or foil one another. Gordon describes with uncanny accuracy the freedom and weightlessness of abstract thought after the bodily consciousness of motherlife—the clarity and comfort of working alone at one's desk after the dense, sensual absorption of being with one's children. Both intellectual work and the tasks of motherhood have redemptive value in this novel. The protagonist cares passionately about both; and what is more remarkable, in her practice of them we begin to see their communalities.

If ever there was a representation of "maternal thinking" in action—a description of a process engaging a mother's care, thought, judgment in a realm other than raising her children—Mary Gordon's representation of Anne Foster's working process in this novel is an example of "maternal thinking."[3] As a biographer and art critic no less than as a mother, Anne Foster calls upon her capacity for what Sara Ruddick has described as "attentive love"—a blending of looking, holding (as opposed to acquiring), self-restraint, humility, and empathy that comprises the maternal discipline.

Gordon reverses the usual metaphoric relations between work and motherhood in this novel and makes the biographer's research and writing figure her maternal activity. The "work" side of the work-and-motherhood equation glows with special intensity. The subject Gordon creates for Anne Foster to work on — Caroline Watson — has tremendous magnetism; anyone would want to know more about her. In many ways, she is the novel's greatest triumph: a woman impressionist created out of whole cloth, believable in a recreated Paris of the 1920s (Gordon even invents a a brief relationship with Gertrude Stein), complete with an *oeuvre* of plausible paintings that deal with formal and personal issues at one and the same time, like the greatest art. Anne Foster's work matters because Caroline Watson's work matters: she is a great painter. A combination of Mary Cassatt, Cecelia Beaux, Suzanne Valadon, and Paula Modersohn-Becker, she has produced work of lasting reputation. In psychological and artistic complexity, Caroline Watson, this artist at the center of the novel (the formal cause of the action), figures the interpenetration of subjective and formal issues, as Anne Foster thinks back and forth between the life and the art. In my first reading of this book, what delighted me most was the description of Anne Foster's piecing together the painterly progress of Caroline Watson's work in connection to the events of her life, acts of imagination familiar to me as a biographer. It seemed to me that Gordon understood and relished the biographer's task. Caroline Watson is also, obviously, the creation of a literary mind — quintessentially fictive in her constitutive parts and in the process by which she is built up. I also saw in Gordon's invention a loving tribute to her own husband's biographical work on the eighteenth-century writer, Laurence Sterne, another strand weaving together life and art in this text.

Caroline Watson, a great painter and a bad mother, is invented in part to ask: Does nothing excuse a woman for not putting maternal responsibilities first? Are there no urgencies that matter next to this? What if she is engaged in revolutionary political actions? What if she is a great artist? As Anne's friend and neighbor Barbara Greenspan observes: "No one gives a shit if Monet wasn't a good father" (171).

Gordon exaggerates the dilemma of living as a mother or living as an artist by structuring Caroline Watson's life as a choice between her art and her son: she was not legally permitted to take Stephen out of the country, and she was unable to paint in America. It was one or the other — a more extreme version of Anne Foster's dilemma with her exhibition catalogue, her two children, and her intrusive babysitter. For Gordon wants us to acknowledge our asymmetrical expectations of women and the consequences for their creative work. "The truth of the matter was that for a woman to have accomplished something, she had to get out of the way of her own body. This was the trick people wanted to know about" (50).

Gordon's own solution to this impasse is to problematize the distinctions—to blur the lines—between life and art, children and writing, and to show how they figure one another. No intellectual issue without its biographical dimension; no personal choice without its abstract, formal meaning. She talks about writing as if it were a kind of mothering: creating and molding, but also operating in the dark much of the time, and finally letting go and permitting the characters to have their independent existence. The same qualities of heart and mind that make Anne Foster a good mother make her a good critic and biographer: the ability to read another, to tune into another's necessities, to understand another's reality. Her recognition of, say, Grunewald's influence on Caroline Watson's style is not unlike to her intuitions about her children, whose otherness she always insists on, and for whom she repeatedly asserts she cannot "take credit." One assumes that Mary Gordon's "negative capability" as an artist—her ability to let her characters evolve beyond the structures she originally envisioned for them—partakes of this same appreciation of otherness. When she writes of Anne Foster's feeling for her children, Gordon suggests her own approach to the fixed dates, famous cultural events, and historical givens of the early twentieth-century art world in Paris, that constitute the limits of her materials.

> She loved the intransigence of their natures, all that could never be molded and so was free from her. She liked to stand back a little from her children—it was why some people thought her, as a mother, vague. But she respected the fixity of her children's souls, what they were born with, what she had, from the first months, seen. (17)

Jessica Benjamin's *The Bonds of Love*, a book that argues for a great cultural need for subjective consciousness, for deeper and more immediate recognition of the subjectivity of others—starting with the mother—claims that women are in a unique position to recognize forms of otherness that do not diminish the self. Women who give birth, for example, after carrying the fetus for nine months, experience the newborn as a kind of transitional object, according to Benjamin, both inside and outside the boundaries of their own identities. "Never will she feel more strongly," writes Benjamin, "than in those first days of her baby's life, the intense mixture of his being part of herself, utterly familiar and yet utterly new, unknown, and other" (14). The protagonist in Mary Gordon's book feels like this about her work as well as her children.

In thus describing the intelligent attention, the creative sympathy, that a gifted woman brings both to writing and to raising children, Gordon heals the division between life and art, mind and body, that is assumed in the culture and replicated in the sexual division of labor. Although, as Suleiman has shown us, the plot of this novel painfully testifies to the cost of this division, I would argue that Gordon reaffirms in her dominant metaphors and details, and in the resonances of her prose, the continuities between the life of a writer and the life of a mother. As Anne says to herself about Caroline Watson, "This woman, whom I know and do not know at all, is part of my life like my own children" (45).

Susan Stanford Friedman has analyzed the meaning for women and men of describing creative and intellectual work with the language of procreation. In tracing the meaning of a gender-differentiated use of metaphors of pregnancy and childbirth for literary creativity, she asserts that women always deploy these metaphors for liberatory ends: "to challenge fundamental binary oppositions of patriarchal ideology between word and flesh, creativity and procreativity, mind and body" (51). Men, on the other hand, often use these metaphors to describe the creative process, she argues, in a spirit that appropriates childbirth for themselves while at the same time denying women scope for any creativity other than biological creativity. Either you give birth with your womb or with your brain, their metaphors insist, but not both. But when women represent their creativity with images of childbirth, according to Friedman, they do so to claim for themselves the possibility of creating with the brain as well as the womb; the imagery is, in their hands, "subversive."

The erotic investment in *Men and Angels* is almost entirely in these two competing but parallel activities: work and family life—or at least life with children. Both radiate libidinous energy. Yet an economy has been worked out between them; neither focuses all the pleasure or drains the energy of the other. The sensations of motherhood and of authorship are described with the language of fleshly love. We are told that Anne's obsession with her work is like a love affair, a "vehicle of infidelity" that intrudes and "siphons off" Anne's attention from her family. "Seeing these paintings, something grew in Anne, . . . a push or desire, like the hunger for a definite but hard-to-come-by food" (23). Gordon's language suggests the push of labor, the desire of sex, the cravings of pregnancy. She invokes these aspects of the life of the body in describing the first stirrings of Anne's biography project. And her descriptions of the bodily experiences of work are more than matched by descriptions of the bodily pleasure taken in being a mother. Anne's sensual enjoyment of the deliciousness of the smell, feel, sound, and sight of her children is evocative of Mary Cassatt's tactile definition of babies' bottoms, cheeks, arms. "The urge to touch one's child, she often thought, was like, and wasn't like, the hunger that one felt to touch a lover" (16). Even Laura's unrequited love for her mother has this bodily dimension, in the way she loved her mother's cool flesh, her quick movements, her small tanned arms.

But if work and children share these sexual valences, the usual sources of sexual energy are missing from this book. Michael Foster, Anne's husband, is shipped off to another country, where his sexual needs are taken care of in a shadowy romance only briefly threatening to preoccupied Anne. Mr. Corcoran, the substitute man in Anne's life—a caricature of the perfect husband, as he fixes the wiring and takes care of the children—will not go to bed with Anne, although she asks him to. The only sexually attractive male actor in the book, he lives celibate, faithful to an impaired wife. None of the central women characters in the book have husbands or lovers who are present—not Anne, Jane, Caroline, or even Laura. It is as if there just isn't enough erotic energy to go around. After juggling the claims of work and motherhood, the imagination is exhausted; there simply is not enough left over for "love" or sex.

This absence of a sexual focus is also dictated by conventions about fictional narrators. It seems unlikely that Gordon could have sustained the authority of the female subject as an artist or intellectual—whether Anne or Caroline Watson—if she had introduced romance into the picture. The difficult psychological balancing act which is the subject of this novel—of attention and imagination, of self and other, of work and mothering—would have dissolved in the heat of sex. Then too, in our culture (which admires nubile androgyny and constructs motherhood as asexual), sexual passion is supposed to exclude thought. No one besides Grace Paley has yet managed convincingly to portray the coexistence of the mother-self and the sexual self. Paley does it by sacrificing the narcissistic vanity—the object status—of the sexual self and by domesticating any romantic sense of elevated mystery about sexual pleasure. Gordon is not ready to give these up yet; they are present in her insistence on Anne's beauty and her discerning sense of style. The closest thing in Gordon's novel to the obsessiveness of a female subject in love is Laura's abject devotion to the "Spirit." And Gordon's final solution to Laura's imperviousness and compulsion is to reduce her to a lifeless object.

In addition to describing the erotic energy of both work and motherhood, Gordon connects the labors of childraising and writing with a sustained analogy between reproduction and literary production. In the beginning, when Anne Foster first thinks about Caroline Watson's life, reads her diaries, and looks at her paintings, these early conceptional stirrings are described as impregnation: "Something embedded itself, dug in, and sharpened" (25). Gordon represents other aspects of literary production as part of the reproductive process as well. She imagines the relations between author and subject as a kind of kinship, and the interconnectedness of women writers as generational. The debt that creativity—writing this book, for instance—owes to the experience of maternity is acknowledged in the subject matter. All four major female characters—Anne, Laura, Caroline, Jane—are seen as parts of their respective families, as daughters of mothers and mothers of daughters. They are related to one another, too, insofar as each represents a different patterning of work and family. All red-haired women, they might be part of one complex whole. As Jane says to Anne, "We're terribly alike; we could be mother and daughter" (129). Each represents a different aspect of the problem; the issues of their lives bear a family resemblance to one another.

Gordon can be read in this novel as self-consciously locating herself in a tradition of women writers, displaying her maternal sources, modeling her literary relations on maternal relations. Just as all the characters in *Men and Angels* are profoundly affected by their mothers' lives — no-one can separate herself from the life that went on before — so this novel was profoundly influenced by two mother-obsessed authors of the previous generation, Elizabeth Bowen and Virginia Woolf. Bowen's *The Death of the Heart*, with its clean, antiseptic prose, may have supplied the original of the young matron and her younger dependent, yoked together by circumstance, living in the same house, each impassively watching the other, and exhibited to the reader in alternating chapters. In addition to Bowen's image of the unbridgeable distance between people, the book owes something to Virginia Woolf's tribute to her own mother, that mosaic of nonverbal sensings, intimations, feelings, and thought, *To the Lighthouse*.

In the spirit of that earlier Mrs. Ramsey, Anne Foster admires her son for his developing male intelligence that knows how to build a solar (sun/son) clock. Likewise, the language about his "courtliness", his ardent nature, his "fine, inflexible standards"— and the male ascription of these qualities — comes from Woolf, as does the imagery of wings and beaks to connote emotion: "She heard nothing, could see nothing but a circle of confused wings, whirring horribly, and the sharp beak somewhere about to strike" (202). And at the center of the book is the Thanksgiving dinner at Jane's house, a lovely literary obeisance to Woolf's famous *boeuf en daube*, the dinner party in *To the Lighthouse*, created by Mrs. Ramsey's art, making out of the self-consuming materials of dailiness a memory for all of them to hold in their hearts forever.

> Everyone sat shyly; the formal beauty made them quiet. Then Jane brought out the turkey, human, comic on its platter. Talk began. The bird was praised; it was coveted; choices were made of dark meat or white. Dishes were passed, and people made arrangements on their plate that pleased them. Jane stood, said a blessing, and Anne felt them all grow ornamented with good fortune, like a spray of diamonds on the dark hair of a woman. (101)

Gordon is perhaps the first feminist novelist of our generation to explore deeply in her fiction what it feels like to be a mother and an intellectual or writer. Susan Stanford Friedman has shown how women use childbirth metaphors to reaffirm their right to intellectual and artistic life. Gordon's novel corroborates and extends this insight by fully imagining both sides of the equation—both motherhood and writing. They not only figure one another but also resemble one another, continue one another, reinforce one another. By constructing the unified consciousness of a woman who loves both her children and her work, she shows how raising children is like developing ideas, and how thinking and acting for the welfare of one's children engages one's mind and heart with the totality and intensity of any other creative work. She shows how a compassionate intellectual acts maternally in trying to put together how a painter sees the world or an artist imagines another life. She shows how a writer makes what is constructed by our culture as a woman's empathic effort—trying to understand what influences and directs another person's thought and perception, what matters in another's life.

Gordon literally maps one kind of process onto the other, in Anne Foster's intensely self-conscious effort to understand the painter and forgive the mother, as well as to live her own life while engaging in the work of biographical reconstruction. This integration of elements—reading thought as maternal attention and maternal attention as thought—is an irreducibly feminist statement, however complacent the overtones in the description of Anne's happy traditional family in their nice old house. By equally privileging intellectual "making" with domestic work like cooking or childcare in her narrative, Gordon integrates these two aspects of a woman's life at a formal level. Aware as she is of the multiplicity of perspectives that life has to offer, this writer has chosen to tell her story with the voice of a mother, speaking to us of the lives of her children and of the beings in her other inner life.

Notes

I am grateful to Janice Thaddeus for her careful reading of an earlier draft of this article.

1. For a thorough analysis of the possible meanings of the absence of the maternal voice in literary discourse, see Hirsch, *Mother/Daughter Plot*.

2. Tillie Olsen's story "I Stand Here Ironing" (1953–54) images the circumstances of poverty, in the soliloquy of a single, white, working-class mother who notes sadly that her pressing economic necessities preclude closer attention to her child's psychological needs.

3. The term "maternal thinking" and its philosophical conceptualization come from Sara Ruddick's crucially important essay, "Maternal Thinking."

Chapter 13

Maternal Reading:
Lazarre and Walker

Maureen T. Reddy

Advocating the mere tolerance of
difference between women is the
grossest reformism. It is a
total denial of the creative function
of difference in our lives.
Difference must be not merely
tolerated, but seen as a
fund of necessary polarities between
which our creativity can spark
like a dialectic.
—Audre Lorde

In "Reading Ourselves: Toward a Feminist Theory of Reading," Patrocinio P. Schweickart suggests that one task facing feminist critics is the development of "reading strategies consonant with the concerns, experiences, and formal devices that constitute" works by women, if we are to break the "vicious circle" of androcentric texts generating androcentric interpretive strategies, which produce a preference for an androcentric canon (45). The twelve essays included in Flynn and Schweickart's *Gender and Reading* individually and collectively contribute to this project, but there are striking lacunae: no essay focuses on the salience of race for both reader and writer, and none examines what effect the experience of mothering might have on reading or on writing. These omissions replicate both the avoidance of real engagement with issues of race by white feminists generally[1] and the silencing of mothers among nonfeminist (and some feminist) literary scholars. In so doing, these omissions preserve other, equally vicious circles: Eurocentric texts generate Eurocentric interpretive strategies, which produce a preference for a Eurocentric canon. "Childcentric" texts—by which I mean those that privilege the subjectivity of someone *not* a parent—generate childcentric interpretive strategies, which produce a preference for a childcentric canon.

The present essay takes as its central concern several of the topics omitted in *Gender and Reading*; it is intended as a contribution to two ongoing feminist debates: (1) how white women might learn to read black women's writing, and (2) how feminists might learn to read mothers' stories while respectfully examining and incorporating into theory differences among women.[2] I want to position this essay at the intersection of these issues, using parts of Sara Ruddick's *Maternal Thinking* as the basis of a strategy for reading some of Jane Lazarre's and Alice Walker's novels, while also using those novels to test the limits of Ruddick's theory. The novels—Alice Walker's *Meridian* (1976), *The Color Purple* (1982), and *The Temple of My Familiar* (1989); and Jane Lazarre's *The Mother Knot* (1976) and *The Powers of Charlotte* (1987)—are by and about women who are daughters, mothers, and artists; in every case, the woman author's, and her hero's, experience of motherhood is central to, and inseparable from, her life as an artist, with this experience impinging upon the actual and imagined texts in a variety of subtle and complex ways.

Ruddick's book is not about literature, but I believe her concept of maternal thinking has implications for reading certain literary works by women. In using Ruddick's theory of maternal thinking to analyze Lazarre's and Walker's novels and the novels to critique the theory, I necessarily focus most closely on those concerns shared to some degree by all three authors; in so doing, though, I do not mean to imply that the authors' concerns are identical or to minimize important differences among them. Instead, I hope to use those differences as the "fund" Lorde speaks of in the passage used as an epigraph to this essay, (*Sister/Outsider*, III), searching for those mothers' tools that might help to dismantle the master's house. That is, maternal thinking potentially provides a model for reading that truly attends to difference, rather than merely tolerating it.

Following Simone Weil and Iris Murdoch, Ruddick describes attentive love, which she posits as knitting together maternal thought (*Maternal Thinking*, 119), as "a kind of knowing that takes truthfulness as its aim but makes truth serve lovingly the person known" (120). The opposite of attentive love is fantasy: "Fantasy is reverie designed to protect the psyche from pain, self-induced blindness designed to protect it from insight" (120). Ruddick distinguishes attentive love from empathy by stressing "the importance of knowing another *without* finding yourself in her" (121); attentive love "lets difference emerge without searching for comforting commonalities, dwells upon the *other*, and lets otherness be" (122). Attentive love, in short, is a habit of mind one might also describe as loving detachment. This way of thinking seeks to understand difference but not to change it, to recognize the immutable separation of knower and known without trying to subsume the other into the self. Attentive love, then, is a useful stance for readers of texts originating in cultures different from their own, as it offers a position from which to "dwell upon the *other*, and let otherness be." This stance allows the reader to interact with the text, not simply attempt to fit the text to preexisting frameworks.

How might one learn this reading strategy? Ruddick argues that one learns to think maternally through mothering work, the daily, ongoing care of children; but in treating maternal thought as a resource for peace, she also implies that there may be other ways to learn—and to teach—maternal thought. I believe that all of these novels—and others written from mothers' perspectives—offer readers, mothers or not, access to maternal thinking. Although I do not want to undercut Ruddick's theory by challenging its basic argument—that the practice of mothering gives rise to a particular way of thinking—I think it is possible to add to that argument by suggesting that one also may learn some aspects of maternal thinking through reading. Ruddick suggests that "maternal conversations" and "maternal stories" are important aspects of learning and then articulating maternal thinking, particularly because they provide a route to collectivity: "Learning to make up, share, and revise good maternal stories is a social project" (*Maternal Thinking*, 101). Defining "good" maternal stories as those that strive toward including realism, compassion, and delight (98), Ruddick acknowledges that these virtues may be extremely difficult to achieve. Further, as Ruddick points out, many mothers lack access to the leisure and space requisite for maternal conversation or storytelling, and therefore lack opportunity to hear other mothers' stories, or to tell and to revise their own:

> Many mothers are cut off from other mothers, because they do their mothering work in isolation or because they are driven by competition or inhibited by self-doubt or simply because they are exhausted. They do not have the company in which shared stories can be collectively judged and improved. (101–102)

Reading mothers' stories may offer an isolated mother links to other mothers, access to their stories, and perhaps even encouragement to tell her own maternal stories. Certainly Lazarre's and Walker's novels function in part as lessons in both reading and thinking.[3] These lessons may provide a kind of substitute both for the work of mothering to those who are not mothers, and/or for the company in which maternal stories might be shared, and therefore might also make possible the inclusion of those who feel "left out" of Ruddick's theory. One does not have to be a mother to read *Meridian*, *The Mother Knot*, *The Powers of Charlotte*, *The Color Purple*, or *The Temple of My Familiar*; but one does need to learn to think like a mother and to value that perspective.

Maternal thinking influences the novels' themes, plots, and structures, and shapes them differently from traditional novels; readers need to learn how to think maternally in order to understand both the novels' structures and their characters' development. Critics have had a remarkably hard time dealing with several of these novels, precisely because the method of thinking that inspires them is little understood or attended to, even by feminists. "Mothers," says Ruddick, "have been a powerless group whose thinking, when it has been acknowledged at all, has most often been recognized by people interested in interpreting and controlling rather than listening" (*Maternal Thinking*, 26). Black mothers' thinking has been attended to even less frequently than white mothers', and more often (and more extensively) controlled. These facts, combined with the limited and largely mistaken views of the novel's history and generic boundaries, as detailed in the introduction to this volume, often have led critics to misidentify or to ignore these novels' central concerns and their artistic achievements.

Most early reviewers labeled Lazarre's *The Mother Knot* a memoir and ignored its novelistic aspects, particularly its careful, fictional structure. Lazarre has said that she has always thought of *The Mother Knot* as an autobiographical novel (personal interview, 12 December 1988), but it was reviewed as straight autobiography and even marketed as such by its original publisher, McGraw-Hill. As late as 1976, then, most critics lacked the background and the imaginative capacity necessary to understand on its own terms a novel that told a story about mothering from a mother's perspective, in obedience to the rhythms of a mother's life, and with close attention to the details of daily life with a small child. In the same year (1976) that Lazarre saw her novel labeled a memoir, Alice Walker saw *Meridian* both treated as autobiography (Tate, 184) and dismembered by critics unable to deal with it as a coherent whole (Tate, 177).[4] *Meridian*'s structure, which Walker likens to a crazy-quilt, seems to have stymied most critics, causing them to do violence to the novel by focusing on just one part of what is actually a careful design (Tate, 176–78). Quilts, of course, are peculiarly female art forms, whose *function* is a major part of their beauty: a quilt is an art object meant for "everyday use," to borrow the title of one of Walker's short stories, and is associated with maternal inheritance.[5] Walker's use of the quilt metaphor in describing *Meridian* offers further support for Mary Helen Washington's view that Walker, along with other black women writers, gains her "authority of authorship" from her mother, who also "provides a model for the black woman's presence in this society" (147). Black women writers, according to Washington, write as the daughters of mothers whose own artistry was expressed in quilts, gardens, and the like; these writing daughters learn to tell their mothers' stories, to speak for their mothers.[6]

The Color Purple met less critical resistance on formal grounds than did *Meridian* or *The Mother Knot*, perhaps because its epistolary form, harking back to eighteenth-century novels like Fanny Burney's *Cecilia* and Samuel Richardson's *Clarissa*, seemed at least superficially familiar to white reviewers. But the letters in *The Color Purple* differ strikingly in both form and content from those early models, with the largest group of the letters written to God in the language of the folk by a young, semiliterate black woman, who writes in order to make some sense of, and therefore to bear, the abuse she suffers first from her stepfather and then from her husband. These letters document Celie's developing maternal perspective; in writing, Celie is "saving the life that is [her] own," to borrow another Walker title: through writing, she learns to trust her own perceptions and to value herself enough to fight her oppressors. Michael Awkward points out that Celie's achievement of a communal voice, an important thematic concern in *The Color Purple*, comes about in part through the form in which she writes, which calls for a response (145) and which can absorb other forms, such as the diary novel, letters from others, conversations, and blues lyrics. The epistolary form, as Mae G. Henderson notes in her article on *The Color Purple*, is "a tradition associated with women, allows a feminine narrative voice, and establishes a bond and intimacy between women" (68). Walker does not simply adopt this form, however: she also adapts it, revising the form's conventions "in such a way as to turn the sentimental novel on its head" (Henderson, 68). Henderson sees Walker's use of quilting in the novel — Celie, Sofia, and Shug contribute to making a quilt called "Sister's Choice" — as a "fitting emblem of the bonding between women" (76); quilting also stands as a fitting emblem of the author's method and of her novel's structure.

For the protagonist of Lazarre's *The Powers of Charlotte*, painting serves a function similar to that served for Celie by writing. Beginning in early adolescence, Charlotte paints both the world around her and her long-dead parents, trying through art to make life manageable. These paintings, described in great detail in the novel, form a narrative of their own that parallels the written narrative. We can read the paintings — multiple versions of the same subjects — as a metaphor for the structure of the novel itself, which approaches its central issues — mothering, art, and politics, to put it briefly — from different perspectives across time. Each of the three parts of *The Powers of Charlotte* depicts Charlotte's search for a satisfying and empowering story of origins, from a distinct position that is symbolic of Charlotte's conception of her needs at that time. In the first part, we are given a linear story about her search for a father; in the second, a recursive and inclusive — of other stories, letters, journals, conversations — story about her search for a mother;

and in the third, a more expansive, more political, *and* more personal narrative about self-acceptance and political action. The novel resembles a palimpsest, with earlier versions of events visible beneath or behind later ones.[7]

Meridian also incorporates metaphors for its own structure, in the Sojourner tree and in Anne-Marion's photograph of the tree-stump's concentric circles. The living tree, like the novel, is named for a woman and has hidden roots and numerous branches, all organically connected and unified by the trunk. Once cut down, the tree refuses to die—a tiny branch grows from its stump— and its stump reveals not a linear history, but a history better represented by circles within circles. This organic, cyclical view of history, rooted in both Native American and African conceptions of nature, life, and death, underpins *The Temple of My Familiar*, in which we learn that the character Lissie has been a black woman, a white man, even a lion. Lissie is a "sister/mystic/ warrior/woman/mother," but also a "goddess" who contains "everybody and everything" (371). Numerous critics scoffed nervously at the "New Age" philosophy of this novel, missing the point that Walker draws on the *sources* of New Age thought: an Afrocentric understanding of the interrelatedness of all things. Doris davenport, in her *Women's Review of Books* review of *The Temple of My Familiar*, says that critics have trouble with that novel because of their refusal to understand or accept its "Afracentric" perspective, which she defines as "the state of being comfortably, wholly female and Black at once, with no schizophrenia, no alternating realities, and no questions about it, either" (13).

That critics' inappropriate expectations shaped their responses to *Meridian* is clearest in Marge Piercy's half-joking complaint that the book needed a marriage or a funeral to end it (Tate, 180). Piercy's criticism is somewhat more perceptive than that of many others, in its implicit recognition of the novel's position in a specifically female literary history—women's heroines do usually end in marriage or death—but misses Walker's crucial revision of that history and her choice of a plot quite different from white female revisions of the *bildungsroman*. Indeed, none of these novels ends in a marriage or a funeral: *Meridian* ends with Truman preparing himself to bear the burdens Meridian has borne, as Meridian herself casts them off to return "to the world cleansed of sickness" (219). *The Color Purple* ends with the reunion of Celie and her long-lost sister and children, a story continued in *The Temple of My Familiar*, one of whose characters is Celie's granddaughter. In turn, that novel's closing scene shows a younger man trying to help an old man to read one of Lissie's paintings, as he begins to regain his sight; in order to really see the world, this scene suggests, one must look upon it with attentive love. *The Mother Knot* ends with Jane, her husband, and her son on a plane, heading toward a visit with Jane's sister in San Franscisco. *The Powers of Charlotte* ends in Nicaragua, with Charlotte sketching a soldier's face, bearing witness to violence in the best way she can.

Although all these endings draw in some ways on the convention of resolving comedy in a public celebration that symbolizes the reconstitution of community, their avoidance of the overdetermined social rituals associated with traditional genres (funerals for tragedies, marriages for comedies) symbolizes the novels' resistance to closure. All five novels are open-ended, inviting the reader to "write beyond the ending," in Rachel Blau DuPlessis's phrase, as the protagonists continue to change. In Ruddick's formulation, "The work of fostering growth provokes or requires a welcoming response to change" (*Maternal Thinking*, 89). In order to welcome change and to change with it, "a mother needs to assume the existence of a partly conscious, continuous mind . . . In assuming their continuous mental reality, mothers construe their children as constructive agents of their world and their life in it" (91–92). Readers of these novels are taught to think like mothers—to think maternally—in that we are encouraged to expect continuous change, to recognize the heroes *and ourselves* as agents constructive of our worlds, to accept *process* as the underlying structural principle—and goal—of both art and life.

Walker's and Lazarre's protagonists learn to accept and to value continuous change, while also learning how to effect change both in themselves and in the world; they become, in short, maternal thinkers. The novels reflect their protagonists' central task in their nonlinear structures and multivocal forms. The hero of each novel must *learn* how to think in this new way, just as the reader must *learn* that way of thinking if she is to make sense of the text. In other words, maternal thinking does not come naturally, nor is it inherent in all women's nature—or alien to all men's, as Walker's Suwelo illustrates—but instead is a disciplined method of reflection that can, and must, be learned.

One barrier to learning to think maternally may arise from a woman's experience as a daughter, from witnessing her own mother's shortcomings. As Ruddick points out, "Mothers often value destructive ways of thinking and misidentify virtues," even "in certain respects mischaracterize what counts as success and failure" (*Maternal Thinking*, 25). Mrs. Hill of *Meridian* falls into the traps of inauthenticity and domination, as we see in her failure to tell her daughter the truth about her own experience: "With her own daughter she certainly said things she herself did not believe. She refused help and seemed, to Meridian, never to understand. But all along she understood perfectly" (51). *The Color Purple* opens with a destructive, hateful injunction to silence, supposedly for the sake of the mother: "You better not never tell nobody but God. It'd kill your mammy." The demand for silence is in fact not maternal, but paternal, as Celie eventually discovers for herself. The novel demonstrates the necessity of "telling," as silence serves only to perpetuate abuse and to protect the abuser.

Learning to recognize and to reject destructive ways of thinking, then finding constructive ways of thinking that allow the correct identification of virtues, are ongoing tasks for all these heroes. These tasks require that the woman first learn to be a daughter *and* a feminist, prerequisites for politicized maternal thought. To do so, a woman must learn to care about her own mother and about all the women who came before her. According to Ruddick, this "includes learning to expect and respect maternal thinking. And this means really listening when mothers speak" (*Maternal Thinking*, 39). Learning to be a feminist daughter "could be considered an act of resistance" (40) against the myths of motherhood that oppress not only mothers but *all* women, as it does *not* require accepting those myths or romanticizing mothers, ignoring their failures, or perpetuating their experiences. Black women may have some advantage over white women in learning to be feminist daughters, because mothering among African-Americans historically has been a collective responsibility, with "othermothers" often playing "central roles in defusing the emotional intensity of relationships between blood mothers and their daughters and in helping daughters understand the Afrocentric ideology of motherhood" (Collins, "Motherhood," 8). Additionally, according to Patricia Hill Collins, "since Black mothers have a distinctive relationship to white patriarchy, they may be less likely to socialize their daughters into their proscribed role as subordinates" ("Motherhood," 7). Of course, some black mothers, like *Meridian*'s Mrs. Hill, accept Eurocentric constructions of motherhood; however, the daughters of these black mothers may still benefit from the presence of "othermothers," such as Miss Winter in *Meridian*, who forgives Meridian when her own mother can not or will not.

The specific ways in which the heroes evolve into maternal thinkers, and their experiences as birth mothers, illuminate some influences of cultural, class, and racial factors on women's experiences of mothering that Ruddick acknowledges but does not explore in detail.[8] However, although their paths greatly differ—separating along lines of class and race—all arrive at similar places, putting into practice the kind of transformative social and political vision that Ruddick believes an enlightened, feminist use of maternal thinking may produce. Taken together, then, the five novels provide support for Ruddick's use of a universalizing vocabulary in her analysis of maternal thinking.[9] After acknowledging her own privileges—of race, class, economic position—and the enormous differences in circumstances among mothers internationally, Ruddick nonetheless argues for a "maternal" work and a "maternal" identity across race, class, and culture:

> I take a child's demand that her life be protected as a demand *children* make upon the world—a demand intrinsic to the promise of birth that mothers in many cultures around the world can and, so far as I can tell, do organize to meet. I hope to endorse the universal demand of children for protection while recognizing that many mothers try to preserve their children's lives and to comfort them in circumstances more terrible than I can imaginatively apprehend. (*Maternal Thinking*, 55).

In sum, "To claim a maternal identity is not to make an empirical generalization but to engage in a political act"; indeed, "for any mother, declaring maternity is a particular act that, at least in our troubled world, is almost always located in a social nexus of violence and oppression" (56). Mothering with a clear-sighted understanding of that nexus "can be a training in attending to unsettling differences . . . maternal identification can be transformed into a commitment to protect the lives of 'other' children, to resist on behalf of *children* assaults on body or spirit that violate the promise of birth" (57). To read from the standpoint of maternal identification is to engage in a similar political act; reading can also be a type of "training in attending to unsettling differences."

The most obvious differences in the heroes' development into maternal thinkers lies in their experiences as birth mothers: the circumstances in which they conceive, their pregnancies and birthing labor, and their relationships to their children sharply differ, reflecting the historically different experiences of black and white, poor and rich women in the U.S. Lazarre's Jane and Charlotte, both middle-class, urban, Jewish, white women, are able to choose to conceive within the context of loving and stable marriages. Jane makes the choice passively, knowingly using an ill-fitting diaphragm and ignoring instructions for its use: "After all, I was married to a man I loved. I knew I wanted children someday, so why not now?" (16). Both Jane and Charlotte, though not rich, have enough money for comfort, access to excellent medical care, and the support of their husbands during their pregnancies. None of these advantages, of course, eliminates or even obscures the deeply painful struggles each woman experiences with herself, her husband, and her social milieu as a result of her pregnancy, but they do make it possible for her to give her attention to those struggles, to see them clearly, and to attempt to resolve them. Neither Meridian nor Celie, both rural, southern, black women with mixed-class backgrounds, even imagines choice.

Beginning at age fourteen, Celie is repeatedly raped by her stepfather, by whom she becomes pregnant twice, giving birth each time alone. We can read the world of pain and the profound ignorance of her own body that Celie suffers in her terse description of her first child's birth: "When I start to hurt and then my stomach start moving and then that little baby come out my pussy chewing on it fist you could have knock me over with a feather" (4). Meridian's "pregnancy came as a total shock to her" (16), as no one has told her anything about sex or its consequences: "Her mother never even used the word [sex], and her lack of information on the subject of sex was accompanied by a seeming lack of concern about her daughter's morals. Having told her absolutely nothing, she had expected her to *do* nothing" (60). Although she does not want a baby, Meridian has no real choice; given her profound lack of information, she probably does not even know abortion exists, much less how to go about obtaining one. She soon finds herself expelled from school, married to a young man she does not love, and drawn into her husband's family while he begins a sexual relationship with another woman.

If Ruddick is right in saying that all mothers are "adoptive," in the sense of engaging in a social act when they commit themselves to caring for a child ("to adopt is to commit oneself to protecting, nurturing, and training particular children" [*Maternal Thinking*, 51]), and I believe she is, then we need to ask what effects denial of the opportunity of adoption might have on mothers — an especially crucial question in considering black women's lives. Celie's children are taken from her immediately after their births by their father, who she believes murders the first ("He took it while I was sleeping. Kilt it out there in the woods" [4]) and sells the second (5), learning only much later that both were given to a childless couple who loved and raised them well. Although it is Meridian who describes motherhood as "slavery" (69), it is Celie whose experience most closely approximates that of actual slaves, who often conceived as the result of their masters' rape, gave birth under terrible conditions, and then saw their children snatched from them, sold away by their fathers/owners. Celie herself, again like her foremothers, is then sold into marriage and expected to serve as mother-surrogate to other children, after being denied the chance to care for her own babies. Losing her children and the younger sister she has mothered makes Celie unable to risk caring for anyone. To survive, Celie closes off her emotions, trying to imagine herself as "wood" or "a tree" (22).

The choice *not* to adopt one's own children may be as painful and have as lasting consequences as the absence of choice, as we see in Meridian's experience.[10] Whereas Celie's life resembles that of her ancestors, Meridian is haunted by what she perceives as a betrayal of those ancestors, in her decision not to "adopt" her son. Soon after Meridian gives birth — described in a chapter ironically titled "The Happy Mother" — she fantasizes ways to murder him or to kill herself, thinking, "So this . . . is what slavery is like" (69). Terrified by her fury at her son, whose helplessness she recognizes, she nevertheless treats him roughly "because everyone who came to visit assumed she loved him, and because he did not feel like anything to her but a ball and chain" (69). Meridian eventually gives this child up for adoption "with a light heart. She did not look back, believing she had saved a small person's life" (90–91); she has also saved a big person's life — her own. Meridian's decision to save both child and mother by separating them is a direct consequence of maternal thought. Although she does not realize it, Meridian's struggle to care for her child and her successful struggle not to hurt either him or herself are not monstrously unique but typical of mothering work (Ruddick, *Maternal Thinking*, 25–30). Perhaps paradoxically, choosing to give her child to someone who can and will care for him is an act of preservative love at least equal to caring for him herself. Furthermore, Meridian's son's adoption has precedence in black culture, where extended kin networks often take over childrearing. Gloria Joseph points out that, in part due to the effects of racial and economic oppression, "frequently it is immaterial whether [black women] are biological mothers, sisters, or members of the extended family" (76). Similarly, Patricia Hill Collins sees "othermothers" as related to an Afrocentric ideology of motherhood, noting that the boundaries between biological mothers and other women who care for children tend to be fluid in African-American communities ("Motherhood," 5). Meridian, then, may be more true to her foremothers' experience than was her own mother, who could not tell the truth or admit her need for help.

Nevertheless, Meridian is plagued for a long time by "a voice that cursed her existence — an existence that could not live up to the standards of motherhood that had gone before" (91). Whose voice is this? Her own mother has called her a "monster" for giving up this child, and Meridian believes she has betrayed her maternal history, generations of enslaved women who suffered torture for their children and of "free" women for whom "freedom" meant the right to keep their children. The "voices," however, are not those of her foremothers but the voices of those women's enslavers; the capitalist, racist, and sexist system that enslaved her maternal ancestors, even when they were nominally free, is the same system that demands Meridian's conformity to the Eurocentric myth of motherhood. These voices are echoed by Meridian's mother, who has accepted their corrupt version of history and their distorted version of black motherhood.

Eventually, Meridian discovers what it is she really owes her foremothers, and it is not silent acceptance of white, patriarchally-defined motherhood, as she once imagined, but action as a community othermother. According to Collins, African-American othermothers who feel responsible for nurturing children within an extended (biological or "fictive") family "have stimulated a more generalized ethic of care where Black women feel accountable to all the Black community's children" ("Motherhood," 5). This ethic of care explains the phenomenon of "community othermothers," women who are led to social activism through the experience of mothering. Meridian's role as a community othermother is made possible by her development into a maternal thinker. This habit of mind—care, attentiveness to detail, acceptance of change and growth; in short, maternal thinking, translated into a public sphere—makes it impossible for Meridian to say that she would kill for the revolution until she recognizes the value of her own life and the necessity of the revolution if anyone is to live, not merely (and not even always) survive. This way of thinking frees her from narrow boundaries of self, causing Meridian to feel that her continuing existence, her development of self, is what she owes her foremothers, as that existence "extended beyond herself to those around her because, in fact, the years in America had created them One Life" (200).

Like Meridian, Celie does not learn to think maternally through the kind of mothering work Ruddick describes—daily, ongoing responsibility for and care of children—but instead through other kinds of caring labor. Celie experiences attentive love from Shug as she offers that kind of love to Shug. Seeing Celie's reality prompts Shug to change her own behavior in order to avoid hurting Celie (an act of preservative love); recognizing Shug's reality allows Celie to imagine, and ultimately to achieve, a way of life founded on self-respect and self-love instead of on fear and domination. Celie's maternal thought takes tangible form in the pants she makes and gives to her friends. That this pants-making expresses maternal thought, particularly attentive love, is clear in Celie's notion of "the perfect pair of pants" for Shug. Celie figures out what Shug needs—beauty, versatility, comfort—by observing her closely, and then makes pants that meet all those needs. Celie's sewing turns into a cottage industry, "Folkspants, Unlimited," but remains deeply anti-capitalistic and expressive of a politicized maternal thought, motivated not by making the greatest possible profit on mass-produced goods, but by love and care. As Celie tells Nettie, "Every stitch I sew will be a kiss" (182). In *The Temple of My Familiar*, Walker suggests that Afrocentric, maternal thought may be learned by men as well as by women. Suwelo evolves into such a thinker during the course of the novel, while Hal is beginning to value that thought and to understand himself as capable of it by novel's end. Lissie, who contains "everybody and everything," serves as a community othermother/artist who mothers through storytelling and painting. Lissie's goal is a grand one that indeed may require many more lifetimes: to save the earth itself and all its inhabitants from violence.

Walker also shows maternal thinking enlightening one white woman, by helping her to understand some realities of black women's lives. *Meridian*'s Lynne Rabinowitz, like Jane of *The Mother Knot*, is a white, Jewish, middle-class wife of a black man and mother of a biracial child. Different in most respects despite these surface similarities, both Jane and Lynne are radical-ized by mothering black children. Through her absolute love for her daughter Camara, Lynne finally repudiates and grows beyond her perception of south-ern black people as Art. Although she has much earlier recognized the rac-ism latent in this view—she repeatedly warns herself, "I will pay for this . . . It is probably a sin to think of a people as Art" (130)—Lynne has been unable to transform her thinking until after Camara's birth. In committing herself to care for Camara, Lynne finally casts off old ways of thinking and being. She also becomes vulnerable to the racist predations that threaten black mothers, and to the violence that endangers their children. Lynne not only imagines, but lives as, one of the "many mothers [who] try to preserve their children's lives and to comfort them in circumstances more terrible" than Ruddick can "imaginatively apprehend" (55).

Mothering Camara leads Lynne to the kind of thinking Ruddick identifies as a possible resource for peace (157–61), as Lynne learns to see the injustice in the world and to struggle against it on behalf of *all* children. Lynne's at-tempts to protect Camara fail horribly when Camara is attacked and mur-dered. The experience of loss brings Lynne and Meridian together as feminist mothers: "They knew her suffering did not make her unique; but knowing that crimes of passion or hatred against children are not considered unique in a society where children are not particularly valued, failed to comfort them" (174). Lynne finally and permanently renounces the privileges of her own racial and class background, having seen clearly that those privileges rest upon and perpetuate violence and hatred. When last we see Lynne in *Meridian*, a year after Camara's death, she is struggling to understand and to articulate what she has learned through tragic experience.

Through mothering her son, Jane learns about the insidious, all-pervasive, threatening nature of racism. Insulated by her class from many of the im-mediate threats posed to Benjamin's safety by a racist society, Jane is not in-sulated from the more subtle forms of racism that might interfere with foster-ing his growth. The constant reminders of racism Jane encounters as the white mother of a black child help her to resist some of the temptations in-herent in mothering, particularly the temptation to allow concern for one's own child to obliterate concern for other children. Jane's love of her child, her attention to his particular needs, leads her to an antiracist stance on behalf of all children.

Perhaps because Lazarre's background is fairly close to Ruddick's own, of the four novels discussed here, *The Mother Knot* most closely parallels in fiction Ruddick's theory of maternal thinking and its transformative poten-tial as a peace resource.[11] For Jane, mothering Benjamin comprises a series of struggles, with herself and with the world. She struggles against the temptation to dominate him and to hurt him, while struggling also to see him as a being separate from herself, with his own personality, deserving of (and needing) respect. Jane comes to see training her child as a work of conscience, as Ruddick describes it. She works through periods of inauthenticity (as when she hits him for hitting another child, acting on her own embarrassment and frustration, not on his needs) and of viewing Benjamin as "a lump of clay, molded by me and taking shape only according to my discretion" (137). Jane learns to appreciate Benjamin's own strengths and weaknesses as more than simple reflections of her mothering. Most importantly, by attending to her own and to her child's real needs, Jane learns to recognize fantasies and myths about motherhood as both false and dangerous, and to reject them; she becomes a maternal thinker. The hard-won insights she gains through mothering her son lead Jane to a concern for *all* children—acted out in the novel in building a cooperative daycare center—that translates into a renewed commitment to resist war and injustice, especially sexism and racism.[12]

One important way that Ruddick theorizes maternal thinking as a peace resource is in the training in nonviolence it may encompass. Mothering offers more temptations to violence than most other kinds of work: a larger, more physically and psychologically powerful person lives in constant, intimate contact with a smaller, less powerful person (or people) whose actions are often incomprehensible, baffling, maddening. Although some mothers do indeed abuse their children, the fact—and the wonder—is that most do not. They may be tempted to physical or psychological violence, but most mothers control themselves most of the time. *How* mothers learn to eschew violence, to resist the temptation of domination, might translate into political activity for peace. We see Jane frequently fantasizing violence in *The Mother Knot*—violence against her child, herself, her husband, even strangers—while teaching herself not to *act* violently, but to let the fantasies themselves take the place of action.[13] Her thoughts, however, terrify her, much as Meridian's fantasies of murder or suicide scare her. Jane is certain she is unique in her struggles: "But ordinary mothers, I was certain, did not move through their days hoping to remain in control for just one more hour" (102). The truth is that ordinary mothers *do* live this way, but find it difficult to speak of the reality of their days, silenced by the myth of motherhood that they are all too conscious of failing. Maternal storytelling represents one form of resistance to such myths.

Instead of the process of learning maternal thinking that we find in *Meridian*, *The Mother Knot*, and *The Color Purple*, *The Powers of Charlotte* describes maternal thinking as habitual with Charlotte in adult life; presumably she had learned it through a combination of her work as artist and as mother. In the novel's final section, "Charlotte's Place," we learn that her place is the world. Charlotte has a recurring dream of nuclear holocaust, which sends her to her son's room, where she holds "his large sleeping body in her arms, protecting him from nuclear destruction" (238). Realistically, of course, Charlotte cannot protect her son from nuclear war by holding him. But this concern for her own child leads her to take action for peace, first by doing a series of paintings called "History," which "climaxed with a painting called 'Holocaust'—a lone, bedraggled woman in the lower right corner sweeping tides of blood off an armory floor" (313), and then by going to Nicaragua with her cousin, where she sees American warships and hates "her country for making necessary the military efficiency of which the young soldiers were clearly so proud" (315). Charlotte becomes a witness for peace, much as Jane becomes a witness for motherhood, Meridian a witness for the Civil Rights Movement, and Lissie a witness for history—in the sense of being a person who brings to others the truth as she knows it, who tells of her actual experiences as a way of demolishing dangerous myths. Charlotte's form of witnessing is painting, and she sketches rapidly as she walks the streets of Managua: "She had to try to keep penetrating the layers or succumb to the threatening pain in her eyes. She would draw this country, its houses, its children, its guns, but when she returned home she would put Ivan's eyes in the soldier's face" (315–16). The projected painting concretizes maternal thought; in putting her son's eyes in the soldier's face, Charlotte extends her love of her son outward, to concern for the safety and growth of all children, and adults.

Reading these novels from the perspective of maternal thought opens up areas of the text that go unremarked in many other analyses. Reading these novels also may be a training in maternal thinking that might then serve as a useful model for reading texts from cultural traditions different from the reader's own. For instance, the question of how white women readers might best read black women's writing, although widely discussed among feminist theorists, remains unresolved, with just one area of agreement: that white women must beware of eliding differences. Ought white women read themselves as "other" in black women's texts, as Minrose Gwin has suggested recently? Or does this purposeful engagement in an alienating project destroy the hope of insights to be gained from attending to *both* "white" and "women," seeing "themselves in ways they had not before," as Barbara Christian says in her response to Gwin (*"Response to 'Black Women's Texts'," * 36)? Maternal thinking's training of attentive love provides an approach to cultural difference founded on respect and on an appreciation of difference that does not require alienation. In addition to its usefulness as a reading stance, maternal thinking also allows readers to extend their reading into the feminist project of social and political change. All these novels validate Ruddick's perception of maternal thinking as a resource for peace, while also offering some support for her claim that all wars are rooted in racism. Peace politics, then, are antiracist politics. Lazarre and Walker allow readers to experience the links among mothering, war, and racism and to imagine ways in which maternal thinking might enable women to resist racism and violence.

Notes

1. This complaint has been eloquently and repeatedly stated by numerous black and several white feminists; see, e.g., Audre Lorde's *Sister Outsider*; and Gloria T. Hull, Patricia Bell Scott, and Barbara Smith, eds., *But Some of Us Are Brave*. Elizabeth Spelman's *Inessential Woman* analyzes in exhaustive detail the phenomenon in feminist scholarship of assuming white experience as a norm, as well as its consequences.

2. Some important recent contributions to the former debate are Minrose Gwin's essay and Barbara Christian's response in *NWSA Journal*, and Holloway and Demetrakopoulos's *New Dimensions of Spirituality*. Incorporation of differences among women into theory is the basis of Marianne Hirsch's *The Mother/Daughter Plot*; Hirsch singles out African-American women's writing of the 1960s–1980s as one tradition in which the mother figure is important and in which we can find a maternal discourse (176–77).

3. I want to make absolutely clear my assumption that black women do not need to learn how to read white texts, as from earliest childhood such lessons in reading are given by all society's institutions; furthermore, were black women in need of such instruction, it certainly would not be for me to offer it. My concern here is white women's reading of black women's texts, as *no* institution takes upon itself responsibility for such a lesson.

4. See Brenda Daly's essay in this volume.

5. See Walker's "In Search of Our Mothers' Gardens," and Barbara Christian's "Alice Walker: The Black Woman Artist as Wayward," 461–63.

6. Washington draws on Walker, "In Search of Our Mothers' Gardens," in making this argument. Of course, speaking *for* mothers is not identical to speaking *as* mothers, as Marianne Hirsch points out (16), but I understand speaking for mothers to be a necessary intermediary step toward privileging maternal subjectivity.

7. Lazarre reports having had great difficulty placing *The Powers of Charlotte* with a publisher, as she had been pegged a "memoirist" after *The Mother Knot*. One famous editor at a major publishing house rejected the book as "too autobiographical," yet Lazarre says it is not autobiography but fiction with very few autobiographical elements (personal interview, 12 Dec. 1988).

8. Ruddick comments that such a discussion lies outside the scope of her work, and she provides sensible reasons for her decision (*Maternal Thinking*, 51–57).

9. This vocabulary also gains some support from Patricia Hill Collins's essay, "The Social Construction of Black Feminist Thought," wherein Collins notes the connections between the thought of different subordinate groups (756) and discusses black feminist thought in terms very similar to those employed by Ruddick in her discussion of feminist versions of maternal thinking.

10. The pain such a choice entailed for one white woman is the subject of Shirley Glubka's "Out of the Stream: An Essay on Unconventional Motherhood." Although

Glubka's piece is autobiographical and *Meridian* is a novel, comparison of the specific varieties of guilt each woman feels reveals significant cultural differences. Glubka expresses no sense of betraying her foremothers, for example.

11. Ruddick and Lazarre are friends and colleagues at the Eugene Lang College of the New School for Social Research. Ruddick's introduction to the Beacon reprint of Lazarre, *The Mother Knot*, points to other ways in which the novel reflects maternal thought.

12. See Lazarre, *The Mother Knot*, 44–49, for an extended discussion of the links among sexism, racism, and war. Ruddick asserts several times her belief that racism is at the center of all wars.

13. In one wonderful episode, Jane imagines castrating all the men who sexually harass her on the street, and finally blowing up a whole section of the city. When a grocer tells Benjamin his mother is pretty: "I lopped off his penis with an ax which I whipped out of the carriage bag where it had waited for an occasion just such as this one" (Lazarre, *The Mother Knot*, 105).

Chapter 14

Teaching Alice Walker's *Meridian*:
Civil Rights According to Mothers

Brenda O. Daly

Yes. She had bitten her baby's cheek,
bitten out a plug, before she
strangled it with a piece of curtain
ruffle. So round and clean it had
been, too. But not red, alas, before
she bit. And wasn't it right to seek
to devour a perishable?
—Alice Walker

The sick woman was saying "I have this
dream that if the Father blesses me
I'll die the week before the second
Sunday in May because I want to be
buried on Mother's Day. I don't know
why I want that, but I do.
—Alice Walker, *Meridian*

One mother kills her child. Another longs to die on Mother's Day. These maternal tragedies in Alice Walker's *Meridian* illustrate what Adrienne Rich describes as "the violence of the institution of motherhood" (*Of Woman Born*, 267). In her analysis of the history and causes of maternal violence, *Of Woman Born*, Rich argues that if we do not listen to the stories of mothers who kill their children, if we regard them as "insane," we will never understand the historical conditions that drive mothers to commit acts of violence: conditions such as lack of economic and emotional support, rape, ignorance, lack of birth control, sanctions against birth control and abortion. All these problems are compounded, of course, by racism. Nevertheless, as Sara Ruddick reminds us in her essay, "Preservative Love and Military Destruction," maternal nonviolence is taken for granted, assumed to be natural and instinctive. "A striking fact about mothers," writes Ruddick, "is that they remain peaceful in situations in which they are powerful, namely in battles with their own and other children" (243). Nevertheless, as Ruddick points out, "little has been written about . . . maternal power from a mother's point of view" (243).

Alice Walker's *Meridian* is, therefore, an important novel, for it tells the story of the Civil Rights Movement from the point of view of a mother—or, more accurately, from the point of view of a variety of different mothers, old and young, white and black, violent and nonviolent, self-denying and self-defining. As Barbara Christian has argued, in the context of the Civil Rights Movement, Meridian "is able to probe the meaning of motherhood, not solely in a biological context, but in terms of love and justice" ("An Angle of Seeing," 6). We learn also that, although Meridian chooses to give her son away in order to mother herself, she nevertheless sees herself in both the mother who kills her child and the mother who hopes to die on Mother's Day. In a chapter ironically titled, "The Happy Mother," we learn that Meridian too had "thought of murdering her own child" and, in an effort to suppress this thought, had considered instead "methods of killing herself" (69). Magazines like *"Sepia, Tan, True Confessions, Real Romances* and *Jet"* had not helped Meridian solve this terrible problem; they all told her that she was "a mindless body, a sex creature, something to hang false hair and nails on" (71). What had awakened Meridian were televised reports of the deaths of three small children in 1960, in which Meridian recognized her own urge to kill her son. Alarmed by this public image of her private impulse, she chose instead to join the revolution. Yet the revolutionaries themselves—specifically Truman Held and a man named "Swinburn"—do not share Meridian's maternal angle of vision, nor do they have any interest in listening to or learning from a teenaged black woman who is, in their estimation, an ignorant high-school dropout.

Why is it that these men, like those in my literature courses, are so often deaf to the voices of women, especially the voices of mothers? One reason is that, as Barbara Christian says, the discourses that define motherhood actually interfere with our ability to hear what mothers say or write, and, tragically, this deafness—which I shall call the maimed or monologic consciousness—leads to violence on the part of the oppressed. As an oppressed group, mothers sacrifice themselves more often than their children, but sacrificial mothers—like those in *Meridian*—are so much the norm that the oppression of mothers remains invisible to most readers. My own efforts to teach Alice Walker's remarkable novel alerted me to the difficulties students have in reading the discourses of mothers. Alice Walker herself describes how frequently *Meridian* is misread. She explains to Claudia Tate that reviewers never treat the novel "in its entirety" (Tate, 177). Tate notes one exception to the many misreadings of the novel: Barbara Christian's essay, "An Angle of Seeing," which Tate says "does an incredibly rich and full interpretation of

Meridian" (178). Such a comment might lead one to ask whether it is necessary to be a black woman and a mother, as Barbara Christian is, in order to read and understand Walker's novel; but I would argue that, if, as Judith Fetterley insists, women have been taught to read as men, and if a black man like Truman Held can be taught to read romantically, as white men do,[1] then all of us—regardless of gender or race—can be taught to read as maternal thinkers.[2]

That gender, race, and ethnicity do make a difference in how we read is well illustrated in responses to *Meridian*. As Walker explains in her interview with Claudia Tate, one reviewer "concentrated totally on the influences of Camus on the work. His whole thing was guilt and expiation." Other reviewers saw "political issues of the sixties" or "Indians" or "the invention of legend" or the tree that "grows miraculously" (Tate, 177). From these remarks it seems obvious not only that readers have failed to see the novel "in its entirety," but that they also have failed to see how, to Walker, the issue of violent or nonviolent revolution is not limited to the 1960s nor to the issue of oppressed races, black or Indian. Nor is Walker writing for women only, whether black, white, or Jewish. As Walker explains to Tate: "Every Jewish 'girl' I meet under fifty is Lynne or thinks she is. And they claim a) Lynne's a stereotype, or b) she's just like them." Nor is the novel strictly about relationships between men and women, black or white, or black and white, Walker insists. Some reader-response critics might argue (in the spirit of romantic individualism) that each of us creates a different text, but Walker has a right to ask readers at least to attempt to see the parts of her novel as they relate to the whole and, more importantly, to see themselves as individuals who do have some relationship to society. Unless students recognize this fact—that through language we are constructed as a self, an "I" that is a social role rather than uniquely individual—they remain prisoners of language, rather than authors of themselves.

Certainly this lesson is one that Meridian learns, not through her education for "ladies" at Saxon, but through her struggle for maternal consciousness. This revolutionary struggle requires, as Walker's comments to Tate suggest, that we learn to read differently. Walker speculates that her own writerly resistance to the conventions of realism, the novel's linear and chronological movement, for example, creates difficulties for readers. She says that *Meridian* is not realism but instead a "collage" (Tate, 178), or "a crazy-quilt story . . . that can jump back and forth in time, work on many different levels, and one that can include myth" (176). The myth that Walker has in mind is not white but Native American. As Walker explains, "Another reason I think nobody has been able to deal with *Meridian* as a total work is the whole sublayer of Indian consciousness, which as I get older becomes more and more pro-

nounced in my life" (179). This consciousness leads, Walker says, past "Charl-
ton Heston" or any image of God as male, or as a person, toward, she says,
"the desert, the trees." Says Walker, "You get the birds, the dirt, you get everything. And that's all God" (178–79). This consciousness, which thinks through
the body, finds God in "the color purple," and this consciousness, which
thinks back through the mothers, finds God in all races, in all matter, and
in all mothers, including Louvinie and Feather Mae.

  Yet some feminists, such as Margaret Homans, argue instead that "though
the novel can represent and defuse the threat of female silence, it can do so
only by denying figuration—by denying the operation of its own language"
(204). Homans, who makes this point in her essay, "'Her Very Own Howl':
The Ambiguities of Representation in Recent Women's Fiction," argues, further,
that in *Meridian*, as in *Sula*, "both Walker and Morrison conclude their presentations of language use in ways that radically call into question the very
possibility of that representation" (195).[3] What I will argue instead is that
Walker illustrates brilliantly how women's writing, rather than privileging
the literal and denying figuration, employs figuration to critique a sexist and
racist society. For example, Walker employs the word "Camara" to challenge
the aesthetics of the "camera," a disembodied, distanced, and objectified art
practiced by Truman, after the fashion of male romanticism. As a photo-
grapher and painter, Truman "kills" women in his art in order to create the
fantasy "Woman." An art based upon a vision of "Camara"—the name of the
racially-mixed daughter born to Lynne and Truman, who is raped and killed
at the age of eight—will be radically different, will be child-centered, communal, spiritual. Since the name "Camara" also refers to the African writer,
Camara Laye, the word is simultaneously literal, figurative, and intertextual.
Walker's use of the double (Camara/camera) figuration illustrates one way
that dialogism[4] operates in the novel, and one way that Walker finds a different ground, the African-American, for representing maternal discourse.

  According to Homans, however, the reason women go unheard or unread
is that their language is not possible. For example, when at the end of *Meridian* Truman is unable to read the letters of Anne-Marion to Meridian, Homans
defines the problem not as his, but rather as the impossibility of representing
women's language. She says:

> The two women understand each other, but the man, sympathetic though
> he is, misconstrues their communication. He finds a blank where there
> is writing, and (even more sinister) he sees a target where there is a living
> tree. He has not even perceived the stump's most significant feature, the
> new branch that suggests, both as a conventional symbol of renewal and
> as a disruption of the bull's-eye pattern, the continuation of women's voices.
> ("Howl," 195)

Truman does not understand their discourse, not because it is impossible, but because he has learned to think and speak monologically, that is, romantically. He doesn't listen to women, regarding them as objects (aesthetic, sexual), at least until the death of his daughter, Camara.

The loss of his daughter prepares Truman to listen to Meridian, but his readiness to read women's writing begins only when Truman sees himself in/as mothers—including those who have murdered their own children, or who have been sacrificed to motherhood. Even this perception, however, does not yet differentiate Truman from the "foundling fathers," who, at the beginning of the novel, pointed their cannon at Meridian and the children, as if they could not tell the difference between a target and a living crowd, just as Truman cannot at first tell the difference between a bull's-eye pattern and a living tree stump. At the novel's end, Truman has only begun the task which had been Meridian's: to learn the art of maternal thought. Thus, Walker identifies the task as True-man's, whereas Homans locates the problem not in men or male-trained readers, but in women's self-effacing, uncertain writing. To make this argument Homans must ignore the novel's structure. This structure, though it first focuses upon individuals (Meridian and Truman), in its final section shifts to an emphasis upon community. In the final section of the novel, "Ending," Walker's multiple endings put into question the notion of "ending" itself. Not only does Meridian see herself multiplied in the lives of mothers, she also sees herself among those who mourn for King, and as the unidentified black man who says simply, "My son died," and in the grieving of Lynne and Truman for their daughter, and in the community's music. This music not only has continued, it has changed. Gone from the music is the despair Meridian had once heard in her father's voice; instead Meridian hears a militant assertiveness, legacy of the Civil Rights Movement. Voices mingle; they continue each other; they form a chorus of protest against injustice.

Certainly, then, *Meridian* is not, as Homans insists, a novel which illustrates the impossibility of women's language; quite the contrary, it illustrates its possibility—its actuality—and its strong tradition. And I believe that, given time and instruction in feminist courses, a "true man" *can* learn to read writing from the maternal point of view. What Walker's novel affirms, in the change in Truman during the two decades depicted in *Meridian*, is that men who learn the destructiveness of the romantic ego have the capacity to learn the discipline of maternal thought. Since such thought arises from social practice, and since most men have not practiced mothering, Sara Ruddick argues that men are likely to acquire the discipline in ways "radically different" from the ways of daughters who, whether they decide to become mothers or not, must at least consider the issue of childcare. My own experience in teaching *Meridian* illustrates Ruddick's point: young women and old, regardless of race, usually see mothering as central to this novel. By contrast, male readers do not see the issue at all. Student readings of *Meridian* are sharply differentiated, more by gender than by race. As Toni Cade Bambara told Claudia Tate, concern for children also differentiates the writing of women and men:

> One of the crucial differences that strikes me immediately among poets, dramatists, novelists, story tellers is the handling of children. I can't nail it down, but the attachment to children and to two-plus-two reality is simply stronger in women's writing; but there are exceptions. And finally, there isn't nearly as large a bulk of gynocentric writing as there is phallic-obsessive writing. . . . We've only just begun . . . to fashion a woman's vocabulary to deal with the "silences" of our lives. (Tate, 243)

As Bambara says, women have only just begun to fashion a woman's vocabulary to deal with the silences of our lives, but such representation is not impossible. It is, however, complex, and as critics such as Barbara Christian have noted, the discourse of mothering is deeply embedded in such discourses as religion, law, science, and literature.

Writers of these discourses have not often regarded mothers themselves as thinking subjects; therefore, as Ruddick notes, it was important for her to "stress that mothers *think*, that a maternal perspective is not only a matter of feeling, of virtue" ("Preservative Love," 237). As Ruddick explains in *Maternal Thinking*, such thinking is a discipline that, like other disciplines, asks certain questions rather than others, establishes criteria for truth, and cares about and acts upon the findings it makes. Ruddick characterizes maternal thought as concern for the preservation of children and for fostering their growth and acceptability. Ruddick also states clearly in her essay, "Maternal Thinking," that she is speaking of a maternal discourse transformed by feminism—which insists upon the authority and authenticity of women, and of women who mother—and that she also believes that the primary goal of feminists should be, not to bring men into the nursery, but to "bring a *transformed* maternal thought into the public realm" (226). The classroom is a logical public space for putting into practice such a feminist goal. However, in *Philosophy and Feminist Thinking*, Jean Grimshaw questions whether such a model—premised as it is upon participants without equal power—can serve for adult relationships.

In particular, Grimshaw asks whether maternal thought ought to serve as a basis for women's relationships with men, for the mothering of men can be damaging to women. She says, "A woman who is dependent on a man may develop great skill in attending to and caring for him, in 'reading' his behavior and learning how to interpret his moods and gratify his desires before he needs to ask" (252). Certainly this is true, but adult relationships in the public realm, such as college and university classrooms, do not place women teachers in relationships of dependency that replicate personal relationships. Ideally, the classroom is a space where teacher and students are cooperatively interdependent, but, in fact, given age differences and hierarchical grading systems, a woman teacher usually is more powerful than her students. Grimshaw doesn't take into account Ruddick's emphasis upon the realities of power in adult relationships, nor does Grimshaw consider Ruddick's careful articulation of "authenticity" and "humility," as they shape maternal thought. Women who mother adults are not practicing maternal thought; rather, they are denying the reality of power, denying the limits of their control of an adult, and often failing to act authentically by asserting their own adult needs. Women who care for men as if they were children, or who behave as seductive objects of male romantic fantasies, are both, in this sense, "inauthentic." Meridian claims authenticity rather than simply playing a feminine part when she faces the guns of the city fathers. In this public scene (which might be Kent State or Tiananmen Square), in which Meridian leads the children to see "the mummy woman," preservative love and military destructiveness are most sharply differentiated.

Yet Walker, like Ruddick, avoids sharp gender opposition, complicating the problem of maternal thought in a number of ways. First, of course, we see that women are capable of violence, while men are capable of maternal thought. Meridian's father is such a man. He feels his kinship to others, such as the Cherokees who have lost their land, and he has what Barbara Christian calls "insight into the preciousness, the value of life, which is the cornerstone of the value of freedom" ("An Angle of Seeing," 247). As Christian insists, "This particular way of seeing the world does not necessarily proceed from being a biological mother; rather it is a state of mind that women can lose if biological motherhood is forced upon them as their necessary state, a state in which they are restricted by being responsible for society's children" (247). But if enforced motherhood causes some women to "lose" such insight—or, perhaps, to fail to develop a view of the preciousness of life—it is more often the case that men fail to become maternal thinkers. One reason for this failure is that, in order to become an autonomous or well-bounded male in this culture, the mother within must be silenced, repressed, denied. For this reason, young men who read *Meridian* do not identify with the problems of mothers in the novel. As Kathryn Allen Rabuzzi says in *Motherself*, "Woman-connected imagery simply is not 'seen' because it fails to match the expectations and assumptions of any androcentrically patterned community in which it appears" (35). This "androcentrically patterned community" is, of course, endorsed by our literary canon, so that, as Cathy Davidson argues, "*what* we read shapes *how* we read" (*Revolution*, 256), until male readers simply cannot perceive patterns unrelated to their own development.

Rabuzzi makes the same argument in *Motherself*: "If a society existed in which the way of the mother were the norm, tales of mothers would predominate the way tales of heroes do in cultures throughout the world" (63). Such is not the case, and, since Alice Walker's novel fails to match the expectations of student readers, especially males, they tend to reject it. Nevertheless, my efforts to teach *Meridian* have been instructive; therefore, I would like to briefly describe my attempts to "bring a *transformed* maternal thought into the public realm," a process far more complicated than I had anticipated. I first taught *Meridian* in 1985, in a University of Minnesota night-school extension course which met once a week in northern Minneapolis, a racially-mixed, poorer suburb. Enrolled in my course in "The Novel" were three black women of different ages, about seven white men, and approximately fifteen white women. One of the black women, a secondary school teacher, opened our discussion of *Meridian* with the statement, "Our babies are having babies." Another middle-aged woman, also a mother, joined the discussion, agreeing that the problem of too-early motherhood had been effectively depicted in *Meridian*. When I recognized that only mothers were responding, I asked others to join the discussion. With some hesitation (these students tended to lack self-confidence), they began to criticize the novel. Rather than acknowledging their own limitations as readers, they blamed the novel, describing it as "disjointed," "confusing," and "hard to follow." I asked them to identify specific passages or chapters, arguing that Walker was writing from a different tradition, and I offered as evidence passages from the novel itself.

At least one student was receptive to my argument. Denise (as I shall call her) argued in her final paper that "complaints" during our discussion were "unfair" to a work "that does so many beautiful things for the problems of racism and sexism," and she attributed reader problems to "inadequate analysis, rather than a literary deficiency of Alice Walker's."[5] A black woman, not yet twenty and the mother of two children, Denise wrote an eloquent defense of the novel, in which she stated that Walker's apparently "crazy" story weaves together "America's most prevalent 'threads' of injustice," such as sexism and racism, as well as the themes of motherhood and female relationships to "tie them into one cause for humanity." Denise illustrated her thesis by focusing upon three episodes, which she saw as interrelated: the mummy woman in the novel's opening scene, the photo that Truman takes of Lynne as the black children comb her hair, and the near-rape of Lynne that Tommy Odds atempts to incite. I shared Denise's concern with motherhood, sexism, and male violence. Denise noted, as I had, that in one scene Truman sees Lynne in aesthetic terms, when black children, like petals of a "gigantic flower," take turns combing her hair. However, I did not see, as Denise did, that Lynne is like the "mummy woman." Denise argued that, to Truman, Lynne is all "exterior," something as valuable dead as alive, and she noted that the black children combing Lynne's hair make a fetish of it, just as Merilene's husband does when he combs the mummy woman's hair. I had not made the connection between the "mummy woman" and Lynne, because I was reading as a white woman.

As a white woman reader, I had emphasized gender in the scene where, as Truman moved closer to photograph Lynne and the black children, "a hopeless feeling about opposites and what they do to each other" (129), stopped him. I interpreted Truman's desire for aesthetic distance as an effort at mastery which compensates him for his sense of vulnerability. As Susan Griffin argues, "When a women's beauty brings a man into the realm of the material, he must live in his body. He must know himself as matter" (8). The romantic self, with its well-bounded ego, tries to deny its participation in this material reality, primarily through mastery of the (M)other. You may recall that the ego, as Freud defines it in *Civilization and Its Discontents*, is normally "autonomous and unitary, marked off from everything else," except during the "pathological state" of falling in love. This romantic language shows why Freud rejects "men's receiving an intimation of their connection with the world around them," a notion which does not fit, as he says, "the fabric of our psychology" (9). Alice Walker rejects Freud's notion of the self, demonstrating how Meridian's relational consciousness enables her to experience ecstasy in the burial mounds of the Sacred Serpent. Here Meridian had, when the sun reached its meridian, felt the walls spin, and herself entering a new world. The name "meridian," which Walker defines in her preface, is not exclusively the name of an individual, but also a place name, and, furthermore, the name of a changing time/place. Thus, the ecstasy Meridian experiences—like the ecstasy of black mourners after the death of Martin Luther King—is a consciousness of her participation in matter, sacred mat(t)er, along with others in her community. A consciousness of one's material identity does not mean that one's individual identity is permanently sacrificed; rather, the "I" temporarily loses itself in its intense identification with what is, at once, both within and beyond the "I."

Artists report such loss of ego during the creative process. The process of childbirth was also, for me, ecstatic. For the first time, my consciousness of an organic identity—my participation in the fluid transformation of matter— put me into contact with a spirituality far deeper than the one I had known through Christianity. Romanticism, I also realized, was limited, failing to take into account what Chopin in *The Awakening* identifies as the dead-end of romantic individualism: the motherself. Once I recognized how romantic scripts interfere with our ability to read the motherself, I resolved to teach *Meridian* along with *The Awakening*, not only to emphasize racial differences, but also to demonstrate how Walker decodes romanticism in chapters such as "Clouds," "The Driven Snow," and "The Conquering Prince." Furthermore, I saw, in Walker's chapter title, "Awakening," an explicit allusion to Chopin's novel. I taught these novels as a pair in 1986, when, during a one-year appointment at a small liberal arts college in southern Minnesota, I designed a course called "The Novel." This time I had only white students in my class: twelve women and twelve men. At the close of the course, I asked students (mostly juniors and seniors in their early twenties) to write a comparison of two novels, and I suggested such creative approaches as writing from the place of one (possibly marginalized) character to another, just as Jean Rhys had written *Wide Sargasso Sea* from the point of view of Charlotte Bronte's "mad woman in the attic" in *Jane Eyre*.

One young man (whom I shall call Jim) wrote his paper as a letter from Alice Walker to Kate Chopin. Jim completely avoided the issue of motherhood, despite my emphasis upon Walker's parody of Chopin's "mother-woman" in her "mummy-woman" scene. I believe that Jim, like Truman Held, failed to recognize the problem of motherhood because of his own need for mastery. As Elizabeth Flynn notes in Flynn and Schweickart, *Gender and Reading*, "Male students often react to disturbing stories by rejecting them or dominating them" (285). Jim's desire for dominion caused him to assume too much authority. For example, writing as Alice Walker, Jim *commended* Edna for seeking knowledge of her own desire. Based on class discussion, Jim interpreted the scene in which Meridian goes to help register voters as her "awakening," as Walker's chapter title suggests, but he disregarded the sexism of Truman and Swinburn, despite my comments in class. Jim saw it as a "kindness" that Meridian was put to work as a typist, although she was a poor typist. He missed the irony of Walker's transformation of Swinburne (whose poetry is cited at Edna's birthday part in *The Awakening*) into a civil rights worker. Although I had called attention to this scene in class, Jim also made no mention of how Swinburn (whose name is spelled without the final "e") mars Meridian's perfectly typed copy by crossing out the final "e" on "Negro."

However, Jim did note some historical and class differences; he wrote, "Times have changed and a small southern town is far removed from the upper class neighborhoods of New Orleans." He then compared the sexual experiences of Edna and Meridian, concluding that, because Meridian's initiation into sex comes very early and is so cruel, she "learns that there is more to life than sex," whereas Edna's fantasies continue until her thirtieth birthday. However, Jim is reading romantically when he says that Meridian's desire is "brought to the surface by Truman." Jim also assumes that Meridian's early sexual awakening (not motherhood) makes it possible for her to redirect her sexual energies into civil rights. "This cause, the improvement of the treatment of blacks, provides Meridian with every bit as much of an awakening as Edna experiences," Jim wrote (as Alice Walker) to Kate Chopin. The confusion in Jim's analysis obeys a certain logic. First, despite his good intentions, he denies Meridian's agency by claiming that Truman awakens her. Then, perhaps overemphasizing racism, Jim explores the differences between Edna and Meridian, losing sight of the greatest similarity: motherhood. Despite the fact that both women have lost their virginity, Jim finds it necessary to claim that, though black, Meridian has "every bit as much of an awakening" as Edna. His own internalized identity themes prevent Jim from even recalling the awakening of motherhood, which we did talk about in class.

Nor does Jim understand Walker's point in a chapter called "The Recurring Dream" where, he notes, one sentence is repeated three times: "She dreamed she was a character in a novel and that her existence presented an insoluble problem, one that would be solved only by her death at the end" (117). I argued, in class, that Walker was underscoring how novelistic conventions of closure mirror social (realistic) conventions which provide women with limited choices: either marriage or death. Jim held Chopin responsible for Edna's death. Writing as Alice Walker, he said, "I put Meridian in a weak physical condition, almost dying," he wrote, but at the end, she "walks off, leaving behind symbols of traditional traps: the bed, where she lay dying, and Truman, whom she might have married." By contrast, Jim wrote, Edna dies, even though "she is strong enough to leave Robert to go to the side of Madame Ratignolle." It did not occur to Jim that Edna might have been undone by the sexual/textual logic of the romantic unitary self, for he ended by asking, "Why . . . must Edna die?" Sadly, the class was over, just as Jim appeared ready to explore Edna's violence against herself. Jim had opened our discussion with the comment, "Walker makes it harder to be a male than to be white." In my experience, Jim's response is typical of white male readers (I've had no young black men in my courses); however, Jim's honesty certainly is not typical.

More often, male readers—who see themselves as the "oppressors"—react defensively, attacking the novel rather than exploring their feelings. To test my hypothesis, I interviewed my son and two of his friends—all white males in their mid-twenties. One of them stated that, as readers of *Meridian*, they were the white "oppressors." After some initial defensiveness, they did come to sympathize with Meridian, whom they first saw as "totally whacko" and "looney tunes." They felt, they said, like that man, the "traveler" who stood on the sidelines. White (male) readers perhaps need to identify with Truman Held, the traveler and implied reader, before they try to understand Meridian.

However, in a small and private discussion, I did find that these young men were more willing to share their feelings, including their sympathy with Meridian. I believe that small group discussion is, therefore, an important strategy for successfully teaching this novel. After listening to these young men talk about *Meridian* for two hours, I told my son, "You didn't once mention motherhood." He said, "You're right, but I think if I read the novel a second time, I'll see it." That was my hope when I decided that, the next time I taught *Meridian*, I would (1) emphasize how, as readers, our own identities—gender, race, class, history—enter into our interpretations; (2) arrange the readings for the course so that students would perceive, as Barbara Christian states, in "Response to 'Black Women's Texts,'" that "point of view is pivotal" (33); (3) teach students to recognize aspects of the "romance" that Walker parodies; (4) use collaborative learning to diffuse defensive reactions and allow students to share their feelings, especially their confusion; and (5) ask students for brief written responses during their reading in order to structure my lectures as dialogues with their questions.

My next opportunity to teach *Meridian* came in fall 1989, at Iowa State University. I designed a topics course called "Women, Romance, and the American Novel," crosslisted under English and women's studies. Although an upper-division course in literature ordinarily would attract mostly majors, at Iowa State—where science dominates—English courses often consist mostly of nonmajors. Given this anticipated audience, I began with a popular romance novel and moved, in reverse chronological order, through different periods of American history. Texts included *The Flame and the Flower* by Kathleen Woodiwiss; the film, *Gone With the Wind; The Great Gatsby; The Awakening; The Bostonians; Our Nig; The Blithedale Romance*. Shifting to contemporary novels that employ what Rachel Blau DuPlessis calls "post-romantic" strategies, we next read *Meridian* and, finally, *Marya, A Life*, by Joyce Carol Oates. Of the thirty students enrolled in the course, twenty-six were white women, two were black women, and two were white men. At mid-term, students were expected to define some feature of romance in the novel—the quest, for example, or patterns of ascent and descent—as defined by Northrop Frye's *The Secular Scripture*. Following the mid-term, I emphasized Fetterley's idea of the "resisting reader," asking students to compare features of male- and female-authored novels and to compare points of view, including differences between black and white perspectives on the "romance." Despite the fact that I had pointed out the sexist and racist implications of the "mammy" figures in *The Flame and The Flower* and *Gone With the Wind*, quite a number of students named these as the "best" works we'd covered by mid-term.

This response did not surprise me, since, even in recent studies of the romance novel—such as Janice Radway's *Reading the Romance* and Carol

Thurston's *The Romance Revolution*—the focus is so much upon gender that racism disappears from their analysis. However, as students began to note the presence of mothers in women-authored novels (and the absence of mothers in novels by men), I introduced Madonne Miner's argument that the fantasy of a "mammy" is a desire for a stable presence that "engages us in repeated cycles of desire and denial: desire for an all-provident mother, denial of her actual existence" (200). Many women students chose to write final papers examining their identities as daughters and/or mothers, as this relationship shapes their own (sometimes unconscious) desires. But others chose to examine the relationship between racism and romance, acknowledging that Harriet Wilson's Frado and Alice Walker's Meridian had radically altered their perspectives. One young man, who never gave up his preference for *The Great Gatsby*, wrote (in a brief in-class response): "After reading about Frado, I now see how much my own experiences as a white, middle-class male have shaped my view of romance." He explained that he might fantasize about beautiful women; Frado must struggle to survive. Other students saw Frado as "in love with" James Bellmont but unable openly to acknowledge her desire.

After having read and talked about *Our Nig*, along with excerpts from slave narratives, and having provided historical background for the civil rights era, I felt students were ready for Alice Walker's novel. First, I explained that they, like Truman Held, were travelers, spectators who would not, initially, be able to understand Meridian's behavior in the opening scene, a scene that Karen Stein calls the novel's "nerve center." I also asked them to see Louvinie as a "mammy," viewed from the angle of vision of a black woman who is both a mother and a writer. By comparing Louvinie—whose stories were designed "to entrap people who hoped to get away with murder" (2)—and Margaret Mitchell's "Mammy," I underscored the difficulties for white readers. As Eve Kosofsky Sedgwick says in *Between Men*, white women readers of *Gone With the Wind* may perceive "the centrality and total alienation of female sexuality" in this popular novel, but the problem is even more complex from "an even slightly more ec-centric or disempowered perspective" (8).

That perspective is, of course, a black woman's. I took care to orient students to this point of view early in the reading process. I explained, for example, Barbara Christian's argument in "Response to 'Black Women's Texts'" that black women become the bearers of "funkiness," but that "because Meridian's maternal ancestors are at the bottom of society's rung, they can see what white women above them may not see, that white women's privilege is rooted in *their* society's definition [of woman] which demeans them by denying them sensuality, an essential part of themselves" (34). Having already noted that, in novels like *The Great Gatsby* and *The Flame and the Flower*, women were "objects" of the questing male, rather than questors themselves, and having also perceived how both Scarlett O'Hara and Edna Pontellier are punished for becoming questors, students recognized how the "angel in the house" is denied her own desire, her sensuality. Yet as Sedgwick says, "As for Mammy, her mind and life . . . are totally in thrall to the ideal of the 'lady,' to the degree that her personal femaleness loses any meaning whatever that is not in relation to Scarlett's role" (9). Of course, having said all this is not the same as having taught it in such a way that students genuinely learn — or imagine — what it means to be a black woman, and a mother, in a sexist and racist society.

My next step in teaching *Meridian*, after students had finished reading part two, "Truman," was to explain Walker's "collage" technique. I asked students to note the novel's three parts — as well as the language of chapter titles — and to explore these "pieces in the collage," these "patches in the quilt." In addition to the topics "Meridian" and "Truman," students chose to discuss "Lynne" (the highest number chose this topic), "The Sacred Serpent," and "Civil Rights." I then directed students to choose a topic and join a small group (four to five students) in piecing together parts of the novel. Small group collaboration did, in fact, eliminate defensiveness. For example, the group "piecing together" Truman's character argued, simply, that Truman "was confused," as confused as they as readers were. Students analyzing Meridian said that she "became a mother of the community," and the group examining "The Sacred Serpent" argued that the novel used a variety of images of burial, growth, and regeneration. Another small group decided that the area of "Civil Rights," had to be subdivided into (1) debates over violence and nonviolence, and (2) tensions between public revolution and painful private struggles, such as the conflict between Meridian and her mother. Lynne, they decided, became the victim of reverse racism and sexism, but, at the same time, she was a woman who joined the movement without understanding herself or others.

During the next class period, when students had completed the novel, I asked them to respond in writing to the question: What pattern did your group create (or see) in *Meridian*, and how do you see this pattern elaborated in the novel's last section, "Ending"? One young woman found parallels between the Sacred Serpent, Meridian, and Truman. She wrote (during the fifteen minutes allowed for an in-class response): "Meridian and Sojourner are like the Phoenix, they suffer at the hands of the people they love most . . . but they survive to sprout again. . . . In the end, Truman faints in her sacred place, surrounded by her poems as Meridian was surrounded by the dead Indians in the Serpent's coil." When I presented my closing lecture — the novel "in its entirety," the whole collage or quilt — I began by focusing upon Meridian as, in their terms, "a mother of the community." I linked Meridian's actions in the novel's final section to the opening scene in which she leads the children to view the "mummy woman." This mummy woman might be

Edna Pontellier, washed up on shore, I said, and Meridian wants to teach the children that such an image of Woman is "fake." Furthermore, as mother to the community, I argued, Meridian brings together—in the militant music of the church—the memories of those who have died: not only Martin Luther King but also women and children, such as "the child, whose body was beginning to decompose" (191), which she placed beside the mayor's gavel, or "the child who murdered her child" (211), or the child Camara. Finally, I said, when Truman takes Meridian's sacred place, his "ending" is a beginning, for, as Walker tells us, he has already begun "to experience moments with Meridian when he felt intensely maternal" (213).

This novel, I said, is about how Truman learns from Meridian to mother the community, but only after he has unlearned the ways of "The Conquering Prince." Did I persuade my students? Most of the women agreed with me, although some saw the issue of motherhood as only an aspect of the novel. One woman declared, "Motherhood is irrelevant to *Meridian*," and another said, "When I read the novel, I was only aware of it peripherally. . . . Maybe, like the typical child, I'm only appreciative in an accidental way." Still another woman said, directly, "*Meridian* is about mothering" (she herself is a single mother), but one woman (not a mother) resisted my argument, especially concerning Truman. She said, "I overlooked Truman's 'maternal' instincts . . . I believe I see it now, but on initial reading I disbelieved Truman so much that by the time I got to the last part, I just saw Truman as trying to make up for everything he'd done wrong, trying to make himself look concerned and caring so that Meridian would take him back." Her skepticism is understandable. What most disturbed me was her notion of "maternal instincts," a phrase that made me realize, belatedly, that I had not done enough to differentiate between the novel's different concepts of motherhood.

Furthermore, although I had designed a course with the specific goal of teaching students to recognize how their own identities shape their reading experiences, I failed to persuade the two white men in my class that motherhood is central in this novel. One young man wrote, "To be honest, I didn't see motherhood as a major concept in this novel." However, in his next sentence, he did concede: "I do think that the way Meridian's mother treated her was cruel, and the conflict they have (about the baby) caused her to act the way she did throughout her life. I don't think she mothered the community." The other white male reader echoed this argument. He said, "*Meridian* is a novel about guilt, obligation and sacrifice. A large part of the book deals with Meridian's sense of guilt for letting down her mother, but I think that is just one part. . . . I think Meridian's guilt theme (and subsequent sacrifices) could have been derived from something else, such as guilt from a failed effort with a close friend." However, I apparently did succeed in creating a genuinely dialogic classroom; most students appeared willing to insist upon the authority of their readings even when it meant disagreeing with me. Perhaps, at best, I will succeed only in teaching male students not to use the royal "we." For example, when one of my male readers concluded his in-class response, "I think we are reading way too much into this novel," I wrote back, "All of us are reading 'into' this novel. You cannot speak for 'we,' but only for yourself. When you use 'we' in this way, you deny the patterns that most women in this class saw in *Meridian*." Given my view of authority, I cannot insist that young men agree with me. Nevertheless, teaching the discipline of maternal thought to both men and women remains an ideal for me.

And I have resolved that the next time I teach *Meridian*, I will more aggressively decode the language of romance, particularly its inauthentic portrayals of the "mother woman," which Walker critiques in her parody, "the mummy woman." I will point out more forcefully to students that as part of her heroic task, Meridian must learn to recognize distinctions between authentic and inauthentic mothers.[6] Meridian's mother, Mrs. Hill, is inauthentic, for she accepts the values of the dominant culture, acting out a Christian martyrdom that burdens Meridian with guilt. In fact, when Meridian strives for authenticity, refusing to accept maternal or Christian martyrdom, her mother rejects her. As Ruddick says, "chronic self-denial" is actually a vice, and Walker shows us how it becomes a vice. Only Miss Winter, a woman teacher who has refused to give up her gold, her musical gift, is able to save Meridian from death, able to mother her with the words, "I forgive you" (125). Unlike her mother, Meridian affirms her "treasure," a treasure Walker redefines when Miss Margaret Treasure, at the age of "sixty-nine" (or is it "seventy-two," as her sister says?), finally acts upon her sexual desire. No longer "pure as the driven snow," no longer a virgin, and fearing she is pregnant, Miss Treasure does not want to lose her economic autonomy: "'They say I got to marry him,' she sobbed, 'but I don't want to now,'" to which Meridian and Truman answer, "'Then don't!'" (209). In this tragicomic scene, Walker not only redefines the nature of a woman's treasure—always, in romance, her virginity—but also insists that the desires of a woman take precedence over the community's definition of a "lady," a mother-woman. As Meridian and Truman affirm Miss Treasure's right to her own wishes, they act out two salient features of maternal thinking: authenticity and humility. With such behavior, in sharp contrast to Truman's earlier arrogance, he earns the love and respect of members of the black community. Although Truman is not a biological mother, in this instance he seems capable of acting as a maternal thinker.

Or rather, one might say that it is with Meridian's example that Truman is able to act in this way. At first, students don't see that Truman Held, with his fantasies of black "earth mothers" and virgins "pure as driven snow," must resist romantic stereotypes. Truman illustrates just how difficult it will be for some men to unlearn romantic thought. For example, critic Norman Harris concludes his reading of *Meridian* with the romantic formula: "She [Meridian] will keep the voice of the people alive and soothe the warriors with her song" (117). Walker leaves open the question of whether, without Meridian's teaching, Truman (or any man) can remain true to the values that Meridian has practiced in the community. Certainly, children have not been central in Truman's thoughts, but Meridian refuses to mother Truman; instead, she leaves her maternal responsibilities in his hands. Walker's novel argues that there's a point at which maternal thinkers like Martin Luther King should just "walk off," refusing to martyr themselves for others, whether these others are friends, lovers, husbands, or communities. This moment in *Meridian* is one of demystification: by taking on the heroic role herself, Meridian discovers that sacrificial heroes are maintained by sacrificial mothers. She realizes that her reversal of heroic and maternal roles will not transform sacrificial logic. The discipline of maternal thought teaches Meridian that nurturers must nurture themselves; otherwise, they no longer foster growth but instead paralyze their children's, and their culture's, development.

In choosing to "bring a *transformed* maternal thought" into this public realm, Meridian moves beyond monologic consciousness. She finds a new "ending," a higher, dialogic consciousness that allows her to affirm both herself and others. Throughout the novel, Meridian carries on a debate, both with Anne-Marion and with herself, over the question of revolutionary violence. I believe that her experience as a mother, including her impulses to kill her son, plays a major role in Meridian's resistance to violence. When asked, "Will you kill for the Revolution?" (27), Meridian cannot say "yes" as readily as Anne-Marion can, for she imagines the consequences. "Meridian alone was holding on to something the others had let go," Walker explains. Meridian is "*held* by something in the past," by her memories of the black community.

By the memory of old black men in the South who, caught by surprise in the eye of a camera, never shifted their position but look directly back; by the sight of young girls singing in a country choir, their hair shining with brushings and grease, their voices the voices of angels. When she was transformed in church, it was always by the purity of the singers' souls, which she could actually *hear*, the purity that lifted their songs like a flight of doves above her music-drunken head. If they committed murder—and to her even revolutionary murder was murder—what would the music be like? (27–28).

Meridian sees, not with the single eye of a camera, but with loving eyes, and with loving ears; she sees herself as/in family, kinship, community. Such consciousness finds its representation in what Julia Kristeva in *Desire in Language* calls "carnivalesque discourse" that rebelliously "breaks through the laws of language" (65) to destroy social cohesion "maintained by virtue of the sacrifice" (138), the sacrifice Walker parodies in the "mummy woman" scene. Walker transforms the autonomous "I" of the romantic into an intersubjective "we," through her insistence upon civil rights for mothers. As Thadious M. Davis says, "By the end of the novel, Meridian's personal identity has become a collective identity" (49).[7]

Notes

1. Is it fair for a white person to decide what's black and what isn't? I would argue that it is Alice Walker, and not I, her white reader, who has decided that Truman reads romantically, constructing "Woman" as a white man does. But, fortunately, as I was considering this issue, Barbara Christian's essay "Response to 'Black Women's Texts'" appeared in the first issue of the *NWSA Journal*. Christian interprets Truman as "the incipient black revolutionary who nonetheless desires the norm which society exalts, a definition which demeans not only black women, or white women, but also himself. In desiring women who 'read *The New York Times*'... he gestures his preference for a woman knowledgeable of the world yet not sullied by its 'funk'" (34).

2. See Maureen Reddy's "Maternal Reading" in this volume. In David Bleich's essay on teaching *The Bluest Eye*, he illustrates one aspect of maternal thinking when he argues that the notion of an individual reader must be replaced with a theory of intersubjectivity. He says, for example, "We must learn how even as individuals, we remain part of the other sex, other races, and other ways of life" (14). Not surprisingly, Bleich reports that white men were the least willing to imagine themselves as part of a collective identity.

3. In *Bearing the Word*, where Homans offers a more complete explanation of her Lacanian theory of women's relationship to language, she emphasizes the tendency of women writers to privilege the literal. I am arguing instead that women—that is, maternal thinkers—think dialogically, insisting upon "both/and" logic: both the literal and the figurative, both the child and the word. I do not accept Homans' argument that Kristeva's notion of the semiotic applies only to the writing of men. In *Desire in Language*, Kristeva herself illustrates in "Place Names" how it is that laughter—for children of both sexes—marks the semiotic disposition "chronologically and logically long before the mirror stage" (283).

4. The name "Camara" challenges the subject/object split of the romantic subject implied in the term "camera," and indicates a subject constructed dialogically, as *both* different from (and outside) the object *and* the same as (and inside) the object. Since, in this instance, the object is a child, a child once carried within the mother's womb, Alice Walker's redefinition of (maternal) subjectivity becomes apparent. Whereas Truman represses his participation in the "object" (whether woman or nature), Meridian acknowledges that she is part of what she observes. Walker also identifies this as an

African way of knowing through her allusion to the African artist, Camara Laye. See especially Tzvetan Todorov's explanation of this aspect of Bakhtin's notion of dialogism in *Mikhail Bakhtin: The Dialogical Principle*, 102–5. See also Julia Kristeva's *Desire in Language*, especially "The Bounded Text," and "Word, Dialogue, and Novel," and "From One Identity to Another."

5. I requested permission to quote Denise, as well as all other students whose work I cite.

6. In *The Female Hero in American and British Literature*, Carol Pearson and Katherine Pope argue that, for the female ego, a significant struggle is to achieve reconciliation with her mother, but only by differentiating between authentic and inauthentic mothers, between patriarchal mothers and maternal thinkers. They also point out that "the heroic woman who is a mother is rarely married" (200).

7. This issue of boundaries of the self inevitably creates confusion. In *Motherself*, Kathryn Allen Rabuzzi explains the difficulty this way: "This [alternative] selfhood, known as motherself, is a bit of a paradox for it contradicts our intuitive notion that selfhood is single. Furthermore, it also counters accepted belief that the instances in which selfhood is not single involve serial selves. . . . Motherself, by contrast, involves a simultaneous two-in-one relationship, composed of mother and child" (48). As Rabuzzi explains, change is inherent in this view of selfhood, because of its relational nature. Rabuzzi also says that the motherself is difficult to articulate because "she is neither one nor the other [and] this perpetual ambivalence differs greatly from the single-minded purposiveness of the unitary self" (57). Anne-Marion's erasure in her letter to Meridian is a good example of such ambivalence — or "dual-consciousness." So are Meridian's changing and apparently inconsistent views of revolutionary violence.

Chapter 15

Teaching / (M)othering:
The Feminist Classroom as Unbounded Text

Sheryl O'Donnell

Like the young female writer
whom Virginia Woolf is describing in
the excerpt from the speech, "Professions
for Women," we women who would teach
as women find ourselves in a bare room
that is not empty. We can clean
out the male curriculum, banking education,
the process/product paradigm, the myth of
objectivity. We can give the old furniture
away to Goodwill, or domesticate it, turning
old school desks into planters
and telephone tables. We can silence
the clanging lockers, period bells, "now-hear-this"
loudspeakers. We can make it a demilitarized
zone. But still we are not in an
empty space. . . . [T]here are no empty houses, only
those houses that our mothers left us.
—Madeleine R. Grumet

Always already forgetting, despite Virginia Woolf's "Angel in the House" and, more recently, Toni Morrison's *Beloved*, I somehow deny how we dwell in our mother's houses: uneasily. I erase the implications of this essay's title, with the M separated from the other; the other in the mother, and pretend that the classroom (*my* classroom, the feminist classroom as an abstract ideal) is benign. I dream of this classroom as an empty space with no phantoms, a safe place where students can think out loud together. Speech after long silence. "Maternal thinking" in practice.

I forget that this dream, like all feminist utopias, is literary: pastoral in its laminated images of teachers and students at leisure, epic in its characterization of the feminist classroom as *locus amantis*, beloved place. The pleasures of imagining the feminist classroom as such a "haven in a heartless world" of traditional academic life are perhaps Victorian; in Victorian times public (male) spaces were separate from private (female) ones. And such dreams play upon Victorian fantasies of ideal maternity: plenitude, safety, enclosure, self-sufficiency. So the occasional worm in the garden—a student who refuses to "get it," an unsisterly research paper, an abandoned group project— need not be monstrous. I am enchanted to read a student's evaluation of our "Women Writers and Readers" course: "Sherry, you sure know how to put the hay down where the sheep can reach it." Her image constructs a delightfully vulgar (maternal?) pastoral: after all, manly pastorals such as *Lycidas* or *The Shepherd's Calendar* do not linger over the messy details of feeding. But this image also disturbs me by recalling the very hierarchy of power and knowledge which feminists seek to transcend. Maybe *I* should feel sheepish. But why be horrified by this vision of students as sheep? They are, after all, the most garrulous of animals who ruminate. Grumet recalls the etymological connections between "read" and "ruminate," to remind us that "the ruminant does not give up the world to think about it. On the hoof it stores the world that it consumes in multiple stomachs until it has found a place of safety to bring back what has been swallowed in haste for a good chew."[1] Food for thought: my fantasies of the feminist classroom as benign may deny students' images of themselves as radical Others. I domesticate them by imagining the Good Mother (me) hearing words of praise from Grateful Daughters (and Sons). So their wild desires for inter-species commerce are tamed, and my utopian fantasies stay intact by an act of willful repression and countertransference.[2] Denying students' otherness, I make them lesser versions of myself.[3]

Pastoral fantasies of the feminist classroom as privileged space are easy for me to construct, and thus all the more insidious, because I can trick myself into thinking that I am making political sense out of personal experience (always a feminist dictum). I live in a state whose "rural" qualities, like my feminist pastoral fantasies, are largely illusory, highly artificial, and utterly ahistorical. So how to account for the contradictions created by an economy which denies the possibility of living on the land at the same time that romantic images of rural life permeate the national scene? The myth of self-sufficiency, the notion of farmers and ranchers as independent, self-reliant individuals, is so strong that my students can hardly trade papers with each other in the classroom for fear that someone will steal their ideas. Their suspicion of others, their unwillingness to respect their own ideas or to converse with each other, their seeming emotional stinginess (and thus my ambivalent gratitude for their praise) are based, I think, on an ideology of private property (including ideas) as sacred and of the coherent ego as autonomous.

Grumet observed that the very aspects of nurturance that are practiced by mother/teachers are purged from the children in schools, even as these aspects are required to be there.

"I resent your reading my paper out loud to the class," wrote one student in her journal a few years ago. "I worked a long time on it and I know that some people haven't even started on their papers yet. How do you know they won't use my ideas?" These are not the words of a shy young woman confessing her secret thrill at being singled out for in-class praise, as I had hoped. Instead, I had invaded her privacy, broadcasting her secret genius to cheaters and laggards who might use her ideas to their own easy advantage. To many students, the feminist classroom, with its emphasis on shared experiences and group discussion, was an academic perversity. Like other "nice girls," this student felt betrayed and exposed by the very authority who was supposed to guarantee her uniqueness by policing all plagiarists and punishing the tardy. Her rhetorical question, "How do you know they won't use my ideas?" made a cautionary tale of my heedlessness.

A similar warning recently appeared in a male student's journal: "My limited, sheltered background did not prepare me for the radical feminist attitudes some women in this class possess. I am used to the more traditional roles of men and women, and have been exposed mainly to women who are comfortable, content, and happy with the roles they have. I am not happy when they feel they must conquer, eliminate, and withhold sex from men in order to get what they want." Here again is a student's defense against licentious classroom talk. He too imagines himself in a predatory world peopled by enemies seemingly aided and abetted by the teacher herself. And his script, like the previous one, mandates a law-and-order rule of protection against perverse group exchange. Being "happy," for many of my students, means being safe and alone in a carefully monitored, predictable crowd of vaguely well-meaning strangers.

I quote these student texts, with their embedded stories of classroom dangers, because they represent dozens of such laments I have read over the years. Read, not heard. For here in the stoic Midwest, classroom silence is one palpable form of resistance which students can claim as their own.[4] Laboring under the injunction to silence—"If you can't say anything nice, don't say anything at all"—both male and female students position themselves as feminized subjects, outwardly silent and inwardly seething against public speech. Their journals thus provide ghost narratives of imagined classroom encounters—what went unsaid, what they could have said, would have said, had the phantoms in the classrooms disappeared. What's so interesting about these injunctions to silence is that they are part of what makes the feminist classroom an unbounded text.[5] Our work goes on, in, around, beneath, and beyond the dreams of enclosure which both my students and I have constructed.

Strikingly, students often use maternal metaphors to account for their learning.[6] And, like many recent theories of feminist pedagogy, their accounts are essentially narratives of progress of some kind or another. Once a woman's silence is broken, so the story goes, she can free herself from constraints operating both within and outside her own discourse. Speaking as a woman, rather than for or about women, she thus gives birth to herself, names herself.[7] And, because "we cannot live without stories," as Leslie Silko has argued, understanding women's narratives as ontological categories rather than as mere descriptors is politically urgent. Since women's narratives are every-where—in novels, letters, journals, academic papers, and the everyday speech of family life and classroom study—they refuse academic laws of separate life, pastoral dreams of safe enclosure, once they have been set in motion. I want to explore this maternal discourse as it was generated in an under-graduate class on "Women Writers and Readers" I taught at the University of North Dakota in fall 1988. Using student papers, reports, and reading jour-nals, I will argue that this construct, "maternal discourse," and the narratives it produced, are neither as innocent nor as benign as I had imagined. But its power was much more revolutionary, its pleasures and dangers uncertain for all.

I planned the course around questions of desire, quoting Leslie Silko's let-ter to James Wright: "Maybe it has taken me this long to discover that we are liable to love anything—like characters in old Greek stories who set eyes on an oak tree or a bucket and fall in love hopelessly. There are no limits to our love" (Silko, 14). Our work, as I explained to the class, would be to ex-plore the powers of such arbitrary desires, making Freud's question, "What does woman want?", into our cry, "What!? Does woman *want*?!" I listed women writers whose works refused to limit female passion or to censure its excesses, and I distributed this course overview:

WOMEN WRITERS AND READERS: QUESTIONS OF DESIRE
We will examine various fictions of feminine desire, studying how it is produced and for whose benefit it circulates. We will be especially inter-ested in the differences between pleasure and what French theory calls *jouissance*.

Required Texts
Fielding Burke (Olive Tilford Dargan), *Call Home the Heart*
Carolyn Chute, *The Beans of Egypt, Maine*
Isabel de Courtivron and Elaine Marks, eds., *New French Feminisms*
Louise Erdrich, *Love Medicine*
Dexter Fisher, ed., *The Third Woman: Minority Women Writers in the United States*

Toni Morrison, *Beloved*
Monique Wittig, *Les Guerrilleres*

Grading
   Class participation (20%), journal (20%), in-class report (20%), paper (20%),
   final exam (20%)

Meeting twice a week for an hour and a half, the class numbered twenty-eight, and included twelve young white women, four young white men, two Native Americans (a young woman and a young man), three Métis (French and Chippewa) women, two middle-aged white women, one white grandmother, and four white women graduate students. *Jouissance* as class list. The whites were of German or Scandinavian background. The students had chosen a variety of majors, predominantly education, humanities, and social sciences. All but two were from farms or small towns in North Dakota and Minnesota, and most were aspiring professionals from working-class backgrounds, the first in their families to attend university. Many had families and children to care for or held part-time jobs to pay their tuition. The younger students went home almost every weekend, and no students described themselves as having strong emotional ties to the campus. Many of the younger students imagined their "real" lives beginning after graduation, and all seemed to feel distanced from academic life. The desires they claimed at the first class session fit what Roland Barthes would call bourgeois needs for comfort and security: new cars and other consumer goods, self-actualization, successful careers as bank presidents and business executives or best-selling novelists. All of the students, including the self-proclaimed feminists, described their goals and ambitions as personal.

After the first class meeting, I assigned journal questions for the semester's reading assignments, so that our discussions would be framed by the students' own texts. At first, they waited until after class discussions to write in their journals, afraid that they wouldn't have the "right answers" to record. Then, when they decided, sometimes disgustedly, that there were no "right answers," they struggled with what they might write.

This struggle to produce their own readings and to authorize them was a crucial, ongoing one, embodying the central and mysterious tropes of mother/teacher/daughter/student relations described by Nell Noddings as dialogue between the "one-caring" and the "cared-for." But the maternal project of nurturing relatedness rather than detachment, as Noddings and Grumet have cautioned, has unsettling effects. In our class, two conventions of discourse prevailed to contain them: polite guardedness in the classroom and raging confessions in the journals. Since both conventions rule midwestern culture at large—the stop signs on our straight, flat country roads are often riddled with bulletholes—I made massive efforts to reverse the sites of this discourse. I wanted what Deanne Bogdan calls "self-emotive, expressive, autobiographical and therapeutic forms of discourse" (9) to inhabit the classroom, and I hoped the journal entries could be more analytic and experimental. To this end, we examined ways in which the voices of authority and desire often opposed each other in the assigned novels, and students produced similar narratives in their journals. One, titled "Confessions from a Madwoman," literally split the narrator from voices which produced, then diagnosed, her manic boredom:

I go back to the bedroom and make the bed. I'm tired at this point and would like to climb back into bed. I notice [my boyfriend's] jockey underwear hanging on the doorknob. I want to scream. I clean the kitchen. I clean the toilet. I clean and clean.* I go to school. One must be a career woman. I work while I go to school to become a career woman.** I'm tired. I'm mad. Who cares? I forgot to mention that I also cut out shopping coupons.

*A major resource for reducing wives' overload is, of course, husbands' cooperation in the home (Fogarty, Rappaport, Rappaport, *Sex, Career, and Family*, 147).

**Most upwardly-mobile women who have worked for any length of time realize that if they want to succeed, they have to work harder and smarter, put in longer hours, and do a better job than men who have the same job. And what they get in return is less money and less recognition. (Higginson and Quick, *The Ambitious Woman's Guide to a Successful Career*, 28).

I was shocked to see how easily this journal entry could transform the *Diary of a Mad Housewife* into "Fragments of a Student's Discourse." Is this a postfeminist text, so knowing and cynical that self-awareness can congeal into self-pitying, helpless rage? The last line, "I forgot to mention that I also cut out shopping coupons," conflates, once and for all, the student/girlfriend/wife/cook/maid metaphors, and the history of this young woman's education mocks its own desires. An icon of its own pain, the text freezes past, present, and future into a hopeless litany of defeat and isolation.

In hindsight I understand how my own dismayed reading of this journal entry reproduced a mother/teacher's fantasies of daughter/student "progress," fantasies which demand that their projects replicate my own. But Noddings asks mothers/teachers to "undergo a motivational displacement toward the project of the cared-for; starting from a position of respect or regard for the project of the other" (Noddings, 176). Read less judgmentally, this entry asks some compelling questions: How far can the ironic disjunctions among the voices in these two columns be stretched? Does the narrator in the left-hand column generate her own footnotes to complete her story, as I first thought, or to mock, even abandon it? And if the footnote prophecies literally authorize madness, what's to confess?

Another journal entry on the same assignment told a surreal story of defiant longing. The "she" in the first paragraph is the "I" of the second paragraph, so that the split voices of authority and desire emerge, then shift locales:

> She was a girl who could give a seasoned lumberjack with arms like steel a run for his money in any logging event. She was from a place where exercise was a part of survival, not a form of entertainment. She didn't know how to swim, but she'd been up to her neck in green slimy river water trying to help hoist a heifer and her calf out of the muck. With neck muscles bulging, she'd helped the new mother escape, and heifer and girl alike lay on the bank with stomachs heaving and thighs shivering against the exhaustion that was beginning to hold their limbs.
>
> You're a vindictive bitch. I've always wanted to say that to the little salt-and-pepper-haired woman who left me crying by the empty cake plate. Mom said, "You shouldn't tease your brothers."
>
> "But Mama, I only hid theirs. It was a joke! You helped me! You're the one who said to put the cake in the china cabinet. You said it would be funny."
>
> "That girl will be the death of me. I can never get her out of that chair and she's always reading. She even reads while she's doing her chores in the barn. She just sits and turns the pages. She reads five books to the other girls' one."
>
> Dad says to leave her alone. "She'll grow out of it in time."

What's so striking, if predictable, since we were reading Dargan's *Call Home the Heart* and had watched the Bryn Mawr "Women of Summer" video, is the heroic energy in this entry, its determination to celebrate a daughter's desire for power. But this entry, like the previous one, isolates its protagonist in a fundamentally Gothic scene. The details of ordinary life—waking up to the sound of an alarm clock in the first entry, tending animals in the second, and reading, in both entries—are sinister. Disembodied voices, suffocating enclosures, and dark prophecies by betraying parents, all are metaphors for the stifling rage at mothers which these texts announce.

If the assigned novels for the course opposed the voices of authority to the voices of desire, many student journal entries somehow blamed their mothers for this opposition. One entry, titled "The Excesses of Motherly Love," written as we read Morrison's *Beloved*, alternately rejects and longs for these "excesses":

> My mother tells me and others that I was very independent as a small child. She says all I wanted from her was food and diaper changes. There

were many times I didn't want the food, either, although I remember being four or five years old, running through the back yards of the neighborhood (very white, middle-class, Athens, Georgia, early 70s), running into the kitchen for a quick lunch. One slice of Velveeta cheese product. That's all I wanted. Mom made me eat at least one slice of cheese every day for lunch.

I remember vaguely a time when I must have been two or three when Mom interrupted my Empire State Building block project to feed me.

I hated being inside. I hated soap operas. They always reminded me of the fact that I couldn't kiss anybody yet, that it was an adult pleasure. I wanted to kiss my mom when I was two. I remember one specific night when I almost really tried to get her to kiss me—long and hard like on the soaps.

It pissed me off that people didn't know I wanted to kiss someone. It still does. I felt like maybe I was different from everyone else because I wanted to kiss someone, but nobody my age kissed like I wanted to. I still feel that way, like I want to kiss every woman I meet, but nobody can kiss without a prolonged ritual of meeting, talking, dating, etc.

At age two I wanted the "real" kisses. I think of Shirley McLaine and Debra Winger in "Terms of Endearment." Now those were real kisses.

I always felt that my mother never gave me enough of the real thing. My definition of the real thing changed from time to time, but I felt that Mom wasn't honest enough with me.

At some point I wanted the real story of make-up. What to use, how, when, and where. Mom never told me—so like with everything else, I experimented. I was always imaginative, bold, and quite frankly, bizarre. Ladybugs and flowers I painted on my face.

At age four I had told my mother that she didn't need make-up—she was beautiful without it. She said she didn't know what she would do without me—and squashed me in her big body right in the middle of a supermarket parking lot. Then I was embarrassed.

This daughter's story of her wish for "real kisses," the virtual kisses of television soaps and films, corrects her mother's reported talk of infant self-sufficiency. The daughter's self-representations—of creativity and mobility in particular—thus oppose, yet are produced by, her mother's version of their early life together. Memories of maternal lack are punctuated, most interestingly, by memories of maternal plenitude, so that metaphors of fantasy and "make-up" never quite control the story's libidinal economy. When the mother appears outside the house, once to interrupt her daughter's building project, once to hug her in a supermarket parking lot, the daughter's creative self-absorption is "squashed," and the story ends its precocious seduction, embarrassed by the mother's "big body."

Throughout the semester, student journal entries mirrored parent-child struggles thematized by the assigned novels and short stories. These entries were often what Toni Morrison calls "rememories," stories that happen "when you lose sight of some things and memory others" (Morrison, 201). One middle-aged woman rememoried a magical train trip to San Francisco in 1943, when her mother and aunt left husbands and waitress jobs in Minneapolis to work in wartime shipyards:

> Mother said she had never been up so high in all her life and she was scared to death. They found her another job. But Aunt Connie held out for the duration. Six feet tall and quite beautiful, she was my Rosie the Riveter in the flesh. I admired her for her Betty Grable looks and I always thought a drawing of her in a bathing suit should be painted on the nose of a bomber. She seemed like a tower of strength to me. How I remember my mother and aunt taking turns standing on a chair while the other drew a black seam up the back of her leg to simulate nylons, which neither could afford or find.

Awash in the Hollywood war propaganda of female beauty and sacrifice, this rememory chooses power (Aunt Connie) over cowardice (Mother). But the last privileged glance is at both women, and it is an admiring one, like the respect Alice Walker's narrator feels for the rootworker Tante Rosie, whose trade she studies to expose in "The Revenge of Hannah Kemhoff." The illusion of having nylons or the illusion of working a curse must be created as a powerful reality whose contours are determined by shared cultural practices, not individual efforts.

Giving students rememory assignments like this one helped them understand the fictional constructs of their own perceived "truths," especially the truths of their experiences. To reduce the tension and anxiety that this understanding produced, they often added moral tags or conclusions to their rememories to clarify themselves: "Just never send a card to your own child when one short handwritten note can say a lot more." "I certainly viewed some very alarming things this semester: girls trying to lose weight so their boyfriends would come back; girls living on coffee and water for days in order to fit into a certain dress; self-induced vomiting and laxatives. I would like to grab them by the shoulders and shake them."

This moral tone entered the classroom itself toward semester's end and was the first discursive element shared by student writing and conversation. Initially, however, the conversations were private, between me and the students meeting in my office or elsewhere on campus. The class had gradually arranged itself into factions, with self-proclaimed feminists monitoring any deviations from the perceived Party Line.[8] These deviations occurred frequently, since we were reading minority women writers and French theorists whose texts hardly underscored the individualistic versions of feminism that some students uncritically embraced. When one young woman noted that the only thing she remembered about feminists was being a five-year-old stuck in a corner to cry, while her mother "screamed in a circle with her consciousness-raising group," the feminists in the class rolled their eyes, then approached me outside the class to ask what could be done to "shut her up." Hedging the question, I recalled that Silko's "Gallup, New Mexico, Indian Capitol of the World" and the opening chapters of Chute's *The Beans of Egypt, Maine* both raise this very question of betrayal. I asked them to assume the child's point of view when reading these scenes. Having done so, could they understand the narrative logic of their classmate's attack on "feminism"? And what might be the function of *sound*—the crying child and the screaming mother—in their classmate's story?

Because I chose texts which offered more radical versions of desire than my students had claimed for themselves, they did not read uncritically. In the assigned novels, for instance, relationships among mothers and daughters were not merely adversarial or "daughter-centered," as many white students had expected.[9] Strong family ties linked distant relatives across generations, both dead and living. And the psychological development of female protagonists was always wedded to social movements, ethnic and folk practices, labor history, and race relations. Three male students who said they enrolled in the course because they thought that, as English majors, they should know something about women writers, balked at all this "background information," and they suspected that they personally were being held accountable for all sins against women, past and present. As we talked in my office, I asked them to trace the mechanisms of their interpretations of our class discussions. What gears were turning to make them feel marked as culprits, and thus justified in rejecting the social and historical forces operating in the assigned texts? What advantages did they gain by thinking of their private lives as separate from the social forces within which they are constituted? And what reading could they offer of Morrison's portrayal of African-American men in *Beloved*?

If the male students felt threatened as a group and thus formed one to defend themselves, the Métis students, already affiliated within the larger context of university politics, spoke as one. They worried about the negative impressions white students might have of minority writers, since all of the assigned texts were so "depressing." I agreed that they might be right, given Robert Towers' essay on Erdrich's *Love Medicine* in the *New York Review of Books*, which reads the novel according to the very stereotypes the Métis students feared:

> From the medley of individual faces and voices a few generic, or tribal, features gradually emerge. The men get drunk as often as possible, and when drunk they are likely to be violent or to do wildly irresponsible or

self-destructive things. . . . Meanwhile the women, with the exception of the stalwart Marie, are likely to take up with any man who comes along. (Quoted in McKenzie, 54)

We used this quote in class, exploring how the key terms in Towers' assessment of *Love Medicine* simplify Erdrich's novel by flattening its lyric power. The multiple narrators, muted chronologies, and ambivalent motives demand much more careful scrutiny than Towers allows. Questions of a writer's responsibility to her family history emerged in the class discussion, with "the truth hurts" versus "the truth heals" claiming various voices. The Métis students, all of whom live on the reservation of *Love Medicine*'s setting, were glad to point out the novel's subtleties, especially its humor, that white readers might miss. And the student who had led the protest against the novel's depressing contagion put this entry in her journal:

> My parents lived through a lot together, for raising nine children isn't always easy for anyone. Especially when one parent is an alcoholic. My mom kept us together and always taught us right from wrong. She always said we were never too old for a "knuckle sandwich"!
> In 1972 my dad was drinking so my mom took us to Rugby to stay a few days. My dad was never abusive to us; he just got drunk in his bedroom and my mom felt that was nothing for us to see so she used to take us out of town to stay for a few days for a "treat." While we were gone the trailer house blew up with my dad in it. The paramedics didn't even know there was anyone in the house till they saw his hand sticking out the door. He got 90% of his body burned. He was in the hospital for two years. Through this my mom took care of us kids, ran the filling station and drove 200 miles a week to see my dad.
> They survived.
> Then my dad had a triple bypass in 1982 and had a stoke on the operating table and another seven days later. My mom sat by his side. He lay in a coma for six weeks.
> They survived.
> In May of 1986 my dad had a seizure and was in Minneapolis for two months where they found a blood clot running from the base of his neck to the tip of his head due to his burn accident.
> They survived.
> In April of this year my dad died, leaving a little bit of him in all of us. My baby Jordan was his last grandchild that he got to see. He had never been to the hospitals when any of his seven daughters were having babies because he was scared and hated hospitals. But, when I came out of the delivery room, he and Mom were there. I cried because I knew then he was trying to tell me something in his own way. I hope and pray that he's done suffering now and I thank God for his being my father and Mom being my mother. I hope I turn out to be as good a parent as they have been to me and my brothers and sisters.
> They survived.

The trope, "They survived," moves from calamity to calamity, capping one disaster just in time for another's appearance, as in a soap opera, where events do not shape character but illustrate it. By subordinating the time of her father's death to his unexpected appearance at the hospital, where she can read his wishes as benign, the student survives her own misgivings about "depressing" subjects and gives birth, literally, to hope.

The happy closure this narrative seeks typifies what most student journal entries managed to do. Existential dread and romantic isolation, the pose which many students adopted in the classroom, didn't show up in their writings. When I assigned an entry beginning "No one ever understood my _____," to include "But there were times" somewhere in the middle, students used a problem/solution narrative design which allowed forbidden desires to surface. This entry by a middle-aged woman is almost formulaic:

> No one ever understood my fits of anger. They used to say I was a shrew who could only be agreeable when I got my own way. But it's not true. Like many women, much of my life was lived to meet the expectations of other people. To be misunderstood as a shrew was to have the desires I did insist on discounted.
>
> When I was a girl, I remember telling my mother that I wanted to grow up and marry a minister and live on the coast of Vermont. I accomplished the first part of my wish but, alas, could never accomplish the last because there is no coast in Vermont. At the time, however, being married to a minister seemed good and safe. Good because nothing was more beautiful than church, safe because no one could not like good people like the minister and his wife.
>
> By the time I met the man who would become my husband, I had forgotten my wish. When I thought about marrying him, the ideas that life would be good and safe seemed to be new and original. So I proposed and he accepted.
>
> I soon realized that being married to a minister meant living at a subsistence level. My husband was over-valued, in a way, as a "man of God," but not valued enough to be paid a living wage. I was over-valued as the wife of a man of God, almost to the point of having children by immaculate conception. I was often alone because he was expected to keep daily office hours, yet much of the church's business was conducted at night. Socializing with other pastors and their wives meant comparing miseries: whose salary was the most inadequate, whose parsonage was the most neglected. Socializing with parishoners meant being a wallflower at wedding dances while other men exchanged dances with each other's wives, or being the only non-family at family gatherings.
>
> But there were times.
>
> I learned to pursue a secular life because life within parish boundaries was entirely too tame and predictable. I began working to supplement our income, but found I enjoyed socializing with heathens—non-Lutherans, even non-Christians. Heathen are full of surprises, even surprises they were

willing to admit. Favorite heathen were those who could swear in my presence without excusing their "French." They were freer people for swearing. Once a person could swear, revelations of character, even weaknesses of character, became easier to make and that person becomes real.

I discovered I was full of surprises, too. I learned to swear and the world was suddenly full of people who were real, both in and out of church. So I demanded to live in the world, not just in the church.

While the Métis student's chaotic life shaped the desire for convention and propriety which generated her survival story, this middle-class white student equates "freedom" with "heathens" who swear. Platitudes about "going native" govern both texts, but from very different vantage points—one disapproving what the other desires. Thus both texts tell stories of linear progress through time. Ironically, as the semester progressed, the students began speaking to each other as well as to me, thereby embodying the "improved" versions of themselves which the liberal arts curriculum demands, and which "my" feminist classroom tacitly urged.

With my complicity, the students' classroom discourse constructed me as mother/teacher and themselves as student/daughters, with all the attendant complexities that recent feminist theory has taught us to see. I was not prepared for the narrative power of this construct, however, as it fashioned various forms of *j'accuse*. The shared space of the classroom changed from a theater to a courtroom, with the confessions and testimonials of the student journals glossing the assigned texts for the course. Students traded stories of insult, rejection, and powerlessness, and I struggled against my own fantasies of omnipotent power to "solve" the dilemmas the class had created in their lives. The course had politicized the curriculum so that they were "too critical" of their other classes. What they once had happily perceived as knowledge now was power masking its authority. And what was I going to do to fix things?

Well, we'd examine these victim narratives in the light of French theory, which resists common-sense discourse and posits the "I" as capable of taking any number of positions in the endless stream of narrative possibilities. Displacement, not confrontation, might be mimed, so that the righteous self-absorption of victim stories might disperse itself along a spectrum of echo or montage. So we listened to each other's victim stories the last two weeks of the class, not as glum compatriots or potential recruits, but as literary critics whose attention is drawn to narrative form. For example, one student reported taking a geology field trip with six male students, her seven-year-old son, and a professor who, around the campfire, lectured on the evils of women's makeup. The student's story featured her as a diminished, frightened isolate who was abashed that her son should see her humiliated by a man he admired. But what if the horrified gaze of the professor were turned to his own desire to be "made up"? Let the prof tremble! We will show him our lipsticks!

A middle-aged student brought news of her son's girlfriend, newly signed up in the Army, harassed in the barracks and on the parade field. With the help of a classmate who had been in the Marines, we constructed a series of parodic moves the girlfriend might make, moves that would not jeopardize her military standing but would call the harassers' actions into question. A young student's stepfather, learning of her enrollment in "Women Writers and Readers," said that no one but ugly rejects and lesbians would do such a thing. A male student was mocked for taking "poles and holes," campus argot for women's studies classes. The stories were myriad and fixed in place.

Retold within the classroom and linked with assigned writings by Cixous and Irigaray, especially, these stories took new collective form and moved from the posture of innocence to that of design. As various voices questioned or modified or contradicted the narrative, both on the page and in our mouths, the mother/teacher/student/daughter constructs assumed new forms and possibilities. My fantasies of omnipotence and their fantasies of grudging dependency dissolved. One of the most interesting sessions we held was on rape narrative, imagining alternatives to the isolate figure's choices which usually foreground the plot. Several Christian students, naming rape as women's equivalent of Jesus' suffering, changed an "I deserved to be raped because I was drunk in the men's dorm" to a collective tale called "How They Clothed the Naked in Walsh Hall."

But this heterogeneity was not always welcome, and the dream of cheerful solidarity, of pastoral enclosure and possessive individualism, was hard to kill. For, in its wake, came the feminists classroom as unbounded text, feminist pedagogy as an unfinished project. We're still chewing on this story, produced at semester's end by a student who fashions herself at the intersection of power and desire. Having idolized her father all her life, she can't swallow the stories of incest told her, finally, by her sisters:

> Here I am, with five sisters and I'm the only one he hasn't touched. Why? Was he just too old, or did he love me more or did he love me less or did he love any of us? I don't know why he would do it, or why my mother didn't stop him. I just know I don't want to know any more about it, ever. I look at him now, and I get all twisted up in knots. I've talked to some of my friends about it, but I don't know if they believe me or think I'm over-reacting. After all, can I be a silent victim? I avoid my oldest sister like the plague, and can't look my mother in the eye. I'm all confused and can't even cry. Do I have the right to? You tell me.

OK, I write. But you have already written yourself out of the silence you speak of. Note the narrative shape of your rhetorical question, the powerful force of your demands.[10] If the "I" and the "you" of this text are two parts of your own warring psyche, you can write about this battle between numbness and feeling, shame and outrage. Assume the position of "you" in your text. Now what can "you" say? Now what can "you" write?

Notes

1. Grumet's chapter, "Feminism and the Phenomenology of the Familiar," in Grumet, *Bitter Milk*, asks a question this paper wants to take up: "Tied to the constraints of the phenomena—that which appears in consciousness—how could the phenomenologist cope with the sentimentalism that so sweetens our sense of reproduction that we can neither discern its ingredients nor metabolize it in our theory?" (64).

2. See Gallop, *The Daughter's Seduction*, and also Kahane for psychoanalytic critiques of this mother-centered gesture.

3. Careful discussions and applications of French theories of the subject are offered in the works of Silverman, Ellis, and Weedon.

4. Giroux and Grumet both have critiqued the assumption that all forms of student resistance are emancipatory. Spivak calls for "the pedagogy of the humanities as the arena of cultural explanations that question the explanations of culture" (*In Other Worlds*, 117).

5. Kristeva's interrogation of "The Bounded Text" made me think about conventions of the feminist classroom which demand textbook answers from students and teachers alike.

6. Grumet (62–63) notes the absence of such metaphors in contemporary curriculum theory.

7. Rich, *Of Woman Born*; Lazarre, *The Mother Knot*; and the special issue of *Feminist Studies* on motherhood (vol. 4, no. 2 [June 1978]) provide examples of such narratives.

8. The same phenomenon appears in other forms elsewhere, as Offen remarks in a recent exchange with McLaughlin:

> As for McLaughlin's insinuations that I am something less than a feminist, let me suggest that she consult the history of women and of feminism before excommunicating those who persist in seeing some fundamental connections between the category "women" and motherhood. Most women in this time live this connection, however socially constructed; indeed, there exists a grand tradition of relational feminism built on critiquing and reconstructing it, especially in Europe. To say this is not to deny that in today's highly individualistic Anglo-American societies, an increasingly great range of differences in opinion, outlook, and experience exists among women, particularly on this subject. This is especially so among feminist intellectuals—who are now more vocal and, I would argue, more divided than at any previous time in history. (5)

9. hooks; and Lugones and Spelman make this point.

10. By writing, students produce texts which signify their power to interpret, and not just recall and recite, their experience. "Experience," they learn, is not merely some external reality to be retrieved and made "conscious" through language. See McNaron and Morgan for recent analyses of such narratives.

Bibliography

Abel, Elizabeth. "*The Golden Notebook:* 'Female Writing and "the Great Tradition."'"
In *Critical Essays on Doris Lessing,* edited by Claire Sprague and Virginia Tiger,
pp. 101–7. Boston: G. K. Hall, 1986.

Achebe, Chinua. *Things Fall Apart.* 1958. Rptd. New York: Fawcett, 1988.

Allen, Jeffner. "Motherhood: The Annihilation of Women." In *Mothering: Essays in Feminist Theory,* edited by Joyce Trebilcot, 315–30. Totowa, N. J.: Rowman and Allanheld, 1984.

Allen, Paula Gunn. *The Sacred Hoop: Recovering the Feminine in American Indian Traditions.* Boston: Beacon, 1986.

Alpert, Judith L., ed. *Psychoanalysis and Women: Contemporary Reappraisals.* New York: Analytic Press, 1986.

Angelou, Maya. *Gather Together in My Name.* 1974. Rptd. New York: Bantam, 1975.

———. *The Heart of a Woman.* New York: Random House, 1981.

———. *I Know Why the Caged Bird Sings.* New York: Bantam, 1970.

———. *Singin' and Swingin' and Getting' Merry Like Christmas.* 1976. Rptd. New York: Bantam, 1977.

Antell, Judith A. "Momaday, Welch, and Silko: Expressing the Feminine Principle Through Male Alienation." *American Indian Quarterly* (Summer 1988):213–24.

Arcana, Judith. *Our Mothers' Daughters.* Berkeley, Calif.: Shameless Hussy Press, 1979.

Atwood, Margaret. *The Edible Woman.* Boston: Little, Brown, 1969.

———. *The Handmaid's Tale.* New York: Ballantine, 1987.

Auerbach, Eric. *Mimesis: The Representation of Reality in Western Literature.* Garden City, N.Y.: Doubleday/Anchor, 1953.

Auerbach, Nina. "Artists and Mothers: A False Alliance." *Women and Literature* 6 (1978):3–15.

Autism Research Review International. San Diego, Calif.: Institute for Child Behavior Research.

Awkward, Michael. "Roadblocks and Relatives: Critical Revision in Toni Morrison's *The Bluest Eye.*" In *Critical Essays on Toni Morrison,* edited by Nellie Y. McKay, pp. 57–68. Boston: G.K. Hall, 1988.

Bakhtin, Mikhail. *The Dialogic Imagination.* Edited by Michael Holquist. Translated by Caryl Emerson and Michael Holquist. Austin: University of Texas Press, 1981.

Baldwin, James. "Everybody's Protest Novel." In *Notes of a Native Son,* pp. 13–23. Boston: Beacon Press, 1955.

Barnes, Djuna. *Nightwood.* New York: New Directions, 1937.

Bataille, Gretchen M., and Kathleen Mullen Sands. *American Indian Women: Telling Their Lives.* Lincoln: University of Nebraska Press, 1984.

Bateson, F., et al. "Toward a Theory of Schizophrenia." In *Theory and Practice of Family Psychiatry*, edited by J.G. Howells, pp. 745–64. New York: Brunner/Mazel, 1971.

Baym, Nina. "The Madwoman and Her Languages: Why I Don't Do Feminist Literary Theory." In *Feminist Issues in Literary Scholarship*, edited by Shari Benstock, pp. 45–61. Bloomington: Indiana University Press, 1987.

Beauvoir, Simone de. *The Coming of Age*. New York: G.P. Putnam's Sons, 1972.

———. *The Second Sex*. New York: Vintage, 1982.

Beavers, Dorothy Johnson. *Autism: Nightmare Without End*. Port Washington, N.Y.: Ashley Books, 1982.

Belenky, Mary Field; Blythe McVicker Clinchy; Nancy Rule Goldberger; and Jill Mattuck Tarule. *Women's Ways of Knowing: The Development of Self, Voice, and Mind*. New York: Basic Books, 1986.

Bell, Bernard W. *The Afro-American Novel and Its Tradition*. Amherst: University of Massachusetts Press, 1987.

Bell, Quentin. *Virginia Woolf: A Biography*. New York: Harcourt Brace Jovanovich, 1972.

Benjamin, Jessica. *The Bonds of Love: Psychoanalysis, Feminism, and the Problem of Domination*. New York: Pantheon, 1988.

Bennett, Paula. *My Life a Loaded Gun: Female Creativity and Feminist Poetics*. Boston: Beacon, 1986.

Bertelsen, Eva. "The Persistent Personal Voice: Lessing on Rhodesia and Marxism: Excerpts from an Interview with Doris Lessing." London, 9 January 1984. *Doris Lessing Newsletter* 9:2 (Fall 1985):8–10.

Bettleheim, Bruno. *The Empty Fortress: Infantile Autism and the Birth of the Self*. New York: Macmillan, 1967.

Betts, Carolyn. *A Special Kind of Normal*. New York: Scribners, 1979.

Bevis, William. "Native American Novels: Homing In." In *Recovering the Word: Essays on Native American Literature*, edited by Brian Swann and Arnold Krupat, pp. 580–620. Berkeley: University of California Press, 1987.

Bleich, David. "Sexism and Racism in Literary Responses to Morrison's *The Bluest Eye*." *Iowa English Bulletin* 37 (1989):1–23.

Block, Ruth H. "American Feminine Ideals in Transition: The Rise of the Moral Mother, 1785–1815." *Feminist Studies* 2 (1978):100–126.

Bogdan, Deanne. "From the Inside Out: On First Teaching Women's Literature and Feminist Criticism." *ADE Bulletin* 94 (1989):4–11.

Boston Lesbian Psychologies Collective. *Lesbian Psychologies: Explorations and Challenges* Urbana: University of Illinois Press, 1987.

Bowen, Elizabeth. *The Death of the Heart*. New York: Knopf, 1952.

Brant, Beth. *A Gathering of Spirit: Writing and Art by North American Indian Women*. N.p.: Sinister Wisdom Books, 1984.

Braxton, Joanne; Nicola Braxton; and Andree McLaughlin, *Wild Women in the Whirlwind: Afra-American Culture and the Contemporary Literary Renaissance*. New Brunswick, N.J.: Rutgers University Press, 1990.

Brent, Linda. *Incidents in the Life of a Slave Girl*. New York: Harcourt Brace Jovanovich, 1973.

Brodzki, Bella, and Celeste Schenck, eds. *Life/Lines; Theorizing Women's Autobiographies*. Ithaca, N.Y.: Cornell University Press, 1988.

Broner, E.M. *Her Mothers*. Bloomington: Indiana University Press, 1985.

———. *A Weave of Women*. 1978. Bloomington: Indiana University Press, 1985.

Brooks, Ellen W. "The Image of Woman in Lessing's *Golden Notebook.*" *Critique: Studies in Modern Fiction* 15:1 (1973):101–9.

Brown, Rita Mae. *Rubyfruit Jungle.* New York: Bantam, 1977.

———. *Six of One.* New York: Bantam, 1978.

Burke, Carolyn. "Rethinking the Maternal." In *The Future of Difference,* edited by Alice Jardine and Hester Eisenstein, pp. 107–14. New Brunswick, N.J.: Rutgers University Press, 1985.

Butler, Octavia. *Kindred.* Boston: Beacon, 1988.

Callahan, Mary. *Fighting for Tony.* New York: Simon and Schuster, 1987.

Carby, Hazel V. *Reconstructing Womanhood.* New York: Oxford University Press, 1987.

Chernin, Kim. *In My Mother's House: A Daughter's Story.* New York: Harper, 1984.

Chesler, Phyllis. *The Sacred Bond.* New York: Random House, 1988.

Chodorow, Nancy. *The Reproduction of Mothering: Psychoanalysis and the Sociology of Gender.* Berkeley: University of California Press, 1978.

———. "Family Structure and Feminine Personality." In *Woman, Culture, and Society,* edited by Michelle Zimbalist Rosaldo and Louise Lamphere, pp. 43–66. Stanford, Calif.: Stanford University Press, 1974.

Chodorow, Nancy, and Susan Contratto. "The Fantasy of the Perfect Mother." In *Rethinking the Family,* edited by Barrie Thorne and Marilyn Yalom, pp. 54–73. New York: Longman, 1982.

Chopin, Kate. *The Awakening.* 1899. Rptd. New York: Norton, 1976.

Christian, Barbara. "Alice Walker: The Black Woman Artist as Wayward." In *Black Woman Writers,* edited by Mari Evans, pp. 457–77. Garden City, N.Y.: Anchor, 1984.

———. "An Angle of Seeing: Motherhood in Buchi Emecheta's *The Joys of Motherhood* and Alice Walker's *Meridian.*" In Christian, *Black Feminist Criticism,* pp. 221–52.

———. *Black Feminist Criticism: Perspectives on Black Women Writers.* New York: Pergamon, 1985.

———. *Black Women Novelists: The Development of a Tradition, 1892–1976.* Westport: Greenwood, 1985.

———. "Response to 'Black Women's Texts.'" *NWSA Journal* 1:1 (1988):32–36.

Cixous, Helene. "The Laugh of the Medusa." In *New French Feminisms,* edited by Elaine Marks and Isabelle de Courtivron, pp. 245–64. New York: Schocken, 1981.

———. "Sorties." In *New French Feminisms,* edited by Elaine Marks and Isabelle de Courtivron, pp. 90–98. New York: Schocken, 1981.

Colette. *The Complete Claudine.* Translated by Antonia White. New York: Farrar, Straus and Giroux, 1976.

Collins, Patricia Hill. "The Meaning of Motherhood in Black Culture and Black Mother-Daughter Relationships." *Sage* 4:2 (1987):3–10.

———. "The Social Construction of Black Feminist Thought." *Signs* 14:4 (1989):745–73.

Corea, Gena. *The Mother Machine.* New York: Harper and Row, 1985.

Dally, Ann. *Inventing Motherhood: The Consequences of an Ideal.* New York: Schocken, 1983.

Dash, Irene G.; Deena Dash Kushner; and Deborah Dash Moore. "How Light a *Lighthouse* for Today's Women?" In *The Lost Tradition: Mothers and Daughters in Literature.* Edited by Cathy N. Davidson and E. M. Broner, pp. 176–88. New York: Frederick Ungar, 1980.

davenport, doris. "Afracentric Visions." *Women's Review of Books* 6:12 (1989):13–14.

Davidson, Cathy. *Revolution and the Word: The Rise of the Novel in America*. New York: Oxford University Press, 1986.

Davidson, Cathy N., and E.M. Broner, eds. *The Lost Tradition: Mothers and Daughters in Literature*. New York: Ungar, 1980.

Davies, Carole Boyce. "Mothering and Healing in Recent Black Women's Fiction." *Sage* 2:1 (Spring 1985):41–43.

———. "Wrapping One's Self in Mother's Akatado-Cloths: Mother-Daughter Relationships in the Works of African Women Writers." *Sage* 4:2 (1987):11–19.

Davin, Anna. "Imperialism and Motherhood." *History Workshop: A Journal of Socialist Historians* 5 (Spring 1978):9–66.

Davis, Angela. "The Black Woman's Role in the Community of Slaves." *Black Scholar* 2:4 (December 1971):5.

Davis. Thadious M. "Alice Walker's Celebration of Self in Southern Generations." In *Women Writers of the Contemporary South*, edited by Peggy Whitman Prenshaw. Jackson: University Press of Mississippi, 1985.

Dearborn, Mary. *Pocahontas's Daughters: Gender and Ethnicity in American Culture*. New York: Oxford University Press, 1986.

de Lauretis, Teresa. *Alice Doesn't*. Bloomington: Indiana University Press, 1984.

DeSalvo, Louise. *Virginia Woolf: The Impact of Childhood Sexual Abuse on Her Life and Work*. Boston: Beacon, 1989.

Devi, Mahasweta. "Breast Giver." Translated by Gayatri Chakravorty Spivak. In *Other Worlds: Essays in Cultural Politics*, edited by Spivak, pp. 222–40. New York: Routledge, 1988.

DiBattista, Maria. *Virginia Woolf's Major Novels: The Fables of Anon*. New Haven, Conn.: Yale University Press, 1980.

Dietz, Bernd, and Fernando Galvan, "*Entrevista*: A Conversation with Doris Lessing." *Doris Lessing Newsletter* 9:1 (Spring 1985):4–6.

Dill, Bonnie Thornton. "Race, Class, and Gender: Prospects for an All-Inclusive Sisterhood." *Feminist Studies* 9:2 (1983):131–50.

Dillard, Annie. *Living By Fiction*. New York: Harper and Row, 1982.

Dinnerstein, Dorothy. *The Mermaid and the Minotaur: Sexual Arrangements and Human Malaise*. New York: Harper and Row, 1976.

Drabble, Margaret. *The Ice Age*. New York: Knopf, 1977.

———. *The Middle Ground*. New York: Penguin, 1980.

———. *A Natural Curiosity*. New York: Viking, 1989.

———. *The Radiant Way*. New York: Penguin, 1987.

———. *The Realms of Gold*. New York: Popular Library, 1977.

DuPlessis, Rachel Blau. *Writing Beyond the Ending: Narrative Strategies of Twentieth-Century Women Writers*. Bloomington: Indiana University Press, 1985.

Eagleton, Terry. *Literary Theory: An Introduction*. Minneapolis: University of Minnesota Press, 1983.

Edwards, Lee R. *Psyche as Hero: Female Heroism and Fictional Form*. Middleton, Conn.: Wesleyan University Press, 1984.

Ehrenreich, Barbara, and Deidre English. *For Her Own Good: One Hundred Fifty Years of the Experts Advice to Women*. Garden City, N.Y.: Doubleday/Anchor, 1978.

Eichenbaum, Luise, and Susie Orbach. *Understanding Women: A Feminist Psychoanalytic Approach*. New York: Basic Books, 1983.

Elshtain, Jean Bethke. "The Social Relations of the Classroom: A Moral and Political

Perspective." In *Studies in Socialist Pedagogy*, edited by T.M. Norton and Bertell Ollman, pp. 49–62. New York: Monthly Review Press, 1978.

Ellis, Kate. "Politicizing Deconstruction." *Specialist Review* 2 (1989):23–38.

Erdrich, Louise. *The Beet Queen*. New York: Henry Holt, 1986.

———. "An Interview with Louise Erdrich and Michael Dorris." With Hertha D. Wong. *North Dakota Quarterly* 55:1 (Winter 1987):196–218.

———. *Love Medicine*. New York: Holt, Rinehart & Winston, 1984.

———. *Tracks*. New York: Henry Holt, 1988.

———. "Whatever Is Really Yours: An interview with Louise Erdrich." In *Survival This Way: Interviews with American Indian Poets*, edited by Joseph Bruchac. Tucson: University of Arizona Press, 1987.

Featherstone, Helen. *A Difference in the Family: Living with a Disabled Child*. New York: Penquin, 1981.

Feldstein, Richard, and Judith Roof, eds. *Feminism and Psychoanalysis*. Ithaca, N.Y.: Cornell University Press, 1989.

Ferguson, Ann. "On Conceiving Motherhood and Sexuality: A Feminist Materialist Approach." In *Mothering: Essays in Feminist Theory*, edited by Joyce Trebilcot, pp. 153–82. Totowa, N.J.: Rowman and Allanheld, 1984.

Fetterley, Judith. *The Resisting Reader: A Feminist Approach to American Literature*. Bloomington: Indiana University Press, 1978.

———, ed. *Provisions: A Reader from Nineteenth-Century American Women*. Bloomington: Indiana University Press, 1985.

Firestone, Shulamith. *The Dialectic of Sex: The Case for Feminist Revolution*. New York: Bantam, 1970.

Fisher, Dexter, ed. *The Third Woman: Minority Women Writers of the United States*. Boston: Houghton Mifflin, 1980.

Fitting, Peter. "For Men Only: A Guide to Reading Single-Sex Worlds." *Women's Studies* 14 (1987):101–118.

Fleishman, Avrom. *Virginia Woolf: A Critical Reading*. Baltimore, Md.: Johns Hopkins University Press, 1977.

Flynn, Elizabeth A., and Patrocinio P. Schweickart, eds. *Gender and Reading: Essays on Readers, Texts, and Contexts*. Baltimore, Md.: Johns Hopkins University Press, 1986.

Freud, Sigmund. *Civilization and Its Discontents*. Edited by James Strachey. German publication, 1930. New York: Norton, 1961.

———. *Dora: An Analysis of a Case of Hysteria*. New York: Collier, 1964.

———. "Three Essays on the Theory of Sexuality." *The Standard Edition of the Complete Psychological Works*. Translated by James Strachey, pp. 125–245. London: Hogarth, 1953.

Friday, Nancy. *My Mother/My Self*. New York: Dell, 1987.

Friedman, Susan Stanford. "Creativity and the Childbirth Metaphor: Gender Difference in Literary Discourse." *Feminist Studies* 13:1 (1987):49–82.

Frye, Northrop. *The Secular Scripture: A Study of the Structure of Romance*. 1976. Cambridge, Mass.: Harvard University Press, 1978.

Gallop, Jane. *The Daughter's Seduction*. Ithaca, N.Y.: Cornell University Press, 1982.

———. *Reading Lacan*. Ithaca, N.Y.: Cornell University Press, 1985.

———. "Reading the Mother Tongue: Psychoanalytic Feminist Criticism." *Critical Inquiry* 13:4 (1987):314–29.

Garner, Shirley Nelson. "Feminism, Psychoanalysis, and the Heterosexual Imperative." In *Feminism and Psychoanalysis*, edited by Richard Feldstein and Judith Roof, pp. 164–81. Ithaca, N.Y.: Cornell University Press, 1989.

Garner, Shirley Nelson; Claire Kahane; and Madelon Sprengnether, eds. *The (M)other Tongue: Essays in Feminist Psychoanalytic Interpretation*. Ithaca, N.Y.: Cornell University Press, 1985.

Garnett, Angelica. *Deceived With Kindness: A Bloomsbury Childhood*. San Diego, Calif.: Harcourt Brace Jovanovich, 1985.

Gauthier, Xaviere. "Is There Such a Thing as Women's Writing?" In *New French Feminisms*, edited by Elaine Marks and Isabelle de Courtivron, pp. 161–64. New York: Schocken, 1981.

Gerson, Mary-Joan; Judith L. Alpert; and Mary Sue Richardson. "Mothering: The View From Psychological Research." *Signs* 9:3 (1984):434–53.

Gilligan, Carol. *In a Different Voice: Psychological Theory and Women's Development*. Cambridge, Mass.: Harvard University Press, 1982.

Gilman, Charlotte Perkins, *The Yellow Wallpaper*. Old Westbury, N.Y.: Feminist Press, 1973.

Giroux, Henry. *Teachers as Intellectuals: Toward a Critical Pedagogy of Learning*. Granby, Mass.: Bergin and Garvey, 1988.

Glubka, Shirley. "Out of the Stream: An Essay on Unconventional Motherhood." *Feminist Studies* 9:2 (1983):223–34.

Goodman, Ellen. "The Doris Lessing Hoax." *Doris Lessing Newsletter* 9:1 (Spring 1985):3.

Gordon, Mary. *Men and Angels*. New York: Random, 1985.

———. "David." In *Fathers: Reflections by Daughters*, edited by Ursula Owen, pp. 106–14. New York: Pantheon, 1985.

Grandin, Temple. *Emergence: Labelled Autistic*. Novato, Calif.: Arena Press, 1986.

Greene, Gayle. "Women and Men in Doris Lessing's *Golden Notebook*: Divided Selves." In *The (M)Other Tongue: Essays in Feminist Psychoanalytic Interpretation*, edited by Shirley Nelson Garner, Clare Kahane, and Madelon Sprengnether, pp. 280–305. Ithaca, N.Y.: Cornell University Press, 1985.

Greenfeld, Josh. *A Child Called Noah*. New York: Holt, Rinehart and Winston, 1972.

———. *A Client Called Noah*. New York: Holt, Rinehart and Winston, 1989.

———. *A Place for Noah*. New York: Holt, Rinehart and Winston, 1978.

Griffin, Susan. *Pornography and Silence: Culture's Revenge Against Nature*. New York: Harper and Row, 1981.

Grimshaw, Jean. *Philosophy and Feminist Thinking*. Minneapolis: University of Minnesota Press, 1986.

Grumet, Madeleine R. *Bitter Milk: Women and Teaching*. Amherst: University of Massachusetts Press, 1988.

Gubar, Susan. "The Birth of the Artist as Heroine: (Re)Production, the *Kunstlerroman* Tradition, and the Fiction of Katherine Mansfield." In *The Representation of Women in Fiction: Selected Papers from the English Institute*, edited by Carolyn G. Heilbrun and Margaret R. Higonnet, pp. 19–59. Baltimore, Md.: Johns Hopkins University Press, 1981.

Gwin, Minrose C. "A Theory of Black Women's Texts and White Women's Readings, or . . . the Necessity of Being Other." *NWSA Journal* 1:1 (1988):21–31.

Hansen, Elaine Tuttle. "(Post)Feminism in Atwood's *Bodily Harm*." *Novel* 19 (1985):5–21.

Harris, Norman. *Connecting Times: The Sixties in Afro-American Fiction*. Jackson: University of Mississippi Press, 1988.

Henderson, Mae G. "*The Color Purple*: Revisions and Redefinitions." In *Modern Critical Views: Alice Walker*, edited by Harold Bloom, pp. 67–80. New York: Chelsea House, 1989.

Herman, Judith Lewis, with Lisa Hirschman. *Father-Daughter Incest*. Cambridge, Mass.: Harvard University Press, 1982.

Hirsch, Marianne. *The Mother/Daughter Plot: Narrative, Psychoanalysis, Feminism*. Bloomington: Indiana University Press, 1989.

———. "Mothers and Daughters: A Review Essay." *Signs* 7:1 (1981):200–222.

Holloway, Karla F.C., and Stephanie A. Demetrakopoulos. *New Dimensions of Spirituality: A Biracial and Bicultural Reading of the Novels of Toni Morrison*. Westport, Conn.: Greenwood, 1987.

Holmquist, Ingrid. *From Society to Nature: A Study of Doris Lessing's Children of Violence*. Goteborg, Sweden: Acta Universitatis Gorthoburgensis, 1980.

Homans, Margaret. *Bearing the Word: Language and Female Experience in Nineteenth-Century Women's Writing*. Chicago: University of Chicago Press, 1986.

———. "'Her Very Own Howl': Ambiguities of Representation in Recent Women's Fiction," *Signs* 9:21 (1983):186–205.

hooks, bell. *Feminist Theory from Margin to Center*. Boston: South End Press, 1985.

Hull, Gloria T.; Patricia Bell Scott; and Barbara Smith. *But Some of Us Are Brave: Black Women's Studies*. Old Westbury, N.Y.: Feminist Press, 1982.

Hunt, Nancy Rose. "Domesticity and Colonialism in Belgian Africa: Usumbura's Foyer Social, 1946–1960." *Signs* 15:3 (1990):447–74.

Idowu, E. Bolaji. *Oladumare: God In Yoruba Belief*. London: Longman, 1962.

Jacobus, Mary. "*Dora* and the Pregnant Madonna." In *Reading Woman: Essays in Feminist Criticism*, edited by Mary Jacobus, pp. 137–93. New York: Columbia University Press, 1986.

Johnston, Basil. *Ojibway Heritage*. New York: Columbia University Press, 1976.

Joseph, Gloria I. "Black Mothers and Daughters: Traditional and New Populations." *Sage* 1:2 (1984):17–21.

Joseph, Gloria I. and Jill Lewis. *Common Differences: Conflicts in Black and White Feminist Perspectives*. Garden City, N.Y.: Anchor, 1981.

Kahane, Claire. "Questioning the Maternal Voice." *Genders* 3 (1988):82–91.

Kaplan, Carey. "A Vision of Power in Margaret Drabble's *Realms of Gold*." *Journal of Women's Studies in Literature* 4 (1978):233–42.

Kingston, Maxine Hong. *The Woman Warrior*. 1975. Rptd. New York: Random House, 1977.

Knapp, Mona. *Doris Lessing*. New York: Ungar, 1984.

Koonz, Claudia. *Mothers in the Fatherland: Women, the Family, and Nazi Politics*. New York: St. Martin's, 1987.

Kristeva, Julia. "The Bounded Text." In *Desire in Language: A Semiotic Approach to Literature and Art*. Edited by Leon Roudiez. Translated by Thomas Gora, Alice Jardine, and Leon Roudiez, pp. 37–63. New York: Columbia University Press, 1987.

———. "Herethique de l'amour." *Tel Quel* 74 (1977):30–49.

———. *In the Beginning Was Love: Psychoanalysis and Faith*. Translated by Arthur Goldhammer. New York: Columbia University Press, 1987.

———. "Motherhood According to Giovanni Bellini." In *Desire in Language: A Semiotic Approach to Literature and Art*. Edited by Leon Roudiez. Translated by Thomas Gora, Alice Jardine, and Leon Roudiez, pp. 237–70. New York: Columbia University Press, 1980.

———. *Revolution in Poetic Language*. Translated by Margaret Waller. New York: Columbia University Press, 1984.

———. "Stabat Mater." In Kristeva, *Tales of Love*, pp. 234–63. Translated by Leon Roudiez. New York: Columbia University Press, 1987.

———. "Word, Dialogue and Novel." In Kristeva, *The Kristeva Reader*, edited by Toril Moi, pp. 34–61. New York: Columbia University Press, 1986.

Lacan, Jacques. "The mirror stage as formative function of the I as revealed in psychoanalytic experience." In Lacan, *Ecrits*, pp. 1–7. Translated by Alan Sheridan. New York: Norton, 1977.

———. *Feminine Sexuality: Jacques Lacan and the Ecole Freudienne*. Edited by Juliet Mitchell and Jacqueline Rose. Translated by Jacqueline Rose. New York: Norton, 1985.

Laing, R.D., and A. Esterson. *Sanity, Madness, and the Family. Families of Schizophrenics*, vol. 1. New York: Basic Books, 1964.

Landes, Ruth. *The Ojibwa Woman*. 1938. Rptd. New York: AMS Press, 1969.

Lasch, Christopher. *Haven in a Heartless World*. New York: Basic Books, 1977.

Lazarre, Jane. *The Mother Knot*. 1976. Rptd. Boston: Beacon, 1986.

———. *The Powers of Charlotte*. Freedom, Calif.: Crossing Press, 1987.

LeGuin, Ursula K. "The Hand that Rocks the Cradle Writes the Book." *New York Times Review of Books*, 22 Jan. 1989.

Lessing, Doris. "Afterword to *The Story of an African Farm*." In Lessing, *A Small Personal Voice*, pp. 97–120. New York: Vintage, 1975.

———. *The Diaries of Jane Somers*. New York: Vintage, 1984. [Includes *The Diary of a Good Neighbor* and *If the Old Could*.]

———. *The Four-Gated City*. New York: Bantam, 1970.

———. *The Golden Notebook*. New York: Ballantine, 1971.

———. *Landlocked*. New York: New American Library/Plume, 1966.

———. *The Making of the Representative for Planet B*. New York: Knopf, 1982.

———. "My Father," London *Sunday Telegraph*, 1 September 1963. Rptd. *Vogue* Magazine, 15 February 1964.

———. *Martha Quest*. New York: New American Library/Plume, 1964.

———. *Memoirs of a Survivor*. 1974. Rptd. New York: Bantam, 1976.

———. "My Mother's Life," part 1. *Granta* 14 (Winter 1984):52–68.

———. *A Proper Marriage*. New York: New American Library/Plume, 1964.

———. *A Ripple from the Storm*. New York: New American Library/Plume, 1966.

———. *Shikasta*. New York: Random House, 1981.

———. "The Small Personal Voice." In Lessing, *A Small Personal Voice: Doris Lessing: Essays, Reviews, Interviews*, edited by Paul Schleuter, pp. 3–21. New York: Vintage, 1975.

———. *A Small Personal Voice: Doris Lessing: Essays, Reviews, Interviews*. Edited by Paul Schleuter. New York: Vintage, 1975.

———. *The Summer Before the Dark*. New York: Bantam, 1973.

Lew, Mike, *Victims No Longer: Men Recovering from Incest and Other Sexual Child Abuse*. New York: Newvraumont, 1988.

Lidz, T.; S. Fleck; and A.R. Cornelison. *Schizophrenia and the Family*. Monograph Series on Schizophrenia, no. 7. New York: International Universities Press, 1965.

Lilienfeld, Jane. "Reentering Paradise: Cather, Colette, Woolf and Their Mothers." In *The Lost Tradition: Mothers and Daughters in Literature*, edited by Cathy N. Davidson and E.M. Broner, pp. 160–75. New York: Ungar, 1980.

————. "The Deceptive Beauty: Mother Love and Mother Hate in *To the Lighthouse*." *Twentieth-Century Literature* 23 (1977):345–76.

Litwin, Dorothy. "Autonomy: A Conflict for Women." In *Psychoanalysis and Women: Contemporary Reappraisals*, edited by Judith L. Alpert, pp. 183–213. Hillsdale, N.J.: Analytic Press, 1986.

Lorde, Audre. "Man Child: A Black Lesbian Feminist's Response." In *Sister Outsider*, pp. 72–80. Freedom, Calif.: Crossing Press, 1984.

————. *Sister/Outsider*. Freedom, Calif.: Crossing Press, 1984.

————. *Zami: A New Spelling of My Name*. New York: Crossing Press, 1983.

Lovell, Ann. *In a Summer Garment: The Experience of an Autistic Child*. London: Secker and Warburg, 1978.

Lugones, Maria C., and Elizabeth V. Spelman. "Have We Got a Theory for You! Feminist Theory, Cultural Imperialism and the Demands for 'The Woman's Voice.'" *Women's Studies International Forum* 6:6 (1983):573–81.

Lupton, Mary Jane. "Singing the Black Mother: Maya Angelou and Autobiographical Continuity." Paper presented at National Women's Studies Association Convention, Baltimore, Md., 1989.

Lurie, Nancy Oestreich, ed. *Mountain Wolf Woman*. Ann Arbor: University of Michigan Press, 1961.

Mahler, M.S. "Autism and Symbiosis, Two Extreme Disturbances of Identity." *International Journal of Psycho-Analysis* 39 (1958):77–83.

Malak, Arnin. "Margaret Atwood's 'The Handmaid's Tale' and the Dystopian Tradition." *Canadian Literature* 112 (Spring 1987):9–16.

Markos, Alice Bradley. "The Pathology of Feminine Failure in the Fiction of Doris Lessing." *Critique: Studies in Modern Fiction* 16:1 (1974): 88–99.

Marshall, Paule. "From the Poets in the Kitchen." In Marshall, *Reena and Other Stories*. New York: Feminist Press, 1983. Rptd. in *Mothers: Memories, Dreams, Reflections by Literary Daughters*, edited by Susan Cahill, pp. 204–17. New York: Meridian, 1988.

Mason, Mary G. "The Other Voice: Autobiographies of Women Writers." In *Life/Lines: Theorizing Women's Autobiographies*, edited by Bella Brodzki and Celeste Schenck, pp. 19–44. Ithaca, N.Y.: Cornell University Press, 1988.

McDowell, Deborah E. "Negotiating Between Tenses: Witnessing Slavery After Freedom—*Dessa Rose*." Paper presented at the National Women's Studies Association Convention, Baltimore, Md., June 1989.

————. "Reading Family Matters." In *Changing Our Own Words*, edited by Cheryl A. Wall, pp. 75–97. New Brunswick, N.J.: Rutgers University Press, 1989.

McGowan, Martha J. "Atonement and Release in Alice Walker's *Meridian*." *Critique: Studies in Modern Fiction* 23:1 (1981):25–36.

McKenzie, James. "Lipsha's Good Road Home: The Revival of Chippewa Culture in *Love Medicine*." *American Indian Culture and Research Journal* 10:3 (1986):53–63.

McKinstry, Susan Jaret. "Community and Autonomy in Louise Erdrich's *The Beet Queen*." Paper presented at Native American Literature Section, Midwest Modern Language Association Convention, Columbus, Ohio, November 1987.

McLaughlin, Lisa. Letter to the Editor. *Women's Review of Books* 6:9 (1989):5.

McMillan, Terry. *Mama*. New York: Washington Square Press, 1987.

McNaron, Toni A., and Yarrow Morgan. *Voices in the Night: Women Speaking About Incest*. Minneapolis, Minn.: Cleis Press, 1982.

Miles, Rosalind. *The Female Form: Women Writers and the Conquest Novel*. New York: Routledge & Kegan Paul, 1987.

Miller, Alice. *Thou Shalt Not Be Aware: Society's Betrayal of the Child*. Translated by Hildegarde and Hunter Hannum. New York: Signet, 1984.

Miller, Isabel. *Patience and Sarah*. New York: Fawcett, 1969.

Miller, Jean Baker. *Toward a New Psychology of Women*. Boston: Beacon, 1977.

Miller, Sue. *The Good Mother*. New York: Harper and Row, 1986.

Moi, Toril. *Sexual/Textual Politics: Feminist Literary Theory*. London: Methuen, 1985.

Monaghan, George. "Saving Kenny from Himself." *Sunday Magazine, Minneapolis Star and Tribune*. 5 March 1989.

Moran, Mary Hurley. *Margaret Drabble: Existing Within Structures*. Carbondale: Southern Illinois University Press, 1983.

Morgan, Ellen. "Alienation of the Woman Writer in *The Golden Notebook*." In *Doris Lessing: Critical Studies*, edited by Annis Pratt and L.S. Dembo, pp. 54–63. Madison: University of Wisconsin Press, 1974.

Morgan, Sam B. *The Unreachable Child: An Introduction to Early Childhood Autism*. Memphis State University Press, 1981.

Morphett, Lurline. *Face to Face*. South Australia: Education Department of South Australia, 1986.

Morrison, Toni. *Beloved*. New York: Knopf, 1987.

———. *The Bluest Eye*. New York: Pocket Books, 1970.

———. *Song of Solomon*. New York: Random House, 1977.

———. *Sula*. New York: New American Library, 1973.

Morson, Gary Saul, ed. *Bakhtin: Essays and Dialogues on His Work*. Chicago: University of Chicago Press, 1981.

Naremone, James. *The World Without Self: Virginia Woolf and the Novel*. New Haven, Conn.: Yale University Press, 1973.

Naylor, Gloria. "A Conversation with Toni Morrison." *Southern Review* 21:3 (July 1985):567–930.

———. *Mama Day*. New York: Ticknor and Fields, 1986.

———. *The Women of Brewster Place*. New York: Penguin, 1982.

Nichols, Michael. *Family Therapy: Concepts and Methods*. New York: Gardner Press, 1984.

Noddings, Nell. *Caring: A Feminine Approach to Ethics and Moral Education*. Berkeley: University of California Press, 1984.

O'Brien, Mary. "Feminist Theory and Dialectical Logic." In *Feminist Theory: A Critique of Ideology*, edited by Nannerl O. Keohane, Michelle Z. Rosaldo, and Barbara Gelpi. Chicago: University of Chicago Press, 1981, 1982.

———. *The Politics of Reproduction*. Boston: Routledge & Kegan Paul, 1981.

Offen, Karen. Letter to the Editor. *Women's Review of Books* 6:9 (1989):5.

Olsen, Tille. "I Stand Here Ironing." In *Tell Me a Riddle*. New York: Dell, 1976.

———. *Tell Me a Riddle*. New York: Dell, 1976.

Overholt, Thomas W., and J. Baird Callicott. *Clothed-in-Fur and Other Tales: An Introduction to an Ojibwa World View*. Washington, D.C.: University Press of America, 1982.

Paley, Grace. *Enormous Changes at the Last Minute*. New York: Dell, 1975.

———. *Later the Same Day*. New York: Farrar Straus Giroux, 1986.

———. *The Little Disturbances of Man: Stories of Women and Men at Love.* New York: Doubleday, 1959.

———. "Midrash on Happiness." In *The Writer in Our World*, edited by Reginald Gibbons, pp. 151–53. Boston: Atlantic Monthly Press, 1986.

———. "Mom." *Esquire*, December 1975. Rptd. as "Other Mothers," *Feminist Studies* 4:2 (1978):166–69.

Park, Clara Claiborne. Review of *Autism: Nightmare Without End*, by Dorothy Johnson Beavers. *Journal of Autism and Developmental Disorders* 15 (1985):113–19.

———. *The Siege: The First Eight Years of an Autistic Child.* 1967. Rptd. Boston: Little, Brown, 1982.

Park, Clara Claiborne, with Leon N. Shapiro, M.D. *You Are Not Alone: Understanding and Dealing with Mental Illness.* Boston: Little, Brown, 1976.

Pearson, Carol, and Katherine Pope. *The Female Hero in American and British Literature.* New York: R.R. Bowker, 1981.

Penley, Constance. "Teaching in your Sleep: Feminism and Psychoanalysis." In *Theory in the Classroom*, edited by Cary Nelson, pp. 129–49. Chicago: University of Illinois Press, 1986.

Perry, Ruth. "Balancing Acts." *Women's Review of Books* 5:10–11 (July 1988):29f.

Pettis, Joyce. "Difficult Survival: Mothers and Daughters in *The Bluest Eye*." *Sage* 4:2 (1987):26–29.

Piercy, Marge. *Woman on the Edge of Time.* New York: Ballantine, 1983.

Pratt, Annis, and L.B. Dembo. *Doris Lessing: Critical Studies.* Madison: University of Wisconsin Press, 1974.

Rabuzzi, Kathryn Allen. *Motherself: A Mythic Analysis of Motherhood.* Bloomington: Indiana University Press, 1988.

Radway, Janice. *Reading the Romance.* Chapel Hill: University of North Carolina Press, 1984.

Rapping, Elayne Antler. "'Unfree Women': Feminism in Doris Lessing's Novels." *Women's Studies* 3 (1975):29–44.

Renvoize, Jean. *Incest: A Family Pattern.* London: Routledge & Kegan Paul, 1982.

Rich, Adrienne. "Compulsory Heterosexuality and Lesbian Existence." *Signs* 5 (1980): 631–60.

———. *Of Woman Born: Motherhood as Experience and Institution.* New York: Norton, 1976.

Roscoe, Will. "We'wha and Klah: The American Indian Berdache as Artist and Priest." *American Indian Quarterly* 12:2 (Spring 1988):127–50.

Rose, Ellen Cronan. "A Lessing in Disguise." Review of *The Diaries of Jane Somers*, by Doris Lessing. *Women's Review of Books* 1:5 (February 1985):7–8.

Rose, Phyllis. *Woman of Letters: A Life of Virginia Woolf's Novels.* Stanford, Calif.: Stanford University Press, 1986.

Rosen, Ellen I. "'Martha's Quest' in Lessing's *Children of Violence*." *Frontiers* 3:2 (1978):54–59.

Rothman, Barbara Katz. *Recreating Motherhood: Ideology and Technology in a Patriarchal Society.* New York: Norton, 1989.

Rubenstein, Roberta. *Boundaries of the Self: Gender, Culture, Fiction.* Chicago: University of Illinois Press, 1987.

Ruotolo, Lucio. *The Interrupted Moment: A View of Virginia Woolf's Novels.* Stanford, Calif.: Stanford University Press, 1986.

Ruddick, Sara. *Maternal Thinking: Toward a Politics of Peace.* Boston: Beacon, 1989.

———. "Maternal Thinking." *Feminist Studies* 6:2 (1980):342–67. Rptd. in *Mothering: Essays in Feminist Theory,* edited by Joyce Trebilcot, 213–29. Totowa, N.J.: Rowman and Allanheld, 1984.

———. "Preservative Love and Military Destructiveness: Some Reflections on Mothering and Peace." In *Mothering: Essays in Feminist Theory,* edited by Joyce Trebilcot, 231–61. Totowa, N.J.: Rowman and Allanheld, 1984.

Rule, Jane. *The Desert of the Heart.* New York: World, 1965.

———. *This Is Not For You.* Tallahassee, Fla.: Naiad, 1988.

Sands, Kathleen Mullen. Review of *Love Medicine,* by Louise Erdrich. *Studies in American Indian Literatures* 9:1 (1985):12–24.

Sayers, Janet. "Feminism and Mothering: A Kleinian Perspective." *Women's Studies International Forum* 7 (1984):237–41.

Schweickart, Patrocinio P. "Reading Ourselves: Toward a Feminist Theory of Reading." In *Gender and Reading: Essays on Readers, Texts, and Contexts,* edited by Elizabeth Flynn and Patrocinio P. Schweickart, 31–62. Baltimore, Md.: Johns Hopkins University Press, 1986.

Sedgwick, Eve Kosofsky. *Between Men: English Literature and Male Homosocial Desire.* New York: Columbia University Press, 1985.

Segal, Lynne. *Is the Future Female? Troubled Thoughts on Contemporary Feminism.* New York: Peter Bedrick Books, 1987.

Showalter, Elaine. *A Literature of Their Own: British Women Novelists from Bronte to Lessing.* London: Virago, 1978.

Silverman, Kaja. *The Subject of Semiotics.* New York: Oxford University Press, 1983.

Sizemore, Christine W. "Reading the City as Palimpsest: The Experiential Perception of the City in Doris Lessing's *Four-Gated City.*" In *Women Writers and the City: Essays in Feminist Literary Criticism,* edited by Susan Merrill Squier, pp. 176–90. Knoxville: University of Tennessee Press, 1984.

Smith, Patricia Clark. "Ain't Seen You Since: Dissent Among Female Relatives in American Indian Women's Poetry." In *American Indian Literature: Critical Essays and Course Designs,* edited by Paula Gunn Allen, pp. 108–26. New York: Modern Language Association, 1983.

Sommer, Doris. "Not Just a Personal Story." In *Life/Lines: Theorizing Women's Autobiography,* edited by Bella Brodzki and Celeste Schenck, pp. 107–30. Ithaca, N.Y.: Cornell University Press, 1988.

Spelman, Elizabeth V. *Inessential Woman: Problems of Exclusion in Feminist Thought.* Boston: Beacon, 1988.

Spender, Dale. *Mothers of the Novel.* New York: Pandora, 1986.

Spiegel, David. "Mothering, Fathering, and Mental Illness." In *Rethinking the Family: Some Feminist Questions,* edited by Barrie Thorne with Marilyn Yalom, pp. 95–110. New York: Longman, 1982.

Spieler, Susan. "The Gendered Self: A Lost Maternal Legacy." In *Psychoanalysis and Women: Contemporary Reappraisals,* edited by Judith L. Alpert, pp. 33–56. Hillsdale, N.J.: Analytic Press, 1986.

Spillers, Hortense J. "Mama's Baby, Papa's Maybe: An American Grammar Book." *diacritics* 17 (Summer 1987):65–81.

Spivak, Gayatri Chakravorty. *In Other Worlds: Essays in Cultural Politics.* New York: Methuen, 1987.

_____. "A Literary Representation of the Subaltern: A Woman's Text from the Third World." In Spivak, *In Other Worlds: Essays in Cultural Politics*, pp. 222–68. New York: Routledge, 1988.

Stanton, Domna. "Difference on Trial: A Critique of the Maternal Metaphor in Cixous, Irigaray, and Kristeva." In *The Poetics of Gender*, edited by Nancy K. Miller, pp. 157–82. New York: Columbia University Press, 1986.

Stein, Karen. "*Meridian*: Alice Walker's Critique of Revolution." *Black American Literature Forum* 10 (1986):129–41.

Stimpson, Catharine R. "Doris Lessing and the Parables of Growth." In *The Voyage In: Fictions of Female Development*, edited by Elizabeth Abel, Marianne Hirsch, and Elizabeth Langland, pp. 186–205. Hanover, N.H.: University Presses of New England, 1983.

Sukenick, Lynn. "Feeling and Reason in Doris Lessing's Fiction." In *Doris Lessing: Critical Studies*, edited by Annis Pratt and L.B. Dembo, pp. 98–108. Madison: University of Wisconsin Press, 1974.

Suleiman, Susan Rubin. "On Maternal Splitting: A Propos of Mary Gordon's *Men and Angels*." *Signs* 14:1 (Autumn 1988):25–41.

_____. "Writing and Motherhood." In *The (M)Other Tongue: Essays in Feminist Psychoanalytic Interpretation*, edited by Shirley Nelson Garner, Claire Kahane, and Madelon Springnether, pp. 352–77. Ithaca, N.Y.: Cornell University Press.

Tate, Claudia. *Black Women Writers at Work*. 1983. Rptd. New York: Continuum, 1988.

Taylor, Cynthia. "History in *Love Medicine*." Paper presented at the Native American Literature Section, Midwest Modern Language Association Convention, St. Louis, Mo., November 1988.

Thorne, Barrie, with Marilyn Yalom, eds. *Rethinking the Family: Some Feminist Questions*. New York: Longman, 1982.

Thurston, Carol. *The Romance Revolution: Erotic Novels for Women and the Quest for a New Sexual Identity*. Urbana: University of Illinois Press, 1987.

Todorov, Tzvetan. *Mikhail Bakhtin: The Dialogical Principle*. Translated by Wlad. Godzich. Minneapolis: University of Minnesota Press, 1984.

Trebilcot, Joyce, ed. *Mothering: Essays in Feminist Theory*. Totowa, N.J.: Rowman and Allanheld, 1984.

Truth, Sojourner. "Ain't I a Woman?" In *Black Sister*, edited by Erlene Stetson, pp. 24–25. Bloomington: Indiana University Press, 1981.

Tyler, Anne. Review of *Later the Same Day*, by Grace Paley. *New Republic* 192 (29 April 1985):38–39.

Vecsey, Christopher. *Traditional Ojibway Religion and Its Historical Changes*. Philadelphia: American Philosophical Society, 1983.

Vizenor, Gerald. *The Everylasting Sky: New Voices from People Named the Chippewa*. New York: Rowell-Collier Press, 1972.

Volkmar, Fred R., and Donald J. Cohen. "The Experience of Infantile Autism: A First-Person Account by Tony W." *Journal of Autism and Developmental Disorders* 15 (1985):47–54.

Wade-Gayles, Gloria. "The Truths of Our Mothers' Lives: Mother-Daughter Relationships in Black Women's Fiction." *Sage* 1:2 (1984):8–12.

Walker, Alice. *The Color Purple*. New York: Harcourt Brace Jovanovich, 1982.

_____ *Meridian*. 1976. Rptd. New York: Pocket Books, 1986.

_____. *In Search of Our Mothers' Gardens*. New York: Harcourt Brace Jovanovich, 1983.

————. *The Temple of My Familiar.* New York: Harcourt Brace Jovanovich, 1989.

Warren, William W. *History of the Ojibway Nation.* 1885. Rptd. Minneapolis, Minn.: Ross and Haines, 1970.

Washington, Mary Helen. "I Sign My Mother's Name." In *Mothering the Mind*, edited by Ruth Perry and Martine Watson Brownley, pp. 142–63. New York: Holmes and Meier, 1984.

Weedon, Chris. *Feminist Practice and Poststructural Theory.* New York: Basil Blackwell, 1987.

West, Paul, *Words for a Deaf Daughter.* New York: Harper and Row, 1970.

Williams, Sherley Anne. *Dessa Rose.* New York: William Morrow, 1986.

Williams, Walter L. *The Spirit and the Flesh: Sexual Diversity in American Indian Culture.* Boston: Beacon, 1986.

Wilson, Harriet, *Our Nig: Sketches from the Life of a Free Black.* Edited by Henry Louis Gates, Jr. New York: Random House, 1983.

Winnicott, D.W. *Babies and Their Mothers.* Edited by Clare Winnicott, Ray Shepherd, and Madeleine Davis. Reading, Mass.: Addison-Wesley, 1987.

————. *The Child, the Family, and the Outside World.* Reading, Mass.: Addison-Wesley, 1987.

————. *Playing and Reality.* Reading, Mass.: Addison-Wesley, 1987.

Wittig, Monique. *Les Guerrilleres.* Translated by Peter Owen. New York: Avon, 1971.

Woolf, Virginia. Mrs. Dalloway. New York, Harcourt Brace Jovanovich, 1925.

————. *To the Lighthouse.* New York: Harcourt Brace Jovanovich, 1955.

Wright, Sarah E. *This Child's Gonna Live.* New York: Feminist Press, 1986.

Yglesias, Helen. "Odd Woman Out." *Women's Review of Books* 6:10–11 (1989).

Contributors

Judith Arcana, director of the Union Institute Center for Women, Washington, D.C., is the author of two books: *Our Mothers' Daughters*, a study of the mother-daughter relationship; and *Every Mother's Son*, an analysis of the role of mothers in the socialization of men. She recently completed *Cultural Dreamer; Grace Paley's Life Stories*, a biographical study of the activist Grace Paley and her fiction. In the past few years, Arcana has presented and published articles about Beowulf, Chaucer's Troilus, Jacobean tragedy, Keats, D.H. Lawrence, and Sherwood Anderson. She also has written essays, made speeches, and participated in panel discussions about mother blaming, abortion, racial and ethnic stereotypes of women, teaching women's studies, Jewish women in the United States, the Old Religion, and other women's issues.

Paula Bennett, University College, Northeastern University, Boston, is the author of two books on gender and creativity: *My Life a Loaded Gun: Female Creativity and Feminist Poetics* and *Emily Dickinson: Woman Poet*. Her essays have appeared in various collections, including *Women's Revisions of Shakespeare* and *Lesbian Texts and Contexts*.

Brenda O. Daly, assistant professor of English at Iowa State University, has published articles on the mother and legal discourse in *Hurricane Alice*; on gender and scientific discourse in the forthcoming collection, *Feminism and Bakhtin*; on mothers in young adult romances in *The English Journal*; and on mothers and women's time in *The Paradigm Exchange*. At present, Daly is writing a book on Joyce Carol Oates for the Ad Feminam series edited by Sandra Gilbert.

Carole Boyce Davies is associate professor of English, Afro-American and African studies, and comparative literature at the State University of New York at Binghamton. She is co-editor of *Ngambika: Studies of Women in African Literature* and *Out of the Kumbla: Caribbean Women and Literature*, and author of several articles on African, Caribbean, and Afro-American literature.

Mary Jane Elkins is associate professor of English and associate dean of arts and sciences at Florida International University in Miami, where she is also a member of the Women's Studies Advisory Board. She has published articles on Margaret Drabble, Anne Tyler, and Elizabeth Bishop, and is currently working on a book-length study of Drabble's narrative strategies.

Cecilia Konchar Farr, assistant professor of English at Brigham Young University, is at work on a book on modernist women's autobiographical fiction. She has published in *American Transcendental Quarterly, Explicator, Studies in American Jewish Literature, Hurricane Alice, Belles Lettres,* and *Re-Visions, Journal of the Women's Studies Program at Michigan State University,* which she also edited. With the birth of her first child, Daley, in June 1990, she has taken up mothering.

Shirley Nelson Garner is professor of English and director of the Center for Advanced Feminist Studies at the University of Minnesota. She is an editor of *The (M)other Tongue: Essays in Feminist Psychoanalytic Interpretation* (with Clarie Kahane and Madelon Sprengnether) and of *Interpreting Women's Lives: Feminist Theory and Personal Narratives.* She has written articles on Shakespeare and on women writers, and is a founding editor of *Hurricane Alice,* a feminist quarterly.

Gayle Greene has published articles on Shakespeare, contemporary women writers, and feminist literary theory. A professor of English at Scripps College, she co-edited *The Woman's Part: Feminist Criticism of Shakespeare* and *Making a Difference: Feminist Literary Criticism.* She has just completed a book, *Breaking the Circle: Feminist Fiction and the Tradition.*

Elaine Tuttle Hansen teaches medieval English literature and contemporary women writers at Haverford College, where she chairs the Department of English. She is the author of *The Solomon Complex: Reading Wisdom in Old English Poetry* and has recently completed a second book, *Chaucer and the Fictions of Gender.* Hansen has published several essays on women writers, including "Fiction and (Post) Feminism in Margaret Atwood's *Bodily Harm,*" "The Uses of Imagination: Margaret Drabble's *The Ice Age,*" and "The Double Narrative Structure of Marge Piercy's *Small Changes.*"

Jane McDonnell teaches women's studies at Carleton College, where for thirteen years she directed the Women's Studies Program and where she offers a multidisciplinary seminar called "The Politics of Motherhood." She has published articles and reviews in *Novel, Genre,* and the now-defunct little magazines *Perspective* and *The Carleton Miscellany.* She is writing a work of creative nonfiction concerning her high-achieving autistic son.

Sheryl O'Donnell is associate professor of English at the University of North Dakota, where she serves on the women's studies faculty. She co-edited *Menopause: A Cross-Cultural Perspective* and has published studies of eighteenth-century women writers and twentieth-century American clubwomen. Her essay, "Your Idea in My Mind: John Locke and Damaris Cudworth Masham," appeared in *Mothering the Mind,* edited by Ruth Perry and Martine Brownley.

Ruth Perry, a mother and a biographer, writes about the influence of gender on the production of art. She is the author of *Women, Letters, and the Novel* and a biography of an early English feminist, *The Celebrated Mary Astell*; is the editor of

George Ballard's *Memoirs of Several Ladies of Great Britain* (1752); and is co-editor and theorist of a volume of essays on nurturing creativity, *Mothering the Mind*. She was founding director of the Women's Studies Program at the Massachusetts Institute of Technology, where she is currently professor of literature and women's studies. A specialist in eighteenth-century English literature, her current project is to explain late eighteenth-century developments in English fiction in terms of changes in the family and the state.

Maureen T. Reddy, assistant professor of English and director of the Women's Studies Program at Rhode Island College, is author of *Sisters in Crime: Feminism and the Crime Novel*, which was nominated for a Mystery Writers of America Edgar Award in 1989. Her articles and reviews have appeared in *The Journal of Narrative Technique, Black American Literature Forum, Studies in Short Fiction, MELUS, The Women's Review of Books*, and *Hurricane Alice* (of which she is East Coast editor).

Judith Roof teaches English at the University of Delaware. She is co-editor of *Feminism and Psychoanalysis* and author of *A Lure of Knowledge: Lesbian Sexuality and Theory* and essays on Beckett, Pinter, Duras, Lacan, Freud, and feminist theory.

Hertha D. Wong is assistant professor of English at the University of California, Berkeley, where she teaches American literature, Native American literatures, and autobiography. Her essays on Native American autobiography have appeared in *American Literary History, American Indian Research and Culture Journal*, and *MELUS*. She has also published an interview with Louise Erdrich and Michael Dorris. Her book, *Native American Autobiography: Pre-Contact Traditions and Contemporary Innovations*, is forthcoming.

Index